Ford Focus Automotive Repair Manual

---

by M R Storey
and John H Haynes

Member of the Guild of Motoring Writers

Models covered:

Ford Focus - 2012 through 2014

Does not include information specific to Focus Electric models

---

(36035 - 9T1)

ABCDE
FGHIJ
KLMNO
PQRS

Haynes Publishing Group
Sparkford Nr Yeovil
Somerset BA22 7JJ England

Haynes North America, Inc
861 Lawrence Drive
Newbury Park
California 91320 USA

Acknowledgements

Technical writers who contributed to this project include John Wegmann and Bob Henderson.

© **Haynes North America, Inc. 2015**

With permission from J.H. Haynes & Co. Ltd.

A book in the Haynes Automotive Repair Manual Series

Printed in the U.S.A.

ISBN-13: 978-1-62092-122-7
ISBN-10: 1-62092-122-7

Library of Congress Control Number: 2015933467

Contents

Haynes writer and photographer with a Ford Focus

About this manual

Its purpose

The purpose of this manual is to help you get the best value from your vehicle. It can do so in several ways. It can help you decide what work must be done, even if you choose to have it done by a dealer service department or a repair shop; it provides information and procedures for routine maintenance and servicing; and it offers diagnostic and repair procedures to follow when trouble occurs.

We hope you use the manual to tackle the work yourself. For many simpler jobs, doing it yourself may be quicker than arranging an appointment to get the vehicle into a shop and making the trips to leave it and pick it up. More importantly, a lot of money can be saved by avoiding the expense the shop must pass on to you to cover its labor and overhead costs. An added benefit is the sense of satisfaction and accomplishment that you feel after doing the job yourself.

Using the manual

The manual is divided into Chapters. Each Chapter is divided into numbered Sections, which are headed in bold type between horizontal lines. Each Section consists of consecutively numbered paragraphs.

The reference numbers used in illustration captions pinpoint the pertinent Section and the Step within that Section. That is, illustration 3.2 means the illustration refers to Section 3 and Step (or paragraph) 2 within that Section.

Procedures, once described in the text, are not normally repeated. When it's necessary to refer to another Chapter, the reference will be given as Chapter and Section number. Cross references given without use of the word "Chapter" apply to Sections and/or paragraphs in the same Chapter. For example, "see Section 8" means in the same Chapter.

References to the left or right side of the vehicle assume you are sitting in the driver's seat, facing forward.

Even though we have prepared this manual with extreme care, neither the publisher nor the author can accept responsibility for any errors in, or omissions from, the information given.

NOTE

A **Note** provides information necessary to properly complete a procedure or information which will make the procedure easier to understand.

CAUTION

A **Caution** provides a special procedure or special steps which must be taken while completing the procedure where the Caution is found. Not heeding a Caution can result in damage to the assembly being worked on.

WARNING

A **Warning** provides a special procedure or special steps which must be taken while completing the procedure where the Warning is found. Not heeding a Warning can result in personal injury.

Introduction

The models covered by this manual are equipped with either a transversely mounted 2.0L four-cylinder, normally aspirated engine, or a 2.0L turbocharged engine. The engine drives the front wheels through either a 5- or 6-speed manual transaxle or 6-speed automatic transaxle.

Suspension is independent at all four wheels; MacPherson struts and transversley mounted control arms are used at the front end, while a multi-link suspension with coil springs and shock absorbers is used at the rear. Front and rear stabilizer bars are used to prevent excessive body roll. The rack-and

-pinion steering gear is mounted to the front subframe.

Brakes are disc-type at the front and either disc or drum at the rear. Power assist and an Anti-lock Braking System (ABS) are standard on all models.

Vehicle identification numbers

Modifications are a continuing and unpublicized process in vehicle manufacturing. Since spare parts manuals and lists are compiled on a numerical basis, the individual vehicle numbers are essential to correctly identify the component required.

Vehicle Identification Number (VIN)

This very important identification number is stamped on a plate attached to the dashboard inside the windshield on the driver's side of the vehicle (see illustration). It can also be found on the certification label located on the driver's side door post and on the right (passenger) side of the firewall. The VIN also appears on the Vehicle Certificate of Title and Registration. It contains information such as where and when the vehicle was manufactured, the model year and the body style.

VIN engine and model year codes

Two particularly important pieces of information found in the VIN are the engine code and the model year code. Counting from the left, the engine code letter designation is the 8th digit and the model year code letter designation is the 10th digit.

On the models covered by this manual the engine codes are:

2 ....2.0L four-cylinder engine (naturally aspirated)

9 ....2.0L four-cylinder engine (turbocharged)

On the models covered by this manual the model year codes are:

C 2012
D 2013
E 2014

Certification label

The certification label is attached to the driver's door jamb (see illustration) . The plate contains the name of the manufacturer, the month and year of production, the Gross Vehicle Weight Rating (GVWR), the Gross Axle Weight Rating (GAWR) and the certification statement.

The Vehicle Identification Number (VIN) is located on a plate on top of the dash, visible through the windshield

The vehicle certification label is located on the driver's door jamb

Recall information

Vehicle recalls are carried out by the manufacturer in the rare event of a possible safety-related defect. The vehicle's registered owner is contacted at the address on file at the Department of Motor Vehicles and given the details of the recall. Remedial work is carried out free of charge at a dealer service department.

If you are the new owner of a used vehicle which was subject to a recall and you want to be sure that the work has been carried out, it's best to contact a dealer service department and ask about your individual vehicle - you'll need to furnish them your Vehicle Identification Number (VIN).

The table below is based on informa-tion provided by the National Highway Traffic Safety Administration (NHTSA), the body which oversees vehicle recalls in the United States. The recall database is updated constantly. For the latest information on vehicle recalls, check the NHTSA website at www.nhtsa.gov, www.safercar.gov, or call the NHTSA hotline at 1-888-327-4236.

Recall date	Recall campaign number	Model(s) affected	Concern
APR 05, 2012	12V149000	2012 Focus	On some models, a seal in the wiring harness connector to the passenger side wiper motor may be missing. Water or other contaminants may accumulate in the connector, resulting in an intermittant or inoperative passenger side wiper motor, reducing visibility and increasing the risk of a crash.
MAR 07, 2013	13V085000	2013 Focus	On some models, the left rear door child lock was built incorrectly. As a result, the child lock may not engage when the operator uses normal force to activate the child lock. The operator may incorrectly believe the child lock is engaged. However, the door may be opened from the inside, increasing the risk of injury to an unrestrained child.

Recall date	Recall campaign number	Model(s) affected	Concern
AUG 01, 2013	13V335000	2012, 2013 Focus	On some models equipped with High Intensity Discharge (HID) headlights, the front side marker lamps may not function. Without the proper illumination of the side maker lamps, the vehicle may be less visible in night time conditions, increasing the risk of a crash.
AUG 22, 2014	14V514000	2014 Focus	Some models may have steering gears that were incorrectly assembled. This may cause impaired steering, increasing the risk of a crash.
SEP 02, 2014	14V525000	2014 Focus	On some models, the Fuel Delivery Module (FDM) may crack between the filter body and the filter cap, possibly resulting in low fuel pressure. A reduction in fuel pressure may result in a vehicle stall, increasing the risk of a crash.

Buying parts

Replacement parts are available from many sources, which generally fall into one of two categories - authorized dealer parts departments and independent retail auto parts stores. Our advice concerning these parts is as follows:

Retail auto parts stores: Good auto parts stores will stock frequently needed components which wear out relatively fast, such as clutch components, exhaust systems, brake parts, tune-up parts, etc. These stores often supply new or reconditioned parts on an exchange basis, which can save a considerable amount of money. Discount auto parts stores are often very good places to buy materials and parts needed for general vehicle maintenance such as oil, grease, filters, spark plugs, belts, touch-up paint, bulbs, etc. They also usually sell tools and general accessories, have convenient hours, charge lower prices and can often be found not far from home.

Authorized dealer parts department: This is the best source for parts which are unique to the vehicle and not generally available elsewhere (such as major engine parts, transmission parts, trim pieces, etc.).

Warranty information: If the vehicle is still covered under warranty, be sure that any replacement parts purchased - regardless of the source - do not invalidate the warranty!

To be sure of obtaining the correct parts, have engine and chassis numbers available and, if possible, take the old parts along for positive identification.

Maintenance techniques, tools and working facilities

Maintenance techniques

There are a number of techniques involved in maintenance and repair that will be referred to throughout this manual. Application of these techniques will enable the home mechanic to be more efficient, better organized and capable of performing the various tasks properly, which will ensure that the repair job is thorough and complete.

Fasteners

Fasteners are nuts, bolts, studs and screws used to hold two or more parts together. There are a few things to keep in mind when working with fasteners. Almost all of them use a locking device of some type, either a lockwasher, locknut, locking tab or thread adhesive. All threaded fasteners should be clean and straight, with undamaged threads and undamaged corners on the hex head where the wrench fits. Develop the habit of replacing all damaged nuts and bolts with new ones. Special locknuts with nylon or fiber inserts can only be used once. If they are removed, they lose their locking ability and must be replaced with new ones.

Rusted nuts and bolts should be treated with a penetrating fluid to ease removal and prevent breakage. Some mechanics use turpentine in a spout-type oil can, which works quite well. After applying the rust penetrant, let it work for a few minutes before trying to loosen the nut or bolt. Badly rusted fasteners may have to be chiseled or sawed off or removed with a special nut breaker, available at tool stores.

If a bolt or stud breaks off in an assembly, it can be drilled and removed with a special tool commonly available for this purpose. Most automotive machine shops can perform this task, as well as other repair procedures, such as the repair of threaded holes that have been stripped out.

Flat washers and lockwashers, when removed from an assembly, should always be replaced exactly as removed. Replace any damaged washers with new ones. Never use a lockwasher on any soft metal surface (such as aluminum), thin sheet metal or plastic.

Fastener sizes

For a number of reasons, automobile manufacturers are making wider and wider use of metric fasteners. Therefore, it is important to be able to tell the difference between standard (sometimes called U.S. or SAE) and metric hardware, since they cannot be interchanged.

All bolts, whether standard or metric, are sized according to diameter, thread pitch and length. For example, a standard 1/2 - 13 x 1 bolt is 1/2 inch in diameter, has 13 threads per inch and is 1 inch long. An M12 - 1.75 x 25 metric bolt is 12 mm in diameter, has a thread pitch of 1.75 mm (the distance between threads) and is 25 mm long. The two bolts are nearly identical, and easily confused, but they are not interchangeable.

In addition to the differences in diameter, thread pitch and length, metric and standard bolts can also be distinguished by examining the bolt heads. To begin with, the distance across the flats on a standard bolt head is measured in inches, while the same dimension on a metric bolt is sized in millimeters (the same is true for nuts). As a result, a standard wrench should not be used on a metric bolt and a metric wrench should not be used on a standard bolt. Also, most standard bolts have slashes radiating out from the center of the head to denote the grade or strength of the bolt, which is an indication of the amount of torque that can be applied to it. The greater the number of slashes, the greater the strength of the bolt. Grades 0 through 5 are commonly used on automobiles. Metric bolts have a property class (grade) number, rather than a slash, molded into their heads to indicate bolt strength. In this case, the higher the number, the stronger the bolt. Property class numbers 8.8, 9.8 and 10.9 are commonly used on automobiles.

Strength markings can also be used to distinguish standard hex nuts from metric hex nuts. Many standard nuts have dots stamped into one side, while metric nuts are marked with a number. The greater the number of

dots, or the higher the number, the greater the strength of the nut.

Metric studs are also marked on their ends according to property class (grade). Larger studs are numbered (the same as metric bolts), while smaller studs carry a geometric code to denote grade.

It should be noted that many fasteners, especially Grades 0 through 2, have no distinguishing marks on them. When such is the case, the only way to determine whether it is standard or metric is to measure the thread pitch or compare it to a known fastener of the same size.

Standard fasteners are often referred to as SAE, as opposed to metric. However, it should be noted that SAE technically refers to a non-metric fine thread fastener only. Coarse thread non-metric fasteners are referred to as USS sizes.

Since fasteners of the same size (both standard and metric) may have different

strength ratings, be sure to reinstall any bolts, studs or nuts removed from your vehicle in their original locations. Also, when replacing a fastener with a new one, make sure that the new one has a strength rating equal to or greater than the original.

Tightening sequences and procedures

Most threaded fasteners should be tightened to a specific torque value (torque is the twisting force applied to a threaded component such as a nut or bolt). Overtightening the fastener can weaken it and cause it to break, while undertightening can cause it to eventually come loose. Bolts, screws and studs, depending on the material they are made of and their thread diameters, have specific torque values, many of which are noted in the Specifications at the beginning of each Chapter. Be sure to follow the torque recommen-

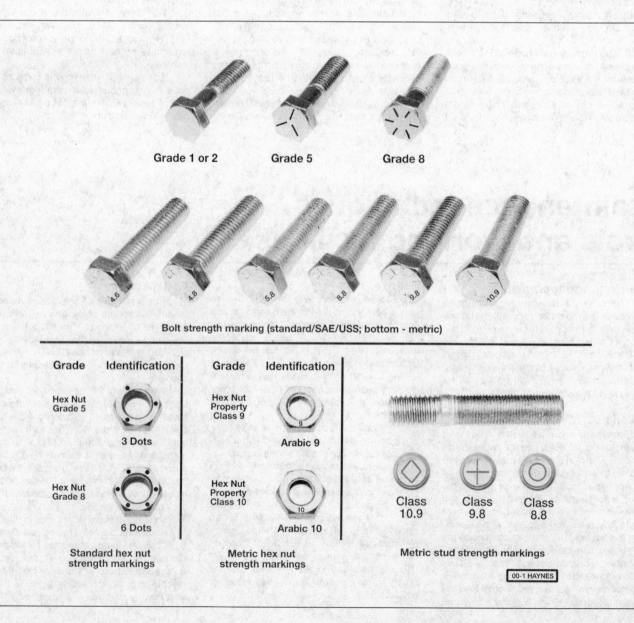

Grade 1 or 2   Grade 5   Grade 8

Bolt strength marking (standard/SAE/USS; bottom - metric)

Grade	Identification
Hex Nut Grade 5	3 Dots
Hex Nut Grade 8	6 Dots

Standard hex nut strength markings

Grade	Identification
Hex Nut Property Class 9	Arabic 9
Hex Nut Property Class 10	Arabic 10

Metric hex nut strength markings

Class 10.9   Class 9.8   Class 8.8

Metric stud strength markings

00-1 HAYNES

dations closely. For fasteners not assigned a specific torque, a general torque value chart is presented here as a guide. These torque values are for dry (unlubricated) fasteners threaded into steel or cast iron (not aluminum). As was previously mentioned, the size and grade of a fastener determine the amount of torque that can safely be applied to it. The figures listed here are approximate for Grade 2 and Grade 3 fasteners. Higher grades can tolerate higher torque values.

Fasteners laid out in a pattern, such as cylinder head bolts, oil pan bolts, differential cover bolts, etc., must be loosened or tightened in sequence to avoid warping the component. This sequence will normally be shown in the appropriate Chapter. If a specific pattern is not given, the following procedures can be used to prevent warping.

Initially, the bolts or nuts should be assembled finger-tight only. Next, they should be tightened one full turn each, in a criss-cross or diagonal pattern. After each one has been tightened one full turn, return to the first one and tighten them all one-half turn, following the same pattern. Finally, tighten each of them one-quarter turn at a time until each fastener has been tightened to the proper torque. To loosen and remove the fasteners, the procedure would be reversed.

Metric thread sizes	Ft-lbs	Nm
M-6	6 to 9	9 to 12
M-8	14 to 21	19 to 28
M-10	28 to 40	38 to 54
M-12	50 to 71	68 to 96
M-14	80 to 140	109 to 154

Pipe thread sizes		
1/8	5 to 8	7 to 10
1/4	12 to 18	17 to 24
3/8	22 to 33	30 to 44
1/2	25 to 35	34 to 47

U.S. thread sizes		
1/4 - 20	6 to 9	9 to 12
5/16 - 18	12 to 18	17 to 24
5/16 - 24	14 to 20	19 to 27
3/8 - 16	22 to 32	30 to 43
3/8 - 24	27 to 38	37 to 51
7/16 - 14	40 to 55	55 to 74
7/16 - 20	40 to 60	55 to 81
1/2 - 13	55 to 80	75 to 108

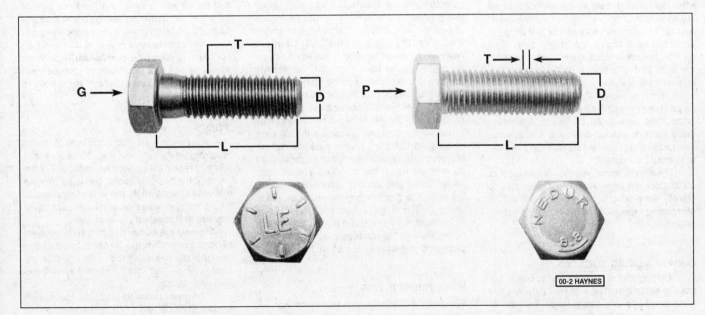

Standard (SAE and USS) bolt dimensions/grade marks

G   Grade marks (bolt strength)
L   Length (in inches)
T   Thread pitch (number of threads per inch)
D   Nominal diameter (in inches)

Metric bolt dimensions/grade marks

P   Property class (bolt strength)
L   Length (in millimeters)
T   Thread pitch (distance between threads in millimeters)
D   Diameter

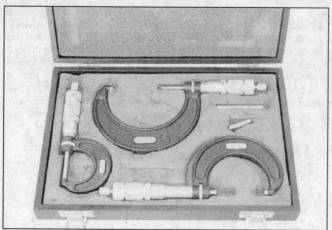

Micrometer set

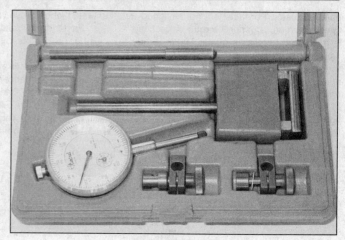

Dial indicator set

Component disassembly

Component disassembly should be done with care and purpose to help ensure that the parts go back together properly. Always keep track of the sequence in which parts are removed. Make note of special characteristics or marks on parts that can be installed more than one way, such as a grooved thrust washer on a shaft. It is a good idea to lay the disassembled parts out on a clean surface in the order that they were removed. It may also be helpful to make sketches or take instant photos of components before removal.

When removing fasteners from a component, keep track of their locations. Sometimes threading a bolt back in a part, or putting the washers and nut back on a stud, can prevent mix-ups later. If nuts and bolts cannot be returned to their original locations, they should be kept in a compartmented box or a series of small boxes. A cupcake or muffin tin is ideal for this purpose, since each cavity can hold the bolts and nuts from a particular area (i.e. oil pan bolts, valve cover bolts, engine mount bolts, etc.). A pan of this type is especially helpful when working on assemblies with very small parts, such as the carburetor, alternator, valve train or interior dash and trim pieces. The cavities can be marked with paint or tape to identify the contents.

Whenever wiring looms, harnesses or connectors are separated, it is a good idea to identify the two halves with numbered pieces of masking tape so they can be easily reconnected.

Gasket sealing surfaces

Throughout any vehicle, gaskets are used to seal the mating surfaces between two parts and keep lubricants, fluids, vacuum or pressure contained in an assembly.

Many times these gaskets are coated with a liquid or paste-type gasket sealing compound before assembly. Age, heat and pressure can sometimes cause the two parts to stick together so tightly that they are very difficult to separate. Often, the assembly can

be loosened by striking it with a soft-face hammer near the mating surfaces. A regular hammer can be used if a block of wood is placed between the hammer and the part. Do not hammer on cast parts or parts that could be easily damaged. With any particularly stubborn part, always recheck to make sure that every fastener has been removed.

Avoid using a screwdriver or bar to pry apart an assembly, as they can easily mar the gasket sealing surfaces of the parts, which must remain smooth. If prying is absolutely necessary, use an old broom handle, but keep in mind that extra clean up will be necessary if the wood splinters.

After the parts are separated, the old gasket must be carefully scraped off and the gasket surfaces cleaned. Stubborn gasket material can be soaked with rust penetrant or treated with a special chemical to soften it so it can be easily scraped off. **Caution:** *Never use gasket removal solutions or caustic chemicals on plastic or other composite components.* A scraper can be fashioned from a piece of copper tubing by flattening and sharpening one end. Copper is recommended because it is usually softer than the surfaces to be scraped, which reduces the chance of gouging the part. Some gaskets can be removed with a wire brush, but regardless of the method used, the mating surfaces must be left clean and smooth. If for some reason the gasket surface is gouged, then a gasket sealer thick enough to fill scratches will have to be used during reassembly of the components. For most applications, a non-drying (or semi-drying) gasket sealer should be used.

Hose removal tips

Warning: *If the vehicle is equipped with air conditioning, do not disconnect any of the A/C hoses without first having the system depressurized by a dealer service department or a service station.*

Hose removal precautions closely parallel gasket removal precautions. Avoid scratching or gouging the surface that the

hose mates against or the connection may leak. This is especially true for radiator hoses. Because of various chemical reactions, the rubber in hoses can bond itself to the metal spigot that the hose fits over. To remove a hose, first loosen the hose clamps that secure it to the spigot. Then, with slip-joint pliers, grab the hose at the clamp and rotate it around the spigot. Work it back and forth until it is completely free, then pull it off. Silicone or other lubricants will ease removal if they can be applied between the hose and the outside of the spigot. Apply the same lubricant to the inside of the hose and the outside of the spigot to simplify installation.

As a last resort (and if the hose is to be replaced with a new one anyway), the rubber can be slit with a knife and the hose peeled from the spigot. If this must be done, be careful that the metal connection is not damaged.

If a hose clamp is broken or damaged, do not reuse it. Wire-type clamps usually weaken with age, so it is a good idea to replace them with screw-type clamps whenever a hose is removed.

Tools

A selection of good tools is a basic requirement for anyone who plans to maintain and repair his or her own vehicle. For the owner who has few tools, the initial investment might seem high, but when compared to the spiraling costs of professional auto maintenance and repair, it is a wise one.

To help the owner decide which tools are needed to perform the tasks detailed in this manual, the following tool lists are offered: *Maintenance and minor repair, Repair/overhaul* and *Special.*

The newcomer to practical mechanics should start off with the *maintenance and minor repair* tool kit, which is adequate for the simpler jobs performed on a vehicle. Then, as confidence and experience grow, the owner can tackle more difficult tasks, buying additional tools as they are needed. Eventually the basic kit will be expanded into the *repair and overhaul* tool set. Over a period of time, the

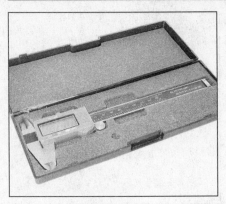

Dial caliper

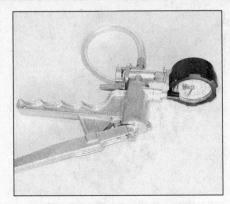

Hand-operated vacuum pump

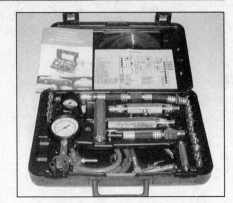

Fuel pressure gauge set

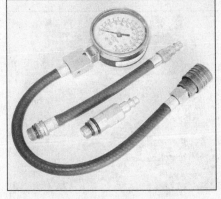

Compression gauge with spark plug hole adapter

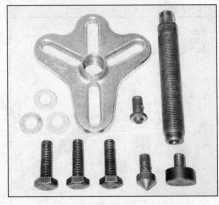

Damper/steering wheel puller

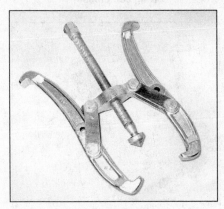

General purpose puller

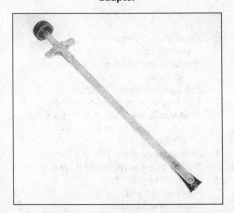

Hydraulic lifter removal tool

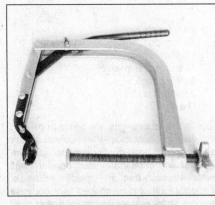

Valve spring compressor

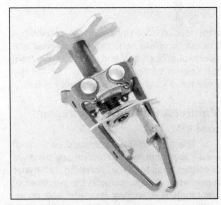

Valve spring compressor

Ridge reamer

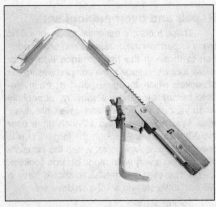

Piston ring groove cleaning tool

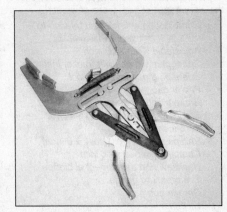

Ring removal/installation tool

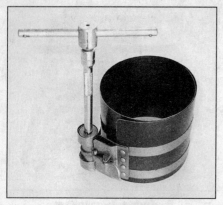

Ring compressor

Cylinder hone

Brake hold-down spring tool

Torque angle gauge

Clutch plate alignment tool

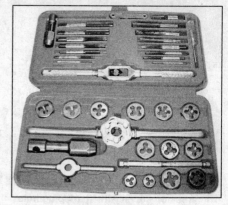

Tap and die set

experienced do-it-yourselfer will assemble a tool set complete enough for most repair and overhaul procedures and will add tools from the special category when it is felt that the expense is justified by the frequency of use.

Maintenance and minor repair tool kit

The tools in this list should be considered the minimum required for performance of routine maintenance, servicing and minor repair work. We recommend the purchase of combination wrenches (box-end and open-end combined in one wrench). While more expensive than open end wrenches, they offer the advantages of both types of wrench.

> *Combination wrench set (1/4-inch to 1 inch or 6 mm to 19 mm)*
> *Adjustable wrench, 8 inch*
> *Spark plug wrench with rubber insert*
> *Spark plug gap adjusting tool*
> *Feeler gauge set*
> *Brake bleeder wrench*
> *Standard screwdriver (5/16-inch x 6 inch)*
> *Phillips screwdriver (No. 2 x 6 inch)*
> *Combination pliers - 6 inch*
> *Hacksaw and assortment of blades*
> *Tire pressure gauge*
> *Grease gun*
> *Oil can*
> *Fine emery cloth*

> *Wire brush*
> *Battery post and cable cleaning tool*
> *Oil filter wrench*
> *Funnel (medium size)*
> *Safety goggles*
> *Jackstands (2)*
> *Drain pan*

Note: *If basic tune-ups are going to be part of routine maintenance, it will be necessary to purchase a good quality stroboscopic timing light and combination tachometer/dwell meter. Although they are included in the list of special tools, it is mentioned here because they are absolutely necessary for tuning most vehicles properly.*

Repair and overhaul tool set

These tools are essential for anyone who plans to perform major repairs and are in addition to those in the maintenance and minor repair tool kit. Included is a comprehensive set of sockets which, though expensive, are invaluable because of their versatility, especially when various extensions and drives are available. We recommend the 1/2-inch drive over the 3/8-inch drive. Although the larger drive is bulky and more expensive, it has the capacity of accepting a very wide range of large sockets. Ideally, however, the mechanic should have a 3/8-inch drive set and a 1/2-inch drive set.

> *Socket set(s)*
> *Reversible ratchet*

> *Extension - 10 inch*
> *Universal joint*
> *Torque wrench (same size drive as sockets)*
> *Ball peen hammer - 8 ounce*
> *Soft-face hammer (plastic/rubber)*
> *Standard screwdriver (1/4-inch x 6 inch)*
> *Standard screwdriver (stubby - 5/16-inch)*
> *Phillips screwdriver (No. 3 x 8 inch)*
> *Phillips screwdriver (stubby - No. 2)*
> *Pliers - vise grip*
> *Pliers - lineman's*
> *Pliers - needle nose*
> *Pliers - snap-ring (internal and external)*
> *Cold chisel - 1/2-inch*
> *Scribe*
> *Scraper (made from flattened copper tubing)*
> *Centerpunch*
> *Pin punches (1/16, 1/8, 3/16-inch)*
> *Steel rule/straightedge - 12 inch*
> *Allen wrench set (1/8 to 3/8-inch or 4 mm to 10 mm)*
> *A selection of files*
> *Wire brush (large)*
> *Jackstands (second set)*
> *Jack (scissor or hydraulic type)*

Note: *Another tool which is often useful is an electric drill with a chuck capacity of 3/8-inch and a set of good quality drill bits.*

Special tools

The tools in this list include those which are not used regularly, are expensive to buy, or which need to be used in accordance with their manufacturer's instructions. Unless these tools will be used frequently, it is not very economical to purchase many of them. A consideration would be to split the cost and use between yourself and a friend or friends. In addition, most of these tools can be obtained from a tool rental shop on a temporary basis.

This list primarily contains only those tools and instruments widely available to the public, and not those special tools produced by the vehicle manufacturer for distribution to dealer service departments. Occasionally, references to the manufacturer's special tools are included in the text of this manual. Generally, an alternative method of doing the job without the special tool is offered. However, sometimes there is no alternative to their use. Where this is the case, and the tool cannot be purchased or borrowed, the work should be turned over to the dealer service department or an automotive repair shop.

> *Valve spring compressor*
> *Piston ring groove cleaning tool*
> *Piston ring compressor*
> *Piston ring installation tool*
> *Cylinder compression gauge*
> *Cylinder ridge reamer*
> *Cylinder surfacing hone*
> *Cylinder bore gauge*
> *Micrometers and/or dial calipers*
> *Hydraulic lifter removal tool*
> *Balljoint separator*
> *Universal-type puller*
> *Impact screwdriver*
> *Dial indicator set*
> *Stroboscopic timing light (inductive*
> *　　pick-up)*
> *Hand operated vacuum/pressure pump*
> *Tachometer/dwell meter*
> *Universal electrical multimeter*
> *Cable hoist*
> *Brake spring removal and installation*
> *　　tools*
> *Floor jack*

Buying tools

For the do-it-yourselfer who is just starting to get involved in vehicle maintenance and repair, there are a number of options available when purchasing tools. If maintenance and minor repair is the extent of the work to be done, the purchase of individual tools is satisfactory. If, on the other hand, extensive work is planned, it would be a good idea to purchase a modest tool set from one of the large retail chain stores. A set can usually be bought at a substantial savings over the individual tool prices, and they often come with a tool box. As additional tools are needed, add-on sets, individual tools and a larger tool box can be purchased to expand the tool selection. Building a tool set gradually allows the cost of the

tools to be spread over a longer period of time and gives the mechanic the freedom to choose only those tools that will actually be used.

Tool stores will often be the only source of some of the special tools that are needed, but regardless of where tools are bought, try to avoid cheap ones, especially when buying screwdrivers and sockets, because they won't last very long. The expense involved in replacing cheap tools will eventually be greater than the initial cost of quality tools.

Care and maintenance of tools

Good tools are expensive, so it makes sense to treat them with respect. Keep them clean and in usable condition and store them properly when not in use. Always wipe off any dirt, grease or metal chips before putting them away. Never leave tools lying around in the work area. Upon completion of a job, always check closely under the hood for tools that may have been left there so they won't get lost during a test drive.

Some tools, such as screwdrivers, pliers, wrenches and sockets, can be hung on a panel mounted on the garage or workshop wall, while others should be kept in a tool box or tray. Measuring instruments, gauges, meters, etc. must be carefully stored where they cannot be damaged by weather or impact from other tools.

When tools are used with care and stored properly, they will last a very long time. Even with the best of care, though, tools will wear out if used frequently. When a tool is damaged or worn out, replace it. Subsequent jobs will be safer and more enjoyable if you do.

How to repair damaged threads

Sometimes, the internal threads of a nut or bolt hole can become stripped, usually from overtightening. Stripping threads is an all-too-common occurrence, especially when working with aluminum parts, because aluminum is so soft that it easily strips out.

Usually, external or internal threads are only partially stripped. After they've been cleaned up with a tap or die, they'll still work. Sometimes, however, threads are badly damaged. When this happens, you've got three choices:

1) *Drill and tap the hole to the next suitable oversize and install a larger diameter bolt, screw or stud.*
2) *Drill and tap the hole to accept a threaded plug, then drill and tap the plug to the original screw size. You can also buy a plug already threaded to the original size. Then you simply drill a hole to the specified size, then run the threaded plug into the hole with a bolt and jam nut. Once the plug is fully seated, remove the jam nut and bolt.*

3) *The third method uses a patented thread repair kit like Heli-Coil or Slimsert. These easy-to-use kits are designed to repair damaged threads in straight-through holes and blind holes. Both are available as kits which can handle a variety of sizes and thread patterns. Drill the hole, then tap it with the special included tap. Install the Heli-Coil and the hole is back to its original diameter and thread pitch.*

Regardless of which method you use, be sure to proceed calmly and carefully. A little impatience or carelessness during one of these relatively simple procedures can ruin your whole day's work and cost you a bundle if you wreck an expensive part.

Working facilities

Not to be overlooked when discussing tools is the workshop. If anything more than routine maintenance is to be carried out, some sort of suitable work area is essential.

It is understood, and appreciated, that many home mechanics do not have a good workshop or garage available, and end up removing an engine or doing major repairs outside. It is recommended, however, that the overhaul or repair be completed under the cover of a roof.

A clean, flat workbench or table of comfortable working height is an absolute necessity. The workbench should be equipped with a vise that has a jaw opening of at least four inches.

As mentioned previously, some clean, dry storage space is also required for tools, as well as the lubricants, fluids, cleaning solvents, etc. which soon become necessary.

Sometimes waste oil and fluids, drained from the engine or cooling system during normal maintenance or repairs, present a disposal problem. To avoid pouring them on the ground or into a sewage system, pour the used fluids into large containers, seal them with caps and take them to an authorized disposal site or recycling center. Plastic jugs, such as old antifreeze containers, are ideal for this purpose.

Always keep a supply of old newspapers and clean rags available. Old towels are excellent for mopping up spills. Many mechanics use rolls of paper towels for most work because they are readily available and disposable. To help keep the area under the vehicle clean, a large cardboard box can be cut open and flattened to protect the garage or shop floor.

Whenever working over a painted surface, such as when leaning over a fender to service something under the hood, always cover it with an old blanket or bedspread to protect the finish. Vinyl covered pads, made especially for this purpose, are available at auto parts stores.

Jacking and towing

Jacking

Warning: *The jack supplied with the vehicle should only be used for changing a tire or placing jackstands under the frame. Never work under the vehicle or start the engine while this jack is being used as the only means of support.*

1   The vehicle should be on level ground. Place the shift lever in Park, if you have an automatic, or Reverse if you have a manual transaxle. Block the wheel diagonally opposite the wheel being changed. Set the parking brake.

2   Remove the spare tire and jack from stowage. Remove the wheel cover and trim ring (if so equipped) with the tapered end of the lug nut wrench by inserting and twisting the handle and then prying against the back of the wheel cover. Loosen, but do not remove, the lug nuts (one-half turn is sufficient).

3   Place the scissors-type jack under the vehicle and adjust the jack height until it engages with the proper jacking point. There is a front and rear jacking point on each side of the vehicle **(see illustration)**.

4   Turn the jack handle clockwise until the tire clears the ground. Remove the lug nuts and pull the wheel off, then install the spare.

5   Install the lug nuts with the beveled edges facing in. Tighten them snugly. Don't attempt to tighten them completely until the vehicle is lowered or it could slip off the jack. Turn the jack handle counterclockwise to lower the vehicle. Remove the jack and tighten the lug nuts in a diagonal pattern.

6   Stow the tire, jack and wrench. Unblock the wheels.

Towing

7   These vehicles can be towed from the front with all four wheels on the ground, or a towing dolly can be used under the front wheels. A sling-type tow truck cannot be used, as body damage will result.

Note: *If emergency towing behind another vehicle, put the vehicle's climate control system in recirculate air mode to keep exhaust fumes from entering the cabin.*

Manual transaxle models

8   Release the parking brake and place the shifter in Neutral. There are no limits on towing distance, but don't exceed 55 miles per hour.

Automatic transaxle models

With push-button start

9   Release the parking brake and, without depressing the brake pedal, push the START/ STOP button.

10   Depress the brake pedal and shift into Neutral.

11   On 2012 models, release the brake pedal and push the START/STOP button again.

12   On 2013 and later models, release the brake pedal, wait for TRANSMISSION READY to appear in the multi-function display, and then push the START/STOP button again.

13   Disconnect the negative battery cable from the remote ground terminal (see Chapter 5).

14   There are no limits on towing distance, but don't exceed 55 miles per hour.

15   When done towing, start the engine within 15 minutes of reconnecting the battery.

Without push-button start

16   Release the parking brake and turn the ignition to the On (II) position.

17   On 2012 models, depress the brake pedal and shift into Neutral.

18   On 2013 and later models, release the brake pedal, wait for TRANSMISSION READY to appear in the multi-function display, and then shift into Neutral.

19   Turn the ignition to the Off (0) position.

20   Disconnect the negative battery cable from the remote ground terminal (see Chapter 5).

21   There are no limits on towing distance, but don't exceed 55 miles per hour.

22   When done towing, start the engine within 15 minutes of reconnecting the battery.

Place the jack on the rocker panel flange, directly behind the triangle mark

Booster battery (jump) starting

Observe these precautions when using a booster battery to start a vehicle:

a) *Before connecting the booster battery, make sure the ignition switch is in the Off position.*

b) *Turn off the lights, heater and other electrical loads.*

c) *Your eyes should be shielded. Safety goggles are a good idea.*

d) *Make sure the booster battery is the same voltage as the dead one in the vehicle.*

e) *The two vehicles MUST NOT TOUCH each other!*

f) *Make sure the transaxle is in Neutral (manual) or Park (automatic).*

g) *If the booster battery is not a maintenance-free type, remove the vent caps and lay a cloth over the vent holes.*

Remove the battery cover, then connect the red-colored jumper cable to the positive (+) terminal of the booster battery and the other end to the positive (+) terminal of the dead battery **(see illustrations)**. Then connect one end of the black jumper cable to the remote ground (-) terminal of the booster vehicle, and the other end of the cable to a good ground, such as a bolt or bracket, on the car with the dead battery.

Start the engine using the booster battery, then run the booster vehicle at a fast idle for a few minutes to instill some charge in the dead battery. Let the engine idle, then disconnect the jumper cables in the reverse order of connection. The vehicle with the dead battery may have to be driven for 20 minutes or more to sufficiently recharge the battery for independent starting.

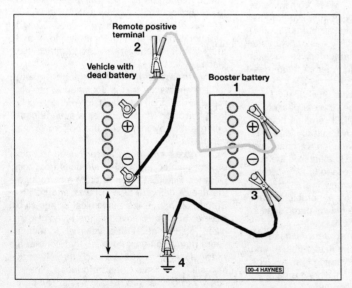

8.2a Make the booster battery cable connections in the numerical order shown (note that the negative cable of the booster battery is NOT attached to the negative terminal of the dead battery)

8.2b Battery positive terminal (A) and remote ground terminal (B)

Automotive chemicals and lubricants

A number of automotive chemicals and lubricants are available for use during vehicle maintenance and repair. They include a wide variety of products ranging from cleaning solvents and degreasers to lubricants and protective sprays for rubber, plastic and vinyl.

Cleaners

Carburetor cleaner and choke cleaner is a strong solvent for gum, varnish and carbon. Most carburetor cleaners leave a dry-type lubricant film which will not harden or gum up. Because of this film it is not recommended for use on electrical components.

Brake system cleaner is used to remove brake dust, grease and brake fluid from the brake system, where clean surfaces are absolutely necessary. It leaves no residue and often eliminates brake squeal caused by contaminants.

Electrical cleaner removes oxidation, corrosion and carbon deposits from electrical contacts, restoring full current flow. It can also be used to clean spark plugs, carburetor jets, voltage regulators and other parts where an oil-free surface is desired.

Demoisturants remove water and moisture from electrical components such as alternators, voltage regulators, electrical connectors and fuse blocks. They are non-conductive and non-corrosive.

Degreasers are heavy-duty solvents used to remove grease from the outside of the engine and from chassis components. They can be sprayed or brushed on and, depending on the type, are rinsed off either with water or solvent.

Lubricants

Motor oil is the lubricant formulated for use in engines. It normally contains a wide variety of additives to prevent corrosion and reduce foaming and wear. Motor oil comes in various weights (viscosity ratings) from 0 to 50. The recommended weight of the oil depends on the season, temperature and the demands on the engine. Light oil is used in cold climates and under light load conditions. Heavy oil is used in hot climates and where high loads are encountered. Multi-viscosity oils are designed to have characteristics of both light and heavy oils and are available in a number of weights from 0W-20 to 20W-50.

Gear oil is designed to be used in differentials, manual transmissions and other areas where high-temperature lubrication is required.

Chassis and wheel bearing grease is a heavy grease used where increased loads and friction are encountered, such as for wheel bearings, balljoints, tie-rod ends and universal joints.

High-temperature wheel bearing grease is designed to withstand the extreme temperatures encountered by wheel bearings in disc brake equipped vehicles. It usually contains molybdenum disulfide (moly), which is a dry-type lubricant.

White grease is a heavy grease for metal-to-metal applications where water is a problem. White grease stays soft under both low and high temperatures (usually from -100 to +190-degrees F), and will not wash off or dilute in the presence of water.

Assembly lube is a special extreme pressure lubricant, usually containing moly, used to lubricate high-load parts (such as main and rod bearings and cam lobes) for initial start-up of a new engine. The assembly lube lubricates the parts without being squeezed out or washed away until the engine oiling system begins to function.

Silicone lubricants are used to protect rubber, plastic, vinyl and nylon parts.

Graphite lubricants are used where oils cannot be used due to contamination problems, such as in locks. The dry graphite will lubricate metal parts while remaining uncontaminated by dirt, water, oil or acids. It is electrically conductive and will not foul electrical contacts in locks such as the ignition switch.

Moly penetrants loosen and lubricate frozen, rusted and corroded fasteners and prevent future rusting or freezing.

Heat-sink grease is a special electrically non-conductive grease that is used for mounting electronic ignition modules where it is essential that heat is transferred away from the module.

Sealants

RTV sealant is one of the most widely used gasket compounds. Made from silicone, RTV is air curing, it seals, bonds, waterproofs, fills surface irregularities, remains flexible, doesn't shrink, is relatively easy to remove, and is used as a supplementary sealer with almost all low and medium temperature gaskets.

Anaerobic sealant is much like RTV in that it can be used either to seal gaskets or to form gaskets by itself. It remains flexible, is solvent resistant and fills surface imperfections. The difference between an anaerobic sealant and an RTV-type sealant is in the curing. RTV cures when exposed to air, while an anaerobic sealant cures only in the absence of air. This means that an anaerobic sealant cures only after the assembly of parts, sealing them together.

Thread and pipe sealant is used for sealing hydraulic and pneumatic fittings and vacuum lines. It is usually made from a Teflon compound, and comes in a spray, a paint-on liquid and as a wrap-around tape.

Chemicals

Anti-seize compound prevents seizing, galling, cold welding, rust and corrosion in fasteners. High-temperature ant-seize, usually made with copper and graphite lubricants, is used for exhaust system and exhaust manifold bolts.

Anaerobic locking compounds are used to keep fasteners from vibrating or working loose and cure only after installation, in the absence of air. Medium strength locking compound is used for small nuts, bolts and screws that may be removed later. High-strength locking compound is for large nuts, bolts and studs which aren't removed on a regular basis.

Oil additives range from viscosity index improvers to chemical treatments that claim to reduce internal engine friction. It should be noted that most oil manufacturers caution against using additives with their oils.

Gas additives perform several functions, depending on their chemical makeup. They usually contain solvents that help dissolve gum and varnish that build up on carburetor, fuel injection and intake parts. They also serve to break down carbon deposits that form on the inside surfaces of the combustion chambers. Some additives contain upper cylinder lubricants for valves and piston rings, and others contain chemicals to remove condensation from the gas tank.

Miscellaneous

Brake fluid is specially formulated hydraulic fluid that can withstand the heat and pressure encountered in brake systems. Care must be taken so this fluid does not come in contact with painted surfaces or plastics. An opened container should always be resealed to prevent contamination by water or dirt.

Weatherstrip adhesive is used to bond weatherstripping around doors, windows and trunk lids. It is sometimes used to attach trim pieces.

Undercoating is a petroleum-based, tar-like substance that is designed to protect metal surfaces on the underside of the vehicle from corrosion. It also acts as a sound-deadening agent by insulating the bottom of the vehicle.

Waxes and polishes are used to help protect painted and plated surfaces from the weather. Different types of paint may require the use of different types of wax and polish. Some polishes utilize a chemical or abrasive cleaner to help remove the top layer of oxidized (dull) paint on older vehicles. In recent years many non-wax polishes that contain a wide variety of chemicals such as polymers and silicones have been introduced. These non-wax polishes are usually easier to apply and last longer than conventional waxes and polishes.

Conversion factors

Length (distance)
Inches (in)	X	25.4	= Millimeters (mm)	X 0.0394	= Inches (in)
Feet (ft)	X	0.305	= Meters (m)	X 3.281	= Feet (ft)
Miles	X	1.609	= Kilometers (km)	X 0.621	= Miles

Volume (capacity)
Cubic inches (cu in; in^3)	X	16.387	= Cubic centimeters (cc; cm^3)	X 0.061	= Cubic inches (cu in; in^3)
Imperial pints (Imp pt)	X	0.568	= Liters (l)	X 1.76	= Imperial pints (Imp pt)
Imperial quarts (Imp qt)	X	1.137	= Liters (l)	X 0.88	= Imperial quarts (Imp qt)
Imperial quarts (Imp qt)	X	1.201	= US quarts (US qt)	X 0.833	= Imperial quarts (Imp qt)
US quarts (US qt)	X	0.946	= Liters (l)	X 1.057	= US quarts (US qt)
Imperial gallons (Imp gal)	X	4.546	= Liters (l)	X 0.22	= Imperial gallons (Imp gal)
Imperial gallons (Imp gal)	X	1.201	= US gallons (US gal)	X 0.833	= Imperial gallons (Imp gal)
US gallons (US gal)	X	3.785	= Liters (l)	X 0.264	= US gallons (US gal)

Mass (weight)
Ounces (oz)	X	28.35	= Grams (g)	X 0.035	= Ounces (oz)
Pounds (lb)	X	0.454	= Kilograms (kg)	X 2.205	= Pounds (lb)

Force
Ounces-force (ozf; oz)	X	0.278	= Newtons (N)	X 3.6	= Ounces-force (ozf; oz)
Pounds-force (lbf; lb)	X	4.448	= Newtons (N)	X 0.225	= Pounds-force (lbf; lb)
Newtons (N)	X	0.1	= Kilograms-force (kgf; kg)	X 9.81	= Newtons (N)

Pressure
Pounds-force per square inch (psi; lbf/in^2; lb/in^2)	X	0.070	= Kilograms-force per square centimeter (kgf/cm^2; kg/cm^2)	X 14.223	= Pounds-force per square inch (psi; lbf/in^2; lb/in^2)
Pounds-force per square inch (psi; lbf/in^2; lb/in^2)	X	0.068	= Atmospheres (atm)	X 14.696	= Pounds-force per square inch (psi; lbf/in^2; lb/in^2)
Pounds-force per square inch (psi; lbf/in^2; lb/in^2)	X	0.069	= Bars	X 14.5	= Pounds-force per square inch (psi; lbf/in^2; lb/in^2)
Pounds-force per square inch (psi; lbf/in^2; lb/in^2)	X	6.895	= Kilopascals (kPa)	X 0.145	= Pounds-force per square inch (psi; lbf/in^2; lb/in^2)
Kilopascals (kPa)	X	0.01	= Kilograms-force per square centimeter (kgf/cm^2; kg/cm^2)	X 98.1	= Kilopascals (kPa)

Torque (moment of force)
Pounds-force inches (lbf in; lb in)	X	1.152	= Kilograms-force centimeter (kgf cm; kg cm)	X 0.868	= Pounds-force inches (lbf in; lb in)
Pounds-force inches (lbf in; lb in)	X	0.113	= Newton meters (Nm)	X 8.85	= Pounds-force inches (lbf in; lb in)
Pounds-force inches (lbf in; lb in)	X	0.083	= Pounds-force feet (lbf ft; lb ft)	X 12	= Pounds-force inches (lbf in; lb in)
Pounds-force feet (lbf ft; lb ft)	X	0.138	= Kilograms-force meters (kgf m; kg m)	X 7.233	= Pounds-force feet (lbf ft; lb ft)
Pounds-force feet (lbf ft; lb ft)	X	1.356	= Newton meters (Nm)	X 0.738	= Pounds-force feet (lbf ft; lb ft)
Newton meters (Nm)	X	0.102	= Kilograms-force meters (kgf m; kg m)	X 9.804	= Newton meters (Nm)

Vacuum
Inches mercury (in. Hg)	X	3.377	= Kilopascals (kPa)	X 0.2961	= Inches mercury
Inches mercury (in. Hg)	X	25.4	= Millimeters mercury (mm Hg)	X 0.0394	= Inches mercury

Power
Horsepower (hp)	X	745.7	= Watts (W)	X 0.0013	= Horsepower (hp)

Velocity (speed)
Miles per hour (miles/hr; mph)	X	1.609	= Kilometers per hour (km/hr; kph)	X 0.621	= Miles per hour (miles/hr; mph)

Fuel consumption*
Miles per gallon, Imperial (mpg)	X	0.354	= Kilometers per liter (km/l)	X 2.825	= Miles per gallon, Imperial (mpg)
Miles per gallon, US (mpg)	X	0.425	= Kilometers per liter (km/l)	X 2.352	= Miles per gallon, US (mpg)

Temperature
Degrees Fahrenheit = (°C x 1.8) + 32

Degrees Celsius (Degrees Centigrade; °C) = (°F - 32) x 0.56

*It is common practice to convert from miles per gallon (mpg) to liters/100 kilometers (l/100km), where mpg (Imperial) x l/100 km = 282 and mpg (US) x l/100 km = 235

DECIMALS to MILLIMETERS

Decimal	mm	Decimal	mm
0.001	0.0254	0.500	12.7000
0.002	0.0508	0.510	12.9540
0.003	0.0762	0.520	13.2080
0.004	0.1016	0.530	13.4620
0.005	0.1270	0.540	13.7160
0.006	0.1524	0.550	13.9700
0.007	0.1778	0.560	14.2240
0.008	0.2032	0.570	14.4780
0.009	0.2286	0.580	14.7320
		0.590	14.9860
0.010	0.2540		
0.020	0.5080		
0.030	0.7620		
0.040	1.0160	0.600	15.2400
0.050	1.2700	0.610	15.4940
0.060	1.5240	0.620	15.7480
0.070	1.7780	0.630	16.0020
0.080	2.0320	0.640	16.2560
0.090	2.2860	0.650	16.5100
		0.660	16.7640
0.100	2.5400	0.670	17.0180
0.110	2.7940	0.680	17.2720
0.120	3.0480	0.690	17.5260
0.130	3.3020		
0.140	3.5560		
0.150	3.8100		
0.160	4.0640	0.700	17.7800
0.170	4.3180	0.710	18.0340
0.180	4.5720	0.720	18.2880
0.190	4.8260	0.730	18.5420
		0.740	18.7960
0.200	5.0800	0.750	19.0500
0.210	5.3340	0.760	19.3040
0.220	5.5880	0.770	19.5580
0.230	5.8420	0.780	19.8120
0.240	6.0960	0.790	20.0660
0.250	6.3500		
0.260	6.6040		
0.270	6.8580	0.800	20.3200
0.280	7.1120	0.810	20.5740
0.290	7.3660	0.820	21.8280
		0.830	21.0820
0.300	7.6200	0.840	21.3360
0.310	7.8740	0.850	21.5900
0.320	8.1280	0.860	21.8440
0.330	8.3820	0.870	22.0980
0.340	8.6360	0.880	22.3520
0.350	8.8900	0.890	22.6060
0.360	9.1440		
0.370	9.3980		
0.380	9.6520		
0.390	9.9060	0.900	22.8600
0.400	10.1600	0.910	23.1140
0.410	10.4140	0.920	23.3680
0.420	10.6680	0.930	23.6220
0.430	10.9220	0.940	23.8760
0.440	11.1760	0.950	24.1300
0.450	11.4300	0.960	24.3840
0.460	11.6840	0.970	24.6380
0.470	11.9380	0.980	24.8920
0.480	12.1920	0.990	25.1460
0.490	12.4460	1.000	25.4000

FRACTIONS to DECIMALS to MILLIMETERS

Fraction	Decimal	mm	Fraction	Decimal	mm
1/64	0.0156	0.3969	33/64	0.5156	13.0969
1/32	0.0312	0.7938	17/32	0.5312	13.4938
3/64	0.0469	1.1906	35/64	0.5469	13.8906
1/16	0.0625	1.5875	9/16	0.5625	14.2875
5/64	0.0781	1.9844	37/64	0.5781	14.6844
3/32	0.0938	2.3812	19/32	0.5938	15.0812
7/64	0.1094	2.7781	39/64	0.6094	15.4781
1/8	0.1250	3.1750	5/8	0.6250	15.8750
9/64	0.1406	3.5719	41/64	0.6406	16.2719
5/32	0.1562	3.9688	21/32	0.6562	16.6688
11/64	0.1719	4.3656	43/64	0.6719	17.0656
3/16	0.1875	4.7625	11/16	0.6875	17.4625
13/64	0.2031	5.1594	45/64	0.7031	17.8594
7/32	0.2188	5.5562	23/32	0.7188	18.2562
15/64	0.2344	5.9531	47/64	0.7344	18.6531
1/4	0.2500	6.3500	3/4	0.7500	19.0500
17/64	0.2656	6.7469	49/64	0.7656	19.4469
9/32	0.2812	7.1438	25/32	0.7812	19.8438
19/64	0.2969	7.5406	51/64	0.7969	20.2406
5/16	0.3125	7.9375	13/16	0.8125	20.6375
21/64	0.3281	8.3344	53/64	0.8281	21.0344
11/32	0.3438	8.7312	27/32	0.8438	21.4312
23/64	0.3594	9.1281	55/64	0.8594	21.8281
3/8	0.3750	9.5250	7/8	0.8750	22.2250
25/64	0.3906	9.9219	57/64	0.8906	22.6219
13/32	0.4062	10.3188	29/32	0.9062	23.0188
27/64	0.4219	10.7156	59/64	0.9219	23.4156
7/16	0.4375	11.1125	15/16	0.9375	23.8125
29/64	0.4531	11.5094	61/64	0.9531	24.2094
15/32	0.4688	11.9062	31/32	0.9688	24.6062
31/64	0.4844	12.3031	63/64	0.9844	25.0031
1/2	0.5000	12.7000	1	1.0000	25.4000

Safety first!

Regardless of how enthusiastic you may be about getting on with the job at hand, take the time to ensure that your safety is not jeopardized. A moment's lack of attention can result in an accident, as can failure to observe certain simple safety precautions. The possibility of an accident will always exist, and the following points should not be considered a comprehensive list of all dangers. Rather, they are intended to make you aware of the risks and to encourage a safety conscious approach to all work you carry out on your vehicle.

Essential DOs and DON'Ts

DON'T rely on a jack when working under the vehicle. Always use approved jackstands to support the weight of the vehicle and place them under the recommended lift or support points.

DON'T attempt to loosen extremely tight fasteners (i.e. wheel lug nuts) while the vehicle is on a jack - it may fall.

DON'T start the engine without first making sure that the transmission is in Neutral (or Park where applicable) and the parking brake is set.

DON'T remove the radiator cap from a hot cooling system - let it cool or cover it with a cloth and release the pressure gradually.

DON'T attempt to drain the engine oil until you are sure it has cooled to the point that it will not burn you.

DON'T touch any part of the engine or exhaust system until it has cooled sufficiently to avoid burns.

DON'T siphon toxic liquids such as gasoline, antifreeze and brake fluid by mouth, or allow them to remain on your skin.

DON'T inhale brake lining dust - it is potentially hazardous (see *Asbestos* below).

DON'T allow spilled oil or grease to remain on the floor - wipe it up before someone slips on it.

DON'T use loose fitting wrenches or other tools which may slip and cause injury.

DON'T push on wrenches when loosening or tightening nuts or bolts. Always try to pull the wrench toward you. If the situation calls for pushing the wrench away, push with an open hand to avoid scraped knuckles if the wrench should slip.

DON'T attempt to lift a heavy component alone - get someone to help you.

DON'T rush or take unsafe shortcuts to finish a job.

DON'T allow children or animals in or around the vehicle while you are working on it.

DO wear eye protection when using power tools such as a drill, sander, bench grinder, etc. and when working under a vehicle.

DO keep loose clothing and long hair well out of the way of moving parts.

DO make sure that any hoist used has a safe working load rating adequate for the job.

DO get someone to check on you periodically when working alone on a vehicle.

DO carry out work in a logical sequence and make sure that everything is correctly assembled and tightened.

DO keep chemicals and fluids tightly capped and out of the reach of children and pets.

DO remember that your vehicle's safety affects that of yourself and others. If in doubt on any point, get professional advice.

Steering, suspension and brakes

These systems are essential to driving safety, so make sure you have a qualified shop or individual check your work. Also, compressed suspension springs can cause injury if released suddenly - be sure to use a spring compressor.

Airbags

Airbags are explosive devices that can **CAUSE** injury if they deploy while you're working on the vehicle. Follow the manufacturer's instructions to disable the airbag whenever you're working in the vicinity of airbag components.

Asbestos

Certain friction, insulating, sealing, and other products - such as brake linings, brake bands, clutch linings, torque converters, gaskets, etc. - may contain asbestos or other hazardous friction material. Extreme care must be taken to avoid inhalation of dust from such products, since it is hazardous to health. If in doubt, assume that they do contain asbestos.

Fire

Remember at all times that gasoline is highly flammable. Never smoke or have any kind of open flame around when working on a vehicle. But the risk does not end there. A spark caused by an electrical short circuit, by two metal surfaces contacting each other, or even by static electricity built up in your body under certain conditions, can ignite gasoline vapors, which in a confined space are highly explosive. Do not, under any circumstances, use gasoline for cleaning parts. Use an approved safety solvent.

Always disconnect the battery ground (-) cable at the battery before working on any part of the fuel system or electrical system. Never risk spilling fuel on a hot engine or exhaust component. It is strongly recommended that a fire extinguisher suitable for use on fuel and electrical fires be kept handy in the garage or workshop at all times. Never try to extinguish a fuel or electrical fire with water.

Fumes

Certain fumes are highly toxic and can quickly cause unconsciousness and even death if inhaled to any extent. Gasoline vapor falls into this category, as do the vapors from some cleaning solvents. Any draining or pouring of such volatile fluids should be done in a well ventilated area.

When using cleaning fluids and solvents, read the instructions on the container carefully. Never use materials from unmarked containers.

Never run the engine in an enclosed space, such as a garage. Exhaust fumes contain carbon monoxide, which is extremely poisonous. If you need to run the engine, always do so in the open air, or at least have the rear of the vehicle outside the work area.

The battery

Never create a spark or allow a bare light bulb near a battery. They normally give off a certain amount of hydrogen gas, which is highly explosive.

Always disconnect the battery ground (-) cable at the battery before working on the fuel or electrical systems.

If possible, loosen the filler caps or cover when charging the battery from an external source (this does not apply to sealed or maintenance-free batteries). Do not charge at an excessive rate or the battery may burst.

Take care when adding water to a non maintenance-free battery and when carrying a battery. The electrolyte, even when diluted, is very corrosive and should not be allowed to contact clothing or skin.

Always wear eye protection when cleaning the battery to prevent the caustic deposits from entering your eyes.

Household current

When using an electric power tool, inspection light, etc., which operates on household current, always make sure that the tool is correctly connected to its plug and that, where necessary, it is properly grounded. Do not use such items in damp conditions and, again, do not create a spark or apply excessive heat in the vicinity of fuel or fuel vapor.

Secondary ignition system voltage

A severe electric shock can result from touching certain parts of the ignition system (such as the spark plug wires) when the engine is running or being cranked, particularly if components are damp or the insulation is defective. In the case of an electronic ignition system, the secondary system voltage is much higher and could prove fatal.

Hydrofluoric acid

This extremely corrosive acid is formed when certain types of synthetic rubber, found in some O-rings, oil seals, fuel hoses, etc. are exposed to temperatures above 750-degrees F (400-degrees C). The rubber changes into a charred or sticky substance containing the acid. *Once formed, the acid remains dangerous for years. If it gets onto the skin, it may be necessary to amputate the limb concerned.*

When dealing with a vehicle which has suffered a fire, or with components salvaged from such a vehicle, wear protective gloves and discard them after use.

Troubleshooting

Contents

This section provides an easy reference guide to the more common problems which may occur during the operation of your vehicle. These problems and their possible causes are grouped under headings denoting various components or systems, such as Engine, Cooling system, etc. They also refer you to the chapter and/or section which deals with the problem.

Remember that successful troubleshooting is not a mysterious black art practiced only by professional mechanics. It is simply the result of the right knowledge combined with an intelligent, systematic approach to the problem. Always work by a process of elimination, starting with the simplest solution and working through to the most complex - and never overlook the obvious. Anyone can run the gas tank dry or leave the lights on overnight, so don't assume that you are exempt from such oversights.

Finally, always establish a clear idea of why a problem has occurred and take steps to ensure that it doesn't happen again. If the electrical system fails because of a poor connection, check the other connections in the system to make sure that they don't fail as well. If a particular fuse continues to blow, find out why - don't just replace one fuse after another. Remember, failure of a small component can often be indicative of potential failure or incorrect functioning of a more important component or system.

Engine

1 Engine will not rotate when attempting to start

1 Battery terminal connections loose or corroded (Chapter 1).
2 Battery discharged or faulty (Chapter 1).
3 Automatic transaxle not completely engaged in Park (Chapter 7A) or clutch pedal not completely depressed (Chapter 8).
4 Broken, loose or disconnected wiring in the starting circuit (Chapters 5 and 12).
5 Starter motor pinion jammed in flywheel ring gear (Chapter 5).
6 Starter solenoid faulty (Chapter 5).
7 Starter motor faulty (Chapter 5).
8 Ignition switch faulty (Chapter 12).
9 Starter pinion or flywheel teeth worn or broken (Chapter 5).

2 Engine rotates but will not start

1 Fuel tank empty.
2 Battery discharged (engine rotates slowly) (Chapter 5).
3 Battery terminal connections loose or corroded (Chapter 1).

4 Leaking fuel injector(s), faulty fuel pump, pressure regulator, etc. (Chapter 4).
5 Broken timing chain (Chapter 2A).
6 Ignition system problem (Chapter 5).
7 Worn, faulty or incorrectly gapped spark plugs (Chapter 1).
8 Broken, loose or disconnected wiring in the starting circuit (Chapter 5).
9 Loose distributor is changing ignition timing (Chapter 5).
10 Defective MAF sensor (see Chapter 6).

3 Engine hard to start when cold

1 Battery discharged or low (Chapter 1).
2 Malfunctioning fuel system (Chapter 4).
3 Faulty coolant temperature sensor or intake air temperature sensor (Chapter 6).
4 Injector(s) leaking (Chapter 4).
5 Faulty ignition system (Chapter 5).
6 Defective MAF sensor (see Chapter 6).

4 Engine hard to start when hot

1 Air filter clogged (Chapter 1).
2 Fuel not reaching the fuel injection system (Chapter 4).
3 Corroded battery connections, especially ground (Chapter 1).
4 Faulty coolant temperature sensor or intake air temperature sensor (Chapter 6).

5 Starter motor noisy or excessively rough in engagement

1 Pinion or flywheel gear teeth worn or broken (Chapter 5).
2 Starter motor mounting bolts loose or missing (Chapter 5).

6 Engine starts but stops immediately

1 Insufficient fuel reaching the fuel injector(s) (Chapters 1 and 4).
2 Vacuum leak at the gasket between the intake manifold/plenum and throttle body (Chapters 1 and 4).

7 Oil puddle under engine

1 Oil pan gasket and/or oil pan drain bolt washer leaking (Chapter 2A).
2 Oil pressure sending unit leaking (Chapter 2A).
3 Valve cover leaking (Chapter 2A).
4 Engine oil seals leaking (Chapter 2A).
5 Oil pump housing leaking (Chapter 2A).

8 Engine lopes while idling or idles erratically

1 Vacuum leakage (Chapters 2A and 4).
2 Air filter clogged (Chapter 1).
3 Fuel pump not delivering sufficient fuel to the fuel injection system (Chapter 4).
4 Leaking head gasket (Chapter 2A).
5 Timing chain and/or sprockets worn (Chapter 2A).
6 Camshaft lobes worn (Chapter 2A).

9 Engine misses at idle speed

1 Spark plugs worn or not gapped properly (Chapter 1).
2 Vacuum leaks (Chapters 2A and 4).
3 Uneven or low compression (Chapter 2A).
4 Problem with the fuel injection system (Chapter 4).
5 Faulty ignition coils (Chapter 5).

10 Engine misses throughout driving speed range

1 Fuel filter clogged and/or impurities in the fuel system (Chapter 1).
2 Low fuel output at the fuel injector(s) (Chapter 4).
3 Faulty or incorrectly gapped spark plugs (Chapter 1).
4 Faulty ignition coils (Chapter 5).
5 Faulty emission system components (Chapter 6).
6 Low or uneven cylinder compression pressures (Chapter 2A).
7 Vacuum leak in fuel injection system, throttle body, intake manifold, IAC/AAC valve or vacuum hoses (Chapter 4).

11 Engine stumbles on acceleration

1 Spark plugs fouled (Chapter 1).
2 Problem with fuel injection system (Chapter 4).
3 Fuel filter clogged (Chapters 1 and 4).
4 Intake manifold air leak (Chapters 2A and 4).

12 Engine surges while holding accelerator steady

1 Intake air leak (Chapter 4).
2 Fuel pump or fuel pressure regulator faulty (Chapter 4).
3 Problem with fuel injection system (Chapter 4).
4 Problem with the emissions control system (Chapter 6).

13 Engine stalls

1   Fuel filter clogged and/or water and impurities in the fuel system (Chapters 1 and 4).
2   Faulty emissions system components (Chapter 6).
3   Faulty or incorrectly gapped spark plugs (Chapter 1).
4   Vacuum leak in the fuel injection system, intake manifold or vacuum hoses (Chapters 2A and 4).
5   Valve clearances incorrectly set (Chapter 1).

14 Engine lacks power

1   Faulty or incorrectly gapped spark plugs (Chapter 1).
2   Problem with the fuel injection system (Chapter 4).
3   Plugged air filter (Chapter 1).
4   Brakes binding (Chapter 9).
5   Automatic transaxle fluid level incorrect (Chapter 1).
6   Clutch slipping (Chapter 8).
7   Fuel filter clogged and/or impurities in the fuel system (Chapters 1 and 4).
8   Emission control system not functioning properly (Chapter 6).
9   Low or uneven cylinder compression pressures (Chapter 2A).
10   Obstructed exhaust system (Chapters 2A and 4).

15 Engine backfires

1   Emission control system not functioning properly (Chapter 6).
2   Problem with the fuel injection system (Chapter 4).
3   Vacuum leak at fuel injector(s), intake manifold or vacuum hoses (Chapters 2A and 4).
4   Valve clearances incorrectly set and/or valves sticking (Chapter 1).

16 Pinging or knocking engine sounds during acceleration or uphill

1   Incorrect grade of fuel.
2   Fuel injection system faulty (Chapter 4).
3   Improper or damaged spark plugs (Chapter 1).
4   Malfunctioning knock sensor (Chapter 6).
5   Vacuum leak (Chapters 2A and 4).

17 Engine runs with oil pressure light on

1   Low oil level (Chapter 1).
2   Idle rpm below specification (Chapter 1).

3   Short in wiring circuit (Chapter 12).
4   Faulty oil pressure sender (Chapter 2B).
5   Worn engine bearings and/or oil pump (Chapter 2A).

18 Engine continues to run after switching off

Faulty ignition switch (Chapter 12), Powertrain Control Module (PCM) (Chapter 6), or Body Control Module (BCM).

Engine electrical system

19 Battery will not hold a charge

1   Alternator drivebelt defective or not adjusted properly (Chapter 1).
2   Battery electrolyte level low (Chapter 1).
3   Battery terminals loose or corroded (Chapter 1).
4   Alternator not charging properly (Chapter 5).
5   Loose, broken or faulty wiring in the charging circuit (Chapter 5).
6   Short in vehicle wiring (Chapter 12).
7   Internally defective battery (Chapters 1 and 5).

20 Alternator light fails to go out

1   Faulty alternator or charging circuit (Chapter 5).
2   Alternator drivebelt defective or out of adjustment (Chapter 1).
3   Alternator voltage regulator inoperative (Chapter 5).

21 Alternator light fails to come on when key is turned on

1   Warning light bulb defective (Chapter 12).
2   Fault in the instrument cluster, dash wiring or bulb holder (Chapter 12).

Fuel system

22 Excessive fuel consumption

1   Dirty or clogged air filter element (Chapter 1).
2   Emissions system not functioning properly (Chapter 6).
3   Fuel injection system not functioning properly (Chapter 4).
4   Low tire pressure or incorrect tire size (Chapter 1).

23 Fuel leakage and/or fuel odor

1   Leaking fuel feed or return line (Chapters 1 and 4).
2   Tank overfilled.
3   Problem with fuel injection system (Chapter 4).

Cooling system

24 Overheating

1   Insufficient coolant in system (Chapter 1).
2   Water pump drivebelt defective or out of adjustment (Chapter 1).
3   Radiator core blocked or grille restricted (Chapter 3).
4   Thermostat faulty (Chapter 3).
5   Electric coolant fan inoperative or blades broken (Chapter 3).
6   Radiator cap not maintaining proper pressure (Chapter 3).

25 Overcooling

Faulty thermostat (Chapter 3).

26 External coolant leakage

1   Deteriorated/damaged hoses; loose clamps (Chapters 1 and 3).
2   Water pump defective (Chapter 3).
3   Leakage from radiator core or coolant reservoir bottle (Chapter 3).
4   Engine drain or water jacket core plugs leaking.

27 Internal coolant leakage

1   Leaking cylinder head gasket (Chapter 2A).
2   Cracked cylinder bore or cylinder head (Chapter 2A).

28 Coolant loss

1   Too much coolant in system (Chapter 1).
2   Coolant boiling away because of overheating (Chapter 3).
3   Internal or external leakage (Chapter 3).
4   Faulty radiator cap (Chapter 3).

29 Poor coolant circulation

1   Inoperative water pump (Chapter 3).
2   Restriction in cooling system (Chapters 1 and 3).

3   Water pump drivebelt defective/out of adjustment (Chapter 1).
4   Thermostat sticking (Chapter 3).

Clutch

30   Pedal travels to floor - no pressure or very little resistance

1   Hydraulic release system leaking or air in the system (Chapter 8).
2   Broken release bearing or fork (Chapter 8).

31   Unable to select gears

1   Faulty transaxle (Chapter 7A).
2   Faulty clutch disc or pressure plate (Chapter 8).
3   Faulty release lever or release bearing (Chapter 8).
4   Faulty shift lever assembly or cable(s) (Chapter 8).

32   Clutch slips (engine speed increases with no increase in vehicle speed)

1   Clutch plate worn (Chapter 8).
2   Clutch plate is oil soaked by leaking rear main seal (Chapter 8).
3   Warped pressure plate or flywheel (Chapter 8).
4   Weak diaphragm spring in pressure plate (Chapter 8).
5   Piston stuck in bore of clutch release cylinder, preventing clutch from fully engaging (Chapter 8).

33   Grabbing (chattering) as clutch is engaged

1   Oil on clutch plate lining, burned or glazed facings (Chapter 8).
2   Worn or loose engine or transaxle mounts (Chapters 2A and 7A).
3   Worn splines on clutch plate hub (Chapter 8).
4   Warped pressure plate or flywheel (Chapter 8).
5   Burned or smeared resin on flywheel or pressure plate (Chapter 8).

34   Transaxle rattling (clicking)

1   Release bearing defective (Chapter 8).
2   Internal transaxle problem.

35   Noise in clutch area

Faulty bearing (Chapter 8).

36   Clutch pedal stays on floor

1   Defective release cylinder (Chapter 8).
2   Hydraulic release system leaking or air in the system (Chapter 8).

37   High pedal effort

1   Piston binding in bore of release cylinder (Chapter 8).
2   Pressure plate faulty (Chapter 8).

Manual transaxle

38   Knocking noise at low speeds

1   Worn driveaxle constant velocity (CV) joints (Chapter 8).
2   Worn side gear shaft counterbore in differential case (Chapter 7A).*

39   Noise most pronounced when turning

Differential gear noise (Chapter 7A).*

40   Clunk on acceleration or deceleration

1   Loose engine or transaxle mounts (Chapters 2A and 7A).
2   Worn differential pinion shaft in case.*
3   Worn side gear shaft counterbore in differential case (Chapter 7A).*
4   Worn or damaged driveaxle inboard CV joints (Chapter 8).

41   Clicking noise in turns

Worn or damaged outboard CV joint (Chapter 8).

42   Vibration

1   Rough wheel bearing (Chapter 10).
2   Damaged driveaxle (Chapter 8).
3   Out of round tires.
4   Tire out of balance.
5   Worn CV joint (Chapter 8).

43   Noisy in neutral with engine running

1   Damaged input gear bearing (Chapter 7A).*
2   Damaged clutch release bearing (Chapter 8).

44   Noisy in one particular gear

1   Damaged or worn constant mesh gears (Chapter 7A).*
2   Damaged or worn synchronizers (Chapter 7A).*
3   Bent reverse fork (Chapter 7A).*
4   Damaged fourth speed gear or output gear (Chapter 7A).*
5   Worn or damaged reverse idler gear or idler bushing (Chapter 7A).*

45   Noisy in all gears

1   Insufficient lubricant (Chapter 7A).
2   Damaged or worn bearings (Chapter 7A).*
3   Worn or damaged input gear shaft and/or output gear shaft (Chapter 7A).*

46   Slips out of gear

1   Worn or improperly adjusted linkage (Chapter 7A).
2   Shift linkage does not work freely, binds (Chapter 7A).
3   Input gear bearing retainer broken or loose (Chapter 7A).*
4   Worn shift fork (Chapter 7A).*

47   Leaks lubricant

1   Side gear shaft seals worn (Chapter 7A).
2   Excessive amount of lubricant in transaxle (Chapter 1).
3   Loose or broken input gear shaft bearing retainer (Chapter 7A).*
4   Input gear bearing retainer O-ring and/or lip seal damaged (Chapter 7A).*
5   Shifter shaft seal leaking (Chapter 7A).

48   Hard to shift

Shift cable(s) worn (Chapter 7A).
* Although the corrective action necessary to remedy the symptoms described is beyond the scope of this manual, the above information should be helpful in isolating the cause of the condition so that the owner can communicate clearly with a professional mechanic.

Automatic transaxle

49 Fluid leakage

1   Automatic transaxle fluid is a deep red color. Fluid leaks should not be confused with engine oil, which can easily be blown onto the transaxle by air flow.

2   To pinpoint a leak, first remove all built-up dirt and grime from the transaxle housing with degreasing agents and/or steam cleaning. Then drive the vehicle at low speeds so air flow will not blow the leak far from its source. Raise the vehicle and determine where the leak is coming from. Common areas of leakage are:

- *PanDipstick tube*
- *Transaxle oil lines*
- *Speed sensor (Chapter 7A)*
- *Driveaxle oil seals (Chapter 7A)*

50 Transaxle fluid brown or has a burned smell

Transaxle fluid overheated (Chapter 1).

51 General shift mechanism problems

1   Chapter 7B deals with checking and adjusting the shift cable on automatic transaxles. Common problems which may be attributed to a poorly adjusted cable are:

- *Engine starting in gears other than Park or Neutral*
- *Indicator on shifter pointing to a gear other than the one actually being used*
- *Vehicle moves when in Park*

2   Refer to Chapter 7B for the shift cable adjustment procedure.

52 Transaxle will not downshift with accelerator pedal pressed to the floor

The transaxle is electronically controlled. This type of problem - which is caused by a malfunction in the control unit, a sensor or solenoid, or the circuit itself - is beyond the scope of this book. Take the vehicle to a dealer service department or a competent automatic transmission shop.

53 Engine will start in gears other than Park or Neutral

Neutral start switch out of adjustment or malfunctioning (Chapter 7B).

54 Transaxle slips, is noisy or has no drive in forward or reverse gears

There are many probable causes for the above problems, but the home mechanic should be concerned with only one possibility - fluid level. Before taking the vehicle to a repair shop, check the level and condition of the fluid as described in Chapter 1. Correct the fluid level as necessary or change the fluid if needed. If the problem persists, have a professional diagnose the cause.

Driveaxles

55 Clicking noise in turns

Worn or damaged outboard CV joint (Chapter 8).

56 Shudder or vibration during acceleration

1   Excessive toe-in (Chapter 10).
2   Worn or damaged inboard or outboard CV joints (Chapter 8).
3   Sticking inboard CV joint assembly (Chapter 8).

57 Vibration at highway speeds

1   Out of balance front wheels and/or tires.
2   Out of round front tires.
3   Worn CV joint(s) (Chapter 8).

Brakes

58 Vehicle pulls to one side during braking

1   Incorrect tire pressures (Chapter 1).
2   Front end out of alignment (have the front end aligned).
3   Front, or rear, tire sizes not matched to one another.
4   Restricted brake lines or hoses (Chapter 9).
5   Malfunctioning caliper assembly (Chapter 9).
6   Loose suspension parts (Chapter 10).
7   Loose calipers (Chapter 9).
8   Excessive wear of brake pad material or disc on one side.

59 Noise (high-pitched squeal when the brakes are applied)

Front and/or rear disc brake pads worn out.

The noise comes from the wear sensor rubbing against the disc (does not apply to all vehicles). Replace pads with new ones immediately (Chapter 9).

60 Brake roughness or chatter (pedal pulsates)

1   Excessive lateral runout (Chapter 9).
2   Uneven pad wear (Chapter 9).
3   Defective disc (Chapter 9).

61 Excessive brake pedal effort required to stop vehicle

1   Malfunctioning power brake booster (Chapter 9).
2   Partial system failure (Chapter 9).
3   Excessively worn pads (Chapter 9).
4   Piston in caliper stuck or sluggish (Chapter 9).
5   Brake pads contaminated with brake fluid, oil or grease (Chapter 9).
6   Brake disc grooved and/or glazed (Chapter 1).
7   New pads installed and not yet seated. It will take a while for the new material to seat against the disc.

62 Excessive brake pedal travel

1   Partial brake system failure (Chapter 9).
2   Insufficient fluid in master cylinder (Chapters 1 and 9).
3   Air trapped in system (Chapters 1 and 9).

63 Dragging brakes

1   Incorrect adjustment of brake light switch (Chapter 9).
2   Master cylinder pistons not returning correctly (Chapter 9).
3   Restricted brakes lines or hoses (Chapters 1 and 9).
4   Incorrect parking brake adjustment (Chapter 9).

64 Grabbing or uneven braking action

1   Malfunction of proportioning valve (Chapter 9).
2   Binding brake pedal mechanism (Chapter 9).

65 Brake pedal feels spongy when depressed

1   Air in hydraulic lines (Chapter 9).
2   Master cylinder mounting bolts loose (Chapter 9).
3   Master cylinder defective (Chapter 9).

66 Brake pedal travels to the floor with little resistance

1   Little or no fluid in the master cylinder reservoir caused by leaking caliper piston(s) (Chapter 9).
2   Loose, damaged or disconnected brake lines (Chapter 9).

67 Parking brake does not hold

Parking brake improperly adjusted (Chapter 9).

Suspension and steering systems

68 Vehicle pulls to one side

1   Mismatched or uneven tires.
2   Broken or sagging springs (Chapter 10).
3   Wheel alignment out-of-specifications.
4   Front brake dragging (Chapter 9).

69 Abnormal or excessive tire wear

1   Wheel alignment out-of-specifications (Chapter 10).
2   Sagging or broken springs (Chapter 10).
3   Tire out-of-balance.
4   Worn strut damper (Chapter 10).
5   Overloaded vehicle.
6   Tires not rotated regularly.

70 Wheel makes a thumping noise

1   Blister or bump on tire.
2   Improper strut damper action (Chapter 10).

71 Shimmy, shake or vibration

1   Tire or wheel out-of-balance or out-of-round.
2   Worn wheel bearings (Chapters 1, 8 and 10).
3   Worn tie-rod ends (Chapter 10).
4   Worn lower balljoints (Chapters 1 and 10).
5   Excessive wheel runout.
6   Blister or bump on tire.

72 Hard steering

1   Lack of lubrication at balljoints or tie-rod ends (Chapter 10).

2   Front wheel alignment out-of-specifications.
3   Low tire pressure(s) (Chapter 1).

73 Poor returnability of steering to center

1   Worn balljoints or tie-rod ends (Chapter 10).
2   Binding in balljoints (Chapter 10).
3   Binding in steering column (Chapter 10).
4   Worn steering gear assembly (Chapter 10).
5   Front wheel alignment out-of-specifications.

74 Abnormal noise at the front end

1   Worn balljoints or tie-rod ends (Chapter 10).
2   Damaged strut mounting (Chapter 10).
3   Worn control arm bushings or tie-rod ends (Chapter 10).
4   Loose stabilizer bar (Chapter 10).
5   Loose wheel nuts.
6   Loose suspension bolts (Chapter 10).

75 Wander or poor steering stability

1   Mismatched or uneven tires.
2   Worn balljoints or tie-rod ends (Chapter 10).
3   Worn strut assemblies (Chapter 10).
4   Loose stabilizer bar (Chapter 10).
5   Broken or sagging springs (Chapter 10).
6   Wheels out of alignment.

76 Erratic steering when braking

1   Wheel bearings worn (Chapter 10).
2   Broken or sagging springs (Chapter 10).
3   Leaking caliper (Chapter 9).
4   Warped brake discs (Chapter 9).

77 Excessive pitching and/or rolling around corners or during braking

1   Loose stabilizer bar (Chapter 10).
2   Worn strut dampers or mountings (Chapter 10).
3   Broken or sagging springs (Chapter 10).
4   Overloaded vehicle.

78 Suspension bottoms

1   Overloaded vehicle.
2   Worn strut dampers, shock absorbers or springs (Chapter 10).

79 Cupped tires

1   Front wheel or rear wheel alignment out-of-specifications.
2   Worn strut dampers or shock absorbers (Chapter 10).
3   Wheel bearings worn (Chapter 10).
4   Excessive tire or wheel runout.
5   Worn balljoints (Chapter 10).

80 Excessive tire wear on outside edge

1   Inflation pressures incorrect (Chapter 1).
2   Excessive speed in turns.
3   Front end alignment incorrect (excessive toe-in). Have professionally aligned.
4   Suspension arm bent (Chapter 10).

81 Excessive tire wear on inside edge

1   Inflation pressures incorrect (Chapter 1).
2   Front end alignment incorrect (toe-out). Have professionally aligned.
3   Loose or damaged steering components (Chapter 10).

82 Tire tread worn in one place

1   Tires out-of-balance.
2   Damaged or buckled wheel. Inspect and replace if necessary.
3   Defective tire (Chapter 1).

83 Excessive play or looseness in steering system

1   Wheel bearing(s) worn (Chapter 10).
2   Tie-rod end loose (Chapter 10).
3   Steering gear loose (Chapter 10).
4   Worn or loose steering intermediate shaft (Chapter 10).

84 Rattling or clicking noise in steering gear

1   Steering gear loose (Chapter 10).
2   Steering gear defective.

Notes

Chapter 1
Tune-up and routine maintenance

Contents

Specifications

Recommended lubricants and fluids

Note: *Listed here are manufacturer recommendations at the time this manual was written. Manufacturers occasionally upgrade their fluid and lubricant specifications, so check with your local auto parts store for current recommendations.*

Engine oil
    Type .... API "certified for gasoline engines"
    Viscosity
        Non-turbocharged engine .... SAE 5W-20
        Turbocharged engine .... SAE 5W-30
Fuel .... Unleaded gasoline, 87 octane
Automatic transaxle fluid .... Motorcraft® Dual Clutch Transmission Fluid / XT-11-QDC
    (WSS-M2C200-D2)
Manual transaxle lubricant .... Motorcraft® Dual Clutch Transmission Fluid XT-11-QDC
Brake/clutch fluid .... DOT 4 LV High Performance Brake Fluid
Engine coolant .... Motorcraft® Orange Antifreeze/Coolant

Caution: *Do not mix coolants of different colors. Doing so might damage the cooling system and/or the engine.*

Capacities*

Engine oil (including filter)	4.5 quarts (4.3 liters)
Coolant	6.8 quarts (6.4 liters)
Automatic transaxle (dry fill)	1.9 quarts (1.8 liters)
Manual transaxle	Up to 2.0 quarts (1.9 liters)

*All capacities approximate. Add as necessary to bring up to appropriate level.

Ignition system

Spark plug type	Check with your auto parts provider
Spark plug gap	
Non-turbocharged engine	0.035 inch (0.9 mm)
Turbocharged engine	0.031 inch (0.8 mm)
Engine firing order	1-3-4-2

Brakes

Disc brake pad friction material minimum thickness	0.059 inch (1.5 mm)
Drum brake shoe lining thickness (minimum)	0.039 inch (1 mm)

Torque specifications

Note: *One foot-pound (ft-lb) of torque is equivalent to 12 inch-pounds (in-lbs) of torque. Torque values below approximately 15 ft-lbs are expressed in inch-pounds, because most foot-pound torque wrenches are not accurate at these smaller values.*

	Ft-lbs (unless otherwise indicated)	Nm
Engine oil drain plug	20	27
Automatic transaxle drain plug	32	43
Manual transaxle drain and fill plug	26	35
Spark plugs		
Non-turbocharged engine	133 in-lbs	15
Turbocharged engine	106 in-lbs	12
Drivebelt tensioner bolts	18	25
Wheel lug nuts	100	135

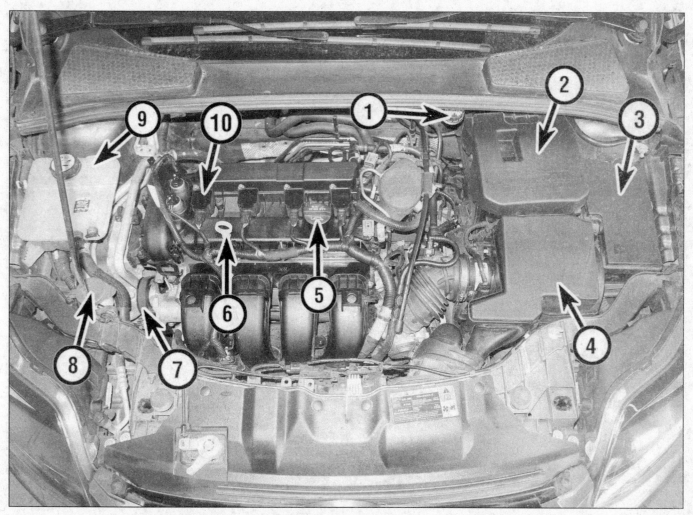

Typical engine compartment components (non-turbo engine)

1	Brake/clutch fluid reservoir	5	Engine oil filler cap	9	Coolant expansion tank
2	Battery	6	Engine oil dipstick	10	Spark plugs (under ignition coils)
3	Fuse/relay block	7	Drivebelt		
4	Air filter housing	8	Windshield washer fluid reservoir		

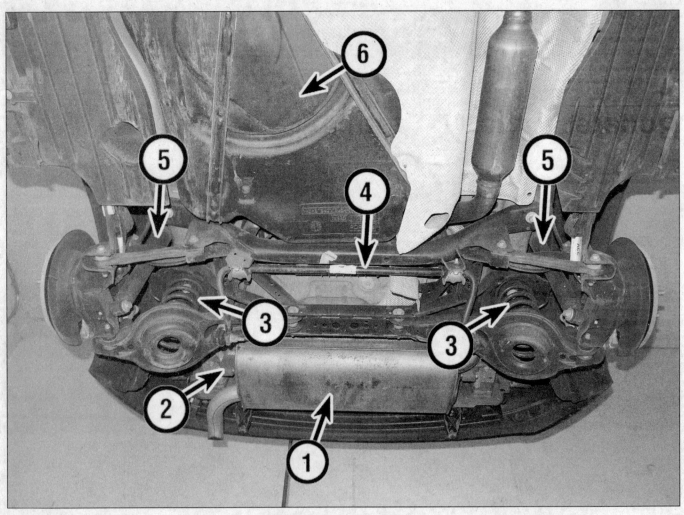

Typical rear underside components

1	Muffler	3	Coil springs	5	Shock absorbers
2	Exhaust system hanger	4	Stabilizer bar	6	Fuel tank

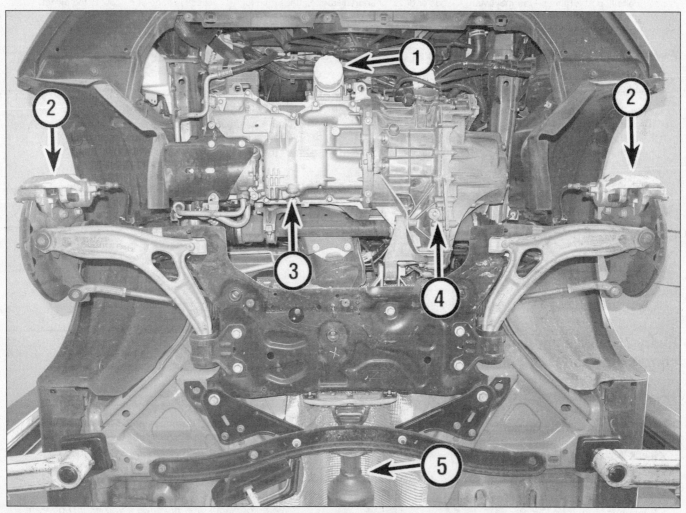

Typical engine compartment underside components

1	Engine oil filter	3	Engine oil drain plug	5	Exhaust system
2	Front disc brake caliper	4	Automatic transaxle drain plug		

1 Maintenance schedule

The maintenance intervals in this manual are provided with the assumption that you, not the dealer, will be doing the work. These are the minimum maintenance intervals recommended by the factory for vehicles that are driven daily. If you wish to keep your vehicle in peak condition at all times, you may wish to perform some of these procedures even more often. Because frequent maintenance enhances the efficiency, performance and resale value of your car, we encourage you to do so. If you drive in dusty areas, tow a trailer, idle or drive at low speeds for extended periods or drive for short distances (less than four miles) in below freezing temperatures, shorter intervals are also recommended.

When your vehicle is new, it should be serviced by a factory authorized dealer service department to protect the factory warranty. In many cases, the initial maintenance check is done at no cost to the owner.

Every 250 miles or weekly, whichever comes first

Check the engine oil level (see Section 4)
Check the engine coolant level (see Section 4)
Check the brake and clutch fluid level (see Section 4)
Check the windshield washer fluid level (see Section 4)
Check the tires and tire pressures (see Section 5)
Check the function of all exterior and interior lights (see Chapter 12).

Every 3000 miles or 3 months, whichever comes first

All items listed above plus:
Change the engine oil and oil filter (see Section 6)

Every 7500 miles or 6 months, whichever comes first

All items listed above plus:
Inspect (and replace, if necessary) the windshield wiper blades (see Section 7)
Check and service the battery (see Section 8)
Check the cooling system (see Section 9)
Rotate the tires (see Section 10)
Check the seat belts (see Section 11)
Check the operation of hinges, latches and looks. Lubricate as necessary (see Chapter 11).

Every 15,000 miles or 12 months, whichever comes first

All items listed above plus:
Check all underhood hoses (see Section 12)
Inspect the brake system (see Section 13)*
Inspect the suspension, steering and driveaxle boots (see Section 14)*
Check the fuel system (see Section 15)
Check the manual transaxle lubricant level (see Section 16)
Check (and replace, if necessary) the air filter (see Section 17)*
Replace the cabin air filter (see Section 18)

Every 30,000 miles or 24 months, whichever comes first

All items listed above plus:
Check the exhaust system (see Section 19)
Change the brake fluid (see Section 21)
Check the engine drivebelts (see Section 22)

Every 50,000 miles or 36 months, whichever comes first

Service the cooling system (drain, flush and refill) (see Section 20) (after initial first replacement at 100,000 miles or 72 months, whichever comes first)

Every 100,000 miles

Replace the spark plugs (see Section 25)

Every 150,000 miles

Replace the automatic transaxle fluid (see Section 23)**
Replace the manual transaxle lubricant (see Section 24)**
This item is affected by "severe" operating conditions as described below. If your vehicle is operated under "severe" conditions, perform all maintenance indicated with an asterisk (*) at 3000 mile/3 month intervals. Severe conditions are indicated if you mainly operate your vehicle under one or more of the following conditions:
Operating in dusty areas
Towing a trailer
Idling for extended periods and/or low speed operation
Operating when outside temperatures remain below freezing and when most trips are less than 4 miles
** *If operated under one or more of the following conditions, change the automatic transaxle fluid every 30,000 miles and manual transaxle fuid every 50,000 miles:*
Operating in dusty areas
In heavy city traffic where the outside temperature regularly reaches 90-degrees F (32-degrees C) or higher
In hilly or mountainous terrain

2   Introduction

1   This Chapter is designed to help the home mechanic maintain the Ford Focus with the goals of maximum performance, economy, safety and reliability in mind.

2   Included is a master maintenance schedule, followed by procedures dealing specifically with each item on the schedule. Visual checks, adjustments, component replacement and other helpful items are included. Refer to the accompanying illustrations of the engine compartment and the underside of the vehicle for the locations of various components.

3   Servicing the vehicle, in accordance with the mileage/time maintenance schedule and the step-by-step procedures will result in a planned maintenance program that should produce a long and reliable service life. Keep in mind that it is a comprehensive plan, so maintaining some items but not others at the specified intervals will not produce the same results.

4   As you service the vehicle, you will discover that many of the procedures can - and should - be grouped together because of the nature of the particular procedure you're performing or because of the close proximity of two otherwise unrelated components to one another.

5   For example, if the vehicle is raised for chassis lubrication, you should inspect the exhaust, suspension, steering and fuel systems while you're under the vehicle. When you're rotating the tires, it makes good sense to check the brakes since the wheels are already removed. Finally, let's suppose you have to borrow or rent a torque wrench. Even if you only need it to tighten the spark plugs, you might as well check the torque of as many critical fasteners as time allows.

6   The first step in this maintenance program is to prepare yourself before the actual work begins. Read through all the procedures you're planning to do, then gather up all the parts and tools needed. If it looks like you might run into problems during a particular job, seek advice from a mechanic or an experienced do-it-yourselfer.

Owner's Manual and VECI label information

7   Your vehicle owner's manual was written for your year and model and contains very specific information on component locations, specifications, fuse ratings, part numbers, etc. The Owner's Manual is an important resource for the do-it-yourselfer to have; if one was not supplied with your vehicle, it can generally be ordered from a dealer parts department or downloaded from the manufacturer's web page.

8   Among other important information, the Vehicle Emissions Control Information (VECI) label contains specifications and procedures for applicable tune-up adjustments and, in some instances, spark plugs. The information on this label is the exact maintenance data

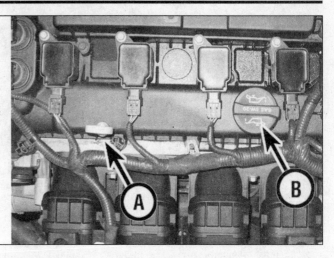

4.2 Engine oil dipstick (A) and oil filler cap (B) locations - non turbo engine

recommended by the manufacturer. This data often varies by intended operating altitude, local emissions regulations, month of manufacture, etc.

9   This Chapter contains procedural details, safety information and more ambitious maintenance intervals than you might find in manufacturer's literature. However, you may also find procedures or specifications in your Owner's Manual or VECI label that differ with what's printed here. In these cases, the Owner's Manual or VECI label can be considered correct, since it is specific to your particular vehicle.

3   Tune-up general information

1   The term tune-up is used in this manual to represent a combination of individual operations rather than one specific procedure.

2   If, from the time the vehicle is new, the routine maintenance schedule is followed closely and frequent checks are made of fluid levels and high wear items, as suggested throughout this manual, the engine will be kept in relatively good running condition and the need for additional work will be minimized.

3   More likely than not, however, there will be times when the engine is running poorly due to lack of regular maintenance. This is even more likely if a used vehicle, which has not received regular and frequent maintenance checks, is purchased. In such cases, an engine tune-up will be needed outside of the regular routine maintenance intervals.

4   The first step in any tune-up or diagnostic procedure to help correct a poor running engine is a cylinder compression check. A compression check (see Chapter 2B) will help determine the condition of internal engine components and should be used as a guide for tune-up and repair procedures. If, for instance, a compression check indicates serious internal engine wear, a conventional tune-up will not improve the performance of the engine and would be a waste of time and money. Because of its importance, the compression check should be done by someone

with the proper equipment and the knowledge to use it properly.

5   The following procedures are those most often needed to bring a generally poor running engine back into a proper state of tune.

Minor tune-up

Check all engine related fluids (see Section 4)
Clean, inspect and test the battery (see Section 8)
Check the cooling system (see Section 9)
Check all underhood hoses (see Section 12)
Check the fuel system (see Section 15)
Check the air filter (see Section 17)
Check the drivebelt (see Section 22)

Major tune-up

All items listed under Minor tune-up, plus . . .
Replace the air filter (see Section 17)
Replace the spark plugs (see Section 25)

4   Fluid level checks (every 250 miles or weekly)

1   Fluids are an essential part of the lubrication, cooling, brake and windshield washer systems. Because the fluids gradually become depleted and/or contaminated during normal operation of the vehicle, they must be periodically replenished. See *Recommended lubricants and fluids* in this Chapter's Specifications before adding fluid to any of the following components.

Note: *The vehicle must be on level ground when fluid levels are checked.*

Engine oil

2   The oil level is checked with a dipstick, which is attached to the engine block **(see illustration)**. The dipstick extends through a metal tube down into the oil pan.

3   The oil level should be checked before the vehicle has been driven, or about 10 minutes after the engine has been shut off. If the oil is checked immediately after driving the vehicle, some of the oil will remain in the

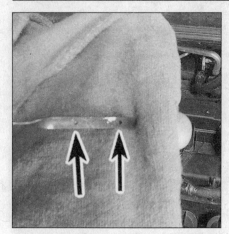

4.4 The oil level should be in the safe range - if it's below the MIN or ADD mark, add enough oil to bring it up to or near the MAX or FULL mark

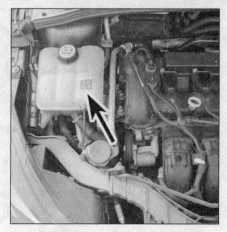

4.8 The cooling system expansion tank is located at the right side of the engine compartment

4.9 When the engine is cold, the coolant level should be kept between the MIN and MAX marks on the reservoir

upper part of the engine, resulting in an inaccurate reading on the dipstick.

4   Pull the dipstick out of the tube and wipe all the oil from the end with a clean rag or paper towel. Insert the clean dipstick all the way back into the tube and pull it out again. Note the oil at the end of the dipstick. At its highest point, the level should be between the MIN and MAX marks on the dipstick **(see illustration)**.

5   It takes one quart of oil to raise the level from the MIN mark to the MAX mark on the dipstick. Do not allow the level to drop below the MIN mark or oil starvation may cause engine damage. Conversely, overfilling the engine (adding oil above the MAX mark) may cause oil fouled spark plugs, oil leaks or oil seal failures. Maintaining the oil level above the MAX mark can cause excessive oil consumption.

6   To add oil, remove the filler cap from the valve cover **(see illustration 4.2)**. After adding oil, wait a few minutes to allow the level to stabilize, then pull out the dipstick and check the level again. Add more oil if required. Install the filler cap and tighten it by hand only.

7   Checking the oil level is an important preventive maintenance step. A consistently low oil level indicates oil leakage through damaged seals, defective gaskets or past worn rings or valve guides. If the oil looks milky in color or has water droplets in it, the cylinder head gasket(s) may be blown or the head(s) or block may be cracked. The engine should be checked immediately. The condition of the oil should also be checked. Whenever you check the oil level, slide your thumb and index finger up the dipstick before wiping off the oil. If you see small dirt or metal particles clinging to the dipstick, the oil should be changed (see Section 6).

Engine coolant

Warning: *Do not allow antifreeze to come in contact with your skin or painted surfaces of the vehicle. Flush contaminated areas imme-*

diately with plenty of water. Don't store new coolant or leave old coolant lying around where it's accessible to children or pets - they're attracted by its sweet smell. Ingestion of even a small amount of coolant can be fatal! Wipe up garage floor and drip pan spills immediately. Keep antifreeze containers covered and repair cooling system leaks as soon as they're noticed.

8   All vehicles covered by this manual are equipped with a pressurized coolant recovery system. A plastic expansion tank located at the right rear corner of the engine compartment is connected by hoses to the cooling system **(see illustration)**. As the engine heats up during operation, the expanding coolant fills the tank.

9   The coolant level in the tank should be checked regularly. The level in the tank varies with the temperature of the engine. When the engine is cold, the coolant level should be at the COLD FULL mark on the reservoir **(see illustration)**. If it isn't, remove the reservoir cap and add the engine coolant listed in this Chapter's Specifications and mix it per the manufacturer's instructions to ensure proper engine cooling.

Warning: *Do not remove the expansion tank cap to check coolant level when the engine is warm.*

10   Drive the vehicle, let the engine cool completely then recheck the coolant level. Don't use rust inhibitors or additives. If only a small amount of coolant is required to bring the system up to the proper level, water can be used. However, repeated additions of water will dilute the antifreeze and water solution. In order to maintain the proper ratio of antifreeze and water, always top up the coolant level with the correct mixture. An empty plastic milk jug or bleach bottle makes an excellent container for mixing coolant.

11   If the coolant level drops consistently, there may be a leak in the system. Inspect the radiator, hoses, filler cap, drain plugs and water pump (see Section 9). If no leaks are noted, have the expansion tank cap pressure

tested by a service station.

12   If you have to remove the expansion tank cap, wait until the engine has cooled completely, then wrap a thick cloth around the cap and unscrew it slowly, stopping if you hear a hissing noise. If coolant or steam escapes, let the engine cool down longer, then remove the cap.

13   Check the condition of the coolant as well. If it's brown or rust colored, the system should be drained, flushed and refilled. Even if the coolant appears to be normal, the corrosion inhibitors wear out, so it must be replaced at the specified intervals.

Brake and clutch fluid

14   The brake master cylinder is mounted on the front of the power booster unit in the engine compartment. On manual transaxle models, the same reservoir is used for the brake and clutch hydraulic systems **(see illustration)**.

15   If the level is low, wipe the top of the reservoir cover with a clean rag to prevent contamination of the brake system before lifting the cover.

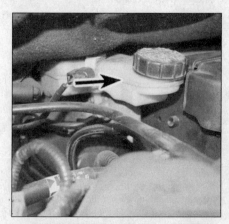

4.14 The fluid level should be kept between the MIN and MAX marks on the plastic reservoir

4.21 The windshield/rear window washer fluid reservoir is located in the right front corner of the engine compartment

4.25 Location of the transaxle fluid leveling plug

16   Add only the specified brake fluid to the reservoir (refer to *Recommended lubricants and fluids* in this Chapter's Specifications or to your owner's manual). Mixing different types of brake fluid can damage the system. Fill the brake master cylinder reservoir only to the MAX line.

Warning: *Use caution when filling the reservoir - brake fluid can harm your eyes and damage painted surfaces. Do not use brake fluid that is more than one year old or has been left open. Brake fluid absorbs moisture from the air. Excess moisture can cause a dangerous loss of braking.*

17   While the reservoir cap is removed, inspect the master cylinder reservoir for contamination. If deposits, dirt particles or water droplets are present, the system should be drained and refilled.

18   After filling the reservoir to the proper level, make sure the lid is properly seated to prevent fluid leakage.

19   The fluid in the brake master cylinder will drop slightly as the brake pads at each wheel wear down during normal operation. If the master cylinder requires repeated replenishing to keep it at the proper level, this is an indication of leakage in the brake or clutch system, which should be corrected immediately. If the brake system shows an indication of leakage check all brake lines and connections, along with the calipers and booster (see Chapter 9). If the hydraulic clutch system shows an indication of leakage check all clutch lines and connections, along with the clutch release cylinder (see Chapter 8).

20   If, upon checking the brake or clutch master cylinder fluid level, you discover the reservoir empty or nearly empty, the systems should be bled (see Chapters 8 and/or 9).

Windshield washer fluid

21   Fluid for the windshield washer system is stored in a plastic reservoir located at the right front of the engine compartment **(see illustration)**.

22   In milder climates, plain water can be used in the reservoir, but it should be kept no more than 2/3 full to allow for expansion if the water freezes. In colder climates, use windshield washer system antifreeze, available at any auto parts store, to lower the freezing point of the fluid. Mix the antifreeze with water in accordance with the manufacturer's directions on the container.

Caution: *Do not use cooling system antifreeze - it will damage the vehicle's paint.*

Automatic transaxle fluid

Note: *It isn't necessary to check the transaxle fluid (unless the transaxle is not working properly or fluid leakage is suspected).*

Caution: *If the vehicle has just been driven for a long time at high speed or in city traffic in hot weather, or if it has been pulling a trailer, an accurate fluid level reading cannot be obtained. Allow the fluid to cool down for about 30 minutes.*

23   Remove the engine splash shield fasteners and shield.

24   Raise the vehicle on a hoist or support it on four jackstands, keeping the vehicle in a level position, and place a drain pan under the transaxle.

25   Remove the oil leveling plug on the side of the transaxle **(see illustration)**. Check the level of the fluid; it should be even with the bottom of the plug hole.

26   If the level is low, add the specified automatic transmission fluid through the oil leveling plug hole with a suctioning gun or large syringe until the fluid starts to drip out of the oil leveling plug hole.

Note: *Allow all excess fluid to drip out of the plug hole.*

27   Once the fluid is even with the oil leveling plug hole install the plug and tighten the plug to torque listed in this Chapter's Specifications

28   The condition of the fluid should also be checked along with the level. If the fluid is black or a dark reddish brown color, or if

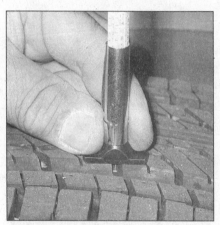

5.2 A tire tread depth indicator should be used to monitor tire wear - they are available at auto parts stores and service stations and cost very little

it emits a burned smell, the fluid should be changed (see Section 23). If you are in doubt about the condition of the fluid, purchase some new fluid and compare the two for color and smell.

5   Tire and tire pressure checks (every 250 miles or weekly)

1   Periodic inspection of the tires may spare you the inconvenience of being stranded with a flat tire. It can also provide you with vital information regarding possible problems in the steering and suspension systems before major damage occurs.

2   The original tires on this vehicle are equipped with 1/2-inch wide bands that will appear when tread depth reaches 1/16-inch, at which point they can be considered worn out. Tread wear can be monitored with a simple, inexpensive device known as a tread depth indicator **(see illustration)**.

UNDERINFLATION

CUPPING

Cupping may be caused by:
- Underinflation and/or mechanical irregularities such as out-of-balance condition of wheel and/or tire, and bent or damaged wheel.
- Loose or worn steering tie-rod or steering idler arm.
- Loose, damaged or worn front suspension parts.

OVERINFLATION

INCORRECT TOE-IN OR EXTREME CAMBER

FEATHERING DUE TO MISALIGNMENT

5.3 This chart will help you determine the condition of your tires, the probable cause(s) of abnormal wear and the corrective action necessary

3   Note any abnormal tread wear **(see illustration)**. Tread pattern irregularities such as cupping, flat spots and more wear on one side than the other are indications of front end alignment and/or balance problems. If any of these conditions are noted, take the vehicle to a tire shop or service station to correct the problem.

4   Look closely for cuts, punctures and embedded nails or tacks. Sometimes a tire will hold air pressure for a short time or leak down very slowly after a nail has embedded itself in the tread. If a slow leak persists, check the valve stem core to make sure it is tight **(see illustration)**. Examine the tread for an object that may have embedded itself in the tire or for a plug that may have begun to leak (radial tire punctures are repaired with a plug that is installed in a puncture). If a puncture is suspected, it can be easily verified by spraying a solution of soapy water onto the puncture area **(see illustration)**. The soapy solution will bubble if there is a leak. Unless the puncture is unusually large, a tire shop or service station can usually repair the tire.

5   Carefully inspect the inner sidewall of each tire for evidence of brake fluid leakage. If you see any, inspect the brakes immediately.

6   Correct air pressure adds miles to the life span of the tires, improves mileage and enhances overall ride quality. Tire pressure cannot be accurately estimated by looking at a tire, especially if it's a radial. A tire pressure gauge is essential. Keep an accurate gauge in the glove compartment. The pressure gauges attached to the nozzles of air hoses at gas stations are often inaccurate.

7   Always check tire pressure when the tires are cold. Cold, in this case, means the vehicle has not been driven over a mile in the three hours preceding a tire pressure check. A pressure rise of four to eight pounds is not uncommon once the tires are warm.

8   Unscrew the valve cap protruding from

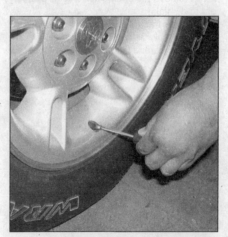

5.4a If a tire loses air on a steady basis, check the valve core first to make sure it's snug (special inexpensive wrenches are commonly available at auto parts stores)

5.4b If the valve core is tight, raise the corner of the vehicle with the low tire and spray a soapy water solution onto the tread as the tire is turned slowly - slow leaks will cause small bubbles to appear

5.8 To extend the life of your tires, check the air pressure at least once a week with an accurate gauge (don't forget the spare!)

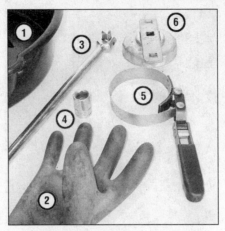

6.2 These tools are required when changing the engine oil and filter

1   **Drain pan** - *It should be fairly shallow in depth, but wide in order to prevent spills*
2   **Rubber gloves** - *When removing the drain plug and filter, it is inevitable that you will get oil on your hands (the gloves will prevent burns)*
3   **Breaker bar** - *Sometimes the oil drain plug is pretty tight and a long breaker bar is needed to loosen it*
4   **Socket** - *To be used with the breaker bar or a ratchet (must be the correct size to fit the drain plug)*
5   **Filter wrench** - *This is a metal band-type wrench, which requires clearance around the filter to be effective*
6   **Filter wrench** - *This type fits on the bottom of the filter and can be turned with a ratchet or breaker bar (different size wrenches are available for different types of filters)*

6.7 Use a proper size box-end wrench or socket to remove the oil drain plug and avoid rounding it off

6.12 Use an oil filter wrench to remove the filter

the wheel or hubcap and push the gauge firmly onto the valve stem **(see illustration)**. Note the reading on the gauge and compare the figure to the recommended tire pressure shown on the tire placard on the driver's side door. Be sure to reinstall the valve cap to keep dirt and moisture out of the valve stem mechanism. Check all four tires and, if necessary, add enough air to bring them up to the recommended pressure.

9   Don't forget to keep the spare tire inflated to the specified pressure (refer to the pressure molded into the tire sidewall).

---

6   Engine oil and filter change (every 3000 miles or 3 months)

Note: *All models are equipped with an oil life indicator system that illuminates a light or message on the instrument panel when the system deems it necessary to change the oil. A number of factors are taken into consideration to determine when the oil should be considered worn out. Generally, this system will allow the vehicle to accumulate more miles between oil changes than the traditional 3000-mile interval, but we believe that frequent oil changes are cheap insurance and will prolong engine life. If you do decide not to change your oil every 3000 miles and rely on the oil life indicator instead, make sure you don't exceed 7,500 miles before the oil is changed, regardless of what the oil life indicator shows.*

1   Frequent oil changes are the most important preventive maintenance procedures that can be done by the home mechanic. As engine oil ages, it becomes diluted and contaminated, which leads to premature engine wear.
2   Make sure that you have all the necessary tools before you begin this procedure **(see illustration)**. You should also have plenty of rags or newspapers handy for mopping up oil spills.
3   Access to the oil drain plug and filter will be improved if the vehicle can be lifted on a hoist, driven onto ramps or supported by jackstands. **Warning:** *Do not work under a vehicle supported only by a jack - always use jackstands!*
4   If you haven't changed the oil on this vehicle before, get under it and locate the oil drain plug and the oil filter. The exhaust components will be warm as you work, so note how they are routed to avoid touching them when you are under the vehicle.
5   Start the engine and allow it to reach normal operating temperature - oil and sludge will flow out more easily when warm. If new oil, a filter or tools are needed, use the vehicle to go get them and warm up the engine/oil at the same time. Park on a level surface and shut off the engine when it's warmed up. Remove the oil filler cap from the valve cover.
6   Raise the vehicle and support it on jackstands. Make sure it is safely supported!
7   Being careful not to touch the hot exhaust components, position a drain pan under the plug in the bottom of the engine, then remove the plug **(see illustration)**. It's a good idea to wear a rubber glove while unscrewing the plug the final few turns to avoid being scalded by hot oil.

8   It may be necessary to move the drain pan slightly as oil flow slows to a trickle. Inspect the old oil for the presence of metal particles .
9   After all the oil has drained, wipe off the drain plug with a clean rag. Any small metal particles clinging to the plug would immediately contaminate the new oil.
10   Clean the area around the drain plug opening, reinstall the plug and tighten it to the torque listed in this Chapter's Specifications.
11   Move the drain pan into position under the oil filter.
12   Loosen the oil filter by turning it counterclockwise with a filter wrench **(see illustration)**. Any standard filter wrench will work. Some engines are equipped with a cartridge type oil filter. On these types, remove the oil filter cover and element.
13   Once the filter is loose, use your hands to unscrew it from the block. Just as the filter is detached from the block, immediately tilt the open end up to prevent the oil inside the filter from spilling out.
14   Using a clean rag, wipe off the mounting surface on the block. Also, make sure that

6.15 Lubricate the oil filter gasket with clean engine oil before installing the filter on the engine

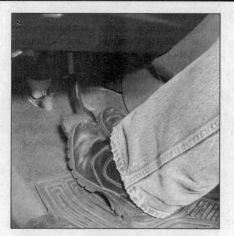

6.23 Press and hold the accelerator and brake pedals

the engine. On push-button start models, with your foot off the brake pedal, depress the button for two seconds.

23   Simultaneously press and hold the accelerator and brake pedals **(see illustration)**.

24   After the "Service: Oil reset in prog" message appears, continue to hold the pedals for 25 seconds, until "Service: Oil reset complete" shows in the display **(see illustrations)**.

25   Take your feet off the pedals to clear the reset message, then turn the ignition to Off. On push-button start models, press the button once to turn off the ignition.

none of the old gasket remains stuck to the mounting surface. It can be removed with a scraper if necessary.

15   Compare the old filter with the new one to make sure they are the same type. Smear some engine oil on the rubber gasket or O-ring seal of the new filter and screw it into place **(see illustration)**. On typical filters, overtightening the filter will damage the gasket, so don't use a filter wrench. Most filter manufacturers recommend tightening the filter by hand only. Normally they should be tightened 3/4-turn after the gasket contacts the block, but be sure to follow the directions on the filter or container. On cartridge type filters, install the new oil filter element and use the oil filter wrench to tighten the filter cover securely. Do not overtighten the oil filter cover.

16   Remove all tools and materials from under the vehicle, being careful not to spill the oil in the drain pan, then lower the vehicle.

17   Add new oil to the engine through the oil filler cap. Use a funnel to prevent oil from spilling onto the top of the engine. Pour four quarts of fresh oil into the engine. Wait a few minutes to allow the oil to drain into the pan, then check the level on the dipstick (see Sec-

tion 4). If the oil level is in the OK range, install the filler cap.

18   Start the engine and run it for about a minute. While the engine is running, look under the vehicle and check for leaks at the oil pan drain plug and around the oil filter. If either one is leaking, stop the engine and tighten the plug or filter slightly.

19   Wait 10 minutes, then recheck the level on the dipstick. Add oil as necessary to bring the level into the OK range.

20   During the first few trips after an oil change, make it a point to check frequently for leaks and proper oil level.

21   The old oil drained from the engine cannot be reused in its present state and should be disposed of. Check with your local auto parts store, disposal facility or environmental agency to see if they will accept the oil for recycling. After the oil has cooled it can be drained into a container (capped plastic jugs, topped bottles, milk cartons, etc.) for transport to one of these disposal sites. Don't dispose of the oil by pouring it on the ground or down a drain!

Oil life monitor resetting

22   Turn the ignition to On without starting

7   Windshield wiper blade inspection and replacement (every 7500 miles or 6 months)

1   The windshield wiper and blade assembly should be inspected periodically for damage, loose components and cracked or worn blade elements.

2   Road film can build up on the wiper blades and affect their efficiency, so they should be washed regularly with a mild detergent solution.

3   If the wiper blade elements are cracked, worn or warped, or no longer clean adequately, they should be replaced with new ones.

Windshield wiper blades

4   Lift the arm assembly away from the glass for clearance, squeeze the release tabs, then slide the wiper blade assembly out of the hook in the end of the arm **(see illustration)**.

5   Attach the new wiper to the arm. Connection can be confirmed by an audible click.

Hatchback window wiper blade

6   Place the wiper blade against the window, then pull the arm away from the blade **(see illustration)**.

6.24a "Service: Oil reset in prog" message

6.24b "Service: Oil reset complete" message

7.4 To release the blade holder, squeeze the release tabs

7.6 Pull the arm away from the wiper blade

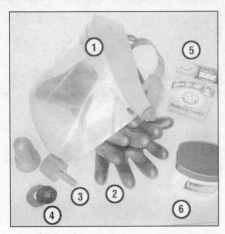

8.1 Tools and materials required for battery maintenance

1 *Face shield/safety goggles - When removing corrosion with a brush, the acidic particles can easily fly up into your eyes*
2 *Rubber gloves - Another safety item to consider when servicing the battery; remember that's acid inside the battery*
3 *Battery post/cable cleaner - This wire brush cleaning tool will remove all traces of corrosion from the battery posts and cable clamps*
4 *Treated felt washers - Placing one of these on each post, directly under the cable clamps, will help prevent corrosion*
5 *Baking soda - A solution of baking soda and water can be used to neutralize corrosion*
6 *Petroleum jelly - A layer of this on the battery posts will help prevent corrosion*

---

8 Battery check, maintenance and charging (every 7500 miles or 6 months)

Warning: *Certain precautions must be followed when checking and servicing the battery. Hydrogen gas, which is highly flammable, is always present in the battery cells, so keep lighted tobacco and all other open flames and sparks away from the battery. The electrolyte inside the battery is actually diluted sulfuric acid, which will cause injury if splashed on your skin or in your eyes. It will also ruin clothes and painted surfaces. When removing the battery cables, always detach the negative cable first and hook it up last!*

1   A routine preventive maintenance program for the battery in your vehicle is the only way to ensure quick and reliable starts. But before performing any battery maintenance, make sure that you have the proper equipment necessary to work safely around the battery **(see illustration)**.
2   There are also several precautions that should be taken whenever battery maintenance is performed. Before servicing the battery, always turn the engine and all accessories off and disconnect the cables from the negative terminal of the battery (see Chapter 5).
3   The battery produces hydrogen gas, which is both flammable and explosive. Never create a spark, smoke or light a match around the battery. Always charge the battery in a ventilated area.
4   Electrolyte contains poisonous and corrosive sulfuric acid. Do not allow it to get in your eyes, on your skin or on your clothes. Never ingest it. Wear protective safety glasses when working near the battery. Keep children away from the battery.
5   Note the external condition of the battery. If the positive terminal and cable clamp on your vehicle's battery is equipped with a rubber protector, make sure that it's not torn or damaged. It should completely cover the terminal. Look for any corroded or loose connections, cracks in the case or cover or loose hold-down clamps. Also check the entire length of each cable for cracks and frayed conductors.
6   If corrosion, which looks like white, fluffy deposits **(see illustration)** is evident, particularly around the terminals, the battery should

be removed for cleaning. Loosen the cable clamp bolts with a wrench, being careful to remove the ground cable first, and slide them off the terminals **(see illustration)**. Then disconnect the hold-down clamp bolt and nut,

8.6a Battery terminal corrosion usually appears as light, fluffy powder

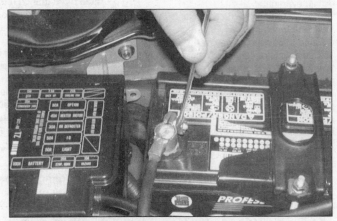

8.6b Removing a cable from the battery post with a wrench - sometimes a pair of special battery pliers are required for this procedure if corrosion has caused deterioration of the nut hex. Always remove the ground (-) cable first and hook it up last!

8.7a When cleaning the cable clamps, all corrosion must be removed (the inside of the clamp is tapered to match the taper on the post, so don't remove too much material)

8.7b Regardless of the type of tool used to clean the battery posts, a clean, shiny surface should be the result

Check for a chafed area that could fail prematurely.

Check for a soft area indicating the hose has deteriorated inside.

Overtightening the clamp on a hardened hose will damage the hose and cause a leak.

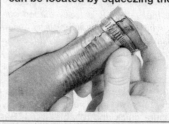

Check each hose for swelling and oil-soaked ends. Cracks and breaks can be located by squeezing the hose.

9.4 Hoses, like drivebelts, have a habit of failing at the worst possible time - to prevent the inconvenience of a blown radiator or heater hose, inspect them carefully as shown here

remove the clamp and lift the battery from the engine compartment.

7   Clean the cable clamps thoroughly with a battery brush or a terminal cleaner and a solution of warm water and baking soda **(see illustration)**. Wash the terminals and the top of the battery case with the same solution but make sure that the solution doesn't get into the battery. When cleaning the cables, terminals and battery top, wear safety goggles and rubber gloves to prevent any solution from coming in contact with your eyes or hands. Wear old clothes too - even diluted, sulfuric acid splashed onto clothes will burn holes in them. If the terminals have been extensively corroded, clean them up with a terminal cleaner **(see illustration)**. Thoroughly wash all cleaned areas with plain water.

8   Make sure that the battery tray is in good condition and the hold-down clamp fasteners are tight. If the battery is removed from the tray, make sure no parts remain in the bottom of the tray when the battery is reinstalled. When reinstalling the hold-down clamp bolts, do not overtighten them.

9   Information on removing and installing the battery can be found in Chapter 5. If you disconnected the cable(s) from the negative and/or positive battery terminals, the power-train control module (PCM) must relearn its idle and fuel trim strategy for optimum drive-ability and performance (see Chapter 5 for this procedure). Information on jump starting can be found at the front of this manual. For more detailed battery checking procedures, refer to the Haynes Automotive Electrical Manual .

Cleaning

10   Corrosion on the hold-down components, battery case and surrounding areas can be removed with a solution of water and baking soda. Thoroughly rinse all cleaned areas with plain water.

11   Any metal parts of the vehicle damaged by corrosion should be covered with a zinc-based primer, then painted.

Charging

Warning: *When batteries are being charged, hydrogen gas, which is very explosive and flammable, is produced. Do not smoke or allow open flames near a charging or a recently charged battery. Wear eye protection when near the battery during charging. Also, make sure the charger is unplugged before connecting or disconnecting the battery from the charger.*

12   Slow-rate charging is the best way to restore a battery that's discharged to the point where it will not start the engine. It's also a good way to maintain the battery charge in a vehicle that's only driven a few miles between starts. Maintaining the battery charge is particularly important in the winter when the battery must work harder to start the engine and electrical accessories that drain the battery are in greater use.

13   It's best to use a one or two-amp battery charger (sometimes called a "trickle" charger). They are the safest and put the least strain on the battery. They are also the least expensive. For a faster charge, you can use a higher amperage charger, but don't use one rated more than 1/10th the amp/hour rating of the battery. Rapid boost charges that claim to restore the power of the battery in one to two hours are hardest on the battery and can damage batteries not in good condition. This type of charging should only be used in emergency situations.

14   The average time necessary to charge a battery should be listed in the instructions that come with the charger. As a general rule, a trickle charger will charge a battery in 12 to 16 hours.

9   Cooling system check (every 7,500 miles or 6 months)

1   Many major engine failures can be caused by a faulty cooling system.

2   The engine must be cold for the cooling system check, so perform the following procedure before the vehicle is driven for the day

or after it has been shut off for at least three hours.

3   Remove the pressure-relief cap from the expansion tank at the right side of the engine compartment. Clean the cap thoroughly, inside and out, with clean water. The presence of rust or corrosion in the expansion tank means the coolant should be changed (see Section 20). The coolant inside the expansion tank should be relatively clean and transparent. If it's rust colored, drain the system and refill it with new coolant.

4   Carefully check the radiator hoses and the smaller diameter heater hoses **(see illustrations** in Chapter 3). Inspect each coolant hose along its entire length, replacing any hose which is cracked, swollen or deteriorated **(see illustration)**. Cracks will show up better if the hose is squeezed. Pay close attention to hose clamps that secure the hoses to cooling system components. Hose clamps can pinch and puncture hoses, resulting in coolant leaks.

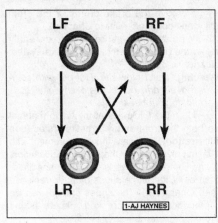

10.2 The recommended tire rotation pattern for these vehicles

5   Make sure that all hose connections are tight. A leak in the cooling system will usually show up as white or rust colored deposits on the area adjoining the leak. If wire-type clamps are used on the hoses, it may be a good idea to replace them with screw-type clamps.

6   Clean the front of the radiator and air conditioning condenser with compressed air, if available, or a soft brush. Remove all bugs, leaves, etc. embedded in the radiator fins. Be extremely careful not to damage the cooling fins or cut your fingers on them.

7   If the coolant level has been dropping consistently and no leaks are detectable, have the expansion tank cap and cooling system pressure checked at a service station.

10   Tire rotation (every 7,500 miles or 6 months)

1   The tires should be rotated at the specified intervals and whenever uneven wear is noticed. Since the vehicle will be raised and the tires removed anyway, check the brakes also (see Section 13).

2   Radial tires must be rotated in a specific pattern (see illustration). Don't include the spare tire in the rotation pattern.

3   Refer to the information in *Jacking and towing* at the front of this manual for the proper procedure to follow when raising the vehicle and changing a tire. If the brakes must be checked, don't apply the parking brake as stated.

4   The vehicle must be raised on a hoist or supported on jackstands to get all four wheels off the ground. Make sure the vehicle is safely supported!

5   After the rotation procedure is finished, check and adjust the tire pressures as necessary and be sure to check the lug nut tightness.

11   Seat belt check (every 7,500 miles or 6 months)

1   Check seat belts, buckles, latch plates and guide loops for obvious damage and signs of wear.

2   See if the seat belt reminder light comes on when the key is turned to the Run or Start position. A chime should also sound.

3   The seat belts are designed to lock up during a sudden stop or impact, yet allow free movement during normal driving. Make sure the retractors return the belt against your chest while driving and rewind the belt fully when the buckle is unlatched.

4   If any of the above checks reveal problems with the seat belt system, replace parts as necessary.

12   Underhood hose check and replacement (every 15,000 miles or 12 months)

Warning: *Replacement of air conditioning hoses must be left to a dealer service department or air conditioning shop that has the equipment to depressurize the system safely. Never remove air conditioning components or hoses until the system has been depressurized.*

General

1   High temperatures under the hood can cause deterioration of the rubber and plastic hoses used for engine, accessory and emission systems operation. Periodic inspection should be made for cracks, loose clamps, material hardening and leaks.

2   Information specific to the cooling system hoses can be found in Section 9

3   Most (but not all) hoses are secured to the fittings with clamps. Where clamps are used, check to be sure they haven't lost their tension, allowing the hose to leak. If clamps aren't used, make sure the hose has not expanded and/or hardened where it slips over the fitting, allowing it to leak.

PCV system hose

4   To reduce hydrocarbon emissions, crankcase blow-by gas is vented through the PCV valve in the valve cover to the intake manifold via a rubber hose on most models. The blow-by gases mix with incoming air in the intake manifold before being burned in the combustion chambers.

5   Check the PCV hose for cracks, leaks and other damage. Disconnect it from the valve cover and the intake manifold and check the inside for obstructions. If it's clogged, clean it out with solvent.

Vacuum hoses

6   It's quite common for vacuum hoses, especially those in the emissions system, to be color coded or identified by colored stripes molded into them. Various systems require hoses with different wall thickness, collapse resistance and temperature resistance. When replacing hoses, be sure the new ones are made of the same material.

7   Often the only effective way to check a hose is to remove it completely from the vehicle. If more than one hose is removed, be sure to label the hoses and fittings to ensure correct installation.

8   When checking vacuum hoses, be sure to include any plastic T-fittings in the check. Inspect the fittings for cracks and the hose where it fits over each fitting for distortion, which could cause leakage.

9   A small piece of vacuum hose (1/4-inch inside diameter) can be used as a stethoscope to detect vacuum leaks. Hold one end of the hose to your ear and probe around vacuum hoses and fittings, listening for the hissing sound characteristic of a vacuum leak. **Warning:** *When probing with the vacuum hose stethoscope, be careful not to come into contact with moving engine components such as drivebelts, the cooling fan, etc.*

Fuel hose

Warning: *Gasoline is flammable, so take extra precautions when you work on any part of the fuel system. Don't smoke or allow open flames or bare light bulbs near the work area, and don't work in a garage where a gas-type appliance (such as a water heater or clothes dryer) is present. Since fuel is carcinogenic, wear fuel-resistant gloves when there's a possibility of being exposed to fuel, and, if you spill any fuel on your skin, rinse it off immediately with soap and water. Mop up any spills immediately and do not store fuel-soaked rags where they could ignite. The fuel system is under constant pressure, so, if any fuel lines are to be disconnected, the fuel pressure in the system must be relieved first (see Chapter 4). When you perform any kind of work on the fuel system, wear safety glasses and have a Class B type fire extinguisher on hand.*

10   The fuel lines are usually under pressure, so if any fuel lines are to be disconnected be prepared to catch spilled fuel. **Warning:** *Your vehicle is equipped with fuel injection and you must relieve the fuel system pressure before servicing the fuel lines. Refer to Chapter 4 for the fuel system pressure relief procedure.*

11   Check all flexible fuel lines for deterioration and chafing. Check especially for cracks in areas where the hose bends and just before fittings, such as where the fuel line attaches to the fuel rail.

12   When replacing a hose, use only hose that is specifically designed for your fuel injection system.

13   Some fuel lines use quick-connect fittings, which require a special tool to disconnect. See Chapter 4 for more information on these types of fittings.

Metal lines

14   Sections of metal line are often used for fuel line that runs underneath the vehicle. Check carefully to make sure the line isn't bent, crimped or cracked.

15   If a section of metal fuel line must be replaced, use seamless steel tubing only, since copper and aluminum tubing do not have the strength necessary to withstand vibration caused by the engine.

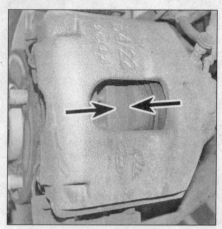

13.5a You will find an inspection hole like this in each caliper through which you can view the thickness of remaining friction material for the inner pad

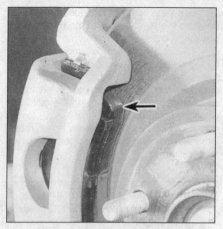

13.5b Be sure to check the thickness of the outer pad material, too

16   Check the metal brake lines where they enter the master cylinder and brake proportioning unit (if used) for cracks in the lines and loose fittings. Any sign of brake fluid leakage calls for an immediate thorough inspection of the brake system.

13   Brake check (every 15,000 miles or 12 months)

Warning: *Dust created by the brake system is harmful to your health. Never blow it out with compressed air and don't inhale any of it. An approved filtering mask should be worn when working on brakes. Do not, under any circumstances, use petroleum-based solvents to clean brake parts. Use brake system cleaner only!*

1   The brakes should be inspected every time the wheels are removed or whenever a defect is suspected. Indications of a potential brake system problem include the vehicle pulling to one side when the brake pedal is depressed, noises coming from the brakes when they are applied, excessive brake pedal travel, a pulsating pedal and leakage of fluid, usually seen on the inside of the tire or wheel. **Note:** *It is normal for a vehicle equipped with an Anti-lock Brake System (ABS) to exhibit brake pedal pulsations during severe braking conditions.*

Disc brakes

2   Disc brakes can be visually checked without removing any parts except the wheels. Remove the hub caps (if applicable) and loosen the wheel lug nuts a quarter turn each.

3   Raise the vehicle and place it securely on jackstands. **Warning:** *Never work under a vehicle that is supported only by a jack!*

4   Remove the wheels. Now visible is the disc brake caliper which contains the pads. There is an outer brake pad and an inner pad.

Both must be checked for wear. **Note:** *Usually the inner pad wears faster than the outer pad.*

5   Measure the thickness of the outer pad at each end of the caliper and the inner pad through the inspection hole in the caliper body **(see illustrations)**. Compare the measurement with the limit given in this Chapter's Specifications; if any brake pad thickness is less than specified, then all brake pads must be replaced (see Chapter 9).

6   If you're in doubt as to the exact pad thickness or quality, remove them for measurement and further inspection (see Chapter 9).

7   Check the disc for score marks, wear and burned spots. If any of these conditions exist, the disc should be removed for servicing or replacement (see Chapter 9).

8   Before installing the wheels, check all the brake lines and hoses for damage, wear, deformation, cracks, corrosion, leakage, bends and twists, particularly in the vicinity of the rubber hoses and calipers.

9   Install the wheels, lower the vehicle and tighten the wheel lug nuts to the torque given in this Chapter's Specifications.

Drum brakes

10   On models with rear drum brakes, make sure the parking brake is off, then tap on the outside of the drum with a rubber mallet to loosen it.

11   Remove the brake drums. If the drum still won't come off, refer to Chapter 9.

12   With the drums removed, carefully clean the brake assembly with brake system cleaner. **Warning:** *Don't blow the dust out with compressed air and don't inhale any of it (it is harmful to your health).*

13   Note the thickness of the lining material on both the front and rear brake shoes **(see illustration)**. Compare the measurement with the limit given in this Chapter's Specifications; if any lining thickness is less than specified, then all of the brake shoes must be replaced (see Chapter 9). The shoes should also be replaced if they're cracked, glazed (shiny areas), or covered with brake fluid.

14   Make sure all the brake assembly springs are connected and in good condition.

15   Check the brake components for signs of fluid leakage. With your finger or a small screwdriver, carefully pry back the rubber cups on the wheel cylinder located at the top of the brake shoes. Any leakage here is an indication that the wheel cylinders should be replaced immediately (see Chapter 9). Also, check all hoses and connections for signs of leakage.

16   Wipe the inside of the drum with a clean rag and denatured alcohol or brake cleaner. Again, be careful not to breathe the dangerous brake dust.

17   Check the inside of the drum for cracks, score marks, deep scratches and hard spots which will appear as small discolored areas. If imperfections cannot be removed with fine emery cloth, the drum must be taken to an automotive machine shop for resurfacing.

18   Repeat the procedure for the remaining wheel. If the inspection reveals that all parts are in good condition, reinstall the brake drums, install the wheels and lower the vehicle to the ground.

Parking brake

19   Slowly pull up on the parking brake and count the number of clicks you hear until the handle is up as far as it will go. The adjustment is correct if you hear the specified number of clicks (see Chapter 9). If you hear more or fewer clicks, it's time to adjust the parking brake (see Chapter 9).

20   An alternative method of checking the

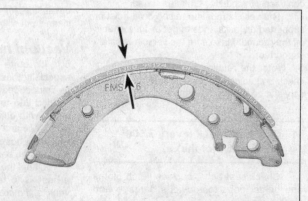

13.13 If the lining is bonded to the brake shoe, measure the lining thickness from the outer surface to the metal shoe, as shown here; if the lining is riveted to the shoe, measure from the lining outer surface to the rivet head

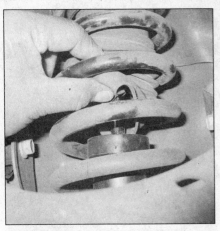

14.6 Check the shocks for leakage at the indicated area

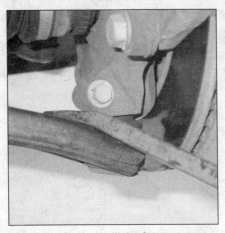

14.11 To check a balljoint for wear, try to pry the control arm up and down to make sure there is no play in the balljoint (if there is, replace it)

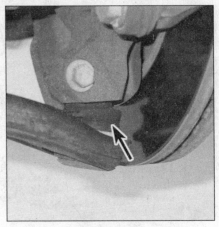

14.12 Check the balljoint boots for damage

parking brake is to park the vehicle on a steep hill with the engine running (so you can apply the brakes if necessary) with the parking brake set and the transaxle in Neutral. If the parking brake cannot prevent the vehicle from rolling, it needs adjustment (see Chapter 9).

14 Steering, suspension and driveaxle boot check (every 15,000 miles or 12 months)

Note: *For detailed illustrations of the steering and suspension components, refer to Chapter 10.*

Shock absorber check

1   Park the vehicle on level ground, turn the engine off and set the parking brake. Check the tire pressures.

2   Push down at one corner of the vehicle, then release it while noting the movement of the body. It should stop moving and come to rest in a level position within one or two bounces.

3   If the vehicle continues to move up-and-down or if it fails to return to its original position, a worn or weak shock absorber is probably the reason.

4   Repeat the above check at each of the three remaining corners of the vehicle.

5   Raise the vehicle and support it securely on jackstands.

6   Check the shock absorbers for evidence of fluid leakage **(see illustration)**. A light film of fluid is no cause for concern. Make sure that any fluid noted is from the shocks and not from some other source. If leakage is noted, replace the shocks as a set.

7   Check the shocks to be sure that they are securely mounted and undamaged. Check the upper mounts for damage and wear. If damage or wear is noted, replace the shocks as a set (front or rear).

8   If the shocks must be replaced, refer to Chapter 10 for the procedure.

Steering and suspension check

9   Check the tires for irregular wear patterns and proper inflation. See Section 5 in this Chapter for information regarding tire wear and Chapter 10 for information on wheel bearing replacement.

10   Inspect the universal joint between the steering shaft and the steering gear housing. Check the steering gear housing for lubricant leakage. Make sure that the dust boots are not damaged and that the boot clamps are not loose. Check the tie-rod ends for excessive play. Look for loose bolts, broken or disconnected parts and deteriorated rubber bushings on all suspension and steering components. While an assistant turns the steering wheel from side to side, check the steering components for free movement, chafing and binding. If the steering components do not seem to be reacting with the movement of the steering wheel, try to determine where the slack is located.

11   Check the balljoints for wear by trying to move each control arm up and down with a prybar **(see illustration)** to ensure that its balljoint has no play. If any balljoint does have play, it's worn out. See Chapter 10 for the control arm replacement procedure (the balljoints aren't replaceable separately).

12   Inspect the balljoint boots for damage and leaking grease **(see illustration)**.

13   At the rear of the vehicle, inspect the suspension arm bushings for deterioration. Additional information on suspension components can be found in Chapter 10.

Driveaxle boot check

14   The driveaxle boots are very important because they prevent dirt, water and foreign material from entering and damaging the constant velocity (CV) joints. Oil and grease can cause the boot material to deteriorate prematurely, so it's a good idea to wash the boots with soap and water. Because it constantly pivots back and forth following the steering action of the front hub, the outer CV boot

14.15 Flex the driveaxle boots by hand to check for cracks and/or leaking grease

wears out sooner and should be inspected regularly.

15   Inspect the boots for tears and cracks as well as loose clamps **(see illustration)**. If there is any evidence of cracks or leaking lubricant, they must be replaced as described in Chapter 8.

15 Fuel system check (every 15,000 miles or 12 months)

Warning: *Gasoline is flammable, so take extra precautions when you work on any part of the fuel system. Don't smoke or allow open flames or bare light bulbs near the work area, and don't work in a garage where a gas-type appliance (such as a water heater or clothes dryer) is present. Since fuel is carcinogenic, wear fuel-resistant gloves when there's a possibility of being exposed to fuel, and, if you spill any fuel on your skin, rinse it off immediately with soap and water. Mop up any spills immediately and do not store fuel-soaked rags where they could ignite. When you per-*

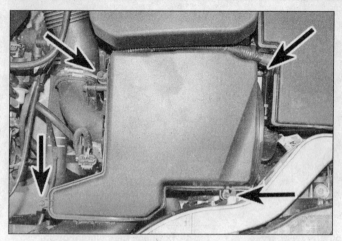

17.1a Remove the fasteners securing the cover . . .

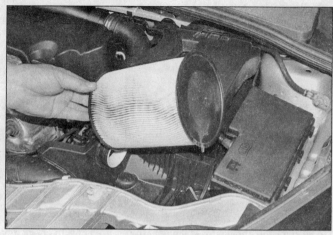

17.1b . . . pull the cover out of the way and lift the element out

form any kind of work on the fuel system, wear safety glasses and have a Class B type fire extinguisher on hand. The fuel system is under constant pressure, so, before any lines are disconnected, the fuel system pressure must be relieved (see Chapter 4).

1   If you smell gasoline while driving or after the vehicle has been sitting in the sun, inspect the fuel system immediately.

2   Remove the fuel filler cap and inspect if for damage and corrosion. The gasket should have an unbroken sealing imprint. If the gasket is damaged or corroded, install a new cap.

3   Inspect the fuel feed line for cracks. Make sure that the connections between the fuel lines and the fuel injection system and between the fuel lines and the fuel tank (inspect from below) are tight and dry.

Warning: *Your vehicle is fuel injected, so you must relieve the fuel system pressure before servicing fuel system components. The fuel system pressure relief procedure is outlined in Chapter 4 .*

4   Since some components of the fuel system - the fuel tank and part of the fuel feed line, for example - are underneath the vehicle, they can be inspected more easily with the vehicle raised on a hoist. If that's not possible, raise the vehicle and support it on jackstands.

5   With the vehicle raised and safely supported, inspect the gas tank and filler neck for punctures, cracks and other damage. The connection between the filler neck and the tank is particularly critical. Sometimes a rubber filler neck will leak because of loose clamps or deteriorated rubber. Inspect all fuel tank mounting brackets and straps to be sure that the tank is securely attached to the vehicle.

Warning: *Do not, under any circumstances, try to repair a fuel tank (except rubber components). A welding torch or any open flame can easily cause fuel vapors inside the tank to explode.*

6   Carefully check all rubber hoses and metal lines leading away from the fuel tank. Check for loose connections, deteriorated hoses, crimped lines and other damage.

Repair or replace damaged sections as necessary (see Chapter 4).

16   Manual transaxle lubricant level check (every 15,000 miles or 12 months)

1   The manual transaxle does not have a dipstick. To check the fluid level, raise the vehicle and support it securely on jackstands. On the front side of the transaxle housing, there is a fill plug about half-way up on the transaxle case; it's the larger of the two hex-head bolts. Remove the plug; if the lubricant level is correct, it should be up to the lower edge of the hole.

Caution: *Do not remove the smaller hex-head bolt above the back-up light switch.*

2   If the transaxle needs more lubricant (if the level is not up to the hole), use a syringe or a gear oil pump to add more. Stop filling the transaxle when the lubricant begins to run out of the hole.

3   Install the plug and tighten it to the torque listed in this Chapter's Specifications. Drive the vehicle a short distance, then check for leaks.

17   Air filter check and replacement (every 15,000 miles or 12 months)

1   The air filter is located inside a housing at the left (driver's) side of the engine compartment. To remove the air filter, remove the fasteners that secure the two halves of the air filter housing together, then separate the cover halves and remove the air filter element **(see illustrations)**.

2   Inspect the outer surface of the filter element. If it is dirty, replace it. If it is only moderately dusty, it can be reused by blowing it clean from the back to the front surface with compressed air. Because it is a pleated paper type filter, it cannot be washed or oiled. If it cannot be cleaned satisfactorily with com-

pressed air, discard and replace it. While the cover is off, be careful not to drop anything down into the housing.

Caution: *Never drive the vehicle with the air filter removed. Excessive engine wear could result and backfiring could even cause a fire under the hood.*

3   Wipe out the inside of the air filter housing.

4   Place the new filter into the air filter housing, making sure it seats properly.

5   Make sure the top half of the housing is seated properly, then secure it with the clamps.

18   Cabin air filter replacement (every 15,000 miles or 12 months)

Note: *Not all models are equipped with a cabin air filter.*

1   Remove the glove box (see Chapter 11).

2   Remove the access door, then pull the filter from the housing **(see illustration)**.

3   Installation is the reverse of removal.

19   Exhaust system check (every 30,000 miles or 24 months)

1   With the engine cold (at least three hours after the vehicle has been driven), check the complete exhaust system from the engine to the end of the tailpipe. Ideally, the inspection should be done with the vehicle on a hoist to permit unrestricted access. If a hoist isn't available, raise the vehicle and support it securely on jackstands.

2   Check the exhaust pipes and connections for evidence of leaks, severe corrosion and damage. Make sure that all brackets and hangers are in good condition and tight **(see illustration)**.

3   At the same time, inspect the underside of the body for holes, corrosion, open seams, etc. which may allow exhaust gases to enter the passenger compartment. Seal all body openings with silicone or body putty.

18.2a Remove the cover . . .

18.2b . . . then remove the filter

4   Rattles and other noises can often be traced to the exhaust system, especially the mounts and hangers. Try to move the pipes, muffler and catalytic converter. If the components can come in contact with the body or suspension parts, secure the exhaust system with new mounts.

5   Check the running condition of the engine by inspecting inside the end of the tailpipe. The exhaust deposits here are an indication of engine state-of-tune. If the pipe is black and sooty or coated with white deposits, the engine may need a tune-up, including a thorough fuel system inspection and adjustment.

20   Cooling system servicing (draining, flushing and refilling) (see Maintenance schedule for service intervals)

Warning: *Do not allow antifreeze to come in contact with your skin or painted surfaces of the vehicle. Rinse off spills immediately with plenty of water. Antifreeze is highly toxic if ingested. Never leave antifreeze lying around in an open container or in puddles on the floor; children and pets are attracted by its sweet smell and may drink it. Check with local authorities about disposing of used antifreeze. Many communities have collection centers which will see that antifreeze is disposed of safely. Never dump used antifreeze on the ground or pour it into drains.*
Caution: *Do not mix coolants of different colors. Doing so might damage the cooling system and/or the engine.*
Note: *Non-toxic antifreeze is now manufactured and available at local auto parts stores, but even this type must be disposed of properly.*

1   Periodically, the cooling system should be drained, flushed and refilled to replenish the antifreeze mixture and prevent formation of rust and corrosion, which can impair the performance of the cooling system and cause engine damage. When the cooling system is serviced, all hoses and the expansion tank cap should be checked and replaced if necessary.

19.2 Check each exhaust system rubber hanger for damage

Draining
Warning: *The engine must be completely cool before performing this procedure.*

2   Apply the parking brake and block the wheels. If the vehicle has just been driven, wait several hours to allow the engine to cool down before beginning this procedure.

3   Once the engine is completely cool, remove the expansion tank cap.

4   Remove the under-vehicle engine splash shield.

5   Move a large container under the radiator drain to catch the coolant. Attach a length of hose to the drain fitting **(see illustration)** to direct the coolant into the container, then open the drain fitting (a pair of pliers may be required to turn it).

6   While the coolant is draining, check the condition of the radiator hoses, heater hoses and clamps (refer to Section 9). Replace any damaged clamps or hoses.

Flushing

7   Fill the cooling system with clean water, following the *Refilling* procedure (see Step 13).

8   Start the engine and allow it to reach normal operating temperature, then rev up the

20.5 The radiator drain fitting

engine a few times.

9   Turn the engine off and allow it to cool completely, then drain the system as described earlier.

10   Repeat Steps 7 through 9 until the water being drained is free of contaminants.

11   In severe cases of contamination or clogging of the radiator, remove the radiator (see Chapter 3) and have a radiator repair facility clean and repair it if necessary.

12   Many deposits can be removed by the chemical action of a cleaner available at auto parts stores. Follow the procedure outlined in the manufacturer's instructions.
Note: *When the coolant is regularly drained and the system refilled with the correct antifreeze/water mixture, there should be no need to use chemical cleaners or descalers.*

Refilling
13   Close and tighten the radiator drain.

14   Place the heater temperature control in the maximum heat position.

15   Add coolant to the expansion tank until the level is at the MAX fill mark on the expansion tank.

16   Install the expansion tank cap and run the engine at 2500 rpm for ten minutes.

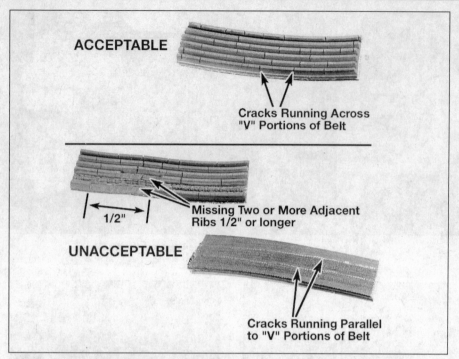

ACCEPTABLE

Cracks Running Across
"V" Portions of Belt

1/2"

Missing Two or More Adjacent
Ribs 1/2" or longer

UNACCEPTABLE

Cracks Running Parallel
to "V" Portions of Belt

22.4 Small cracks in the underside of a V-ribbed belt are acceptable - lengthwise cracks, or missing pieces that cause the belt to make noise, are cause for replacement

Caution: *If at any time the engine begins to overheat, or the coolant level falls below the MIN fill line on the expansion tank, turn off the engine, allow it to cool completely, then add coolant to the expansion tank to the MAX fill line.*

17   Turn the engine off and let it cool. Add more coolant mixture to bring the level to the MAX fill mark on the expansion tank.

18   Repeat Steps 16 and 17 if necessary.

19   Start the engine, allow it to reach normal operating temperature and check for leaks. Also, set the heater and blower controls to the maximum setting and check to see that the heater output from the air ducts is warm. This is a good indication that all air has been purged from the cooling system.

21   Brake fluid change (every 30,000 miles or 24 months)

Warning: *Brake fluid can harm your eyes and damage painted surfaces, so use extreme caution when handling or pouring it. Do not use brake fluid that has been standing open or is more than one year old. Brake fluid absorbs moisture from the air. Excess moisture can cause a dangerous loss of braking effectiveness.*

1   At the specified intervals, the brake fluid should be drained and replaced. Since the brake fluid may drip or splash when pouring it, place plenty of rags around the master cylinder to protect any surrounding painted surfaces.

2   Before beginning work, purchase the specified brake fluid (see *Recommended lubricants and fluids* in this Chapter's Specifications).

3   Remove the cap from the master cylinder reservoir.

4   Using a hand suction pump or similar device, withdraw the fluid from the master cylinder reservoir.

5   Add new fluid to the master cylinder until it rises to the base of the filler neck.

6   Bleed the brake system as described in Chapter 9 at all four brakes until new and uncontaminated fluid is expelled from the bleeder screw. Be sure to maintain the fluid level in the master cylinder as you perform the bleeding process. If you allow the master cylinder to run dry, air will enter the system.

7   Refill the master cylinder with fluid and check the operation of the brakes. The pedal should feel solid when depressed, with no sponginess. Warning: Do not operate the vehicle if you are in doubt about the effectiveness of the brake system.

22   Drivebelt check and replacement (every 100,000 miles)

1   Two serpentine drivebelts are located at the front of the engine and play an important role in the overall operation of the engine and its components. Due to its function and material make up, the belt is prone to wear and should be periodically inspected. One serpentine belt drives the alternator and

water pump and the other belt drives the air conditioning compressor. Although the belts should be inspected at the recommended intervals, replacement may not be necessary for more than 100,000 miles.

Check

2   Since the drivebelts are located very close to the right-hand side of the engine compartment, it is possible to gain better access by raising the front of the vehicle and removing the right-hand wheel, then removing the wheel arch liner in the right fenderwell (see Chapter 11). Be sure to support the front of the vehicle securely on jackstands.

3   With the engine stopped, inspect the full length of the drivebelts for cracks and separation of the belt plies. It will be necessary to turn the engine (using a wrench or socket and bar on the crankshaft pulley bolt, working clockwise only) in order to move the belt from the pulleys so that the belt can be inspected thoroughly. Twist the belt between the pulleys so that both sides can be viewed. Also check for fraying, and glazing which gives the belt a shiny appearance. Check the pulleys for nicks, cracks, distortion and corrosion.

4   Note that it is not unusual for a ribbed belt to exhibit small cracks in the edges of the belt ribs, and unless these are extensive or very deep, belt replacement is not essential **(see illustration)**.

Replacement

Accessory drivebelts

5   Disconnect the negative battery cable from the remote ground terminal (see Chapter 5). Remove the engine cover, if equipped. Loosen the right front wheel lug nuts, then raise the front of the vehicle and support it on jackstands. Remove the right front wheel and the wheel arch liner (see Chapter 11).

6   Remove the air conditioning compressor belt (see Steps 11 and 12)

7   Note how the drivebelt is routed, then remove the belt from the pulleys. If you're working on a non-turbo model, use a wrench on the hex cast into the tensioner and turn the tensioner to release the drivebelt tension. Once tension has been released, remove the belt from the pulleys. If you're working on a turbo model engine, insert a ratchet or breaker bar into the tensioner hole and pull the handle to release the drivebelt tension. Once tension has been released, remove the belt from the pulleys.

8   Fit the new drivebelt onto the crankshaft, alternator, and water pump pulleys, then turn the tensioner back and locate the drivebelt on the pulley. Make sure that the drivebelt is correctly seated in all of the pulley grooves, then release the tensioner.

9   Install the air conditioning compressor belt (see Step 13 and 14).

10   Install the splash shield and wheel, then lower the car to the ground. Tighten the lug nuts to the torque listed in this Chapter's Specifications.

23.6 Location of the transaxle drain plug

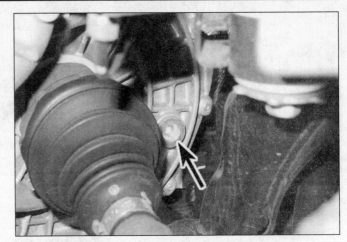

23.7 The fluid fill plug is located on the left side of the transaxle

Air conditioning compressor belt

11   Disconnect the negative battery cable from the remote ground terminal (see Chapter 5). Loosen the right front wheel lug nuts, then raise the front of the vehicle and support it on jackstands. Remove the right front wheel and the wheel arch liner (see Chapter 11). The belt and pulley are protected by a cover. The belt is of a unique design, called a "stretchy belt," which provides tension without the use of a mechanical tensioner.

12   Insert a length of flexible material such as a leather or plastic strap under the belt at the pulley at the end of the compressor, then have an assistant rotate the engine (clockwise) by using a socket and breaker bar on the crankshaft pulley bolt, while you feed the remover strap between the belt and the pulley. Pull the strap quickly to force the belt from the pulley on the compressor.

Caution: *Do not use hard plastic or metal tools to pry the belt off; it can be easily damaged.*

Note: *If the belt is not going to be re-used, you can simply cut it off.*

13   Route the new belt under the compressor, then over the pulley on the crankshaft, and have your assistant rotate the engine again; the belt should pop over the pulley on the crankshaft. Make sure the belt is positioned properly on both pulleys.

14   Reinstall the cover and tighten the fasteners securely.

Accessory drivebelt tensioner

15   Remove the drivebelts (see Steps 5 through 12).

16   On non-turbo models, remove the two bolts securing the tensioner to the engine block. On turbo models, remove the three bolts securing the tensioner to the timing chain cover, then detach the tensioner from the cover.

17   Installation is the reverse of removal. Tighten the tensioner bolts to the torque listed in this Chapter's Specifications .

23   Automatic transaxle fluid change (every 150,000 miles)

Note: *For transmission identification, refer to the Vehicle Identification Numbers information at the front of this manual.*

1   The automatic transaxle fluid should be changed at the recommended intervals.

2   Before beginning work, purchase the specified transmission fluid (see this Chapter's Specifications).

3   Other tools necessary for this job include jackstands to support the vehicle in a raised position, wrenches, a drain pan, newspapers and clean rags.

4   The fluid should be drained immediately after the vehicle has been driven. Hot fluid is more effective than cold fluid at removing built-up sediment.

Warning: *Fluid temperature can exceed 350-degrees F in a hot transaxle. Wear protective gloves.*

5   After the vehicle has been driven to warm up the fluid, raise the front of the vehicle and support it securely on jackstands.

Warning: *Never work under a vehicle that is supported only by a jack!*

6   Place the drain pan under the drain plug in the transaxle pan and remove the drain plug **(see illustration)**. Once the fluid has drained, reinstall the drain plug and tighten it to the torque listed in this Chapter's Specifications .

7   Lower the vehicle and remove the oil leveling plug from the side of the transaxle **(see illustration)**.

8   Add the specified automatic transmission fluid through the oil leveling plug hole with a suctioning gun or large syringe until the fluid starts to drip out of the hole.

Note: *Allow all excess fluid to drip out of the plug hole.*

9   Once the fluid is even with the oil leveling plug hole install the plug and tighten it to torque listed in this Chapter's Specifications.

10   The old fluid drained from the transaxle cannot be reused in its present state and should be disposed of. Check with your local auto parts store, disposal facility or environmental agency to see if they will accept the fluid for recycling. After the fluid has cooled it can be drained into a container (capped plastic jugs, topped bottles, milk cartons, etc.) for transport to one of these disposal sites. Don't dispose of the fluid by pouring it on the ground or down a drain!

24   Manual transaxle lubricant change (every 150,000 miles)

1   This procedure should be performed after the vehicle has been driven so the lubricant will be warm and therefore flow out of the transaxle more easily.

2   Raise the vehicle and support it securely on jackstands. Position a drain pan under the transaxle. Remove the transaxle fill plug on the front of the case; it's about half-way up on the transaxle case and is the larger of the two hex-head bolts.

Caution: *Do not remove the smaller hex-head bolt above the back-up light switch. Remove the drain plug at the bottom of the case and allow the lubricant to drain into the pan.*

3   After the lubricant has drained completely, reinstall the drain plug and tighten it securely.

4   Using a hand pump, syringe or funnel, fill the transaxle with the specified lubricant until it is level with the lower edge of the filler hole. Using a new sealing washer, reinstall the fill plug and tighten it to the torque listed in this Chapter's Specifications

5   Lower the vehicle.

6   Drive the vehicle for a short distance, then check the drain and fill plugs for leakage.

7   The old lubricant drained from the

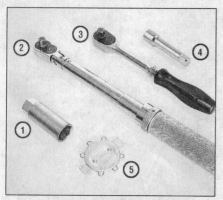

25.2 Tools required for changing spark plugs

1   **Spark plug socket** - *This will have special padding inside to protect the spark plug porcelain insulator*
2   **Torque wrench** - *Although not mandatory, use of this tool is the best way to ensure that the plugs are tightened properly*
3   **Ratchet** - *Standard hand tool to fit the plug socket*
4   **Extension** - *Depending on model and accessories, you may need special extensions and universal joints to reach one or more of the plugs*
5   **Spark plug gap gauge** - *This gauge for checking the gap comes in a variety of styles. Make sure the gap for your engine is included*

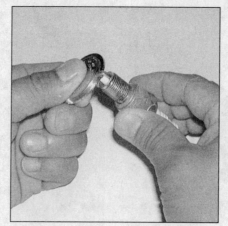

25.5a Using a tapered thickness gauge to check the spark plug gap - slide the thin side into the gap and turn it until the gauge just fills the gap, then read the thickness on the gauge - do not force the tool into the gap or use the tapered portion to widen a gap

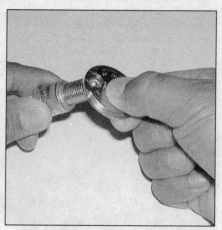

25.5b To change the gap, bend the side electrode only, using the adjuster hole in the tool, and be very careful not to crack or chip the porcelain insulator surrounding the center electrode

---

transaxle cannot be reused in its present state and should be disposed of. Check with your local auto parts store, disposal facility or environmental agency to see if they will accept the lubricant for recycling. After the lubricant has cooled it can be drained into a container (capped plastic jugs, topped bottles, milk cartons, etc.) for transport to one of these disposal sites. Don't dispose of the lubricant by pouring it on the ground or down a drain!

---

25   Spark plug check and replacement (see Maintenance schedule for service intervals)

1   On these models, the spark plugs are located in the valve covers.
2   In most cases, the tools necessary for spark plug replacement include a spark plug socket which fits onto a ratchet (spark plug sockets are padded inside to prevent damage to the porcelain insulators on the new plugs), various extensions and a gap gauge to check and adjust the gaps on the new plugs **(see illustration)**. A torque wrench should be used to tighten the new plugs.
3   The best approach when replacing the spark plugs is to purchase the new ones in advance, adjust them to the proper gap and replace the plugs one at a time. When buying the new spark plugs, be sure to obtain the correct plug type for your particular engine. This information can be found in or in the factory owner's manual.

4   Allow the engine to cool completely before attempting to remove any of the plugs. These engines are equipped with aluminum cylinder heads, which can be damaged if the spark plugs are removed when the engine is hot. While you are waiting for the engine to cool, check the new plugs for defects and adjust the gaps.
5   The gap is checked by inserting the proper-thickness gauge between the electrodes at the tip of the plug **(see illustration)**. The gap between the electrodes should be the same as the one specified on the Emissions Control Information label or in this Chapter's Specifications. The gauge should just slide between the electrodes with a slight amount of drag. If the gap is incorrect, use the adjuster on the gauge body to bend the curved side electrode slightly until the proper gap is obtained **(see illustration)**. If the side electrode is not exactly over the center electrode, bend it with the adjuster until it is. Check for cracks in the porcelain insulator (if any are found, the plug should not be used).
Note: *We recommend using a tapered thickness gauge when checking platinum- or iridium-type spark plugs. Other types of gauges may scrape the thin coating from the electrodes, thus dramatically shortening the life of the plugs. However, if dual-electrode spark plugs are used, a wire-type gauge will have to be used.*
6   All models are equipped with individual ignition coils which must be removed first to access the spark plugs **(see illustration)**.
7   If compressed air is available, use it to blow any dirt or foreign material away from the spark plug hole. The idea here is to eliminate the possibility of debris falling into the cylinder as the spark plug is removed.
8   Place the spark plug socket over the plug and remove it from the engine by turning it in a counterclockwise direction **(see illustration)**.

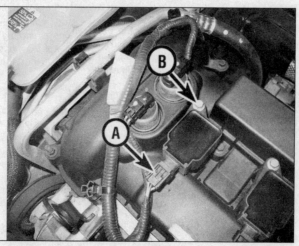

25.6 To remove the coils, depress the tab (A) and disconnect the electrical connector, remove the coil retaining bolt (B), then pull the coil straight up to remove it

25.8 Use a ratchet and extension to remove the spark plugs

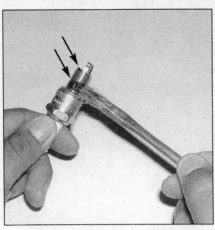

25.10a Apply a thin coat of anti-seize compound to the spark plug threads

25.10b A length of snug-fitting rubber hose will save time and prevent damaged threads when installing the spark plugs

9　Compare the spark plug to those shown in the photos located on the inside back cover of this book to get an indication of the general running condition of the engine.

10　Apply a small amount of anti-seize compound to the spark plug threads **(see illustration)**. Install one of the new plugs into the hole until you can no longer turn it with your fingers, then tighten to the torque listed in this Chapter's Specifications. It is a good idea to slip a short length of rubber hose over the end of the plug to use as a tool to thread it into place **(see illustration)**. The hose will grip the plug well enough to turn it, but will start to slip if the plug begins to cross-thread in the hole - this will prevent damaged threads and the accompanying repair costs.

11　Repeat the procedure for the remaining spark plugs.

Notes

Chapter 2 Part A   Engines

Contents

Specifications

General

2.0L EcoBoost (turbocharged) engine

Engine type	Four-cylinder, in-line, DOHC
Displacement	122 cubic inches (1999 cc)
Engine VIN code	9
Firing order	1-3-4-2
Bore	3.4449 inches (87.5 mm)
Stroke	3.2717 inches (83.1 mm)
Compression ratio	9.3:1
Compression pressure	See Chapter 2B
Oil pressure	See Chapter 2B

2.0L Duratech-HE (non-turbocharged) engine

Engine type	Four cylinder, in-line DOHC
Displacement	122 cubic inches (1999 cc)
Engine VIN code	Z
Firing order	1-3-4-2
Bore	3.4449 inches (87.5 mm)
Stroke	3.2717 inches (83.1 mm)
Compression ratio	12:1
Compression pressure	See Chapter 2B
Oil pressure	See Chapter 2B

FRONT OF VEHICLE

Cylinder locations

Camshafts

2.0L EcoBoost (turbocharged) engine
  Lobe height
    Intake .... 0.326 inch (8.3 mm)
    Exhaust .... 0.291 inch (7.4 mm)
  Bearing journal diameter .... 0.9827 to 0.9835 inch (24.96 to 24.98 mm)
  Journal-to-bore-clearance .... 0.0014 to 0.0031 inch (0.036 to 0.079 mm)
  Runout .... 0.0012 inch (0.03 mm)
  Endplay .... 0.003 to 0.009 inch (0.08 to 0.23 mm)
2.0L Duratec-HE (non-turbocharged) engine
  Lobe height
    Intake .... 0.35 inch (8.9 mm)
    Exhaust .... 0.346 inch (8.8 mm)
  Bearing journal diameter .... 0.9827 to 0.9835 inch (24.96 to 24.98 mm)
  Journal-to-bore-clearance .... 0.0014 to 0.0031 inch (0.036 to 0.079 mm)
  Runout .... 0.0012 inch (0.03 mm)
  Endplay .... 0.003 to 0.009 inch (0.08 to 0.23 mm)

Valve clearances (cold)

2.0L EcoBoost (turbocharged) engine
  Ideal clearance
    Intake .... 0.0095 inch (0.24 mm)
    Exhaust .... 0.0142 inch (0.36 mm)
  Acceptable clearance
    Intake .... 0.007 to 0.012 inch (0.18 to 0.30 mm)
    Exhaust .... 0.012 to 0.017 inch (0.30 to 0.43 mm)
2.0L Duratec-HE (non-turbocharged) engine
  Intake .... 0.009 to 0.013 inch (0.23 to 0.33 mm)
  Exhaust .... 0.012 to 0.016 inch (0.30 to 0.41 mm)

Warpage limits

Cylinder head gasket surfaces (head and block) .... 0.002 inch (0.05 mm)
Exhaust manifold .... 0.030 inch (0.76 mm)

Torque specifications

	Ft-lbs (unless otherwise indicated)	**Nm**

Note: One foot-pound (ft-lb) of torque is equivalent to 12 inch-pounds (in-lbs) of torque. Torque values below approximately 15 ft-lbs are expressed in inch-pounds, because most foot-pound torque wrenches are not accurate at these smaller values.

	Ft-lbs	Nm
Camshaft bearing cap bolts (in sequence - **see illustration 11.25a or 11.25b**)		
2.0L EcoBoost (turbocharged) engine		
Step 1, All bolts	Tighten finger tight	
Step 2, All but front bearing cap	62 in-lbs	7
Step 3, All but front bearing cap	142 in-lbs	16
Step 4, Front bearing cap (3-bolt)	62 in-lbs	7
Step 5, Front bearing cap (3-bolt)	142 in-lbs	16
2.0L Duratech-HE (non-turbocharged) engine		
Step 1	Tighten finger tight	
Step 2	62 in-lbs	7
Step 3	144 in-lbs	16
Camshaft phaser and sprocket bolts		
2.0L EcoBoost (turbocharged) engine		
Step 1	30	40
Step 2	Tighten an additional 60-degrees	
2.0L Duratech-HE (non-turbocharged) engine		
Step 1	37	50
Step 2	Tighten an additional 90-degrees	
Crankshaft pulley bolt*		
Step 1	74	100
Step 2	Tighten an additional 90-degrees	
Cylinder head bolts (in sequence - **see illustration 12.29a**)*		
2.0L EcoBoost (turbocharged) engine		
Step 1	62 in-lbs	7
Step 2	133 in-lbs	15
Step 3	41	56
Step 4	Tighten an additional 90-degrees	
Step 5	Tighten an additional 90-degrees	

Torque specifications

	Ft-lbs (unless otherwise indicated)	Nm
Cylinder head bolts (in sequence - **see illustration 12.29a**)* (continued)		
2.0L Duratech-HE (non-turbocharged) engine		
Step 1	62 in-lbs	7
Step 2	133 in-lbs	15
Step 3	26	35
Step 4	Tighten an additional 90-degrees	
Step 5	Tighten an additional 135-degrees	
Variable Camshaft Timing (VCT) solenoid bolt	89 in-lbs	10
Valve cover bolts (in sequence - **see illustration 4.13a or 4.13b**)	89 in-lbs	10
Turbocharger mounting nuts	37	50
Engine mount		
Mounting nuts	59	80
Mounting bolts	66	89
Exhaust manifold/catalytic converter studs (2.0L Duratech-HE [non-turbocharged] engine)*	150 in-lbs	17
Exhaust manifold/catalytic converter nuts (2.0L Duratech-HE [non-turbocharged] engine)*		
Step 1	41	56
Step 2	41	56
Flywheel/driveplate bolts*		
Step 1	37	50
Step 2	59	80
Step 3	83	111
Intake manifold fasteners	177 in-lbs	20
Crankshaft rear oil seal and retainer	89 in-lbs	10
Oil pan-to-bellhousing bolts	35	47
Timing chain cover-to-oil pan bolts	89 in-lbs	10
Oil pan-to-engine block bolts	177 in-lbs	20
Oil pick-up tube bolts	89 in-lbs	10
Oil pump-to-cylinder block bolts		
Step 1	89 in-lbs	10
Step 2	177 in-lbs	20
Sprocket bolt	18	25
Oil pump chain tensioner and guide bolts	89 in-lbs	10
Timing chain cover (in sequence - **see illustration 9.11a or 9.11b**)		
2.0L EcoBoost (turbocharged) engine		
Bolts 1 through 19	89 in-lbs	10
Bolts 20 through 22	35	47
2.0L Duratech-HE (non-turbocharged) engine		
Bolts 1 through 17	89 in-lbs	10
Bolts 19 through 21	35	47
Bolt 22	18	25
Bolt 18	35	47
Timing chain guide bolts	89 in-lbs	10
Timing chain tensioner bolts	89 in-lbs	10
Transaxle-to-engine bolts	35	47

*Install new fasteners during installation.

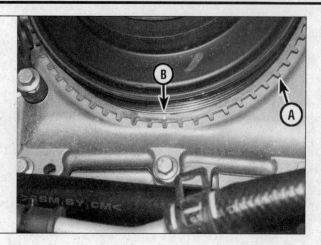

3.10 Crankshaft positions (A) 45-derees before TDC (B) TDC (6 o'clock position)

1   General Information

How to use this Chapter

1   This Chapter is devoted to repair procedures possible while the engine is still installed in the vehicle. Since these procedures are based on the assumption that the engine is installed in the vehicle, if the engine has been removed from the vehicle and mounted on a stand, some of the preliminary dismantling steps outlined will not apply.

2   Information concerning engine/transaxle removal and replacement and engine overhaul, can be found in Chapter 2B.

Engine description

3   These engines are sixteen-valve, double overhead camshaft (DOHC), four-cylinder, in-line type, mounted transversely at the front of the vehicle, with the transmission on the left-hand end. They incorporate an aluminum cylinder head and an aluminum cylinder block.

4   The two camshafts are driven by a timing chain, each operating eight valves via conventional lifters with Variable Camshaft Timing (VCT) phasers on the end of the camshafts to control valve timing. Each camshaft rotates in five bearings that are line-bored directly in the cylinder head and the (bolted-on) bearing caps. This means that the bearing caps are not available separately from the cylinder head, and must not be interchanged with caps from another engine.

5   These engines incorporate an aluminum timing chain cover and oil pan, and the crankshaft main caps are part of a one-piece lower block support. When working on these engines, note that Torx-type (both male and female heads) and hexagon socket (Allen head) fasteners are widely used. A good selection of sockets, with the necessary adapters, will be required, so that these can be unscrewed without damage and, on reassembly, tightened to the torque settings specified.

Lubrication system

6   The oil pump is driven via a chain from the front of the crankshaft, using the same sprocket that drives the timing chain. The pump forces oil through an externally mounted full-flow cartridge-type filter. From the filter, the oil is pumped into a main gallery in the cylinder block/crankcase, from where it is distributed to the crankshaft (main bearings) and cylinder head.

7   The connecting rod bearings are supplied with oil via internal drillings in the crankshaft. Each piston crown and connecting rod is cooled by a spray of oil.

8   The cylinder head is provided with two oil galleries, one on the intake side and one on the exhaust, to ensure constant oil supply to the camshaft bearings and lifters. A retaining valve (inserted into the cylinder head's top surface, in the middle, on the intake side) prevents these galleries from being drained when the engine is switched off. The valve incorporates a ventilation hole in its upper end, to allow air bubbles to escape from the system when the engine is restarted.

2   Repair operations possible with the engine in the vehicle

1   Many major repair operations can be accomplished without removing the engine from the vehicle.

2   Clean the engine compartment and the exterior of the engine with some type of degreaser before any work is done. It will make the job easier and help keep dirt out of the internal areas of the engine.

3   Depending on the components involved, it may be helpful to remove the hood to improve access to the engine as repairs are performed (see Chapter 11). Cover the fenders to prevent damage to the paint. Special pads are available, but an old bedspread or blanket will also work.

4   If vacuum, exhaust, oil or coolant leaks develop, indicating a need for gasket or seal replacement, the repairs can generally be made with the engine in the vehicle. The intake and exhaust manifold gaskets, oil pan gasket, crankshaft oil seals and cylinder head gasket are all accessible with the engine in place.

5   Exterior engine components, such as the intake and exhaust manifolds, the oil pan, the oil pump, the water pump, the starter motor, the alternator and the fuel system components can be removed for repair with the engine in place.

6   Since the camshaft(s) and cylinder head can be removed without pulling the engine, valve component servicing can also be accomplished with the engine in the vehicle. Replacement of the timing chain and sprockets is also possible with the engine in the vehicle.

7   In extreme cases caused by a lack of necessary equipment, repair or replacement of piston rings, pistons, connecting rods and rod bearings is possible with the engine in the vehicle. However, this practice is not recommended because of the cleaning and preparation work that must be done to the components involved.

3   Top Dead Center (TDC) for number 1 piston - locating

Note: *You will need two special tools for this procedure: the camshaft positioning tool (303-1565) or equivalent, and the timing pin (303-507). We don't recommend trying to fabricate a timing pin with a bolt because while you would be able to determine the correct bolt diameter and thread pitch, it is impossible to determine what the length of the bolt should be. These pins come in several lengths, depending on the engine family. There is no way to determine the correct pin length without comparing it to a factory or aftermarket tool designed to be used with this engine. Using a bolt of the wrong length could damage the engine. Also, never use the timing pin as a means to stop the engine from rotating - tool breakage and/ or engine damage can result.*

1   Disconnect the negative battery cable from the remote ground terminal (see Chapter 5).

2   Remove the passenger's side inner fender splash shield (see Chapter 11).

3   Remove the engine splash shield fasteners and splash shield.

4   Remove the air filter outlet duct (see Chapter 4).

5   Remove the drivebelt (see Chapter 1).

6   If you're working on a turbocharged model, remove the power brake booster vacuum pump (see Chapter 3).

7   Remove the valve cover (see Section 4).

8   Remove the rear intake camshaft bearing cap (see Section 11).

9   Prevent the camshaft from turning by using a wrench on the flats of the intake camshaft then loosen and remove the brake vacuum pump adapter from the end of the camshaft.

10   Using a wrench or socket on the crankshaft pulley bolt, rotate the crankshaft clockwise until the (TDC) marked tooth on the crankshaft pulley is 1/8-turn (45-degrees) before the 6 o'clock position **(see illustration)**.

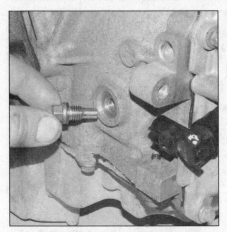

3.11 Remove the timing hole plug

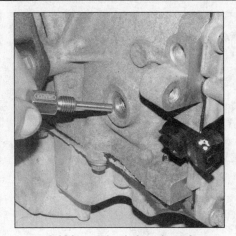

3.12 Insert the timing pin tool

3.13 The (TDC) marked tooth aligned with the center line of the Crankshaft Position (CKP) sensor

11   The TDC timing hole is located near the lower right front corner of the engine block (on the firewall side) hidden behind the driveaxle support bracket; it provides a means of accurately positioning the no. 1 cylinder at TDC. Locate the hole and remove the timing hole plug **(see illustration)**.

12   Screw in the timing pin **(see illustration)**. **Caution:** *Never use the timing pin as a means to stop the engine from rotating - tool breakage and/or engine damage can result.* **Note:** *With the timing pin installed, the engine can still be rotated counterclockwise.*

13   Turn the crankshaft slowly clockwise until the crankshaft counterweight comes into contact with the timing pin and the tooth on the crankshaft pulley is aligned with the center line on the Crankshaft Position (CKP) sensor **(see illustration)** - in this position, the engine is set to TDC on no. 1 cylinder.

14   The camshafts each have a machined slot at the transaxle end of the engine. Both slots will be completely horizontal, and at the same height as the cylinder head machined surface, when the engine is at TDC on the Number 1 cylinder. Manufacturer service tool

303-1565 is used to check this position, and to positively locate the camshafts in position **(see illustrations)**.

15   Before rotating the crankshaft again, make sure that the tools are removed. Do not forget to install the timing hole plug and tighten it securely.

---

4   Valve cover - removal and installation

Removal

1   Disconnect the cable from the negative battery cable from the remote ground terminal (see Chapter 5).

2   On 2.0L EcoBoost engines, remove the cowl panel (see Chapter 12).

3   Remove the individual ignition coil assemblies from the spark plugs (see Chapter 5).

4   Remove the Charge Air Cooler (CAC) inlet and outlet tubes (see Chapter 4), then remove the CAC bracket fasteners and bracket.

5   Disconnect the electrical connectors

from the Variable Camshaft Timing (VCT) solenoids, EVAP canister purge valve, Cylinder Head Temperature (CHT) sensor, Camshaft Position (CMP) sensor, Fuel Rail Pressure (FRP) sensor and the Manifold Absolute Pressure (MAP) sensor, if equipped.

6   Remove the bracket for the wiring harness on the valve cover stud, then set the harness aside.

7   Remove the engine oil dipstick.

8   Working progressively, unscrew the valve cover retaining fasteners, noting the (captive) spacer sleeve and rubber seal, then withdraw the cover.

9   Discard the cover gasket. This must be replaced whenever it is disturbed. Check that the sealing faces are undamaged and that the rubber seal at each bolt hole is serviceable. Replace any worn or damaged seals.

Installation

10   Clean the cover and cylinder head gasket faces carefully, then install a new gasket onto the valve cover, ensuring that it is located correctly by the rubber seals and spacer sleeves.

3.14a Turn the engine so that the camshaft end slots are aligned . . .

3.14b . . . then insert the metal strip into the slots to locate and set the shafts to TDC (typical)

4.13a 2.0L EcoBoost engine valve cover bolt tightening sequence

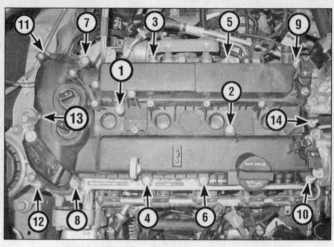

4.13b 2.0L Duratec-HE engine valve cover bolt tightening sequence

11   At the top of the timing chain cover, apply a small bead of RTV sealant to the joints where the valve cover and timing cover meet the engine.

12   Install the cover to the cylinder head, ensuring as the cover is tightened that the gasket remains seated.

13   Working in a diagonal sequence from the center outwards, first tighten the cover bolts by hand only. Once all the bolts are hand-tight, go around once more in sequence **(see illustrations)**, and tighten the bolts to the torque listed in this Chapter Specifications.

14   The remainder of installation is the reverse of removal.

15   Run the engine and check for signs of oil leakage.

5   Valve clearances - checking and adjustment

1   Disconnect the negative battery cable from the remote ground terminal (see Chapter 5).

2   Remove all the spark plugs as described in Chapter 1, then remove the valve cover as described in Section 4.

3   Loosen the right front wheel lug nuts, raise the front of the vehicle and support it securely on jackstands, then remove the wheel. Remove the wheel arch liners (see Chapter 11).

4   Using a wrench or socket on the crankshaft pulley bolt, rotate the crankshaft clockwise and check each lifter when its camshaft lobe is straight up, ensuring that the measurement is between the base circle of the camshaft lobe and the top of the lifter. Use feeler gauges to measure the clearances **(see illustration)**.

5   The clearance must be checked between each camshaft lobe and the lifter it operates. Keep careful notes of the measurements recorded for each lifter.

6   If some measurements fall outside the recommended clearances in this Chapter's Specifications, the camshafts must be removed and the out-of-spec lifters replaced (see Section 11). New lifters are available with various thicknesses to correct the valve clearances. Each lifter is marked with a thickness number. Only refer to the numbers after the

decimal point. A "0.650" marking refers to an actual thickness of 3.650 mm.

7   To arrive at the desired thickness for new lifters: add the thickness of the original lifter (such as 0.650 mm) to the clearance you measured. Subtract the midrange figure for ideal clearance (see this Chapter's Specifications) from that number and you have the proper lifter thickness to order. Every thickness is not available, so choose the closest to your requirement.

8   Refer to Section 11 for installation of the camshafts. Once the camshafts and timing chain have been installed, recheck the valve clearances.

9   The remainder of installation is the reverse of removal. Run the engine and check for oil leaks.

6   Intake manifold - removal and installation

Removal

1   Relieve the fuel system pressure (see Chapter 4).

2   Disconnect the negative battery cable from the remote ground terminal (see Chapter 5).

3   Raise the vehicle and support it safely on jackstands. Remove the lower splash shield.

4   Remove the air filter outlet hose (see Chapter 4).

5   Disconnect the electrical connectors from the swirl control, throttle body (see Chapter 4) and oil pressure sender (see Chapter 2B, Section 2).

6   Disconnect the EVAP tube from the Charge Air Cooler (CAC) outlet tube, then loosen the CAC outlet tube clamp and pull the tube off of the throttle body (see Chapter 4).

7   Disconnect the electrical connectors from the Fuel Rail Pressure (FRP) sensor and the Manifold Absolute Pressure (MAP) sensor (see Chapter 6).

8   Disengage the EVAP line and heater

5.4 Check the valve clearances with a feeler gauge of the specified thickness. If the clearance is correct, you should feel a slight drag as the feeler gauge is slid between the lifter and the camshaft

6.9 Push in on the locking ring while pulling the hose from the intake manifold

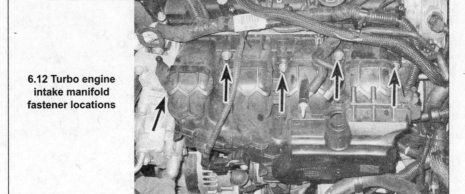

6.12 Turbo engine intake manifold fastener locations

hose retainers underneath the manifold, then remove the EVAP canister purge valve (see Chapter 6).
9   Release the vacuum hoses from the intake manifold by depressing the red quick-connect lock ring and pulling the hose upward at the same time **(see illustration)**.
10   Release the harness clips and set aside the wiring harness at the top of the intake manifold.
11   If equipped, remove the fuel rail heat shield.
12   The intake manifold is secured with five bolts on turbo models **(see illustration)**. On non-turbo models, the intake manifold is secured with six bolts, five at the top and one at the bottom. Remove the bolts and pull the intake manifold away from the engine enough to access and disconnect the EGR pipe (if equipped) and the crankcase vent hose from the oil separator. Squeeze the two clips on the vent hose to release it.

Installation

13   There are individual gaskets for each of the four ports of the intake manifold. Using new manifold gaskets, install the intake manifold. Tighten the bolts and nuts in several stages, working from the center out, to the torque listed in this Chapter's Specifications.
14   Installation is otherwise the reverse of removal.

7   Exhaust manifold - removal and installation

Warning: *Allow the engine to cool completely before beginning this procedure.*
Note: *Turbo models do not use an exhaust manifold; the exhaust passages are an integral part of the cylinder head, and the turbocharger mounts directly to the cylinder head (see Chapter 4).*

Removal

1   Raise the vehicle and place it securely on jackstands.

2   When the engine has cooled, it will be helpful to soak the manifold heat-shield retaining nuts with penetrating oil to loosen any rust. Remove the heat shield. Apply penetrating oil to the exhaust manifold mounting bolts and let sit per the manufacturer's instructions.
3   Disconnect the exhaust pipe from the exhaust manifold (see Chapter 4). Remove and discard the old flange gasket.
4   Unplug the electrical connector from the oxygen sensor and remove the oxygen sensor from the exhaust manifold (see Chapter 6).
5   Remove the exhaust manifold mounting nuts, then remove the exhaust manifold and the old manifold gasket.
6   Use a stud removal tool or two nuts tightened against each other to remove the old studs from the cylinder head.

Inspection

7   Inspect the exhaust manifold for cracks and any other obvious damage. If the manifold is cracked or damaged in any way, replace it.
8   Using a scraper, remove all traces of gasket material from the mating surfaces and inspect them for wear and cracks.
Caution: *When removing gasket material from any surface, especially aluminum, be very careful not to scratch or gouge the gasket surface. Any damage to the surface may cause an exhaust leak. Gasket removal solvents are available from auto parts stores and may prove helpful.*
9   Using a straightedge and feeler gauge, inspect the exhaust manifold mating surface for warpage. Also check the exhaust manifold surface on the cylinder head. If the warpage on any surface exceeds the limits listed in this Chapter's Specifications, the exhaust manifold and/or cylinder head must be replaced or resurfaced at an automotive machine shop.

Installation

10   Install new exhaust studs in the cylinder head and tighten them to the torque listed in this Chapter's Specifications. Install the manifold with a new gasket and new self-locking nuts. Tighten the nuts in several stages, working from the center out, to the torque listed in this Chapter's Specifications.

Note: *Coat the threads of the exhaust manifold studs with an anti-seize compound.*
Note: *Failure to tighten the exhaust manifold bolts to the specified torque a second time may cause leaks to develop.*
11   The remainder of installation is the reverse of removal. Run the engine and check for exhaust leaks.

8   Crankshaft pulley - removal and installation

Removal

Caution: *Once the crankshaft pulley is loosened, the crankshaft (timing) sprocket will be loosened as well. The engine is considered out-of-time at this point. The installation procedure in this Section must be followed exactly to re-time the engine properly. Severe engine damage will occur otherwise.*
Note: *You will need two special tools for the timing procedure (see Section 3): camshaft positioning tool 303-1565, and the timing pin (303-507).*
1   Remove the drivebelt (see Chapter 1).
2   Set the engine to TDC using the camshaft and crankshaft locking tools (see Section 3).
3   The crankshaft must be held to prevent its rotation while the pulley bolt is unscrewed. Use a strap wrench around the crankshaft pulley to hold it from turning.
Caution: *Use of a pry bar or similar tool can damage the crankshaft pulley. The manufacturer recommends using a 1/2-inch-drive air or electric impact gun to remove the pulley bolt.*
Caution: *Failure to hold the crankshaft pulley securely while removing the pulley bolt could result in engine damage. NEVER use the timing pin or the camshaft alignment tool as a means of locking the crankshaft - they are designed for calibration only. Engine damage could occur by using these tools for anything other than their intended purpose.*
4   Unscrew the pulley bolt.
5   Remove the pulley and the "diamond" washer behind it. Obtain a new pulley bolt and washer.

8.9 Install the M6 x 18 mm bolt to verify TDC

Installation

6   Install a new diamond washer onto the nose of the crankshaft.

7   Lightly coat the crankshaft front seal with clean engine oil, then install the crankshaft pulley.

Note: *If the seal shows signs of leakage, you may want to replace it before installing the crankshaft pulley (see Section 10).*

8   Install a new crankshaft pulley bolt and washer and hand tighten only. Attempt to closely align the hole in the pulley with the threaded hole in the timing chain cover.

9   Install a crankshaft pulley alignment bolt (M6 x 18 mm) through the pulley and into the front engine cover (hand-tight only) **(see illustration)**. Rotate the pulley as necessary to do this.

Note: *This correctly aligns the pulley with the crankshaft.*

Caution: *Do not use an impact gun to tighten the crankshaft pulley bolt.*

10   Using the strap wrench to hold the pulley, tighten the crankshaft pulley bolt in stages, to the torque listed in this Chapter's Specifications.

11   Install the CKP sensor (see Chapter 6).

All models

12   Remove the timing pin from the cylinder block.

13   Remove the camshaft alignment tool.

14   Remove the spark plugs and rotate the engine clockwise two complete revolutions by turning the crankshaft pulley bolt with a wrench or large socket.

Caution: *If you feel resistance at any point, stop and find out why. If the valve timing is incorrect, the valves may be contacting the pistons.*

15   Rotate the engine again to achieve TDC (see Section 3).

Note: *Rotate the engine in the clockwise direction only.*

16   Install the timing pin into the cylinder block.

17   With the tooth on the crankshaft pulley in a center line with the Crankshaft Position (CKP) sensor, install the camshaft alignment

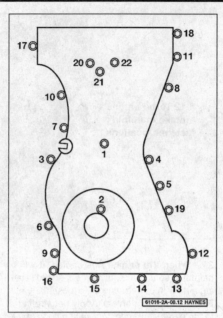

9.11a 2.0L EcoBoost engine timing chain cover bolt tightening sequence

tool and check the position of the camshafts. If the tool cannot be installed, the engine timing must be corrected by repeating the installation procedure.

18   The correct engine timing is achieved when the camshaft alignment tool is in place, timing pin is inserted and the crankshaft pulley TDC tooth is aligned with the CKP sensor, simultaneously.

19   Once correct engine timing is achieved, remove all the alignment tools and bolts and install the timing pin plug.

20   Reinstall all components removed previously.

---

9   Timing chain cover, timing chain and tensioner - removal and installation

---

Warning: *The air conditioning system is under high pressure. DO NOT loosen any fittings or remove any components until after the system has been discharged. Air conditioning refrigerant must be properly discharged into an EPA-approved container at a dealer service department or an automotive air conditioning repair facility. Always wear eye protection when disconnecting air conditioning system fittings.*

Timing chain cover
Removal

1   On non-turbo engines, have the air conditioning system discharged by an automotive air conditioning technician.

2   Disconnect the negative battery cable from the remote ground terminal (see Chapter 5).

3   On non-turbo engines, unclip the coolant expansion tank and set it aside (see Chapter 3), then remove the cowl cover (see Chapter 12).

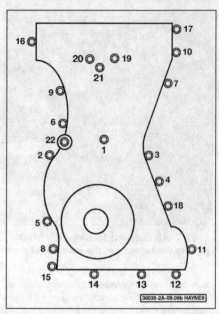

9.11b 2.0L DuraTech-HE engine timing chain cover bolt tightening sequence

4   Loosen the water pump pulley bolts, remove the drivebelt, then remove drivebelt idler pulley (see Chapter 1) and the water pump pulley (see Chapter 3).

5   Remove the crankshaft pulley (see Section 8). After this Step, the engine must remain at TDC with the valve cover removed.

6   Disconnect the Crankshaft Position (CKP) sensor electrical connector, then remove the sensor (see Chapter 6).

7   On non-turbo engines, disconnect the upper (suction) refrigerant line, then unclamp it from the cover.

8   Support the engine from above with a support fixture (see Chapter 2B). Raise the engine enough to remove the right engine mount (see Section 17).

9   Remove the crankshaft front oil seal (see Section 10).

10   Remove the bolts and the timing cover.

Installation

11   Installation is the reverse of removal, noting the following:

a)   Clean the mating surfaces of all sealant. **Note:** *Be careful not to gouge, or use any abrasives on the mating surfaces.*

b)   Install the engine cover within four minutes of applying a 2.5 mm bead of RTV sealant.

c)   Tighten the bolts a little at a time, in sequence **(see illustrations)**, to the torque listed in this Chapter's Specifications.

d)   Install a new crankshaft front oil seal.

e)   Re-time the engine as described in Section 8 and install the Crankshaft Position (CKP) sensor with the necessary alignment tool (see Chapter 6). Do not tighten the sensor mounting bolts until the installation tool is in place.

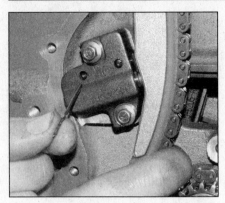

9.13a Compress the tensioner and insert the lock pin

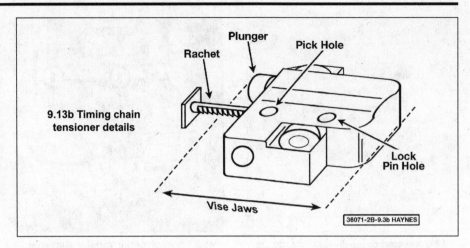

9.13b Timing chain tensioner details

Timing chain and tensioner

Removal

12   Remove the timing chain cover (see Steps 1 through 10).

13   Compress the timing chain tensioner and place a pin (a drill bit or paper clip will work) into the hole to hold it in the compressed position **(see illustration)**.

Note: *The tensioner contacts the right-hand chain guide.*

Caution: *Compress only the round plunger on the tensioner and not the ratchet mechanism. The ratchet is next to the plunger and has square sides. If the ratchet needs to be reset, perform the following (see illustration):*

   a) *Remove the tensioner and place it lightly in a vise using the plunger and tensioner housing.*

   b) *Place a pick-type tool in the hole closest to the ratchet to relieve the tension on the ratchet mechanism.*

   c) *While holding the pick tool in place, move the ratchet back into the tensioner, then install a pin into the other hole to keep the plunger and ratchet compressed.*

   d) *Remove the tensioner from the vise. Do not remove the pick tool until the tensioner is installed or this step will have to be repeated.*

14   Remove the two tensioner mounting bolts, then remove the tensioner.

15   Remove the loose timing chain guide (right). Remove the timing chain.

16   The left chain guide and camshaft sprockets can now be removed if necessary.

Installation

17   Remove the camshaft alignment tool (if installed).

18   Loosen both camshaft phaser and sprocket bolts but don't remove them. Use a wrench on the hexagonal area of the camshaft to hold it while turning the camshaft sprocket bolt **(see illustration)**.

Caution: *Damage to the valves or pistons may occur if the camshafts are rotated during this procedure.*

19   Install the left chain guide (if removed) and tighten to the torque listed this Chapter's Specifications.

20   Install the timing chain.

21   Install the right chain guide and tighten to the torque listed this Chapter's Specifications.

22   Install the timing chain tensioner and tighten the fasteners to the torque listed in this Chapter's Specifications. Remove the pin to release the tensioner to engage the chain guide **(see illustration)**.

23   Install the camshaft alignment tool.

24   Tighten the camshaft phaser and sprocket bolts to the torque listed in this Chapter's Specifications while holding the

camshafts in place with a wrench.

Caution: *Do not rely on the camshaft alignment tool to hold the camshafts while tightening the camshaft sprocket bolts. Tool and engine damage may occur.*

25   The timing chain cover can now be installed (see Step 11).

10   Crankshaft front oil seal - replacement

1   Remove the crankshaft pulley (see Section 8).

2   Use a screwdriver or hook tool to carefully pry out the seal.

Note: *Be careful not to damage the timing chain cover bore where the seal is seated or the nose and sealing surface of the crankshaft.*

3   Another procedure for removing the seal is to drill a small hole on each side of the seal and place a self-tapping screw in each hole. Use these screws as a means of pulling the seal out without having to pry on it.

4   Wipe the sealing surfaces in the engine cover and on the crankshaft. Clean and coat them with clean engine oil.

5   Start installing the new seal by pressing it into the timing chain cover **(see illustration)**.

9.18 Use a large wrench on the hex portion to hold the camshaft while removing/installing the sprocket bolt

9.22 Compress the tensioner to release the lock pin

10.5 Make certain that the oil seal is kept square as it is placed in the bore

10.6 A socket of the correct size can be used to install the new seal

6   Once started, use a seal driver or a suitable socket of the correct size to carefully drive the seal squarely into place **(see illustration)**.
7   The seal should be flush with the engine cover and remain square when installed.
8   Coat the lip of the seal (where it contacts the crankshaft) with clean engine oil.
9   Install the crankshaft pulley (see Section 8).

---

11   Camshafts and lifters - removal, inspection and installation

---

Note: *Whenever the camshafts are to be removed for a procedure, it's a good idea to check the valve clearances before disassembly (see Section 5), so any required new lifters can be ordered from a dealership.*

Removal

1   Remove the timing chain (see Section 9).
Note: *Before removing the timing chain, note the positions of the no. 1 cylinder cam lobes and the slots in the ends of the camshafts (for*

11.3 Location of the Variable Camshaft Timing (VCT) solenoids retaining bolts (A), and the one piece camshaft bearing cap bolts (B)

the alignment tool). When installing the camshafts, the lobes and the slots in the ends of the camshafts must be in the same positions.
2   Remove the camshaft phaser and sprockets.
Note: *The camshaft phaser and sprockets should be marked with indelible ink so that they can be reinstalled in the same position. When loosening the camshaft sprocket bolts, place a wrench on the hexagonal area of the camshaft to prevent it from turning (see illustration 9.18).*
3   Remove the Variable Camshaft Timing (VCT) solenoid(s) fasteners and pull the solenoid(s) out of the front camshaft bearing cap **(see illustration)**.
4   Remove the front one piece camshaft bearing cap bolts and lift the cap from both camshafts **(see illustration 11.3)**.
5   Mark the bearing caps for each position and the direction they face - the bearing caps must be reinstalled in their original positions.
Caution: *The camshafts bearing caps must be loosened in order or the camshafts can be damaged.*

6   Working in the sequence shown, loosen the camshaft bearing cap bolts progressively by half a turn at a time **(see illustrations)**. Work only as described, to release gradually and evenly the pressure of the valve springs on the caps.
7   Withdraw the caps, noting their markings and the presence of the locating dowels, then remove the camshafts.
8   Obtain sixteen small, clean containers, and number them 1 to 16. Using a rubber suction tool (such as a valve-lapping tool), withdraw each lifter in turn and place them in the containers. Do not interchange the lifters.

Inspection

9   Check the camshafts and lifters for signs of obvious wear (scoring, pitting, etc) and for roundness and replace if necessary.
10   Measure the outside diameter of each lifter - take measurements at the top and bottom of each lifter, then a second set at right-angles to the first; if any measurement is significantly different from the others, the lifter is tapered or oval (as applicable) and must be replaced **(see illustration)**. If the necessary equipment is available, measure the inside diameter of the corresponding cylinder head bore. No manufacturer's specifications were available at the time of writing; if the lifters or the cylinder head bores are excessively worn, new lifters and/or a new cylinder head may be required.
11   If the engine's valve components have sounded noisy, it may be just that the valve clearances need adjusting (see Section 5). Although this is part of the routine maintenance schedule in Chapter 1, the extended checking interval and the need for dismantling or special tools may result in the task being overlooked. Now is also a good time to install new valve stem oil seals. A valve stem oil seal remover and slide hammer are needed.
12   Visually examine the camshaft lobes for score marks, pitting, galling (wear due to rubbing) and evidence of overheating (blue, discolored areas). Look for flaking away of the hardened surface layer of each lobe. If any such signs are evident, replace the cam-

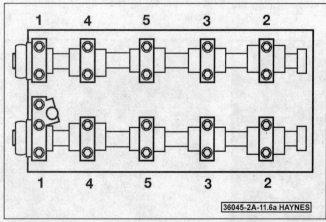

11.6a Camshaft bearing cap bolt loosening sequence - loosen each pair of bolts on the designated bearing cap in sequence - turbo engine

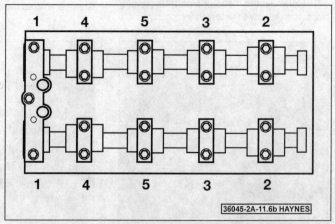

11.6b Camshaft bearing cap bolt loosening sequence - loosen each pair of bolts on the designated bearing cap in sequence - non-turbo engines

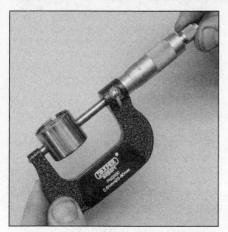

11.10 Measure the lifter outside diameter at several points

11.13 Check that the camshaft bearing oilways are not blocked with debris

ponent concerned. Measure the lobe heights and compare to the measurements listed in this Chapter's Specifications.

13 Examine the camshaft bearing journals and the cylinder head bearing surfaces for signs of obvious wear or pitting. If any such signs are evident, consult an automotive machine shop for advice. Also check that the bearing oilways in the cylinder head are clear **(see illustration)**.

14 Using a micrometer, measure the diameter of each journal at several points. If the diameter of any one journal is less than the amount listed in this Chapter's Specifications, replace the camshaft.

15 To check the bearing journal-to-bore clearance, remove the lifters, use a suitable solvent and a clean lint-free rag to carefully clean all bearing surfaces, then install the camshafts and bearing caps with a strand of Plastigage across each journal. Tighten the bearing cap bolts in the proper sequence **(see illustration 11.25a or 11.25b)** to the torque listed in this Chapter's Specifications (do not rotate the camshafts), then remove the bearing caps and use the scale provided to measure the width of the compressed strands. Scrape off the Plastigage with your fingernail

or the edge of a credit card - don't scratch or nick the journals or bearing caps.

16 If the journal-to-bore clearance of any bearing is found to be worn to beyond the specified service limits, install a new camshaft and repeat the check; if the clearance is still excessive, the cylinder head must be replaced.

17 To check camshaft endplay, remove the lifters, clean the bearing surfaces carefully and install the camshafts and bearing caps. Tighten the cap bolts to the torque specified in this Chapter's Specifications, then measure the endplay using a dial indicator mounted on the cylinder head so that its tip bears on the camshaft right-hand end.

18 Tap the camshaft fully towards the gauge, zero the gauge, then tap the camshaft fully away from the gauge and note the gauge reading. If the endplay is at or beyond the specified service limit, install a new camshaft and repeat the check; if the clearance is still excessive, the cylinder head must be replaced.

Installation

19 Confirm that the crankshaft is still at TDC and that the timing pin is in place (see Section 3).

20 Liberally oil the cylinder head lifter bores and the lifters. Carefully install the lifters to the cylinder head, ensuring that each lifter is replaced to its original bore.

21 Liberally oil the camshaft bearing surfaces in the cylinder head, taking care not to get any on the camshaft cap mating surface.

22 Ensuring that each camshaft is in its original location, install the camshafts, locating each so that lobes for cylinder no. 1 are in the same position as noted in Step 1 and the slot in its left-hand end is parallel to, and just above, the cylinder head mating surface. Check that, as each camshaft is laid in position, the TDC setting tool will fit into the slot. **Caution:** *When the camshaft bearing caps are tightened, it is imperative that the camshafts do not rotate from their TDC positions.*

23 Ensure that the locating dowels are pressed firmly into their recesses and check that all mating surfaces are completely clean, unmarked and free from oil.

24 Apply a little oil to the camshaft journals and lobes, then install each of the camshaft bearing caps to its previously-noted position, so that its numbered side faces outwards, to the front (exhaust) or to the rear (intake).

25 Ensuring that each cap is kept square to the cylinder head as it is tightened down and working in the sequence shown, tighten the camshaft bearing cap bolts slowly and by one turn at a time, until each cap touches the cylinder head **(see illustrations)**. This is the Step 1 torque.

26 Next, using the same sequence, tighten the bearing cap bolts to the Step 2 torque listed in this Chapter's Specifications.

27 Tighten the bearing cap bolts to the Step 3 torque listed in this Chapter's Specifications.

28 Install the sprockets to the camshafts, tightening the retaining bolts loosely.

29 The remainder of the reassembly procedure, including replacement of the timing chain and setting the valve timing, is as described in Section 9.

30 Before installing the valve cover, check the valve clearances (see Section 5).

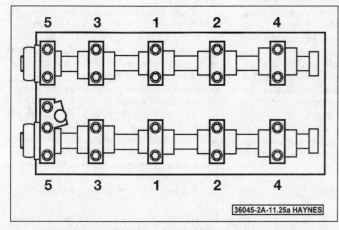

11.25a Camshaft bearing cap bolt tightening sequence - turbo engine

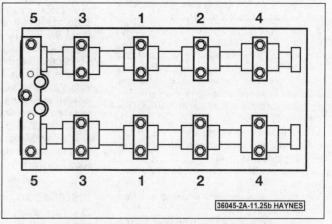

11.25b Camshaft bearing cap bolt tightening sequence - non-turbo engine

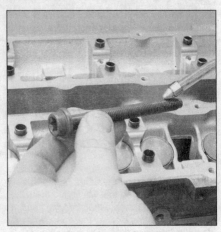

12.28 Apply a light coat of oil to the cylinder head bolt threads

12   Cylinder head - removal and installation

Warning: *Wait until the engine is completely cool before beginning this procedure.*

Removal

1   Disconnect the negative battery cable from the remote ground terminal (see Chapter 5).
2   Relieve the fuel pressure (see Chapter 4).
3   Remove the intake air duct and air filter housing, and on turbo models, the Charge Air Cooler (CAC) inlet and outlet pipes (see Chapter 4).
4   Drain the cooling system (see Chapter 1).
5   On turbo models, remove the turbocharger (see Chapter 4).
6   Remove the coolant recovery tank (see Chapter 3).
7   Remove the timing chain (see Section 9).
Note: *Whenever the camshafts are to be removed for a procedure, it's a good idea to check the valve clearances before disassembly (see Section 5), so any required new lifters can be ordered from a dealership.*
8   Disconnect the Camshaft Position (CMP) sensor (see Chapter 6).
9   Unbolt and remove the VCT solenoid valve(s) from the front camshaft bearing cap, then remove the camshafts and lifters (see Section 11), keeping the lifters in order.
10   Remove the fuel rail and injectors (see Chapter 4).
11   Disconnect the hoses from the coolant outlet housing, then remove the thermostat housing (see Chapter 3).
12   Remove the intake manifold (see Section 6).
13   Remove the exhaust manifold (see Section 7), if equipped.
14   If an engine support fixture or hoist is being used to hold the engine up and it interferes with removal of the cylinder head, use

a floor jack and block of wood to support the engine from below.
15   Loosen the ten cylinder head bolts progressively and by half a turn at a time, working in the reverse order of the tightening sequence **(see illustration 12.29a)**.
Caution: *The head bolts are torque-to-yield bolts that must be replaced with new ones on installation.*
16   Lift the cylinder head from the engine compartment.
17   If the head is stuck, be careful how you choose to free it. Remember that the cylinder head is made of aluminum alloy, which is easily damaged. Striking the head with tools carries the risk of damage, and the head is located on two dowels, so its movement will be limited. Do not, under any circumstances, pry the head between the mating surfaces, as this will certainly damage the sealing surfaces for the gasket, leading to leaks. Try rocking the head free, to break the seal, taking care not to damage any of the surrounding components.
18   Once the head has been removed, remove and discard the gasket. Check for the presence of locating dowels in the cylinder block and cylinder head. If dowels are present, make sure they are returned to their original locations after cleaning the components.

Inspection

19   The mating faces of the cylinder head and cylinder block must be perfectly clean before replacing the head. Use spray-on gasket remover and a hard plastic or wood scraper to remove all traces of gasket and carbon.
20   Take particular care during the cleaning operations, as aluminum alloy is easily damaged. Also, make sure that the carbon is not allowed to enter the oil and water passages - this is particularly important for the lubrication system, as carbon could block the oil supply to the engine's components.
21   To prevent carbon entering the gap between the pistons and bores, smear a little grease in the gap. After cleaning each piston, use a small brush to remove all traces of grease and carbon from the gap, then wipe away the remainder with a clean rag.
22   Check the mating surfaces of the cylinder block and the cylinder head for nicks, deep scratches and other damage. Also check the cylinder head gasket surface and the cylinder block gasket surface with a precision straight-edge and feeler gauges. If either surface exceeds the warpage limit listed in this Chapter's Specifications, the manufacturer states that the component must be replaced. If the gasket mating surface of your cylinder head or block is out of specification or is severely nicked or scratched, you may want to consult with an automotive machine shop for advice.

Installation

23   Wipe clean the mating surfaces of the cylinder head and cylinder block. If equipped, install the alignment dowels into their original locations.

24   The cylinder head bolt holes must be free from oil or water. This is most important, because a hydraulic lock in a cylinder head bolt hole can cause a fracture of the block casting when the bolt is tightened. Note the location of the cylinder head alignment dowels in the block.
25   Position a new gasket on the cylinder block surface, so that the "TOP" mark is facing up.
26   As the cylinder head is such a heavy and awkward assembly to install, it is helpful to make up a pair of guide studs from two 10 mm (thread size) studs approximately 90 mm long, with a screwdriver slot cut in one end - you can use two of the old cylinder head bolts with their heads cut off. Screw these guide studs, screwdriver slot upwards to permit removal, into the bolt holes at diagonally-opposite corners of the cylinder block surface; ensure that approximately 70 mm of stud protrudes above the gasket.
27   Install the cylinder head, sliding it down the guide studs (if used) and locating it on the dowels. Unscrew the guide studs (if used) when the head is in place.
28   Coat the threads with engine oil - do not apply more than a light film of oil **(see illustration)**. Install the new cylinder head bolts and screw them in by hand only until finger-tight.
Note: *New cylinder head bolts must be used.*
29   Working progressively and in the sequence shown, first tighten all the bolts to the specified Step 1 torque setting listed in this Chapter's Specifications **(see illustration)**. On these engines there are five tightening stages, the final two using the angle torque method **(see illustration)**.
30   Replacement of the other components removed is a reversal of removal.
31   Change the engine oil and filter and refill the cooling system (see Chapter 1).

13   Oil pan - removal and installation

Removal

1   Raise the vehicle and support it securely on jackstands.
2   Drain the engine oil (see Chapter 1), then clean and install the engine oil drain plug, tightening it to the torque listed in the Chapter 1 Specifications. Remove and discard the oil filter, so that it can be replaced with the oil.
3   Remove the engine lower splash shield.
4   Remove the air conditioning compressor drivebelt (see Chapter 1).
5   On turbo models, remove the Charge Air Cooler (CAC) lower pipe (see Chapter 4).
6   Remove the air conditioning compressor mounting bolts (see Chapter 3) and move the compressor out of the way. Do not loosen any hoses or couplers.
7   Remove the air filter housing (see Chapter 4).
8   On models with an automatic transaxle, remove the battery and battery tray (see Chapter 5), then disconnect the shift cable

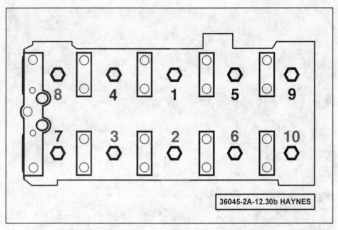

12.29a Cylinder head bolt tightening sequence

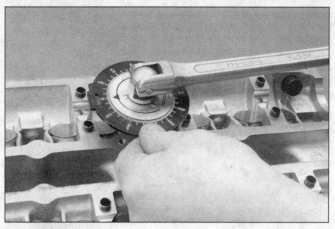

12.29b You can use a torque angle gauge, or you can carefully note the starting and stopping points of the wrench handle

from the shift lever and remove the cable from it's mounting bracket (see Chapter 7B).

9   The transaxle must be moved slightly back from the engine. Support the engine from above with an engine support fixture (connected to the left end of the engine, near the transaxle), and support the transaxle with a floor jack. Loosen the upper engine-to-transaxle mounting bolts and back them off about 0.20-inch (5 mm), loosen the left-side engine-to-bellhousing bolts, then loosen the right-side bolts.

10   Remove the two oil pan-to-bellhousing bolts, and the one bellhousing-to-pan bolt. Also remove the timing chain cover-to-oil pan fasteners.

11   Use a screwdriver to pry between the engine and transaxle until the bellhousing has moved away from the block to the limit of the loosened bolts (about 0.20-inch [5 mm]).

12   Progressively unscrew the oil pan retaining bolts. Use a rubber mallet to loosen the oil pan seal, then lower the oil pan, turning it as necessary to clear the exhaust system. Unfortunately, the use of sealant can make removal of the oil pan more difficult. Be careful when prying between the mating surfaces, other-

wise they will be damaged, resulting in leaks when finished. With care, a putty knife can be used to cut through the sealant.

Installation

13   Thoroughly clean and degrease the mating surfaces of the lower engine block/crankcase and oil pan, removing all traces of sealant, then use a clean rag to wipe out the oil pan. Do not nick or scratch the mating surfaced or leaks will occur.

14   Apply a 1/8-inch wide bead of sealant to the oil pan flange so that the bead is approximately 3/16-inch from the outside edge of the flange. Make sure the bead is around the inside edge of the bolt holes. Also apply sealant to the front flange of the oil pan where it meets the timing chain cover.

Note: *The oil pan must be installed within 4 minutes of applying the sealant.*

15   Install the oil pan bolts, only tightening them finger tight at this time. Align the front surface of the oil pan with the front surface of the engine block before tightening any bolts.

16   Install the timing chain cover-to-oil pan fasteners and tighten them to the torque listed in this Chapter's Specifications.

17   Tighten the oil pan-to engine block bolts, a little at a time, working from the center outwards in a criss-cross pattern, to the torque listed in this Chapter's Specifications.

18   Tighten the oil pan-to-bellhousing bolts and the transaxle-to-engine bolts, a little at a time to draw them together evenly, to the torque listed in this Chapter's Specifications.

19   Lower the vehicle to the ground. Before refilling the engine with oil, wait at least 1 hour for the sealant to cure, or whatever time is indicated by the sealant manufacturer. Trim off the excess sealant with a sharp knife. Install a new oil filter and refill the engine with oil (see Chapter 1).

14   Oil pump - removal and installation

Note: *The oil pump is serviced as a complete unit without any sub-assembly or internal inspection.*

1   Have the air conditioning system discharged by a dealership or suitably equipped repair facility.

2   Drain the engine oil and remove the oil filter (see Chapter 1).

3   On turbo models, disconnect the boost pressure sensor from the turbocharger, then disconnect and remove the Charge Air Cooler (CAC) inlet and outlet hoses (see Chapter 4). Remove the air conditioning compressor (see Chapter 3).

4   Remove the timing chain cover (see Section 9) and the oil pan (see Section 13).

5   Remove the oil pick-up tube **(see illustration)**. Discard the pick-up tube o-ring. A new one must be used during installation.

6   Use a screwdriver to pry the end of the oil pump drive chain tensioner's spring from under the shouldered bolt. Remove the two bolts and the tensioner.

7   Remove the chain from the oil pump sprocket. While holding the oil pump drive sprocket with a suitable tool, remove the sprocket bolt from the oil pump, then remove the sprocket **(see illustration)**.

14.5 The oil pump pick-up tube is held by two mounting bolts (typical)

14.7 Using a holding tool on the oil pump drive sprocket to remove the retaining bolt

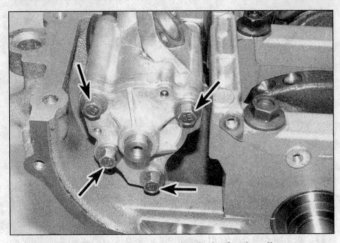

14.8 Remove the four mounting bolts for the oil pump

15.10 Install the new bolts, tightening them by hand

8   Remove the oil pump mounting bolts, then remove the pump (see illustration).

9   Installation is the reverse of removal, noting the following points:

a) *Thoroughly clean all surfaces before installation. Replace all gaskets with new ones.*

b) *Tighten the oil pick-up pipe bolts to the torque listed in this Chapter's Specifications.*

c) *Tighten the oil pump mounting bolts to the torque listed in this Chapter's Specifications in a criss-cross pattern.*

d) *After installing the oil pan (see Section 13), install a new oil filter and refill the crankcase with oil (see Chapter 1).*

e) *Be certain to check for any oil warning lights in the instrument panel after the vehicle has been started and idling.*

15   Flywheel/driveplate - removal, inspection and installation

Caution: *Special bolts are used to install the flywheel/drivepate. Do not use standard bolts to install the flywheel/drivepate.*

Removal

1   Remove the transaxle as described in Chapter 7A or 7B. Now is a good time to check components such as oil seals and replace them if necessary.

2   On manual transaxle models, remove the clutch as described in Chapter 8. Now is a good time to check or replace the clutch components and release bearing.

3   Use a center-punch or paint to make alignment marks on the flywheel and crankshaft to make replacement easier - the bolt holes are slightly offset, and will only line up one way, but making a mark eliminates the guesswork (and the flywheel is heavy).

4   Hold the flywheel/driveplate stationary and unscrew the bolts. To prevent the flywheel/driveplate from turning, insert one of

the transaxle mounting bolts into the cylinder block and have an assistant engage a wide-bladed screwdriver with the starter ring gear teeth while the flywheel or driveplate bolts are loosened.

5   Loosen and remove each bolt in turn and ensure that new replacements are obtained for reassembly. These bolts are subjected to severe stresses and so must be replaced, regardless of their apparent condition, whenever they are removed.

6   Remove the flywheel, remembering that it is very heavy - do not drop it. The driveplate used with automatic transaxles is much lighter.

Inspection

7   Clean the flywheel to remove grease and oil. Inspect the surface for cracks, rivet grooves, burned areas and score marks. Light scoring can be removed with emery cloth. Check for cracked and broken ring gear teeth. Lay the flywheel on a flat surface and use a straight-edge to check for warpage.

8   Clean and inspect the mating surfaces of the flywheel and the crankshaft. If the oil seal is leaking, replace it (see Section 16) before replacing the flywheel. If the engine has high mileage, it may be worth installing a new seal as a matter of course, given the amount of work needed to access it.

9   While the flywheel is removed, carefully clean its inboard face, particularly the recesses that serve as the reference points for the crankshaft speed/position sensor. Clean the sensor's tip and check that the sensor is securely fastened.

Installation

10   On installation, ensure that the engine/transaxle adapter plate is in place (where necessary), then install the flywheel/driveplate on the crankshaft so that all bolt holes align - it will fit only one way - check this using the marks made on removal. Install the new bolts (see illustration).

11   Lock the flywheel by the method used on

disassembly. Working in a diagonal sequence to tighten them evenly and increasing to the final amount in two or three stages, tighten the new bolts to the torque listed in this Chapter's Specifications.

12   The remainder of installation is the reverse of removal.

16   Rear main oil seal - replacement

1   The one-piece rear main oil seal is pressed into the rear main oil seal carrier mounted at the rear of the block. Remove the transaxle (see Chapter 7A or 7B) and the flywheel/driveplate (see Section 15).

2   Remove the oil pan (see Section 13).

3   Unbolt the oil seal and carrier.

4   Clean the mating surface for the oil seal carrier on the cylinder block and the crankshaft. Carefully remove and polish any burrs or raised edges on the crankshaft that may have caused the seal to fail.

5   Lightly coat the inside lip of the new seal with clean engine oil. Use a thin (but durable) two-inch wide plastic strip (or a two-liter plastic beverage bottle cut to size) around the inside circumference of the seal to act as a liner for installation. A Manufacturer tool #303-328 also works well.

6   With the plastic seal liner or tool in place, carefully move the new carrier (with seal factory-installed) into position by sliding it onto the contact surface of the crankshaft.

7   Install the oil seal carrier bolts and finger tighten them while holding the carrier in place. Align the bottom of the seal carrier precisely with the bottom edge of the engine block to ensure that the surfaces are flush before tightening the carrier mounting bolts.

Caution: *The oil pan may leak if the two surfaces are not perfectly flush.*

8   Carefully remove the plastic liner or tool so that the new seal contacts the crankshaft mating surface correctly.

9   Tighten the oil seal carrier to the torque listed in this Chapter's Specifications using

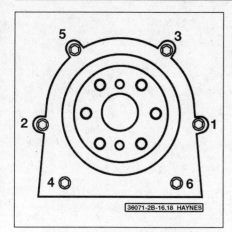

16.9 Rear oil seal carrier tightening
sequence

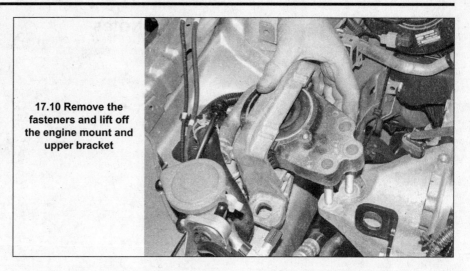

17.10 Remove the
fasteners and lift off
the engine mount and
upper bracket

the proper sequence **(see illustration)**.
10   The remainder of installation is the reverse of removal.

17   Engine mounts - check and replacement

1   Engine mounts seldom require attention, but broken or deteriorated mounts should be replaced immediately or the added strain placed on the driveline components may cause damage or wear.

Check

2   During the check, the engine must be raised slightly to remove the weight from the mounts.
3   Raise the vehicle and support it securely on jackstands, then position a jack under

the engine oil pan. Place a large wood block between the jack head and the oil pan to prevent oil pan damage, then carefully raise the engine just enough to take the weight off the mounts.
Warning: *DO NOT place any part of your body under the engine when it's supported only by a jack!*
4   Unclip the coolant expansion tank and set it aside (see Chapter 3).
5   Check the mounts to see if the rubber is cracked, hardened or separated from the bushing in the center of the mount.
6   Check for relative movement between the mount and the engine or chassis. Use a large screwdriver or prybar to attempt to move the mounts. If movement is noted, lower the engine and tighten the mount fasteners.

Replacement
Note: *Refer to Chapter 7A or 7B for information on the transaxle mounts.*

7   Disconnect the negative battery cable from the remote ground terminal (see Chapter 5), then raise the vehicle and support it securely on jackstands (if not already done).
8   Place a floor jack under the engine with a wood block between the jack head and oil pan and raise the engine slightly to relieve the weight from the mounts.
9   Unclip the coolant expansion tank and set it aside (see Chapter 3).
10   Remove the fasteners and detach the mount from the frame and engine **(see illustration)**.
Caution: *Do not disconnect more than one mount at a time, except during engine removal.*
11   Installation is the reverse of removal. Use thread-locking compound on the mount bolts and be sure to tighten them to the torque listed in this Chapter's Specifications.

Notes

Chapter 2 Part B
General engine overhaul procedures

Contents

Specifications

General

Cylinder compression	Lowest cylinder must be within 75% of the highest cylinder
Oil pressure (hot @ 2000 rpm)	
Non-turbo engine	29 to 39 psi (200 to 268 kPa)
Turbo engine	29 to 60 psi (200 to 414 kPa)
Balance shaft assembly backlash (Turbo models)	0.00019 to 0.0039 inch (0.005 to 0.099 mm)

Torque specifications

Note: *One foot-pound (ft-lb) of torque is equivalent to 12 inch-pounds (in-lbs) of torque. Torque values below approximately 15 ft-lbs are expressed in inch-pounds, because most foot-pound torque wrenches are not accurate at these smaller values.*

	Ft-lbs (unless otherwise indicated)	Nm
Balance shaft assembly mounting bolts (four-cylinder engines)		
Step 1	18	24
Step 2	37	50
Connecting rod cap bolts*		
Non-turbo engine		
Step 1	21	28
Step 2	Tighten an additional 90-degrees	
Turbo engine		
Step 1	89 in-lbs	10
Step 2	21	28
Step 3	Tighten an additional 90 degrees	

* New bolts must be used during final installation.

Torque specifications

Ft-lbs (unless otherwise indicated)   **Nm**

Note: *One foot-pound (ft-lb) of torque is equivalent to 12 inch-pounds (in-lbs) of torque. Torque values below approximately 15 ft-lbs are expressed in inch-pounds, because most foot-pound torque wrenches are not accurate at these smaller values.*

Balance shaft assembly mounting bolts (four-cylinder engines)
Main bearing bolts

Step 1	44 in-lbs	5
Step 2	18	24
Step 3	Tighten an additional 90 degrees	
Oil pressure sending unit**	133 in-lbs	15

***Apply thread sealant.*

1   General information - engine overhaul

1   Included in this portion of are general information and diagnostic testing procedures for determining the overall mechanical condition of your engine.

2   The information ranges from advice concerning preparation for an overhaul and the purchase of replacement parts and/or components to detailed, step-by-step procedures covering removal and installation.

3   The following Sections have been written to help you determine whether your engine needs to be overhauled and how to remove and install it once you've determined it needs to be rebuilt. For information concerning in-vehicle engine repair, see Chapter 2A.

4   The Specifications included in this Part are general in nature and include only those necessary for testing the oil pressure and checking the engine compression. Refer to Chapter 2A for additional engine Specifications.

5   It's not always easy to determine when, or if, an engine should be completely overhauled, because a number of factors must be considered.

6   High mileage is not necessarily an indication that an overhaul is needed, while low mileage doesn't preclude the need for an overhaul. Frequency of servicing is probably the most important consideration. An engine that's had regular and frequent oil and filter changes, as well as other required maintenance, will most likely give many thousands of miles of reliable service. Conversely, a neglected engine may require an overhaul very early in its service life.

7   Excessive oil consumption is an indication that piston rings, valve seals and/or valve guides are in need of attention. Make sure that oil leaks aren't responsible before deciding that the rings and/or guides are bad. Perform a cylinder compression check to determine the extent of the work required (see Section 3). Also check the vacuum readings under various conditions (see Section 4).

8   Check the oil pressure with a gauge installed in place of the oil pressure sending unit and compare it to this Chapter's Specifications (see Section 2). If it's extremely low, the bearings and/or oil pump are probably worn out.

9   Loss of power, rough running, knocking or metallic engine noises, excessive valve train noise and high fuel consumption rates may also point to the need for an overhaul, especially if they're all present at the same time. If a complete tune-up doesn't remedy the situation, major mechanical work is the only solution.

1.10a An engine block being bored. An engine rebuilder will use special machinery to recondition the cylinder bores

1.10b If the cylinders are bored, the machine shop will normally hone the engine on a machine like this

10   An engine overhaul involves restoring the internal parts to the specifications of a new engine. During an overhaul, the piston rings are replaced and the cylinder walls are reconditioned (rebored and/or honed) **(see illustrations)**. If a rebore is done by an automotive machine shop, new oversize pistons will also be installed. The main bearings, connecting rod bearings and camshaft bearings are generally replaced with new ones and, if necessary, the crankshaft may be reground to restore the journals **(see illustration)**. Generally, the valves are serviced as well, since they're usually in less-than-perfect condition at this point. While the engine is being overhauled, other components, such as the starter and alternator, can be rebuilt or replaced as well. The end result should be similar to a new engine that will give many trouble free miles.

Note: *Critical cooling system components such as the hoses, drivebelts, thermostat and water pump should be replaced with new parts when an engine is overhauled. The radiator should be checked carefully to ensure that it isn't clogged or leaking (see Chapter 1). If you purchase a rebuilt engine or short block,*

some rebuilders will not warranty their engines unless the radiator has been professionally flushed. Also, we don't recommend overhauling the oil pump - always install a new one when an engine is rebuilt.

11   Overhauling the internal components on today's engines is a difficult and time-consuming task which requires a significant amount of specialty tools and is best left to a professional engine rebuilder **(see illustrations)**. A competent engine rebuilder will handle the inspection of your old parts and offer advice concerning the reconditioning or replacement of the original engine, never purchase parts or have machine work done on other components until the block has been thoroughly inspected by a professional machine shop. As a general rule, time is the primary cost of an overhaul, especially since the vehicle may be tied up for a minimum of two weeks or more. Be aware that some engine builders only have the capability to rebuild the engine you bring them while other rebuilders have a large inventory of rebuilt exchange engines in stock. Also be aware that many machine shops could take as much as two weeks time

1.10c A crankshaft having a main bearing journal ground

to completely rebuild your engine depending on shop workload. Sometimes it makes more sense to simply exchange your engine for another engine that's already rebuilt to save time.

1.11a A machinist checks for a bent connecting rod, using specialized equipment

1.11b A bore gauge being used to check the main bearing bore

1.11c Uneven piston wear like this indicates a bent connecting rod

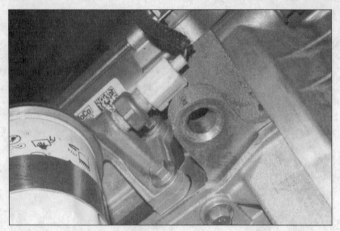

2.2 The oil pressure sending unit is located on the front of the engine block, threaded into the oil filter adapter

3.6 Use a compression gauge with a threaded fitting for the spark plug hole, not the type that requires hand pressure to maintain the seal (typical)

2   Oil pressure check and oil pressure sending unit replacement

1   Low engine oil pressure can be a sign of an engine in need of rebuilding. A low oil pressure indicator (often called an "idiot light") is not a test of the oiling system. Such indicators only come on when the oil pressure is dangerously low. Even a factory oil pressure gauge in the instrument panel is only a relative indication, although much better for driver information than a warning light. A better test is with a mechanical (not electrical) oil pressure gauge.

2   Locate the oil pressure sending unit on the engine block **(see illustration)**.

3   Unscrew the oil pressure sending unit and screw in the hose for your oil pressure gauge. If necessary, install an adapter fitting. Use Teflon tape or thread sealant on the threads of the adapter and/or the fitting on the end of your gauge's hose.

4   Connect an accurate tachometer to the engine, according to the tachometer manufacturer's instructions.

5   Check the oil pressure with the engine running (normal operating temperature) at the specified engine speed, and compare it to this Chapter's Specifications. If it's extremely low, the bearings and/or oil pump are probably worn out. Apply thread sealant to the oil pressure sending unit and install it. Tighten the sending unit to the torque listed in this Chapter's Specifications.

3   Cylinder compression check

1   A compression check will tell you what mechanical condition the upper end of your engine (pistons, rings, valves, head gaskets) is in. Specifically, it can tell you if the compression is down due to leakage caused by worn piston rings, defective valves and seats or a blown head gasket.

Note: *The engine must be at normal operating temperature and the battery must be fully charged for this check.*

2   Begin by cleaning the area around the ignition coils before you remove them (compressed air should be used, if available). The idea is to prevent dirt from getting into the cylinders as the compression check is being done.

3   Remove all of the spark plugs from the engine (see Chapter 1).

4   Remove the air intake duct from the throttle body, then block the throttle wide open.

5   Remove the fuel pump relay (see Chapter 4).

6   Install a compression gauge in the spark plug hole **(see illustration)**.

7   Crank the engine over at least seven compression strokes and watch the gauge. The compression should build up quickly in a healthy engine. Low compression on the first stroke, followed by gradually increasing pressure on successive strokes, indicates worn piston rings. A low compression reading on the first stroke, which doesn't build up during successive strokes, indicates leaking valves or a blown head gasket (a cracked head could also be the cause). Deposits on the undersides of the valve heads can also cause low compression. Record the highest gauge reading obtained.

8   Repeat the procedure for the remaining cylinders and compare the results to this Chapter's Specifications.

9   Add some engine oil (about three squirts from a plunger-type oil can) to each cylinder, through the spark plug hole, and repeat the test.

10   If the compression increases after the oil is added, the piston rings are definitely worn. If the compression doesn't increase significantly, the leakage is occurring at the valves or head gasket. Leakage past the valves may be caused by burned valve seats and/or faces or warped, cracked or bent valves.

11   If two adjacent cylinders have equally low compression, there's a strong possibility that the head gasket between them is blown. The appearance of coolant in the combustion chambers or the crankcase would verify this condition.

12   If one cylinder is slightly lower than the others, and the engine has a slightly rough idle, a worn lobe on the camshaft could be the cause.

13   If the compression is unusually high, the combustion chambers are probably coated with carbon deposits. If that's the case, the cylinder head(s) should be removed and decarbonized (see Chapter 2A).

14   If compression is way down or varies greatly between cylinders, it would be a good idea to have a leak-down test performed by an automotive repair shop. This test will pinpoint exactly where the leakage is occurring and how severe it is.

15   After performing the test, don't forget to unblock the throttle plate.

4   Vacuum gauge diagnostic checks

1   A vacuum gauge provides inexpensive but valuable information about what is going on in the engine. You can check for worn rings or cylinder walls, leaking head or intake manifold gaskets, incorrect carburetor adjustments, restricted exhaust, stuck or burned valves, weak valve springs, improper ignition or valve timing and ignition problems.

2   Unfortunately, vacuum gauge readings are easy to misinterpret, so they should be used in conjunction with other tests to confirm the diagnosis.

3   Both the absolute readings and the rate of needle movement are important for accurate interpretation. Most gauges measure vacuum in inches of mercury (in-Hg). The following references to vacuum assume the diagnosis is being performed at sea level. As elevation increases (or atmospheric pressure decreases), the reading will decrease. For every 1,000 foot increase in elevation above

approximately 2,000 feet, the gauge readings will decrease about one inch of mercury.

4   Connect the vacuum gauge directly to the intake manifold vacuum, not to ported (throttle body) vacuum. Be sure no hoses are left disconnected during the test or false readings will result.

5   Before you begin the test, allow the engine to warm up completely. Block the wheels and set the parking brake. With the transaxle in Park, start the engine and allow it to run at normal idle speed.

Warning: *Keep your hands and the vacuum gauge clear of the fans.*

6   Read the vacuum gauge; an average, healthy engine should normally produce about 17 to 22 in-Hg with a fairly steady needle **(see illustration)**. Refer to the following vacuum gauge readings and what they indicate about the engine's condition:

7   A low steady reading usually indicates a leaking gasket between the intake manifold and cylinder head(s) or throttle body, a leaky vacuum hose, late ignition timing or incorrect camshaft timing. Check ignition timing with a timing light and eliminate all other possible causes, utilizing the tests provided in this Chapter before you remove the timing chain cover to check the timing marks.

8   If the reading is three to eight inches below normal and it fluctuates at that low reading, suspect an intake manifold gasket leak at an intake port or a faulty fuel injector.

9   If the needle has regular drops of about two-to-four inches at a steady rate, the valves are probably leaking. Perform a compression check or leak-down test to confirm this.

10   An irregular drop or down-flick of the needle can be caused by a sticking valve or an ignition misfire. Perform a compression check or leak-down test and read the spark plugs.

11   A rapid vibration of about four in-Hg vibration at idle combined with exhaust smoke indicates worn valve guides. Perform a leak-down test to confirm this. If the rapid vibration occurs with an increase in engine speed, check for a leaking intake manifold gasket or head gasket, weak valve springs, burned valves or ignition misfire.

12   A slight fluctuation, say one inch up and down, may mean ignition problems. Check all the usual tune-up items and, if necessary, run the engine on an ignition analyzer.

13   If there is a large fluctuation, perform a compression or leak-down test to look for a weak or dead cylinder or a blown head gasket.

14   If the needle moves slowly through a wide range, check for a clogged PCV system, incorrect idle fuel mixture, throttle body or intake manifold gasket leaks.

15   Check for a slow return after revving the engine by quickly snapping the throttle open until the engine reaches about 2,500 rpm and let it shut. Normally the reading should drop to near zero, rise above normal idle reading (about 5 in-Hg over) and then return to the previous idle reading. If the vacuum returns slowly and doesn't peak when the throttle is

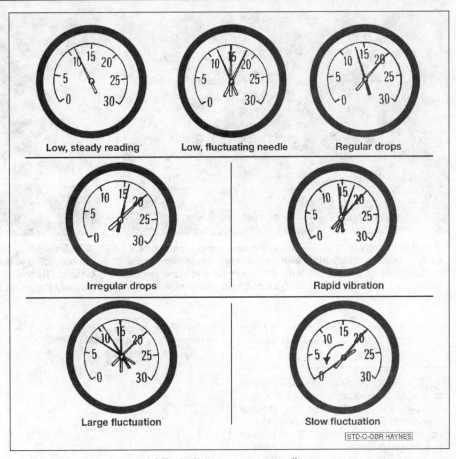

Low, steady reading   Low, fluctuating needle   Regular drops

Irregular drops   Rapid vibration

Large fluctuation   Slow fluctuation

STD-O-OBR HAYNES

4.6 Typical vacuum gauge readings

snapped shut, the rings may be worn. If there is a long delay, look for a restricted exhaust system (often the muffler or catalytic converter). An easy way to check this is to temporarily disconnect the exhaust ahead of the suspected part and redo the test.

5   Engine rebuilding alternatives

1   The do-it-yourselfer is faced with a number of options when purchasing a rebuilt engine. The major considerations are cost, warranty, parts availability and the time required for the rebuilder to complete the project. The decision to replace the engine block, piston/connecting rod assemblies and crankshaft depends on the final inspection results of your engine. Only then can you make a cost effective decision whether to have your engine overhauled or simply purchase an exchange engine for your vehicle.

2   Some of the rebuilding alternatives include:

3   **Individual parts** - If the inspection procedures reveal that the engine block and most engine components are in reusable condition, purchasing individual parts and having a rebuilder rebuild your engine may be the most economical alternative. The block, crankshaft and piston/connecting rod assemblies should all be inspected carefully by a machine shop first.

4   **Short block** - A short block consists of an engine block with a crankshaft and piston/connecting rod assemblies already installed. All new bearings are incorporated and all clearances will be correct. The existing camshafts, valve train components, cylinder head and external parts can be bolted to the short block with little or no machine shop work necessary.

5   **Long block** - A long block consists of a short block plus an oil pump, oil pan, cylinder head, valve cover, camshaft and valve train components, timing sprockets and chain or gears and timing cover. All components are installed with new bearings, seals and gaskets incorporated throughout. The installation of manifolds and external parts is all that's necessary.

6   **Low mileage used engines** - Some companies now offer low mileage used engines which are a very cost effective way to get your vehicle up and running again. These engines often come from vehicles which have been totaled in accidents or come from other countries which have a higher vehicle turn over rate. A low mileage used engine also usually has a similar warranty like the newly remanufactured engines.

7   Give careful thought to which alternative is best for you and discuss the situation with local automotive machine shops, auto parts dealers and experienced rebuilders before ordering or purchasing replacement parts.

6.3a After tightly wrapping water-vulnerable components, use a spray cleaner on everything, with particular concentration on the greasiest areas, usually around the valve cover and lower edges of the block. If one section dries out, apply more cleaner

6.3b Depending on how dirty the engine is, let the cleaner soak in according to the directions and then hose off the grime and cleaner. Get the rinse water down into every area you can get at; then dry important components with a hair dryer or paper towels

6   Engine removal - methods and precautions

1   If you've decided that an engine must be removed for overhaul or major repair work, several preliminary steps should be taken. Read all removal and installation procedures carefully prior to committing to this job. These engines are removed by lowering the engine to the floor, along with the transmission, and then raising the vehicle sufficiently to slide the assembly out; this will require a vehicle hoist as well as an engine hoist. Make sure the engine hoist is rated in excess of the combined weight of the engine and transmission. A transmission jack is also very helpful. Safety is of primary importance, considering the potential hazards involved in removing the engine from the vehicle.

2   Locating a suitable place to work is extremely important. Adequate work space, along with storage space for the vehicle, will be needed. If a shop or garage isn't available, at the very least a flat, level, clean work surface made of concrete or asphalt is required.

3   Cleaning the engine compartment and engine before beginning the removal procedure will help keep tools clean and organized **(see illustrations)**.

4   If you're a novice at engine removal, get at least one helper. One person cannot easily do all the things you need to do to remove a big heavy engine and transmission assembly from the engine compartment. Also helpful is to seek advice and assistance from someone who's experienced in engine removal.

5   Plan the operation ahead of time. Arrange for or obtain all of the tools and equipment you'll need prior to beginning the job **(see illustrations)**. Some of the equipment necessary to perform engine removal and installation safely and with relative ease are (in addition to a vehicle hoist and an engine hoist) a heavy duty floor jack (preferably fitted with a transmission jack head adapter), a sturdy engine stand,

6.5a Get an engine stand sturdy enough to firmly support the engine while you're working on it. Stay away from three-wheeled models: they have a tendency to tip over more easily, so get a four-wheeled unit

a clutch alignment tool (if required), complete sets of wrenches and sockets as described in the front of this manual, wooden blocks, plenty of rags and cleaning solvent for mopping up spilled oil, coolant and gasoline.

6   Plan for the vehicle to be out of use for quite a while. A machine shop can do the work that is beyond the scope of the home mechanic. Machine shops often have a busy schedule, so before removing the engine, consult the shop for an estimate of how long it will take to rebuild or repair the components that may need work.

7   Engine - removal and installation

Warning: *The models covered by this manual are equipped with Supplemental Restraint systems (SRS), more commonly known as airbags. Always disable the airbag system before working in the vicinity of airbag system*

6.5b A clutch alignment tool is necessary if you plan to install a rebuilt engine mated to a manual transaxle

components to avoid the possibility of accidental deployment of the airbag, which could cause personal injury (see Chapter 12).
Warning: *Gasoline is extremely flammable, so take extra precautions when you work on any part of the fuel system. Don't smoke or allow open flames or bare light bulbs near the work area, and don't work in a garage where a gas-type appliance (such as a water heater or clothes dryer) is present. Since gasoline is carcinogenic, wear fuel-resistant gloves when there's a possibility of being exposed to fuel, and, if you spill any fuel on your skin, rinse it off immediately with soap and water. Mop up any spills immediately and do not store fuel-soaked rags where they could ignite. The fuel system is under constant pressure, so, if any fuel lines are to be disconnected, the fuel pressure in the system must be relieved first (see Chapter 4 for more information). When you perform any kind of work on the fuel system, wear safety glasses and have a Class B type fire extinguisher on hand.*

Warning: *The engine must be completely cool before beginning this procedure.*

Note: *Engine removal on these models is a difficult job, especially for the do-it-yourself mechanic working at home. Because of the vehicle's design, the manufacturer states that the engine and transaxle have to be removed as a unit from the bottom of the vehicle, not the top. With a floor jack and jackstands the vehicle can't be raised high enough and supported safely enough for the engine/transaxle assembly to slide out from underneath. The manufacturer recommends that removal of the engine/transaxle assembly only be performed on a vehicle hoist.*

Removal

1 Have the air conditioning system discharged by an automotive air conditioning technician.
2 Park the vehicle on a frame-contact type vehicle hoist. The pads of the hoist arms must contact the body welt along each side of the vehicle.
3 Relieve the fuel system pressure (see Chapter 4). Ensure the negative batter cable is removed from the remote ground terminal (see Chapter 5).
4 Place protective covers on the fenders and cowl and remove the hood (see Chapter 11).
5 Remove the air filter housing and intake duct (see Chapter 4).
6 On turbo models, disconnect and remove the charge air cooler (CAC) inlet and outlet pipes (see Chapter 4).
7 Remove the cowl panels (see Chapter 11), then remove the battery and battery tray (see Chapter 5).
8 Loosen the front wheel lug nuts and the driveaxle/hub nuts, then raise the vehicle on the hoist. Drain the cooling system and engine oil and remove the drivebelt (see Chapter 1).
9 Clearly label, then disconnect all vacuum lines, coolant and emissions hoses, wiring harness connectors, ground straps and fuel lines. Masking tape and/or a touch up paint applicator work well for marking items. Take instant photos or sketch the locations of components and brackets.
10 Disconnect the high-pressure fuel pump quick-connect fitting (see Chapter 4).
11 Remove the alternator and the starter (see Chapter 5).
12 If equipped with automatic transaxle, remove the driveplate-to-clutchplate nuts (see Chapter 7B).
13 On non-turbo models, remove the engine cooling fan and shroud (see Chapter 3).
14 On turbo models remove the cooling module (see Chapter 3).
15 Disconnect the shift cable(s) from the transaxle (see Chapter 7A or 7B). Also disconnect any wiring harness connectors from the transaxle.
16 Remove the air conditioning compressor (see Chapter 3).
17 If equipped with a manual transaxle, disconnect the clutch release cylinder from the transaxle (see Chapter 7A).
18 On non-turbo models remove the exhaust manifold (see Chapter 4).

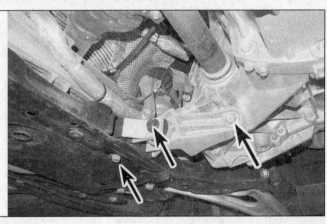

7.22 Remove the fasteners securing the transaxle mount

19 Detach all wiring harnesses and hoses from between the engine/transaxle and the chassis. Be sure to mark all connectors to facilitate reassembly.
20 Remove the driveaxles (see Chapter 8).
21 Attach a lifting sling or chain to the engine. Position an engine hoist and connect the sling to it. If no lifting hooks or brackets are present, you'll have to fasten the chains or slings to some substantial part of the engine - ones that are strong enough to take the weight, but in locations that will provide good balance. Take up the slack until there is slight tension on the sling or chain. Position the chain on the hoist so it balances the engine and the transaxle level with the vehicle.
22 Remove the transaxle mount **(see illustration)**.
23 Recheck to be sure nothing except the upper mount is still connecting the engine to the vehicle. Disconnect and label anything still remaining.
24 Remove the upper engine mount (see Chapter 2A).
25 Slowly lower the engine/transaxle from the vehicle.
Note: *Placing a sheet of hardboard or paneling between the engine and the floor makes moving the powertrain easier.*
26 Once the powertrain is on the floor, disconnect the engine lifting hoist and raise the vehicle hoist until the powertrain can be slid out from underneath.
Note: *A helper will be needed to move the powertrain.*
27 Reconnect the chain or sling and raise the engine/transaxle with the hoist. Support the transmission with a jack (preferably one with a transmission jack head adapter). Separate the engine from the transaxle (see Chapter 7A or 7B).
28 Remove the driveplate/flywheel and mount the engine on a stand.

Installation

29 Installation is the reverse of removal, noting the following points:

a) *Check the engine/transaxle mounts. If they're worn or damaged, replace them.*
b) *Attach the transaxle to the engine following the procedure described in Chapter 7A or 7B.*

c) *Add coolant, oil and transmission fluids as needed (see Chapter 1).*
d) *Run the engine and check for proper operation and leaks. Shut off the engine and recheck fluid levels.*
e) *Have the air conditioning system recharged and leak tested by the shop that discharged it.*

8 Engine overhaul - disassembly sequence

1 It's much easier to remove the external components if the engine is mounted on a portable engine stand. A stand can often be rented quite cheaply from an equipment rental yard. Before the engine is mounted on a stand, the flywheel/driveplate should be removed from the engine.
2 If a stand isn't available, it's possible to remove the external engine components with it blocked up on the floor. Be extra careful not to tip or drop the engine when working without a stand.
3 If you're going to obtain a rebuilt engine, all external components must come off first, to be transferred to the replacement engine. These components include:

- Clutch and flywheel *(models with manual transaxle)*
- Driveplate *(models with automatic transaxle)*
- Emissions-related components
- Engine mounts and mount brackets
- Intake/exhaust manifolds
- Fuel injection components
- Oil filter
- Ignition coils and spark plugs
- Thermostat and housing assembly
- Water pump

Note: *When removing the external components from the engine, pay close attention to details that may be helpful or important during installation. Note the installed position of gaskets, seals, spacers, pins, brackets, washers, bolts and other small items.*

4 If you're going to obtain a short block (assembled engine block, crankshaft, pistons and connecting rods), remove the timing chain, cylinder head, oil pan, oil pump pick-up tube, oil pump and water pump from

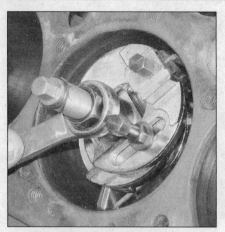

9.1 Before you try to remove the pistons, use a ridge reamer to remove the raised material (ridge) from the top of the cylinders

9.3 Checking the connecting rod endplay (side clearance)

your engine so that you can turn in your old short block to the rebuilder as a core. Engine rebuilding alternatives (see, Section 5) lists additional information regarding the different possibilities to be considered.

9 Pistons and connecting rods - removal and installation

Removal

Note: *Prior to removing the piston/connecting rod assemblies, remove the cylinder head and oil pan (see Chapter 2A).*

1 Use your fingernail to feel if a ridge has formed at the upper limit of ring travel (about 1/4-inch down from the top of each cylinder). If carbon deposits or cylinder wear have produced ridges, they must be completely removed with a special tool **(see illustration)**. Follow the manufacturer's instructions provided with the tool. Failure to remove the ridges before attempting to remove the piston/connecting rod assemblies may result in piston damage.

2 After the cylinder ridges have been

removed, turn the engine so the crankshaft is facing up. On four-cylinder engines, remove the balance shaft assembly (see Section 13).

3 Before the main bearing caps or main-bearing support bridge and connecting rods are removed, check the connecting rod endplay with feeler gauges. Slide them between the first connecting rod and the crankshaft throw until the play is removed **(see illustration)**. Repeat this procedure for each connecting rod. The endplay is equal to the thickness of the feeler gauge(s). Check with an automotive machine shop for the endplay service limit (a typical end play limit should measure between 0.005 to 0.015 inch [0.127 to 0.381 mm]). If the play exceeds the service limit, new connecting rods will be required. If new rods (or a new crankshaft) are installed, the endplay may fall under the minimum allowable. If it does, the rods will have to be machined to restore it. If necessary, consult an automotive machine shop for advice.

4 Check the connecting rods and caps for identification marks. If they aren't plainly marked, use paint or marker to clearly identify each rod and cap (1, 2, 3, etc., depending on the cylinder they're associated with) **(see illustration)**.

5 Loosen each of the connecting rod cap bolts 1/2-turn at a time until they can be removed by hand.

Note: *New connecting rod cap bolts must be used when reassembling the engine, but save the old bolts for use when checking the connecting rod bearing oil clearance.*

6 Remove the number one connecting rod cap and bearing insert. Don't drop the bearing insert out of the cap.

7 Remove the bearing insert and push the connecting rod/piston assembly out through the top of the engine. Use a wooden or plastic hammer handle to push on the upper bearing surface in the connecting rod. If resistance is felt, double-check to make sure that all of the ridge was removed from the cylinder.

8 Repeat the procedure for the remaining cylinders.

9 After removal, reassemble the connecting rod caps and bearing inserts in their respective connecting rods and install the cap bolts finger tight. Leaving the old bearing inserts in place until reassembly will help prevent the connecting rod bearing surfaces from being accidentally nicked or gouged.

10 The pistons and connecting rods are now ready for inspection and overhaul at an automotive machine shop.

Piston ring installation

11 Before installing the new piston rings, the ring end gaps must be checked. It's assumed that the piston ring side clearance has been checked and verified correct as noted during removal.

12 Lay out the piston/connecting rod assemblies and the new ring sets so the ring sets will be matched with the same piston and cylinder during the end gap measurement and engine assembly.

13 Insert the top (number one) ring into the first cylinder and square it up with the cylinder walls by pushing it in with the top of the piston **(see illustration)**. The ring should be near the bottom of the cylinder, at the lower limit of ring travel.

9.4 If the connecting rods and caps are not marked, use permanent ink or paint to mark the caps to the rods by cylinder number (for example, this would be the No. 4 connecting rod)

9.13 Install the piston ring into the cylinder then push it down into position using a piston so the ring will be square in the cylinder

9.14 With the ring square in the cylinder, measure the ring end gap with a feeler gauge

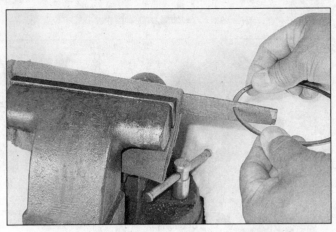

9.15 If the ring end gap is too small, clamp a file in a vise as shown and file the piston ring ends - be sure to remove all raised material

14   To measure the end gap, slip feeler gauges between the ends of the ring until a gauge equal to the gap width is found **(see illustration)**. The feeler gauge should slide between the ring ends with a slight amount of drag. A typical ring gap should fall between 0.010 and 0.020 inch (0.25 to 0.50 mm) for compression rings and up to 0.030 inch (0.76 mm) for the oil ring steel rails. If the gap is larger or smaller than specified, double-check to make sure you have the correct rings before proceeding.

15   If the gap is too small, it must be enlarged or the ring ends may come in contact with each other during engine operation, which can cause serious damage to the engine. If necessary, increase the end gaps by filing the ring ends very carefully with a fine file. Mount the file in a vise equipped with soft jaws, slip the ring over the file with the ends contacting the file face and slowly move the ring to remove material from the ends. When performing this operation, file only by pushing the ring from the outside end of the file towards the vise **(see illustration)**.

16   Excess end gap isn't critical unless it's greater than 0.040 inch (1.01 mm). Again, double-check to make sure you have the correct ring type.

17   Repeat the procedure for each ring that will be installed in the first cylinder and for each ring in the remaining cylinders. Remember to

9.19a Installing the spacer/expander in the oil ring groove

keep rings, pistons and cylinders matched up.

18   Once the ring end gaps have been checked/corrected, the rings can be installed on the pistons.

19   The oil control ring (lowest one on the piston) is usually installed first. It's composed of three separate components. Slip the spacer/expander into the groove **(see illustration)**. If an anti-rotation tang is used, make sure it's inserted into the drilled hole in the ring groove.

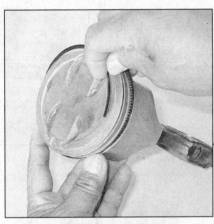

9.19b DO NOT use a piston ring installation tool when installing the oil control side rails

Next, install the upper side rail in the same manner **(see illustration)**. Don't use a piston ring installation tool on the oil ring side rails, as they may be damaged. Instead, place one end of the side rail into the groove between the spacer/expander and the ring land, hold it firmly in place and slide a finger around the piston while pushing the rail into the groove. Finally, install the lower side rail.

20   After the three oil ring components have been installed, check to make sure that both the upper and lower side rails can be rotated smoothly inside the ring grooves.

21   The number two (middle) ring is installed next. It's usually stamped with a mark which must face up, toward the top of the piston. Do not mix up the top and middle rings, as they have different cross-sections.

Note: *Always follow the instructions printed on the ring package or box - different manufacturers may require different approaches.*

22   Use a piston ring installation tool and make sure the identification mark is facing the top of the piston, then slip the ring into the middle groove on the piston **(see illustration)**. Don't expand the ring any more than necessary to slide it over the piston.

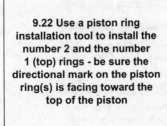

9.22 Use a piston ring installation tool to install the number 2 and the number 1 (top) rings - be sure the directional mark on the piston ring(s) is facing toward the top of the piston

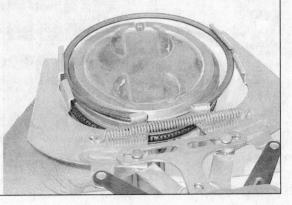

ENGINE BEARING ANALYSIS

Debris

Babbitt bearing embedded with debris from machinings

Microscopic detail of debris

Microscopic detail of gouges

Overplated copper alloy bearing gouged by cast iron debris

Aluminum bearing embedded with glass beads

Microscopic detail of glass beads

Damaged lining caused by dirt left on the bearing back

Misassembly

Result of a lower half assembled as an upper - blocking the oil flow

Excessive oil clearance is indicated by a short contact arc

Polished and oil-stained backs are a result of a poor fit in the housing bore

Result of a wrong, reversed, or shifted cap

Overloading

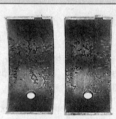

Damage from excessive idling which resulted in an oil film unable to support the load imposed

Damaged upper connecting rod bearings caused by engine lugging; the lower main bearings (not shown) were similarly affected

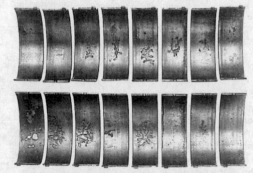

The damage shown in these upper and lower connecting rod bearings was caused by engine operation at a higher-than-rated speed under load

Misalignment

A warped crankshaft caused this pattern of severe wear in the center, diminishing toward the ends

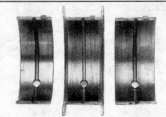

A poorly finished crankshaft caused the equally spaced scoring shown

A tapered housing bore caused the damage along one edge of this pair

A bent connecting rod led to the damage in the "V" pattern

Lubrication

Result of dry start: The bearings on the left, farthest from the oil pump, show more damage

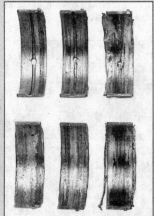

Result of a low oil supply or oil starvation

Severe wear as a result of inadequate oil clearance

Corrosion

Microscopic detail of corrosion

Corrosion is an acid attack on the bearing lining generally caused by inadequate maintenance, extremely hot or cold operation, or inferior oils or fuels

Microscopic detail of cavitation

Example of cavitation - a surface erosion caused by pressure changes in the oil film

Damage from excessive thrust or insufficient axial clearance

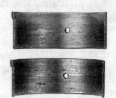

Bearing affected by oil dilution caused by excessive blow-by or a rich mixture

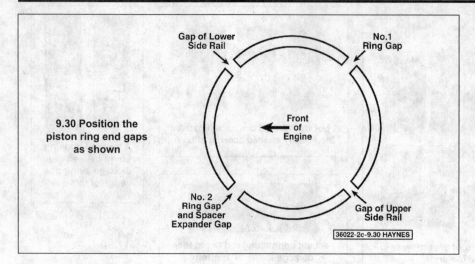

9.30 Position the piston ring end gaps as shown

Gap of Lower Side Rail

No.1 Ring Gap

Front of Engine

No. 2 Ring Gap and Spacer Expander Gap

Gap of Upper Side Rail

36022-2c-9.30 HAYNES

9.35 Use a plastic or wooden hammer handle to push the piston into the cylinder

23   Install the number one (top) ring in the same manner. Make sure the mark is facing up. Be careful not to confuse the number one and number two rings.

24   Repeat the procedure for the remaining pistons and rings.

Installation

25   Before installing the piston/connecting rod assemblies, the cylinder walls must be perfectly clean, the top edge of each cylinder bore must be chamfered, and the crankshaft must be in place.

26   Remove the cap from the end of the number one connecting rod (refer to the marks made during removal). Remove the original bearing inserts and wipe the bearing surfaces of the connecting rod and cap with a clean, lint-free cloth. They must be kept spotlessly clean.

Connecting rod bearing oil clearance check

27   Clean the back side of the new upper bearing insert, then lay it in place in the connecting rod.

28   Make sure the tab on the bearing fits into the recess in the rod. Don't hammer the bearing insert into place and be very careful not to nick or gouge the bearing face. Don't lubricate the bearing at this time.

29   Clean the back side of the other bearing insert and install it in the rod cap. Again, make sure the tab on the bearing fits into the recess in the cap, and don't apply any lubricant. It's critically important that the mating surfaces of the bearing and connecting rod are perfectly clean and oil free when they're assembled.

30   Position the piston ring gaps at 90-degree intervals around the piston as shown **(see illustration)**.

31   Lubricate the piston and rings with clean engine oil and attach a piston ring compressor to the piston. Leave the skirt protruding about 1/4-inch to guide the piston into the cylinder. The rings must be compressed until they're flush with the piston.

32   Rotate the crankshaft until the number one connecting rod journal is at BDC (bottom dead center) and apply a liberal coat of engine oil to the cylinder walls.

33   With the mark on top of the piston facing the front (timing belt or chain end) of the engine, gently insert the piston/connecting rod assembly into the number one cylinder bore and rest the bottom edge of the ring compressor on the engine block.

34   Tap the top edge of the ring compressor to make sure it's contacting the block around its entire circumference.

35   Gently tap on the top of the piston with the end of a wooden or plastic hammer handle **(see illustration)** while guiding the end of the connecting rod into place on the crankshaft journal. The piston rings may try to pop out of the ring compressor just before entering the cylinder bore, so keep some downward pressure on the ring compressor. Work slowly, and if any resistance is felt as the piston enters the cylinder, stop immediately. Find out what's hanging up and fix it before proceeding. Do not, for any reason, force the piston into the cylinder - you might break a ring and/or the piston.

36   Once the piston/connecting rod assembly is installed, the connecting rod bearing oil clearance must be checked before the rod cap is permanently installed.

37   Cut a piece of the appropriate size Plastigage slightly shorter than the width of the connecting rod bearing and lay it in place on the number one connecting rod journal, parallel with the journal axis **(see illustration)**.

38   Clean the connecting rod cap bearing face and install the rod cap. Make sure the mating mark on the cap is on the same side as the mark on the connecting rod **(see illustration 9.4)**.

39   Install the old rod bolts, at this time, and tighten them to the torque listed in this Chapter's Specifications.

Note: *Use a thin-wall socket to avoid erroneous torque readings that can result if the socket is wedged between the rod cap and the bolt head. If the socket tends to wedge itself between the fastener and the cap, lift up on it slightly until it no longer contacts the cap. DO NOT rotate the crankshaft at any time during this operation.*

40   Remove the fasteners and detach the rod cap, being very careful not to disturb the Plastigage.

41   Compare the width of the crushed Plastigage to the scale printed on the Plastigage package to obtain the oil clearance **(see illustration)**. The connecting rod oil clearance is usually about 0.001 to 0.002 inch (0.025 to 0.05 mm). Consult an automotive machine shop for the clearance specified for the rod bearings on your engine. On the covered vehicles, code numbers on the block and crankshaft are used to select the proper bearings, using a chart at a dealership service/ parts department.

42   If the clearance is not as specified, the bearing inserts may be the wrong size (which means different ones will be required). Before deciding that different inserts are needed, make sure that no dirt or oil was between the bearing inserts and the connecting rod or cap when the clearance was measured. Also, recheck the journal diameter. If the Plastigage was wider at one end than the other, the journal may be tapered. If the clearance still exceeds the limit specified, the bearing will have to be replaced with an undersize bearing.

9.37 Place Plastigage on each connecting rod bearing journal parallel to the crankshaft centerline

9.41 Use the scale on the Plastigage package to determine the bearing oil clearance - be sure to measure the widest part of the Plastigage and use the correct scale; it comes with both standard and metric scales

Caution: *When installing a new crankshaft always use a standard size bearing.*

Final installation

43 Carefully scrape all traces of the Plastigage material off the rod journal and/or bearing face. Be very careful not to scratch the bearing - use your fingernail or the edge of a plastic card.

44 Make sure the bearing faces are perfectly clean, then apply a uniform layer of clean moly-base grease or engine assembly lube to both of them. You'll have to push the piston into the cylinder to expose the face of the bearing insert in the connecting rod.

45 Slide the connecting rod back into place on the journal, install the rod cap, install the new bolts and tighten them to the torque listed in this Chapter's Specifications.

Caution: *Install new connecting rod cap bolts. Do NOT reuse old bolts - they have stretched and cannot be reused. Again, work up to the torque in three steps.*

46 Repeat the entire procedure for the remaining pistons/connecting rods.

47 The important points to remember are:

a) *Keep the back sides of the bearing inserts and the insides of the connecting rods and caps perfectly clean when assembling them.*

b) *Make sure you have the correct piston/rod assembly for each cylinder.*

c) *The mark on the piston must face the front (timing belt end) of the engine.*

d) *Lubricate the cylinder walls liberally with clean oil.*

e) *Lubricate the bearing faces when installing the rod caps after the oil clearance has been checked.*

48 After all the piston/connecting rod assemblies have been correctly installed, rotate the crankshaft a number of times by hand to check for any obvious binding.

49 As a final step, check the connecting rod

10.1 Checking crankshaft endplay with a dial indicator

endplay, as described in Step 3. If it was correct before disassembly and the original crankshaft and rods were reinstalled, it should still be correct. If new rods or a new crankshaft were installed, the endplay may be inadequate. If so, the rods will have to be removed and taken to an automotive machine shop for resizing.

10 Crankshaft - removal and installation

Removal

Note: *The crankshaft can be removed only after the engine has been removed from the vehicle. It's assumed that the flywheel or driveplate, crankshaft pulley, timing chain, oil pan, oil pump body, oil filter and piston/connecting rod assemblies have already been removed. The rear main oil seal retainer must be unbolted and separated from the block before proceeding with crankshaft removal.*

1 Before the crankshaft is removed, measure the endplay. Mount a dial indicator with the indicator in line with the crankshaft and just touching the end of the crankshaft as shown **(see illustration)**.

2 Pry the crankshaft all the way to the rear and zero the dial indicator. Next, pry the crankshaft to the front as far as possible and check the reading on the dial indicator. The distance traveled is the endplay. A typical crankshaft endplay will fall between 0.003 to 0.010 inch (0.076 to 0.254 mm). If it is greater than that, check the crankshaft thrust surfaces for wear after it's removed. If no wear is evident, new main bearings should correct the endplay.

3 If a dial indicator isn't available, feeler gauges can be used. Gently pry the crankshaft all the way to the front of the engine. Slip feeler gauges between the crankshaft and the front face of the thrust bearing or washer to determine the clearance **(see illustration)**.

4 Loosen the main bearing cap beam bolts 1/4-turn at a time each, until they can be removed by hand. Loosen the bolts in the reverse of the tightening sequence (see illustration 10.19).

5 Remove the main bearing cap support beam. Try not to drop the bearing inserts if

they come out with the assembly.

6 Carefully lift the crankshaft out of the engine. It may be a good idea to have an assistant available, since the crankshaft is quite heavy and awkward to handle. With the bearing inserts in place inside the engine block and main bearing caps or lower cylinder block, reinstall the main bearing caps or lower cylinder block onto the engine block and tighten the bolts finger tight.

Installation

7 Crankshaft installation is the first step in engine reassembly. It's assumed at this point that the engine block and crankshaft have been cleaned, inspected and repaired or reconditioned.

8 Position the engine block with the bottom facing up.

9 Remove the bolts and lift off the support beam, main bearing caps or lower cylinder block, as applicable.

10 If they're still in place, remove the original bearing inserts. Wipe the bearing surfaces of the block and main bearing cap assembly with a clean, lint-free cloth. They must be kept spotlessly clean. This is critical for determining the correct bearing oil clearance.

10.3 Checking the crankshaft endplay with feeler gauges at the thrust bearing journal

10.17 Place the Plastigage onto the crankshaft bearing journal as shown

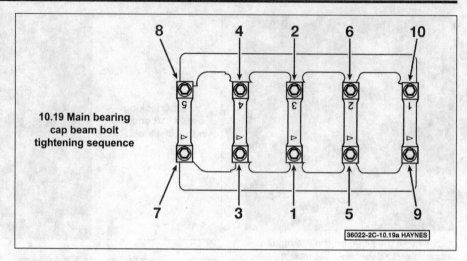

10.19 Main bearing cap beam bolt tightening sequence

36022-2C-10.19a HAYNES

Main bearing oil clearance check

11 Without mixing them up, clean the back sides of the new upper main bearing inserts (with grooves and oil holes) and lay one in each main bearing saddle in the engine block. Each upper bearing (engine block) has an oil groove and oil hole in it.

Caution: *The oil holes in the block must line up with the oil holes in the upper bearing inserts.*

Note: *The thrust bearing on the engine is located on the engine block number 3 (center) journal. Clean the back sides of the lower main bearing inserts and lay them in the corresponding location in the main bearing caps or the lower cylinder block. Make sure the tab on the bearing insert fits into its corresponding recess.*

Caution: *Do not hammer the bearing insert into place and don't nick or gouge the bearing faces. DO NOT apply any lubrication at this time.*

12 Clean the faces of the bearing inserts in the block and the crankshaft main bearing journals with a clean, lint-free cloth.

13 Check or clean the oil holes in the crankshaft, as any dirt here can go only one way - straight through the new bearings.

14 Once you're certain the crankshaft is clean, carefully lay it in position in the cylinder block.

15 Before the crankshaft can be permanently installed, the main bearing oil clearance must be checked.

16 Cut several strips of the appropriate size of Plastigage. They must be slightly shorter than the width of the main bearing journal.

17 Place one piece on each crankshaft main bearing journal, parallel with the journal axis as shown **(see illustration)**.

18 Clean the faces of the bearing inserts in the main bearing caps or the lower cylinder block. Hold the bearing inserts in place and install the caps or the lower cylinder block onto the crankshaft and cylinder block. DO NOT disturb the Plastigage.

19 Apply clean engine oil to all bolt threads prior to installation, then install all bolts finger-tight. Tighten the bolts in the sequence shown

(see illustration) progressing in steps, to the torque listed in this Chapter's Specifications. DO NOT rotate the crankshaft at any time during this operation.

20 Remove the bolts in the reverse order of the tightening sequence and carefully lift the caps or the lower cylinder block straight up and off the block. Do not disturb the Plastigage or rotate the crankshaft.

21 Compare the width of the crushed Plastigage on each journal to the scale printed on the Plastigage package to determine the main bearing oil clearance **(see illustration)**. Check with an automotive machine shop for the oil clearance for your engine.

22 If the clearance is not as specified, the bearing inserts may be the wrong size (which means different ones will be required). Before deciding if different inserts are needed, make sure that no dirt or oil was between the bearing inserts and the cap assembly or block when the clearance was measured. If the Plastigage was wider at one end than the other, the crankshaft journal may be tapered. If the clearance still exceeds the limit specified, the bearing insert(s) will have to be replaced with an undersize bearing insert(s).

Caution: *When installing a new crankshaft always install a standard bearing insert set.*

23 Carefully scrape all traces of the Plastigage material off the main bearing journals and/or the bearing insert faces. Be sure to remove all residue from the oil holes. Use your fingernail or the edge of a plastic card - don't nick or scratch the bearing faces.

Final installation

24 Carefully lift the crankshaft out of the cylinder block.

25 Clean the bearing insert faces in the cylinder block, then apply a thin, uniform layer of moly-base grease or engine assembly lube to each of the bearing surfaces. Be sure to coat the thrust faces as well as the journal face of the thrust bearing.

26 Make sure the crankshaft journals are clean, then lay the crankshaft back in place in the cylinder block.

27 Clean the bearing insert faces and apply the same lubricant to them. Clean the engine

block and the bearing caps/lower cylinder block thoroughly. The surfaces must be free of oil residue.

28 Install the main bearing caps in their proper locations, with the arrows on the caps facing the front of the engine.

29 Prior to installation, apply clean engine oil to all bolt threads wiping off any excess, then install all bolts finger-tight.

30 Tighten the support beam following the correct torque sequence **(see illustration 10.19)**. Tighten the bolts to the torque listed in 2A this Chapter's Specifications.

31 Recheck the crankshaft endplay with a feeler gauge or a dial indicator. The endplay should be correct if the crankshaft thrust faces aren't worn or damaged and if new bearings have been installed.

32 Rotate the crankshaft a number of times by hand to check for any obvious binding. It should rotate with a running torque of 50 in-lbs or less. If the running torque is too high, correct the problem at this time.

33 Install a new rear main oil seal (see Chapter Chapter 2A).

10.21 Use the scale on the Plastigage package to determine the bearing oil clearance - be sure to measure the widest part of the Plastigage and use the correct scale; it comes with both standard and metric scales

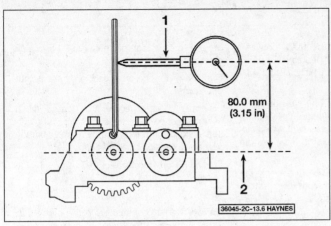

13.6 Method of checking the backlash in the balancer assembly

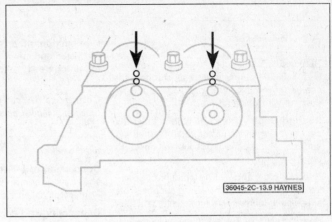

13.9 Remove/install the balance shaft assembly bolts only when the crank is at TDC and these balancer dots align

11 Engine overhaul - reassembly sequence

1   Before beginning engine reassembly, make sure you have all the necessary new parts, gaskets and seals as well as the following items on hand:

Common hand tools
A 1/2-inch drive torque wrench
New engine oil
Gasket sealant
Thread locking compound

2   If you obtained a short block it will be necessary to install the cylinder head, the oil pump and pick-up tube, the oil pan, the water pump, the timing belt and timing cover, and the valve cover (see Chapter 2A). In order to save time and avoid problems, the external components must be installed in the following general order:

Thermostat and housing cover
Water pump
Intake and exhaust manifolds
Fuel injection components
Emission control components
Spark plugs
Ignition coils
Oil filter
Engine mounts and mount brackets
Clutch and flywheel (manual transaxle)
Driveplate (automatic transaxle)

12 Initial start-up and break-in after overhaul

Warning: *Have a fire extinguisher handy when starting the engine for the first time.*

1   Once the engine has been installed in the vehicle, double-check the engine oil and coolant levels (see Chapter 1).
2   With the spark plugs out of the engine and the fuel pump disabled (see Chapter 4 Section 3), crank the engine until oil pressure registers on the gauge or the light goes out.
3   Install the spark plugs, and restore the ignition system and fuel pump functions.

4   Start the engine. It may take a few moments for the fuel system to build up pressure, but the engine should start without a great deal of effort.
5   After the engine starts, it should be allowed to warm up to normal operating temperature. While the engine is warming up, make a thorough check for fuel, oil and coolant leaks.
6   Shut the engine off and recheck the engine oil and coolant levels.
7   Drive the vehicle to an area with minimum traffic, accelerate from 30 to 50 mph, then allow the vehicle to slow to 30 mph with the throttle closed. Repeat the procedure 10 or 12 times. This will load the piston rings and cause them to seat properly against the cylinder walls. Check again for oil and coolant leaks.
8   Drive the vehicle gently for the first 500 miles (no sustained high speeds) and keep a constant check on the oil level. It is not unusual for an engine to use oil during the break-in period.
9   At approximately 500 to 600 miles, change the oil and filter.
10   For the next few hundred miles, drive the vehicle normally. Do not pamper it or abuse it.
11   After 2,000 miles, change the oil and filter again and consider the engine broken in.

13 Balance shaft assembly (Turbo engines) - removal and installation

1   The balance shaft assembly is bolted to the crankshaft main bearing support beam. A gear on the crankshaft meshes with a gear on the balance shaft assembly. When the engine is operating, the assembly smoothes engine vibrations.
2   The balancer is a precision-machined assembly, there are no serviceable parts inside and it should not be disassembled. If the backlash is out of Specification (see Steps 5 through 8), the assembly must be replaced as a complete unit.

Removal

3   Position the crankshaft at top dead center (TDC) (see Chapter 2A). Remove the four mounting bolts.
4   With the engine turned crankshaft side up, lift the assembly straight up from the engine.

Inspection

5   When the balance shaft assembly is in place, the backlash between the drive gear (on the crankshaft) and the driven gear on the assembly can be checked. Remove the timing peg.
6   Attach a 5 mm Allen wrench to the top of the driveshaft with the long end of the wrench pointing straight up. Secure a dial-indicator fixture to the engine so that the tip of the indicator is against the top of the wrench (**see illustration**).
7   Use a pry tool against the crankshaft front counterweight to apply thrust pressure, while turning the crankshaft back-and-forth. Record the measurements of the dial-indicator. Measurements should be taken at the following degrees of engine rotation: 10, 30, 100, 190 and 210 degrees. Compare your results with the allowable range of backlash given in this Chapter's Specifications.
8   If the backlash is out of range, the assembly must be replaced.

Installation

9   When installing the balance shaft assembly, the engine must set to TDC for cylinder number 1. Before installing the assembly, rotate the assembly to align the timing marks on both shafts of the assembly (**see illustration**). Bolt the assembly to the engine and recheck that the timing marks are still aligned and that the crankshaft has not moved. Tighten the bolts in a criss-cross pattern and in two steps to the torque listed in this Chapter's Specifications.
10   The crankshaft timing peg should remain installed to keep the engine at TDC until installation of the timing chain and sprockets is completed.

COMMON ENGINE OVERHAUL TERMS

B

Backlash - The amount of play between two parts. Usually refers to how much one gear can be moved back and forth without moving the gear with which it's meshed.

Bearing Caps - The caps held in place by nuts or bolts which, in turn, hold the bearing surface. This space is for lubricating oil to enter.

Bearing clearance - The amount of space left between shaft and bearing surface. This space is for lubricating oil to enter.

Bearing crush - The additional height which is purposely manufactured into each bearing half to ensure complete contact of the bearing back with the housing bore when the engine is assembled.

Bearing knock - The noise created by movement of a part in a loose or worn bearing.

Blueprinting - Dismantling an engine and reassembling it to EXACT specifications.

Bore - An engine cylinder, or any cylindrical hole; also used to describe the process of enlarging or accurately refinishing a hole with a cutting tool, as to bore an engine cylinder. The bore size is the diameter of the hole.

Boring - Renewing the cylinders by cutting them out to a specified size. A boring bar is used to make the cut.

Bottom end - A term which refers collectively to the engine block, crankshaft, main bearings and the big ends of the connecting rods.

Break-in - The period of operation between installation of new or rebuilt parts and time in which parts are worn to the correct fit. Driving at reduced and varying speed for a specified mileage to permit parts to wear to the correct fit.

Bushing - A one-piece sleeve placed in a bore to serve as a bearing surface for shaft, piston pin, etc. Usually replaceable.

C

Camshaft - The shaft in the engine, on which a series of lobes are located for operating the valve mechanisms. The camshaft is driven by gears or sprockets and a timing chain. Usually referred to simply as the cam.

Carbon - Hard, or soft, black deposits found in combustion chamber, on plugs, under rings, on and under valve heads.

Cast iron - An alloy of iron and more than two percent carbon, used for engine blocks and heads because it's relatively inexpensive and easy to mold into complex shapes.

Chamfer - To bevel across (or a bevel on) the sharp edge of an object.

Chase - To repair damaged threads with a tap or die.

Combustion chamber - The space between the piston and the cylinder head, with the piston at top dead center, in which air-fuel mixture is burned.

Compression ratio - The relationship between cylinder volume (clearance volume) when the piston is at top dead center and cylinder volume when the piston is at bottom dead center.

Connecting rod - The rod that connects the crank on the crankshaft with the piston. Sometimes called a con rod.

Connecting rod cap - The part of the connecting rod assembly that attaches the rod to the crankpin.

Core plug - Soft metal plug used to plug the casting holes for the coolant passages in the block.

Crankcase - The lower part of the engine in which the crankshaft rotates; includes the lower section of the cylinder block and the oil pan.

Crank kit - A reground or reconditioned crankshaft and new main and connecting rod bearings.

Crankpin - The part of a crankshaft to which a connecting rod is attached.

Crankshaft - The main rotating member, or shaft, running the length of the crankcase, with offset throws to which the connecting rods are attached; changes the reciprocating motion of the pistons into rotating motion.

Cylinder sleeve - A replaceable sleeve, or liner, pressed into the cylinder block to form the cylinder bore.

D

Deburring - Removing the burrs (rough edges or areas) from a bearing.

Deglazer - A tool, rotated by an electric motor, used to remove glaze from cylinder walls so a new set of rings will seat.

E

Endplay - The amount of lengthwise movement between two parts. As applied to a crankshaft, the distance that the crankshaft can move forward and back in the cylinder block.

F

Face - A machinist's term that refers to removing metal from the end of a shaft or the face of a larger part, such as a flywheel.

Fatigue - A breakdown of material through a large number of loading and unloading cycles. The first signs are cracks followed shortly by breaks.

Feeler gauge - A thin strip of hardened steel, ground to an exact thickness, used to check clearances between parts.

Free height - The unloaded length or height of a spring.

Freeplay - The looseness in a linkage, or an assembly of parts, between the initial application of force and actual movement. Usually perceived as slop or slight delay.

Freeze plug - See Core plug.

G

Gallery - A large passage in the block that forms a reservoir for engine oil pressure.

Glaze - The very smooth, glassy finish that develops on cylinder walls while an engine is in service.

H

Heli-Coil - A rethreading device used when threads are worn or damaged. The device is installed in a retapped hole to reduce the thread size to the original size.

I

Installed height - The spring's measured length or height, as installed on the cylinder head. Installed height is measured from the spring seat to the underside of the spring retainer.

J

Journal - The surface of a rotating shaft which turns in a bearing.

K

Keeper - The split lock that holds the valve spring retainer in position on the valve stem.

Key - A small piece of metal inserted into matching grooves machined into two parts fitted together - such as a gear pressed onto a shaft - which prevents slippage between the two parts.

Knock - The heavy metallic engine sound, produced in the combustion chamber as a result of abnormal combustion - usually detonation. Knock is usually caused by a loose or worn bearing. Also referred to as detonation, pinging and spark knock. Connecting rod or main bearing knocks are created by too much oil clearance or insufficient lubrication.

L

Lands - The portions of metal between the piston ring grooves.

Lapping the valves - Grinding a valve face and its seat together with lapping compound.

Lash - The amount of free motion in a gear train, between gears, or in a mechanical assembly, that occurs before movement can begin. Usually refers to the lash in a valve train.

Lifter - The part that rides against the cam to transfer motion to the rest of the valve train.

M

Machining - The process of using a machine to remove metal from a metal part.

Main bearings - The plain, or babbit, bearings that support the crankshaft.

Main bearing caps - The cast iron caps, bolted to the bottom of the block, that support the main bearings.

O

O.D. - Outside diameter.

Oil gallery - A pipe or drilled passageway in the engine used to carry engine oil from one area to another.

Oil ring - The lower ring, or rings, of a piston; designed to prevent excessive amounts of oil from working up the cylinder walls and into the combustion chamber. Also called an oil-control ring.

Oil seal - A seal which keeps oil from leaking out of a compartment. Usually refers to a dynamic seal around a rotating shaft or other moving part.

O-ring - A type of sealing ring made of a special rubberlike material; in use, the O-ring is compressed into a groove to provide the sealing action.

Overhaul - To completely disassemble a unit, clean and inspect all parts, reassemble it with the original or new parts and make all adjustments necessary for proper operation.

P

Pilot bearing - A small bearing installed in the center of the flywheel (or the rear end of the crankshaft) to support the front end of the input shaft of the transmission.

Pip mark - A little dot or indentation which indicates the top side of a compression ring.

Piston - The cylindrical part, attached to the connecting rod, that moves up and down in the cylinder as the crankshaft rotates. When the fuel charge is fired, the piston transfers the force of the explosion to the connecting rod, then to the crankshaft.

Piston pin (or wrist pin) - The cylindrical and usually hollow steel pin that passes through the piston. The piston pin fastens the piston to the upper end of the connecting rod.

Piston ring - The split ring fitted to the groove in a piston. The ring contacts the sides of the ring groove and also rubs against the cylinder wall, thus sealing space between piston and wall. There are two types of rings: Compression rings seal the compression pressure in the combustion chamber; oil rings scrape excessive oil off the cylinder wall.

Piston ring groove - The slots or grooves cut in piston heads to hold piston rings in position.

Piston skirt - The portion of the piston below the rings and the piston pin hole.

Plastigage - A thin strip of plastic thread, available in different sizes, used for measuring clearances. For example, a strip of plastigage is laid across a bearing journal and mashed as parts are assembled. Then parts are disassembled and the width of the strip is measured to determine clearance between journal and bearing. Commonly used to measure crankshaft main-bearing and connecting rod bearing clearances.

Press-fit - A tight fit between two parts that requires pressure to force the parts together. Also referred to as drive, or force, fit.

Prussian blue - A blue pigment; in solution, useful in determining the area of contact between two surfaces. Prussian blue is commonly used to determine the width and location of the contact area between the valve face and the valve seat.

R

Race (bearing) - The inner or outer ring that provides a contact surface for balls or rollers in bearing.

Ream - To size, enlarge or smooth a hole by using a round cutting tool with fluted edges.

Ring job - The process of reconditioning the cylinders and installing new rings.

Runout - Wobble. The amount a shaft rotates out-of-true.

S

Saddle - The upper main bearing seat.

Scored - Scratched or grooved, as a cylinder wall may be scored by abrasive particles moved up and down by the piston rings.

Scuffing - A type of wear in which there's a transfer of material between parts moving against each other; shows up as pits or grooves in the mating surfaces.

Seat - The surface upon which another part rests or seats. For example, the valve seat is the matched surface upon which the valve face rests. Also used to refer to wearing into a good fit; for example, piston rings seat after a few miles of driving.

Short block - An engine block complete with crankshaft and piston and, usually, camshaft assemblies.

Static balance - The balance of an object while it's stationary.

Step - The wear on the lower portion of a ring land caused by excessive side and back-clearance. The height of the step indicates the ring's extra side clearance and the length of the step projecting from the back wall of the groove represents the ring's back clearance.

Stroke - The distance the piston moves when traveling from top dead center to bottom dead center, or from bottom dead center to top dead center.

Stud - A metal rod with threads on both ends.

T

Tang - A lip on the end of a plain bearing used to align the bearing during assembly.

Tap - To cut threads in a hole. Also refers to the fluted tool used to cut threads.

Taper - A gradual reduction in the width of a shaft or hole; in an engine cylinder, taper usually takes the form of uneven wear, more pronounced at the top than at the bottom.

Throws - The offset portions of the crankshaft to which the connecting rods are affixed.

Thrust bearing - The main bearing that has thrust faces to prevent excessive endplay, or forward and backward movement of the crankshaft.

Thrust washer - A bronze or hardened steel washer placed between two moving parts. The washer prevents longitudinal movement and provides a bearing surface for thrust surfaces of parts.

Tolerance - The amount of variation permitted from an exact size of measurement. Actual amount from smallest acceptable dimension to largest acceptable dimension.

U

Umbrella - An oil deflector placed near the valve tip to throw oil from the valve stem area.

Undercut - A machined groove below the normal surface.

Undersize bearings - Smaller diameter bearings used with re-ground crankshaft journals.

V

Valve grinding - Refacing a valve in a valve-refacing machine.

Valve train - The valve-operating mechanism of an engine; includes all components from the camshaft to the valve.

Vibration damper - A cylindrical weight attached to the front of the crankshaft to minimize torsional vibration (the twist-untwist actions of the crankshaft caused by the cylinder firing impulses). Also called a harmonic balancer.

W

Water jacket - The spaces around the cylinders, between the inner and outer shells of the cylinder block or head, through which coolant circulates.

Web - A supporting structure across a cavity.

Woodruff key - A key with a radiused backside (viewed from the side).

Notes

Chapter 3
Cooling, heating and air conditioning systems

Contents

Specifications

General

Expansion tank cap pressure rating	18 to 24 psi (124 to 166 kPa)
Cooling system capacity..	See Chapter 1
Refrigerant type..	R-134a
Refrigerant capacity..	Refer to HVAC specification tag

Torque specifications

Note: *One foot-pound (ft-lb) of torque is equivalent to 12 inch-pounds (in-lbs) of torque. Torque values below approximately 15 ft-lbs are expressed in inch-pounds, because most foot-pound torque wrenches are not accurate at these smaller values.*

	Ft-lbs (unless otherwise indicated)	Nm
Air conditioning compressor mounting bolts...	18	24
Air conditioning compressor drain bolt	22	30
Drivebelt tensioner bolts..	18	24
Refrigerant line-to-air conditioning compressor nuts.............................	177 in-lbs	20
Refrigerant line-to-condenser nuts..	133 in-lbs	15
Refrigerant line-to-thermostatic expansion valve nut	97 in-lbs	11
Thermostatic expansion valve bolts	71 in-lbs	8
Thermostat housing cover bolts...	89 in-lbs	10
Water pump fasteners	89 in-lbs	10
Water pump pulley bolts	177 in-lbs	20

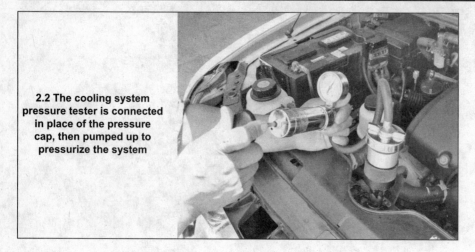

2.2 The cooling system pressure tester is connected in place of the pressure cap, then pumped up to pressurize the system

1   General Information

Warning: *Do not allow antifreeze to come in contact with your skin or painted surfaces of the vehicle. Rinse off spills immediately with plenty of water. Antifreeze is highly toxic if ingested. Never leave antifreeze lying around in an open container or in puddles on the floor; children and pets are attracted by it's sweet smell and may drink it. Check with local authorities about disposing of used antifreeze. Many communities have collection centers which will see that antifreeze is disposed of safely. Never dump used antifreeze on the ground or pour it into drains.*

Engine cooling system

1   All modern vehicles employ a pressurized engine cooling system with thermostatically controlled coolant circulation. The cooling system consists of a radiator, an expansion tank or coolant reservoir, a pressure cap (located on the expansion tank or radiator), a thermostat, a cooling fan, and a water pump.

2   The water pump circulates coolant through the engine. The coolant flows around each cylinder and around the intake and exhaust ports, near the spark plug areas and in close proximity to the exhaust valve guides.

3   A thermostat controls engine coolant temperature. During warm up, the closed thermostat prevents coolant from circulating through the radiator. As the engine nears normal operating temperature, the thermostat opens and allows hot coolant to travel through the radiator, where it's cooled before returning to the engine.

Heating system

4   The heating system consists of a blower fan and heater core located in a housing under the dash, the hoses connecting the heater core to the engine cooling system and the heater/air conditioning control head on the dashboard. Hot engine coolant is circulated through the heater core. When the heater mode is activated, a flap door in the housing opens to expose the heater core to the passenger compartment through air ducts. A fan switch on the control head activates the blower motor, which forces air through the core, heating the air.

Air conditioning system

5   The air conditioning system consists of a condenser mounted in front of the radiator, an evaporator mounted adjacent to the heater core, a thermostatic expansion valve, a compressor mounted on the engine, a receiver-drier (integral with the condenser) and the plumbing connecting all of the above components.

6   A blower fan forces the warmer air of the passenger compartment through the evaporator core (sort of a radiator-in-reverse), transferring the heat from the air to the refrigerant. The liquid refrigerant boils off into low pressure vapor, taking the heat with it when it leaves the evaporator.

2   Troubleshooting

Coolant leaks

1   A coolant leak can develop anywhere in the cooling system, but the most common causes are:

a) A loose or weak hose clamp
b) A defective hose
c) A faulty pressure cap
d) A damaged radiator
e) A bad heater core
f) A faulty water pump
g) A leaking gasket at any joint that carries coolant

2   Coolant leaks aren't always easy to find. Sometimes they can only be detected when the cooling system is under pressure. Here's where a cooling system pressure tester comes in handy. After the engine has cooled completely, the tester is attached in place of the pressure cap, then pumped up to the pressure value equal to that of the pressure cap rating **(see illustration)**. Now, leaks that only exist when the engine is fully warmed up will become apparent. The tester can be left connected to locate a nagging slow leak.

Coolant level drops, but no external leaks

3   If you find it necessary to keep adding coolant, but there are no external leaks, the probable causes include:

a) A blown head gasket
b) A leaking intake manifold gasket (only on engines that have coolant passages in the manifold) cracked cylinder head or cylinder block

4   Any of the above problems will also usually result in contamination of the engine oil, which will cause it to take on a milkshake-like appearance. A bad head gasket or cracked head or block can also result in engine oil contaminating the cooling system.

5   Combustion leak detectors (also known as block testers) are available at most auto parts stores. These work by detecting exhaust gases in the cooling system, which indicates a compression leak from a cylinder into the coolant. The tester consists of a large bulb-type syringe and bottle of test fluid **(see illustration)**. A measured amount of the fluid is added to the syringe. The syringe is placed over the cooling system filler neck and, with the engine running, the bulb is squeezed and a sample of the gases present in the cooling system are drawn up through the test fluid **(see illustration)**. If any combustion gases are present in the sample taken, the test fluid will change color.

6   If the test indicates combustion gas is present in the cooling system, you can be sure that the engine has a blown head gasket or a crack in the cylinder head or block, and will require disassembly to repair.

Pressure cap

Warning: *Wait until the engine is completely cool before beginning this check.*

7   The cooling system is sealed by a spring-loaded cap, which raises the boiling point of the coolant. If the cap's seal or spring are worn out, the coolant can boil and escape past the cap. With the engine completely cool, remove the cap and check the seal; if it's cracked, hardened or deteriorated in any way, replace it with a new one.

8   Even if the seal is good, the spring might not be; this can be checked with a cooling system pressure tester **(see illustration)**. If the cap can't hold a pressure within approximately 1-1/2 lbs of its rated pressure (which is marked on the cap), replace it with a new one.

9   The cap is also equipped with a vacuum relief spring. When the engine cools off, a vacuum is created in the cooling system. The vacuum relief spring allows air back into the system, which will equalize the pressure and prevent damage to the radiator (the radiator tanks could collapse if the vacuum is great enough). If, after turning the engine off and allowing it to cool down you notice any of the cooling system hoses collapsing, replace the pressure cap with a new one.

2.5a The combustion leak detector consists of a bulb, syringe and test fluid

2.5b Place the tester over the cooling system filler neck and use the bulb to draw a sample into the tester

Thermostat

10   Before assuming the thermostat (**see illustration**) is responsible for a cooling system problem, check the coolant level (see Chapter 1), drivebelt tension (see Chapter 1) and temperature gauge (or light) operation.

11   If the engine takes a long time to warm up (as indicated by the temperature gauge or heater operation), the thermostat is probably stuck open. Replace the thermostat with a new one.

12   If the engine runs hot or overheats, a thorough test of the thermostat should be performed.

13   Definitive testing of the thermostat can only be made when it is removed from the vehicle. If the thermostat is stuck in the open position at room temperature, it is faulty and must be replaced.

Caution: *Do not drive the vehicle without a thermostat. The computer may stay in open loop and emissions and fuel economy will suffer.*

14   To test a thermostat, suspend the (closed) thermostat on a length of string or wire in a pot of cold water.

15   Heat the water on a stove while observing thermostat. The thermostat should fully open before the water boils.

16   If the thermostat doesn't open and close as specified, or sticks in any position, replace it.

Cooling fan

Electric cooling fan

17   If the engine is overheating and the cooling fan is not coming on when the engine temperature rises to an excessive level, unplug the fan motor electrical connector(s) and connect the motor directly to the battery with fused jumper wires. If the fan motor doesn't come on, replace the motor.

18   If the radiator fan motor is okay, but it isn't coming on when the engine gets hot, the fan relay might be defective. A relay is used to control a circuit by turning it on and off in response to a control decision by the Pow-

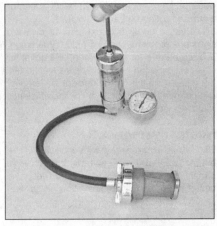

2.8 Checking the cooling system pressure cap with a cooling system pressure tester

ertrain Control Module (PCM). These control circuits are fairly complex, and checking them should be left to a qualified automotive technician. Sometimes, the control system can be fixed by simply identifying and replacing a bad relay.

19   Locate the fan relays in the engine compartment fuse/relay box.

20   Test the relay (see Chapter 12).

21   If the relay is okay, check all wiring and connections to the fan motor. Refer to the wiring diagrams at the end of Chapter 12. If no obvious problems are found, the problem could be the Engine Coolant Temperature (ECT) sensor or the Powertrain Control Module (PCM). Have the cooling fan system and circuit diagnosed by a dealer service department or repair shop with the proper diagnostic equipment.

Belt-driven cooling fan

22   Disconnect the cable from the negative terminal of the battery and rock the fan back and forth by hand to check for excessive bearing play.

23   With the engine cold (and not running), turn the fan blades by hand. The fan should turn freely.

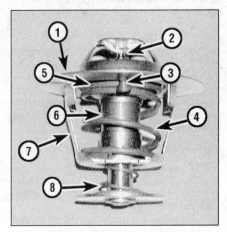

2.10 Typical thermostat:

1	Flange	5	Valve seat
2	Piston	6	Valve
3	Jiggle valve	7	Frame
4	Main coil spring	8	Secondary coil spring

24   Visually inspect for substantial fluid leakage from the clutch assembly. If problems are noted, replace the clutch assembly.

25   With the engine completely warmed up, turn off the ignition switch and disconnect the negative battery cable from the battery. Turn the fan by hand. Some drag should be evident. If the fan turns easily, replace the fan clutch.

Water pump

26   A failure in the water pump can cause serious engine damage due to overheating.

Drivebelt-driven water pump

27   There are two ways to check the operation of the water pump while it's installed on the engine. If the pump is found to be defective, it should be replaced with a new or rebuilt unit.

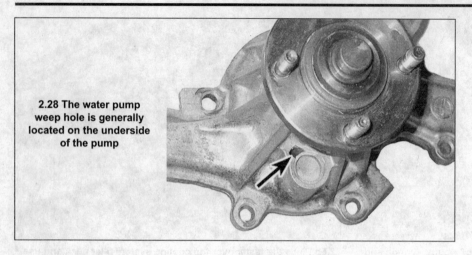

2.28 The water pump weep hole is generally located on the underside of the pump

28   Water pumps are equipped with weep (or vent) holes **(see illustration)**. If a failure occurs in the pump seal, coolant will leak from the hole.

29   If the water pump shaft bearings fail, there may be a howling sound at the pump while it's running. Shaft wear can be felt with the drivebelt removed if the water pump pulley is rocked up and down (with the engine off). Don't mistake drivebelt slippage, which causes a squealing sound, for water pump bearing failure.

Timing chain or timing belt-driven water pump

30   Water pumps driven by the timing chain or timing belt are located underneath the timing chain or timing belt cover.

31   Checking the water pump is limited because of where it is located. However, some basic checks can be made before deciding to remove the water pump. If the pump is found to be defective, it should be replaced with a new or rebuilt unit.

32   One sign that the water pump may be failing is that the heater (climate control) may not work well. Warm the engine to normal operating temperature, confirm that the coolant level is correct, then run the heater and check for hot air coming from the ducts.

33   Check for noises coming from the water pump area. If the water pump impeller shaft or bearings are failing, there may be a howling sound at the pump while the engine is running. **Note:** *Be careful not to mistake drivebelt noise (squealing) for water pump bearing or shaft failure.*

34   It you suspect water pump failure due to noise, wear can be confirmed by feeling for play at the pump shaft. This can be done by rocking the drive sprocket on the pump shaft up and down. To do this you will need to remove the tension on the timing chain or belt as well as access the water pump.

All water pumps

35   In rare cases or on high-mileage vehicles, another sign of water pump failure may be the presence of coolant in the engine oil. This condition will adversely affect the engine in varying degrees.

36   Finding coolant in the engine oil could indicate other serious issues besides a failed water pump, such as a blown head gasket or a cracked cylinder head or block.

37   Even a pump that exhibits no outward signs of a problem, such as noise or leakage, can still be due for replacement. Removal for close examination is the only sure way to tell. Sometimes the fins on the back of the impeller can corrode to the point that cooling efficiency is diminished significantly.

Heater system

38   Little can go wrong with a heater. If the fan motor will run at all speeds, the electrical part of the system is okay. The three basic heater problems fall into the following general categories:

a) *Not enough heat*
b) *Heat all the time*
c) *No heat*

39   If there's not enough heat, the control valve or door is stuck in a partially open position, the coolant coming from the engine isn't hot enough, or the heater core is restricted. If the coolant isn't hot enough, the thermostat in the engine cooling system is stuck open, allowing coolant to pass through the engine so rapidly that it doesn't heat up quickly enough. If the vehicle is equipped with a temperature gauge instead of a warning light, watch to see if the engine temperature rises to the normal operating range after driving for a reasonable distance.

40   If there's heat all the time, the control valve or the door is stuck wide open.

41   If there's no heat, coolant is probably not reaching the heater core, or the heater core is plugged. The likely cause is a collapsed or plugged hose, core, or a frozen heater control valve. If the heater is the type that flows coolant all the time, the cause is a stuck door or a broken or kinked control cable.

Air conditioning system

42   If the cool air output is inadequate:

a) *Inspect the condenser coils and fins to make sure they're clear*
b) *Check the compressor clutch for slippage.*

c) *Check the blower motor for proper operation.*
d) *Inspect the blower discharge passage for obstructions.*
e) *Check the system air intake filter for clogging.*

43   If the system provides intermittent cooling air:

a) *Check the circuit breaker, blower switch and blower motor for a malfunction.*
b) *Make sure the compressor clutch isn't slipping.*
c) *Inspect the plenum door to make sure it's operating properly.*
d) *Inspect the evaporator to make sure it isn't clogged.*
e) *If the unit is icing up, it may be caused by excessive moisture in the system, incorrect super heat switch adjustment or low thermostat adjustment.*

44   If the system provides no cooling air:

a) *Inspect the compressor drivebelt. Make sure it's not loose or broken.*
b) *Make sure the compressor clutch engages. If it doesn't, check for a blown fuse.*
c) *Inspect the wire harness for broken or disconnected wires.*
d) *If the compressor clutch doesn't engage, bridge the terminals of the A/C pressure switch(es) with a jumper wire; if the clutch now engages, and the system is properly charged, the pressure switch is bad.*
e) *Make sure the blower motor is not disconnected or burned out.*
f) *Make sure the compressor isn't partially or completely seized.*
g) *Inspect the refrigerant lines for leaks.*
h) *Check the components for leaks.*
i) *Inspect the receiver-drier/accumulator or expansion valve/tube for clogged screens.*

45   If the system is noisy:

a) *Look for loose panels in the passenger compartment.*
b) *Inspect the compressor drivebelt. It may be loose or worn.*
c) *Check the compressor mounting bolts. They should be tight.*
d) *Listen carefully to the compressor. It may be worn out.*
e) *Listen to the idler pulley and bearing and the clutch. Either may be defective.*
f) *The winding in the compressor clutch coil or solenoid may be defective.*
g) *The compressor oil level may be low.*
h) *The blower motor fan bushing or the motor itself may be worn out.*
i) *If there is an excessive charge in the system, you'll hear a rumbling noise in the high pressure line, a thumping noise in the compressor, or see bubbles or cloudiness in the sight glass.*
j) *If there's a low charge in the system, you might hear hissing in the evaporator case at the expansion valve, or see bubbles or cloudiness in the sight glass.*

3.9 Insert a thermometer in the center vent, turn on the air conditioning system and wait for it to cool down; depending on the humidity, the output air should be 35 to 40 degrees cooler than the ambient air temperature

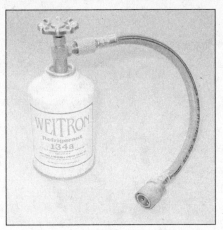

3.11 R-134a automotive air conditioning charging kit

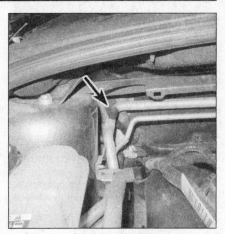

3.13 Location of the low-side charging port

---

3   Air conditioning and heating system - check and maintenance

Air conditioning system

Warning: *The air conditioning system is under high pressure. Do not loosen any hose fittings or remove any components until after the system has been discharged. Air conditioning refrigerant should be properly discharged into an EPA-approved recovery/recycling unit at a dealer service department or an automotive air conditioning repair facility. Always wear eye protection when disconnecting air conditioning system fittings.*

Caution: *All models covered by this manual use environmentally friendly R-134a. This refrigerant (and its appropriate refrigerant oils) are not compatible with R-12 refrigerant system components and must never be mixed or the components will be damaged.*

Caution: *When replacing entire components, additional refrigerant oil should be added equal to the amount that is removed with the component being replaced. Be sure to read the can before adding any oil to the system, to make sure it is compatible with the R-134a system.*

1   The following maintenance checks should be performed on a regular basis to ensure that the air conditioning continues to operate at peak efficiency.

a) *Inspect the condition of the compressor drivebelt. If it is worn or deteriorated, replace it (see Chapter 1).*

b) *Inspect the system hoses. Look for cracks, bubbles, hardening and deterioration. Inspect the hoses and all fittings for oil bubbles or seepage. If there is any evidence of wear, damage or leakage, replace the hose(s).*

c) *Inspect the condenser fins for leaves, bugs and any other foreign material that may have embedded itself in the fins. Use a fin comb or compressed air to remove debris from the condenser.*

d) *Make sure the system has the correct refrigerant charge.*

2   It's a good idea to operate the system for about ten minutes at least once a month. This is particularly important during the winter months because long term non-use can cause hardening, and subsequent failure, of the seals. Note that using the Defrost function operates the compressor.

3   If the air conditioning system is not working properly, proceed to Step 6 and perform the general checks outlined below.

4   Because of the complexity of the air conditioning system and the special equipment necessary to service it, in-depth troubleshooting and repairs beyond checking the refrigerant charge and the compressor clutch operation are not included in this manual. However, simple checks and component replacement procedures are provided in this Chapter. For more complete information on the air conditioning system, refer to the *Haynes Automotive Heating and Air Conditioning Manual*.

5   The most common cause of poor cooling is simply a low system refrigerant charge. If a noticeable drop in system cooling ability occurs, one of the following quick checks will help you determine if the refrigerant level is low.

Checking the refrigerant charge

6   Warm the engine up to normal operating temperature.

7   Place the air conditioning temperature selector at the coldest setting and put the blower at the highest setting.

8   After the system reaches operating temperature, feel the larger pipe exiting the evaporator at the firewall. The outlet (larger-diameter) pipe should be cold (the tubing that leads back to the compressor). If the evaporator outlet pipe is warm, the system probably needs a charge.

9   Insert a thermometer in the center air distribution duct **(see illustration)** while operating the air conditioning system at its maximum setting - the temperature of the output air should be 35 to 40 degrees F below the ambient air temperature (down to approximately 40 degrees F). If the ambient (outside) air temperature is very high, say 110 degrees F, the duct air temperature may be as high as 60 degrees F, but generally the air conditioning is 35 to 40 degrees F cooler than the ambient air.

10   Further inspection or testing of the system requires special tools and techniques and is beyond the scope of the home mechanic.

Adding refrigerant

Caution: *Make sure any refrigerant, refrigerant oil or replacement component you purchase is designated as compatible with R-134a systems.*

11   Purchase an R-134a automotive charging kit at an auto parts store **(see illustration)**. A charging kit includes a can of refrigerant, a tap valve and a short section of hose that can be attached between the tap valve and the system low side service valve.

Caution: *Never add more than one can of refrigerant to the system. If more refrigerant than that is required, the system should be evacuated and leak tested.*

12   Back off the valve handle on the charging kit and screw the kit onto the refrigerant can, making sure first that the O-ring or rubber seal inside the threaded portion of the kit is in place.

Warning: *Wear protective eyewear when dealing with pressurized refrigerant cans.*

13   Remove the dust cap from the low-side charging port and attach the hose's quick-connect fitting to the port **(see illustration)**.

Warning: *DO NOT hook the charging kit hose to the system high side! The fittings on the charging kit are designed to fit only on the low side of the system.*

14   Warm up the engine and turn On the air conditioning. Keep the charging kit hose away from the fan and other moving parts.

Note: *The charging process requires the compressor to be running. If the clutch cycles off, you can put the air conditioning switch on High and leave the car doors open to keep the clutch on and compressor working. The compressor can be kept on during the charging by removing the connector from the pressure switch and bridging it with a paper clip or jumper wire during the procedure.*

15　Turn the valve handle on the kit until the stem pierces the can, then back the handle out to release the refrigerant. You should be able to hear the rush of gas. Keep the can upright at all times, but shake it occasionally. Allow stabilization time between each addition.

Note: *The charging process will go faster if you wrap the can with a hot-water-soaked rag to keep the can from freezing up.*

16　If you have an accurate thermometer, you can place it in the center air conditioning duct inside the vehicle and keep track of the output air temperature. A charged system that is working properly should cool down to approximately 40 degrees F. If the ambient (outside) air temperature is very high, say 110 degrees F, the duct air temperature may be as high as 60 degrees F, but generally the air conditioning is 35 to 40 degrees F cooler than the ambient air.

17　When the can is empty, turn the valve handle to the closed position and release the connection from the low-side port. Reinstall the dust cap.

18　Remove the charging kit from the can and store the kit for future use with the piercing valve in the UP position, to prevent inadvertently piercing the can on the next use.

Heating systems

19　If the carpet under the heater core is damp, or if antifreeze vapor or steam is coming through the vents, the heater core is leaking. Remove it (see Section 9) and install a new unit (most radiator shops will not repair a leaking heater core).

20　If the air coming out of the heater vents isn't hot, the problem could stem from any of the following causes:

a) *The thermostat is stuck open, preventing the engine coolant from warming up enough to carry heat to the heater core. Replace the thermostat (see Section 4).*

b) *There is a blockage in the system, preventing the flow of coolant through the heater core. Feel both heater hoses at the firewall. They should be hot. If one of them is cold, there is an obstruction in one of the hoses or in the heater core, or the heater control valve is shut. Detach the hoses and back flush the heater core with a water hose. If the heater core is clear but circulation is impeded, remove the two hoses and flush them out with a water hose.*

c) *If flushing fails to remove the blockage from the heater core, the core must be replaced (see Section 9).*

4.5 Disconnect the hoses from the thermostat housing cover

Eliminating air conditioning odors

21　Unpleasant odors that often develop in air conditioning systems are caused by the growth of a fungus, usually on the surface of the evaporator core. The warm, humid environment there is a perfect breeding ground for mildew to develop.

22　The evaporator core on most vehicles is difficult to access, and factory dealerships have a lengthy, expensive process for eliminating the fungus by opening up the evaporator case and using a powerful disinfectant and rinse on the core until the fungus is gone. You can service your own system at home, but it takes something much stronger than basic household germ-killers or deodorizers.

23　Aerosol disinfectants for automotive air conditioning systems are available in most auto parts stores, but remember when shopping for them that the most effective treatments are also the most expensive. The basic procedure for using these sprays is to start by running the system in the RECIRC mode for ten minutes with the blower on its highest speed. Use the highest heat mode to dry out the system and keep the compressor from engaging by disconnecting the wiring connector at the compressor.

24　The disinfectant can usually comes with a long spray hose. Remove the cabin air filter (see Chapter), then insert the nozzle into the opening and spray according to the manufacturer's recommendations. Try to cover the whole surface of the evaporator core, by aiming the spray up, down and sideways. Follow the manufacturer's recommendations for the length of spray and waiting time between applications.

25　Once the evaporator has been cleaned, the best way to prevent the mildew from coming back again is to make sure your evaporator housing drain tube is clear.

Automatic heating and air conditioning systems

26　Some vehicles are equipped with an optional automatic climate control system. This system has its own computer that receives inputs from various sensors in the heating and air conditioning system. This computer, like the PCM, has self-diagnostic capabilities to help pinpoint problems or faults within the system. Vehicles equipped with automatic heating and air conditioning systems are very complex and considered beyond the scope of the home mechanic. Vehicles equipped with automatic heating and air conditioning systems should be taken to dealer service department or other qualified facility for repair.

4　Thermostat - replacement

Warning: *Wait until the engine is completely cool before performing this procedure.*

Removal

Note: *The thermostat and thermostat housing are replaced as an assembly.*

1　Disconnect the negative battery cable from the remote ground terminal (see Chapter 5).

2　Drain the cooling system (see Chapter 1). If the coolant is relatively new and still in good condition, save it and reuse it.

3　If you're working on a non-turbocharged model, raise the front of the vehicle and support it securely on jackstands, then remove the under-vehicle splash shield.

4　Cover the alternator and its electrical connectors with plastic-wrap.

5　Loosen the hose clamps, then detach the hoses from the fittings on the housing **(see illustration)**. If they are stuck, grasp them near the ends with a pair of adjustable pliers and twist to break the seal, then pull them off. If the hoses are old or deteriorated, cut them off and install new ones.

6　Remove the thermostat housing bolts, then detach the housing/thermostat assembly.

Installation

7　Clean the sealing surfaces. Also inspect the hoses, replacing them as necessary.

8　Install the thermostat housing, using a new gasket. Tighten the bolts to the torque listed in this Chapter's Specifications. Reconnect the hoses.

9　Refill the cooling system (see Chapter 1).

10　Start the engine and allow it to reach normal operating temperature, then check for leaks and proper thermostat operation.

5　Engine cooling fan and shroud assembly – removal and installation

1　Disconnect the negative battery cable from the remote ground terminal (see Chapter 5).

2　Carefully cut the foam strip that is glued

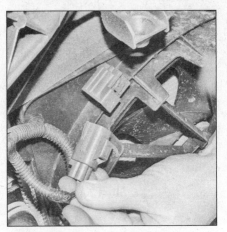

5.6a Disconnect the electrical connector . . .

5.6b . . . and release the wiring harness

5.7a Release the retaining clips

to the top of the fan shroud, radiator and condenser (this will free the shroud from the radiator). Obtain a new foam strip.

3   Raise the front of the vehicle and support it securely on jackstands.

4   Remove the air deflector below the bumper cover and the under-vehicle splash shield.

5   Remove the oil filter for clearance (see Chapter 1). Be prepared to catch and clean up spilled engine oil.

6   Disconnect the electrical connector from the cooling fan module and unclip the harness from the support brackets **(see illustrations)**.

7   Use a screwdriver to slightly open the retaining clips, then push up the fan and shroud assembly to release it **(see illustrations)**. Lower the assembly from the vehicle.

8   Installation is the reverse of the removal procedure. Check the engine oil level, adding as necessary (see Chapter 1).

6   Coolant temperature sending unit - check and replacement

Warning: *Wait until the engine is completely cool before beginning this procedure.*

The coolant temperature indicator system consists of a warning light or a temperature gauge on the dash and a coolant temperature sending unit mounted on the engine. On the models covered by this manual, the Engine Coolant Temperature (ECT) sensor is an information sensor for the Powertrain Control Module (PCM) and also functions as the coolant temperature sending unit for the temperature gauge. Information on the ECT sensor can be found in Chapter 6.

7   Radiator and expansion tank – removal and installation

Warning: *The engine must be completely cool before beginning this procedure.*

Radiator

Removal

1   Drain the coolant system (see Chapter 1).

2   Raise the front of the vehicle and support it securely on jackstands.

3   Remove the radiator fan and shroud assembly as described in Section 5.

4   While not strictly necessary, removal of the front bumper cover (see Chapter 11) is

5.7b With the fan removed the retaining clip can be clearly seen

highly recommended, as this allows better access to the coolant hoses and the condenser retaining clips.

5   Release the clamps and disconnect the upper and lower radiator and vent hoses **(see illustrations)**.

7.5a Remove the main coolant hoses . . .

7.5b . . . and the vent hose

7.6 Unclip the wiring harness

7.9 Remove the support panel

7.10 Remove the bolt from each end

6   Unclip the wiring harness from the radiator support panel **(see illustration)**.
7   If you're working on a turbo model, remove the intercooler as described in Chapter 4. Note this is not essential, but it avoids any possibility of damaging the intercooler as the radiator is removed.
8   Using straps or cable ties, secure the radiator and condenser. They should be supported separately, so that the radiator can be removed while leaving the condenser in place.
9   Unbolt and then remove the radiator/condenser support panel **(see illustration)**.
10   Remove the two bolts from each end of the radiator **(see illustration)**.
11   Working with care and crucially ensuring that no strain is placed on the condenser or AC refrigerant lines work the radiator free from the locating clips at each end. The radiator must be pushed up, before it can be lowered from the vehicle.
12   With the radiator released carefully lower it and then remove it from the vehicle **(see illustration)**. Anticipate some coolant spillage as the radiator is removed.

Inspection

13   With the radiator removed, it can be inspected for leaks and damage. If it leaks or

is damaged the radiator should be replaced – repair is not usually an option.
14   Insects and dirt can be removed from the radiator with a garden hose or a soft brush. Take care not to damage the cooling fins as this is being done.

Installation

15   Installation is the reverse of the removal procedure, noting the following points:
• Be sure the rubber mounts are seated properly at the base of the radiator.
• Refill the cooling system with the recommended coolant (see Chapter 1).
• Start the engine, and check for leaks. Allow the engine to reach normal operating temperature, indicated by the radiator top hose becoming hot. Once the engine has cooled (ideally, leave overnight), recheck the coolant level, and add more if required.

Expansion tank

Removal

16   With the engine completely cool, remove the expansion tank cap and use a suction gun to remove as much coolant as possible from the tank. Alternatively, drain the coolant until the level is below the tank (see Chapter 1).

17   Disconnect the upper hose(s) from the tank **(see illustration)**
18   Pull the expansion tank upwards to release it from the mounting tabs **(see illustration)**.
19   Detach the main coolant hose from the base of the expansion tank.
20   Wash out the tank and inspect it for cracks and chafing – replace it if it's damaged.

Installation

21   Installation is the reverse of the removal procedure. Refill the cooling system with the recommended coolant (see Chapter 1), then start the engine and allow it to reach normal operating temperature, indicated by the radiator upper hose becoming hot. Recheck the coolant level and add more if required, then check for leaks.

---

8   Water pump - replacement

Warning: *Wait until the engine is completely cool before beginning this procedure.*

Removal

1   Disconnect the negative battery cable from the remote ground terminal (see Chapter 5).

7.12 Lower the radiator

7.17 Remove the upper coolant hose(s) (some models only have one)

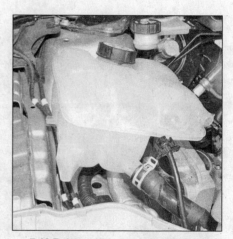

7.18 Release the expansion tank by pulling it upwards

8.4 Pull the refrigerant line out of its retaining clip

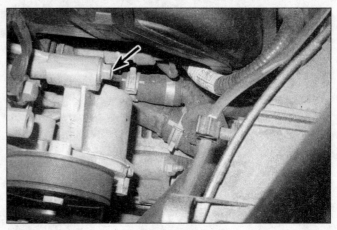

8.8 The drivebelt tensioner is mounted with two bolts (lower bolt not visible here)

2   Drain the cooling system (see Chapter 1).

Non-turbocharged models

3   Remove the coolant expansion tank (see Section 7).
4   Free the refrigerant line from its retaining clip over the right engine mount **(see illustration)**.
5   Remove the right-side engine mount bracket-to-body bolts.
6   Support the engine with a floor jack and block of wood placed under the oil pan.
Note: *Using the floor jack, raise the engine slightly, as necessary, to facilitate the remainder of the procedure.*
7   Loosen the water pump pulley bolts, then remove the drivebelt from the water pump pulley and position it out of the way (see Chapter 1).
8   Remove the drivebelt tensioner **(see illustration)**.
9   Remove the water pump pulley **(see illustration)**.
10   Remove the bolts attaching the water pump to the engine block and remove the pump from the engine **(see illustration)**. If the water pump is stuck, gently tap it with a

soft-faced hammer to break the seal.
11   Clean the bolt threads and the threaded holes in the engine **(see illustration)** and remove all corrosion and sealant. Remove all traces of old gasket material from the sealing surfaces.

Turbocharged models

12   Loosen the water pump pulley bolts, then remove the drivebelt from the pulley (see Chapter 1).
13   Remove the bolts and detach the pulley from the pump.
14   Remove the bolts attaching the water pump to the engine block and remove the pump from the engine **(see illustration 8.10)**. If the water pump is stuck, gently tap it with a soft-faced hammer to break the seal.
15   Clean the bolt threads and the threaded holes in the engine **(see illustration 8.11)** and remove all corrosion and sealant. Remove all traces of old gasket material from the sealing surfaces.

Installation

16   Compare the new pump to the old one to make sure that they're identical.

8.9 Remove the bolts and separate the water pump pulley from the pump

17   Apply a thin film of RTV sealant to hold the new O-ring in place during installation. Carefully mate the pump to the water pump housing.
18   Install the water pump bolts and tighten them to the torque listed in this Chapter's Specifications.

8.10 Remove the water pump bolts

8.11 Clean the water pump bolt threads, the threaded holes in the housing and the pump mating surface of the housing

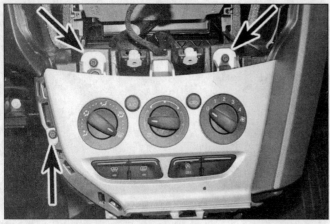

10.3a Remove the screws . . .   **10.3b . . . and disconnect the electrical connectors**

19   The remainder of installation is the reverse of removal. Refill the cooling system when you're done (see Chapter 1).
20   Operate the engine to check for leaks.

9   Heater/ventilation components – removal and installation

Warning: *The air conditioning system is under high pressure. DO NOT loosen any fittings or remove any components until after the system has been discharged. Air conditioning refrigerant must be properly discharged into an EPA-approved container at a dealer service department or an automotive air conditioning repair facility. Always wear eye protection when disconnecting air conditioning system fittings.*

1   Disconnect the negative battery cable from the remote ground terminal (see Chapter 5).

Blower motor

2   Remove the glove box (see Chapter 11) and the Body Control Module (BCM) (see Chapter 12).
3   Working under the right side of the instrument panel, disconnect the electrical connector from the air inlet mode actuator motor,

then remove the screws and the inlet duct.
4   Disconnect the electrical connector from the blower motor.
5   Working under the left side of the instrument panel, release the blower motor retaining tang and rotate the motor counterclockwise to release it from the housing.
6   Working under the right side of the instrument panel, have an assistant reach into the housing and grasp the hub of the fan, then guide the motor and fan out from the right side of the housing.
7   Installation is the reverse of removal.

Blower motor resistor

8   The resistor is located behind the cabin filter housing. Access is gained by removing the glove box as described in Chapter 11.
9   With the glovebox removed, disconnect the electrical connector. Access is still difficult – a short 'stubby' Torx screwdriver will help here. Remove the single screw and pull the resistor from the housing.
10   Installation is the reverse of removal.

Heater core

11   Remove the instrument panel complete with the heater/air conditioning housing (see Chapter 12).

12   Remove the firewall seal from the heater core pipes, then remove the heater mounting bracket.
13   Working on the driver's side of the housing, remove the evaporator core cover and the heater tube cover.
14   Remove the air intake plenum.
15   Remove the heater core cover and remove the heater core from the housing.
16   Installation is the reverse of removal. Use new seals where applicable.

10   Heater/air conditioning control panel – removal and installation

1   Disconnect the negative battery cable from the remote ground terminal (see Chapter 5).
2   Remove the audio unit as described in Chapter 12.
3   Remove the mounting screws, pull the control panel forward and disconnect the electrical connectors **(see illustrations)**.
4   If required, remove the control panel from the trim panel **(see illustration)**.
5   Individual components of the control panel are not available. If any of the switches or controls are faulty then the complete panel must be replaced.
6   Installation is the reverse of the removal procedure.

11   Air conditioning system components – removal and installation

Warning: *The air conditioning system is under high pressure. DO NOT loosen any fittings or remove any components until after the system has been discharged. Air conditioning refrigerant must be properly discharged into an EPA-approved container at a dealer service department or an automotive air conditioning repair facility. Always wear eye protection when disconnecting air conditioning system fittings.*

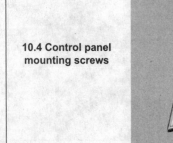

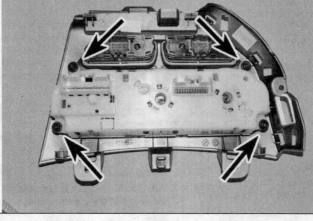

10.4 Control panel mounting screws

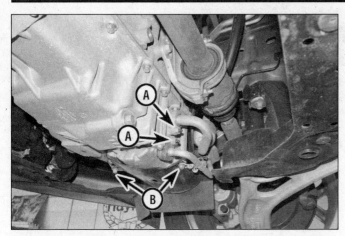

11.17 Air conditioning compressor refrigerant line fitting nuts (A) and shield bolts (B, two of three shown)

11.18 Remove the compressor

Condenser

1   Have the air conditioning system refrigerant discharged and recovered by an air conditioning technician.
2   Disconnect the negative battery cable from the remote ground terminal (see Chapter 5).
3   Apply the parking brake, then raise the front of the vehicle and support it securely on jackstands.
4   Remove the engine undershield and the air deflector from beneath the front bumper. Some models have an additional rail fitted between the engine undershield and the front bumper.
5   Disconnect the refrigerant lines from the condenser. Immediately cap the open fittings, to prevent the entry of dirt and moisture.
6   The condenser is placed between the radiator and, on models so equipped, the active shutter grille. While it is possible to separate the radiator from the condenser (as described for radiator removal in Section 7, the easiest solution is to remove the radiator first and then remove the condenser. Alternatively the radiator, condenser, cooling fan and active shutter grille can be removed as a complete assembly.
7   Remove the front bumper as described in Chapter 11.
8   Support the radiator and condenser assembly and then remove the radiator as described in Section 7.
9   Lower the condenser, taking care not to damage the radiator or the active shutter grille.
10   Installation is the reverse of removal. Replace the O-rings and lubricate them with refrigerant oil. Tighten the refrigerant line-to-condensor nuts to the torque listed in this Chapter's Specifications. If installing a new condenser, pour out the oil from the old condenser and add that amount, plus an additional 2 ounces (60 ml) of R-134a compatible refrigerant oil to it before installing.
11   Have the system evacuated, charged and leak-tested by the specialist who discharged it.

Compressor

12   Have the air conditioning system refrigerant discharged and recovered by an air conditioning technician.
13   Disconnect the negative battery cable from the remote ground terminal (see Chapter 5).
14   Loosen the right-front wheel lug nuts. Apply the parking brake, then raise the front of the vehicle and support it securely on jackstands.
15   Remove the right-front wheel and the wheel arch liner (see Chapter 11).
16   Remove the drivebelt (see Chapter 1).
17   Remove the nuts to disconnect the refrigerant lines from the compressor **(see illustration)**. Plug the line connections to prevent entry of any dirt or moisture. Discard the O-ring seals; new ones must be installed.
18   Unbolt the compressor from the cylinder block/crankcase, unplug its electrical connector, then withdraw the compressor from the vehicle **(see illustration)**.
Note: *Keep the compressor level during handling and storage. If the compressor has seized, or if you find metal particles in the refrigerant lines, the system must be flushed out by an air conditioning technician, and the receiver-drier must be replaced.*

If you are installing a new compressor

19   Remove the drain bolt from the old compressor and drain the oil into a measuring cup. Turn the compressor shaft eight revolutions while doing this to expel all oil.

a)   If the amount of oil measured is less than 3 ounces (89 ml), drain 4 ounces (118 ml) of oil from the new compressor.
b)   If the amount of oil measured is 3 ounces (89 ml), drain 3 ounces (89 ml) of oil from the new compressor.
c)   If the amount of oil measured is 4 ounces (118 ml), drain 2 ounces (60 ml) of oil from the new compressor.
d)   If the amount of oil measured is 5 ounces (148 ml), drain 1 ounce (30 ml) of oil from the new compressor.
e)   If the amount of oil measured is more than 5 ounces (148 ml), don't drain any oil from the new compressor.

Caution: *These figures apply to OEM replacement compressors. If the instructions that came with your new compressor differ, follow them instead.*
20   Tighten the compressor drain bolt to the torque listed in this Chapter's Specifications.

Installing old or new compressor

21   Prior to installation, turn the compressor clutch center six times, to disperse any oil that has collected in the head.
22   Reinstall the compressor in the reverse order of removal; replace all seals that were disturbed. Tighten the compressor mounting bolts to the torque listed in this Chapter's Specifications. Tighten the refrigerant line-to-air conditioning compressor nuts to the torque listed in this Chapter's Specifications.
23   Have the system evacuated, charged and leak-tested by the shop that discharged it.

Receiver-drier

24   Have the air conditioning system refrigerant discharged and recovered by an air conditioning technician.
25   Apply the parking brake, then raise the front of the vehicle and support it securely on jackstands.
26   Remove the under-vehicle splash shield and the air deflector from beneath the bumper cover.
27   Support the radiator and condenser assembly using straps or cable ties and then remove the support panel from the base of the assembly **(see illustration 7.10)**.
28   Remove the plug from the base of the receiver-drier, then remove the snap-ring with

11.28a Remove the receiver drier plug . . .

11.28b . . . then remove the snap-ring

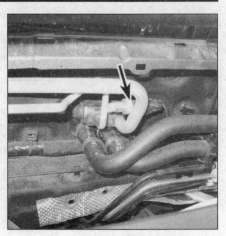

11.32 Location of the refrigerant pressure sensor

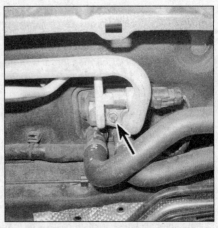

11.40 Refrigerant line fitting nut at the thermostatic expansion valve

snap-ring pliers **(see illustrations)**.

29   Screw a long bolt into the base of the receiver-drier and pull the receiver-drier element from the housing.

30   Reinstall the receiver-drier element in the reverse order of removal. Replace all seals and lubricate them with R-134a compatible refrigerant oil before installing. Reinstall the remainder of the components, and then have the system leak tested and recharged with by the shop that discharged it.

Refrigerant pressure sensor

31   Have the air conditioning system refrigerant discharged and recovered by an air conditioning technician.

32   The sensor is threaded into a fitting on the high-pressure line at the center of the firewall **(see illustration)**.

33   Disconnect the electrical connector and unscrew the sensor.

Caution: *Counterhold the fitting on the refrigerant line to prevent distorting the line.*

34   Installation is the reverse of the removal procedure. Replace the O-rings and lubricate with refrigerant oil.

35   Have the system evacuated, charged and leak-tested by the shop that discharged it.

Thermostatic expansion valve

Note: *The thermostatic expansion valve is located at the center of the firewall.*

36   Have the air conditioning system refrigerant discharged and recovered by an air conditioning technician.

37   On some 2.0L Duratec HE models, the expansion tank must be removed (see Section 7).

38   On 2.0L EcoBoost models, remove the cowel panel (see Chapter 12), the expansion tank (see Section 7) and the engine cover (if equipped).

39   Disconnect the electrical connector from the refrigerant pressure sensor **(see illustration 11.32)**.

40   Unscrew the nut and detach the refrigerant line from the thermostatic expansion valve **(see illustration)**.

41   Remove the two bolts from the center of the thermostatic expansion valve and detach the valve. Remove and discard the old O-rings.

42   Installation is the reverse of the removal procedure. Use new O-rings and lubricate them with refrigerant oil. Tighten the valve bolts and the refrigerant line manifold nut to the torque values listed in this Chapter's Specifications.

43   Have the system evacuated, charged and leak-tested by the shop that discharged it, adding the amount of refrigerant oil that was recovered at the time of discharging.

Chapter 4
Fuel and exhaust systems

Contents

Specifications

Fuel system pressure
  Non-turbocharged engines
    Key On, engine Off .... 72.5 psi (500 kPa)
    Engine running.. 79.8 psi (550 kPa)
  Turbocharged engines
    Key On, engine Off .... 58 psi (400 kPa)
    Engine running.. 55.1 to 79.8 psi (380 to 550 kPa)

Torque specifications

Note: One foot-pound (ft-lb) of torque is equivalent to 12 inch-pounds (in-lbs) of torque. Torque values below approximately 15 ft-lbs are expressed in inch-pounds, because most foot-pound torque wrenches are not accurate at these smaller values.

	Ft-lbs (unless otherwise indicated)	Nm
Fuel rail mounting bolts*	18	24
High-pressure fuel pump mounting bolts*		
Step 1	177 in-lbs	20
Step 2	Tighten an additional 45-degrees	
High-pressure fuel line fittings		
Step 1	133 in-lbs	15
Step 2	Tighten an additional 45-degrees	
High-pressure fuel line bracket bolts	89 in-lbs	10
Throttle body mounting fasteners	89 in-lbs	10 Nm

*Use new bolts.

Torque specifications	Ft-lbs (unless otherwise indicated)	Nm

Note: *One foot-pound (ft-lb) of torque is equivalent to 12 inch-pounds (in-lbs) of torque. Torque values below approximately 15 ft-lbs are expressed in inch-pounds, because most foot-pound torque wrenches are not accurate at these smaller values.*

Turbocharger

	Ft-lbs (unless otherwise indicated)	Nm
Coolant line banjo bolts	21	28
Oil line banjo bolts	18	24
Oil drain tube bolts	89 in-lbs	10
Turbocharger mounting studs-to-cylinder head*	150 in-lbs	17
Turbocharger mounting nuts*	37	50
Turbocharger bypass valve bolts	53 in-lbs	6

*Use new fasteners during installation.

2.3a Remove the retainers from the right-side under-dash panel and remove the panel for access to the Body Control Module (BCM)

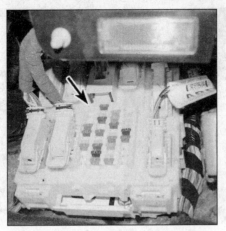

2.3b The fuel pump fuse (A) is located on the BCM; it's fuse no. F56

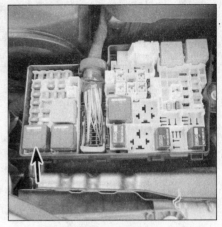

2.3c The PCM main relay is located in the underhood fuse/relay box (be sure to check the fuse box cover or your Owner's Manual for the relay location on your particular vehicle)

1   General Information

Fuel system warnings

1   Gasoline is extremely flammable and repairing fuel system components can be dangerous. Consider your automotive repair knowledge and experience before attempting repairs which may be better suited for a professional mechanic.

- *Don't smoke or allow open flames or bare light bulbs near the work area*
- *Don't work in a garage with a gas-type appliance (water heater, clothes dryer)*
- *Use fuel-resistant gloves. If any fuel spills on your skin, wash it off immediately with soap and water*
- *Clean up spills immediately*
- *Do not store fuel-soaked rags where they could ignite*
- *Prior to disconnecting any fuel line, you must relieve the fuel pressure (see Section 3)*
- *Wear safety glasses*
- *Have a proper fire extinguisher on hand*

Fuel system

2   The fuel system consists of the fuel tank, electric fuel pump/fuel level sending unit (located in the fuel tank), fuel rail and fuel injectors. The fuel injection system is a multi-port system; multi-port fuel injection uses timed impulses to inject the fuel directly into the intake port of each cylinder. The Powertrain Control Module (PCM) controls the injectors. The PCM monitors various engine parameters and delivers the exact amount of fuel required into the intake ports.

3   Fuel is circulated from the fuel pump to the fuel rail through fuel lines running along the underside of the vehicle. Various sections of the fuel line are either rigid metal or nylon, or flexible fuel hose. The various sections of the fuel hose are connected either by quick-connect fittings or threaded metal fittings.

Exhaust system

4   The exhaust system consists of the exhaust manifold, catalytic converter(s), muffler(s), tailpipe and all connecting pipes, flanges and clamps. The catalytic converters are an emission control device added to the exhaust system to reduce pollutants.

2   Troubleshooting

Electric fuel pump

1   The electric fuel pump is located inside the fuel tank. Sit inside the vehicle with the windows closed, turn the ignition key to ON (not START) and listen for the sound of the fuel pump as it's briefly activated. You will only hear the sound for a second or two, but that sound tells you that the pump is working. Alternatively, have an assistant listen at the fuel filler cap.

2   A fuel cut-off system is used in case of an accident. If there has been an accident, the restraint system sends a signal to the Fuel Pump Driver Module (FPDM) and shuts the module off. To reset the FPDM, turn the ignition key to the "OFF" position, then to the "ON" position and start the engine.

Note: *This may take a few attempts.*

3   Check the fuel pump fuse and the Powertrain Control Module (PCM) main relay **(see illustrations)**. If the fuse and relay are okay, check the wiring back to the fuel pump. If the fuse, relay and wiring are okay, the fuel pump is probably defective. If the pump runs continuously with the ignition key in the ON position, the Powertrain Control Module (PCM) is probably defective. Have the PCM checked by a professional mechanic.

Fuel injection system

Note: *The following procedure is based on the assumption that the fuel pump is working and the fuel pressure is adequate (see Section 4).*

4   Check all electrical connectors that are related to the system. Check the ground wire connections for tightness.

5   Verify that the battery is fully charged (see Chapter 5).

6   Inspect the air filter element (see Chapter 1).

7   Check the air induction system between the throttle body and the intake manifold for air leaks. Also inspect the condition of all vacuum hoses connected to the intake manifold and to the throttle body.

8   Remove the air intake duct from the throttle body and look for dirt, carbon, varnish, or other residue in the throttle body, particularly around the throttle plate. If it's dirty, clean it with carb cleaner, a toothbrush and a clean shop towel.

9   Check for the presence of Diagnostic Trouble Codes (DTCs) stored in the Powertrain Control Module (PCM) (see Chapter 6).

3   Fuel pressure relief procedure

Warning: *Gasoline is extremely flammable. See **Fuel system warnings** in Section 1.*

Warning: *These models are equipped with Gasoline Turbocharged Direct Injection (GTDI) engines. Removing the fuel pump control module fuse and running the engine until it dies will remove most of the pressure from both the low and high-pressure sides of the fuel system. Once the pressure on the low-pressure side of the system has been relieved, wait at least 20 minutes before loosening any fuel line fittings in the engine compartment.*

Low-pressure fuel system

1   Remove the fuel filler cap to relieve any pressure built-up in the fuel tank.

2   Remove the fuel pump control module fuse from the Body Control Module (BCM) **(see illustration 2.3b)**.

3.6 Loosen the high pressure fuel tube with a flare-nut wrench while covering it with a shop towel

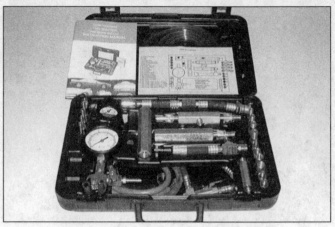

4.1a This fuel pressure testing kit contains all the necessary fittings and adapters, along with the fuel pressure gauge, to test most automotive systems

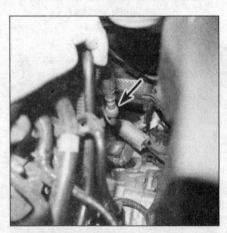

4.1b Detach the fuel feed hose from the metal fuel line near the firewall and connect a fuel pressure gauge between the hose and the metal line

3   Attempt to start the engine; it should immediately stall. Crank the engine several more times to ensure the fuel system has been completely relieved.

4   Disconnect the negative battery cable from the remote ground terminal (see Chapter 5).

5   It's a good idea to cover any fuel connection to be disassembled with rags to absorb the residual fuel that may leak out. Properly dispose of the rags.

High-pressure fuel system

Warning: *Wrap a shop towel around the high-pressure line flare nut prior to loosening the flare nut to absorb fuel when relieving fuel pressure.*

6   Relieve the pressure from the low-pressure side of the system. Remove the insulator from the high-pressure fuel pump, place a flare-nut wrench on the high-pressure fuel tube at the high-pressure pump **(see illustration)**, then wrap the wrench and nut with a shop towel to absorb any remaining fuel pressure while loosening the nut.

7   Loosen the high-pressure fuel tube-to-fuel injection pump flare nut and release the remaining pressure.

Warning: *The manufacturer states that the high-pressure fuel tube must be replaced with a new one whenever it is loosened or removed.*

8   When installing the new fuel tube, tighten the fitting nuts to the torque listed in this Chapter's Specifications.

4   Fuel pressure - check

Warning: *Gasoline is extremely flammable. See* **Fuel system warnings** *in Section 1.*

Note: *The following procedure assumes that the in-tank fuel pump is receiving voltage and runs.*

1   Relieve the fuel system pressure (see Section 3), disconnect the fuel supply hose at the metal fuel line (see Section 5), then use an adapter to connect the fuel pressure gauge between the fuel hose and the metal line **(see illustrations)**.

2   Reinstall the fuel pump control module fuse into the Body Control module (BCM) **(see illustration 2.3b)**.

3   Connect the negative battery cable to the remote ground terminal (see Chapter 5).

4   Start the engine and allow it to idle. Immediately check for leaks. Note the gauge reading as soon as the pressure stabilizes, and compare it with the pressure listed in this Chapter's specifications.

5   If the fuel pressure is not within specifications as noted in this Chapter's Specifications, check the following:

a) *Check for a restriction in the fuel system (kinked fuel line, plugged fuel pump inlet strainer or clogged fuel filter). If no restrictions are found, replace the fuel pump module (see Section 9).*

b) *If the fuel pressure is higher than specified, replace the fuel pump module (see Section 9).*

6   Turn off the engine. Fuel pressure should not fall more than 8 psi over five minutes. If it does, the problem could be a leaky fuel injector, fuel line leak, or faulty fuel pump module.

7   Relieve the fuel system pressure (see Section 3), then disconnect the fuel pressure gauge. Wipe up any spilled gasoline.

8   Reconnect the fuel hose to the metal line.

9   Reconnect the battery (see Chapter 5). Turn the ignition key to the On position and check for fuel leaks.

5   Fuel lines and fittings - general information and disconnection

Warning: *Gasoline is extremely flammable. See* **Fuel system warnings** *in Section 1.*

1   Relieve the fuel pressure before servicing fuel lines or fittings (see Section 3), then disconnect the negative battery cable from the remote ground terminal (see Chapter 5).

2   The fuel supply line connects the fuel pump in the fuel tank to the fuel rail on the engine. The Evaporative Emission (EVAP) system lines connect the fuel tank to the EVAP canister and connect the canister to the intake manifold.

3   Whenever you're working under the vehicle, be sure to inspect all fuel and evaporative emission lines for leaks, kinks, dents and other damage. Always replace a damaged fuel or EVAP line immediately.

4   If you find signs of dirt in the lines during disassembly, disconnect all lines and blow them out with compressed air. Inspect the fuel strainer on the fuel pump pick-up unit for damage and deterioration.

Steel tubing

5   It is critical that the fuel lines be replaced with lines of equivalent type and specification.

6   Some steel fuel lines have threaded fittings. When loosening these fittings, hold the stationary fitting with a wrench while turning the tube nut.

Disconnecting Fuel Line Fittings

Two-tab type fitting; depress both tabs with your fingers, then pull the fuel line and the fitting apart

On this type of fitting, depress the two buttons on opposite sides of the fitting, then pull it off the fuel line

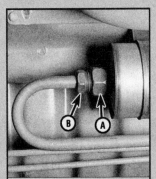

Threaded fuel line fitting; hold the stationary portion of the line or component (A) while loosening the tube nut (B) with a flare-nut wrench

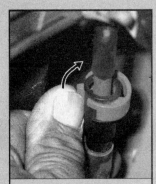

Plastic collar-type fitting; rotate the outer part of the fitting

Metal collar quick-connect fitting; pull the end of the retainer off the fuel line and disengage the other end from the female side of the fitting . . .

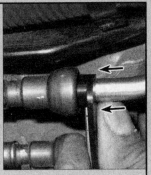

. . . insert a fuel line separator tool into the female side of the fitting, push it into the fitting and pull the fuel line off the pipe

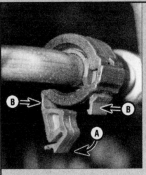

Some fittings are secured by lock tabs. Release the lock tab (A) and rotate it to the fully-opened position, squeeze the two smaller lock tabs (B) . . .

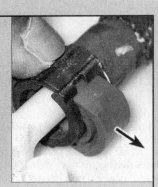

. . . then push the retainer out and pull the fuel line off the pipe

Spring-lock coupling; remove the safety cover, install a coupling release tool and close the tool around the coupling . . .

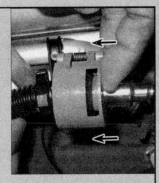

. . . push the tool into the fitting, then pull the two lines apart

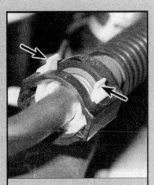

Hairpin clip type fitting: push the legs of the retainer clip together, then push the clip down all the way until it stops and pull the fuel line off the pipe

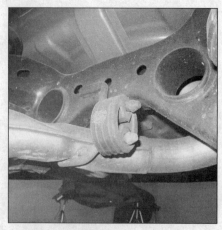

6.1 A typical exhaust system hanger. Inspect regularly and replace at the first sign of damage or deterioration

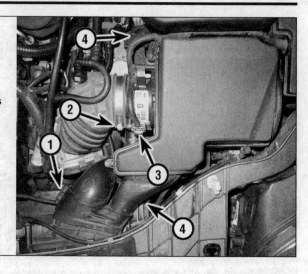

7.1 Air filter housing details

1 Strap (unhook)
2 Duct clamp
3 MAF sensor electrical connector
4 Mounting grommets

Plastic tubing

7   When replacing fuel system plastic tubing, use only original equipment replacement plastic tubing.
Caution: *When removing or installing plastic fuel line tubing, be careful not to bend or twist it too much, which can damage it. Also, plastic fuel tubing is NOT heat resistant, so keep it away from excessive heat.*

Flexible hoses

8   When replacing fuel system flexible hoses, use only original equipment replacements.
9   Don't route fuel hoses (or metal lines) within four inches of the exhaust system or within ten inches of the catalytic converter. Make sure that no rubber hoses are installed directly against the vehicle, particularly in places where there is any vibration. If allowed to touch some vibrating part of the vehicle, a hose can easily become chafed and it might start leaking. A good rule of thumb is to maintain a minimum of 1/4-inch clearance around a hose (or metal line) to prevent contact with the vehicle underbody.

6   Exhaust system servicing - general information

Warning: *Allow exhaust system components to cool before inspection or repair. Also, when working under the vehicle, make sure it is securely supported on jackstands.*
1   The exhaust system consists of the exhaust manifold, catalytic converter, muffler, tailpipe and all connecting pipes, flanges and clamps. The exhaust system is isolated from the vehicle body and from chassis components by a series of rubber hangers **(see illustration)**. Periodically inspect these hangers for cracks or other signs of deterioration, replacing them as necessary.
2   Conduct regular inspections of the exhaust system to keep it safe and quiet. Look

for any damaged or bent parts, open seams, holes, loose connections, excessive corrosion or other defects which could allow exhaust fumes to enter the vehicle. Do not repair deteriorated exhaust system components; replace them with new parts.
3   If the exhaust system components are extremely corroded, or rusted together, a cutting torch is the most convenient tool for removal. Consult a properly-equipped repair shop. If a cutting torch is not available, you can use a hacksaw, or if you have compressed air, there are special pneumatic cutting chisels that can also be used. Wear safety goggles to protect your eyes from metal chips and wear work gloves to protect your hands.
4   Here are some simple guidelines to follow when repairing the exhaust system:
a) *Work from the back to the front when removing exhaust system components.*
b) *Apply penetrating oil to the exhaust system component fasteners to make them easier to remove.*
c) *Use new gaskets, hangers and clamps.*
d) *Apply anti-seize compound to the threads of all exhaust system fasteners during reassembly.*
e) *Be sure to allow sufficient clearance between newly installed parts and all points on the underbody to avoid overheating the floor pan and possibly damaging the interior carpet and insulation. Pay particularly close attention to the catalytic converter and heat shield.*

7   Air filter housing – removal and installation

1   Loosen the air duct hose clamp and disconnect the Mass Airflow (MAF) sensor electrical connector **(see illustration)**.
2   Unhook the rubber retaining strap at the front of the intake snorkel.
3   Pull the air filter housing upwards to remove it. The pegs on the base of the housing fit into rubber grommets. These pegs may prove troublesome to release, and some effort may be needed.

4   When installing, locate the pegs into the grommets and push down firmly to engage them in the grommets. Lubricate them with a silicone-based grease if necessary. Make sure the duct clamp is securely tightened to prevent air leaks.

8   Fuel tank – removal, inspection and installation

Warning: *Gasoline is extremely flammable. See* **Fuel system warnings** *in Section 1.*

Removal

1   Run the fuel level as low as possible prior to removing the tank. There is no drain plug (and siphoning may prove difficult; if it IS attempted, use a siphoning kit, available at most auto parts stores) but it may be possible to partially drain the tank.
2   Relieve the fuel system pressure (see Section 3).
3   Disconnect the negative battery cable from the remote ground terminal (see Chapter 5).
4   Chock the front wheels. Loosen the rear wheel lug nuts, then raise the rear of the vehicle and support it securely on jackstands. Remove the rear wheels.
5   Unhook the exhaust system mounting rubbers from the center and rear hangers, and allow the exhaust system to rest on the rear suspension crossmember.
6   Remove the nuts securing the flange of the exhaust system rear section, then maneuver the rear section to one side, securing it in place using cable ties/wire/string.
7   Remove the bolts and pull the left-side air deflector shield rearwards to release its retaining clip, then remove the protective cover from the EVAP canister **(see illustrations)**.
8   Unscrew the nuts and remove the exhaust center and rear section heat shields from the vehicle underside **(see illustration)**.
9   Loosen the clamp and disconnect the fuel tank filler hose **(see illustration)**. Do

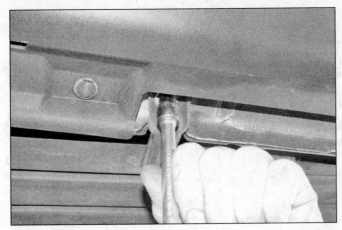

8.7a Remove the bolts and remove the left-side air deflector shield

8.7b Remove the protective cover

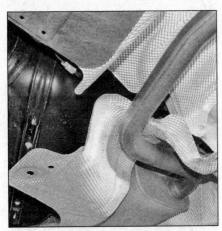

8.8 Remove the nuts and remove the heat shields beneath the fuel tank

8.9 Detach the filler hose

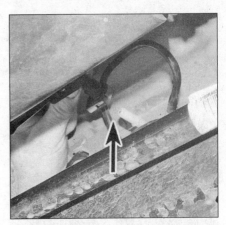

8.10 Depress the release button and disconnect the vent hose from the rear of the tank

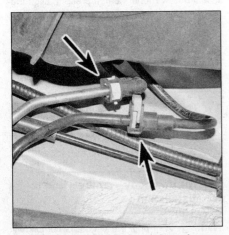

8.11 Disconnect the fuel supply and purge valve hoses at the front of the tank

8.14a Remove the bolts securing the retaining straps at the rear . . .

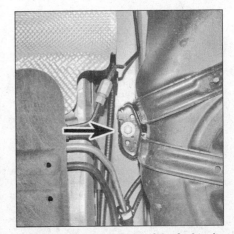

8.14b . . . and at the front of the fuel tank

not use any sharp-edged tools to release the hose from its fitting.

10 Depress the release button and disconnect the fuel tank vent hose from the rear of the tank to the evaporative emissions system **(see illustration)**.

11 Disconnect the fuel supply hose and

EVAP canister purge valve hose from the front of the tank **(see illustration)**.

12 Support the tank using a floor jack and a large sheet of wood to spread the load.

13 Note exactly how the fuel tank retaining straps are arranged to make installation easier. In particular, note their installed order

under the retaining bolt heads, where applicable. The left-side strap is on top at the front mounting point.

14 Unbolt and remove the fuel tank retaining straps **(see illustrations)**, but do not lower the tank at this stage.

15 Partially lower the tank on the jack, tak-

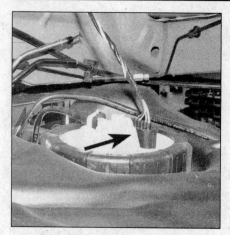

8.15a Disconnect the electrical connector . . .

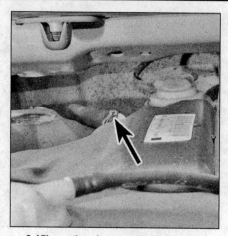

8.15b . . . then loosen the clamp and disconnect the breather hose

9.3 A pair of pliers can be used to unscrew the fuel pump module lock ring

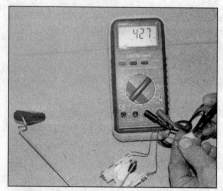

9.5 Measure the resistance of the sending unit at full and zero float arm deflection

ing care that no strain is placed on any fuel lines or wiring. As soon as the electrical connector for the Fuel Tank Pressure (FTP) sensor and the fuel pump/gauge sender on top of the tank is accessible, reach in and disconnect them, then loosen the clamp and disconnect the breather hose from the top of the tank (see illustrations). Where applicable, detach the EVAP canister hose from the top of the tank.

16 Lower the fuel tank to the ground, checking all the way down that no hoses or wiring are under any strain. Remove the tank from under the car.

Inspection

17 While removed, the fuel tank can be inspected for damage or deterioration. Removal of the fuel pump/fuel gauge sender unit (see Section 9) will allow a partial inspection of the interior. If the tank is contaminated with sediment or water, rinse it out with a little clean fuel. Do not under any circumstances try to repair a damaged fuel tank.

Warning: *Check with your local disposal facility or environmental agency to see if they will accept the contaminated fuel.*

18 While the fuel tank is removed from the car, it should be placed in a safe area where sparks or open flames cannot ignite the fumes coming out of the tank. Be especially careful inside garages where a gas-type appliance is located.

19 Check the condition of the lower filler pipe and replace it if necessary.

Installation

20 Installation is the reverse of the removal procedure, noting the following points:

a) *Ensure that all hose and wiring connections are securely joined.*

b) *When reconnecting the quick-connect fittings, press them together until the locking lugs snap into their groove.*

c) *Tighten the tank strap retaining bolts securely.*

d) *If evidence of contamination was found, do not return any previously-drained fuel to the tank unless it is carefully filtered first.*

9 Fuel pump module/fuel gauge sending unit – removal and installation

Note: *Gasoline is extremely flammable. See Fuel system warnings in Section 1.*

1 A combined fuel pump and fuel gauge sending unit module is located in the top face of the fuel tank. The module can only be removed from the tank after the tank has been removed from the vehicle. Refer to Section 8 and remove the fuel tank.

2 With the fuel tank removed, clean around the fuel pump module connections, couplings, flange surface and surrounding areas so no debris falls into the tank, then disconnect the fuel supply pipe (if still attached to the tank) from the fitting by squeezing the quick-release lugs.

3 Remove the pump module lock ring using a lock ring removal tool (available at most auto parts stores), or use a pair of large water pump pliers to unscrew the lock ring by turning it counterclockwise (see illustration).

4 Carefully lift out the fuel pump/gauge sender unit from the tank. Take care that the sending unit float and arm are not damaged as the unit is removed.

5 The level sender unit can be tested by connecting an ohmmeter across the sender terminals, and measuring its resistance (see illustration). Check that the resistance changes smoothly and progressively as the arm is moved through the full range of travel.

6 Installation is the reverse of removal. Install a new rubber seal. If present, align the arrow on the top of the module with the mark on the top of the tank.

10 Fuel tank roll-over valve – removal and installation

1 The roll-over valve is built into the top of the fuel tank. It is not possible to access the valve. Its purpose is to prevent fuel loss if the car becomes inverted in a crash.

11 Throttle body - removal and installation

Warning: *Wait until the engine is completely cool before beginning this procedure.*

1 Disconnect the negative battery cable from the remote ground terminal (see Chapter 5).

2 On non-turbo models, loosen the clamp and remove the air intake duct from the throttle body (see illustration).

3 On turbocharged models, loosen the clamp and remove the Charge Air Cooler (CAC) duct from the throttle body (see illustration).

11.2 Throttle body details (non-turbocharged models)

1. *Intake duct hose clamp*
2. *Electrical connector*
3. *Mounting bolts (two of four visible)*

11.3 Loosen the Charge Air Cooler (CAC) duct clamp (turbo models)

4   Disconnect the electrical connector from the throttle body.

5   Remove the throttle body mounting fasteners and detach the throttle body from the intake manifold. Discard the gasket; it should be replaced with a new one. Cover the intake manifold opening with a clean shop towel.

6   Installation is the reverse of removal. Use a new gasket and tighten the throttle body mounting fasteners to the torque listed in this Chapter's Specifications.

12 High-pressure fuel pump - removal and installation

Warning: *Gasoline is extremely flammable. See* **Fuel system warnings** *in Section 1.*

Removal

1   Relieve the fuel system pressure (see Section 3).

2   Disconnect the negative battery cable from the remote ground terminal (see Chapter 5).

3   Remove the noise insulator from the fuel injection pump **(see illustration)**.

4   Disconnect the fuel injection pump electrical connector **(see illustration)**.

5   Disconnect the fuel feed line from the fuel pump.

Warning: *Wrap the high-pressure fuel line fitting with a rag as they are loosened.*

6   Loosen the fittings at each end of the high-pressure fuel line, remove the fuel line bracket bolt, then remove the high-pressure fuel line.

Note: *The manufacturer recommends replacing the high-pressure fuel line whenever it is removed.*

7   Loosen the fuel pump bolts **(see illustration 12.4)**, alternating one turn at a time until the bolts and pump can be removed. The bolts must be replaced after they have been removed.

Caution: *The fuel pump is under heavy spring pressure - if the bolts are not loosened evenly and one complete turn at a time, the pump or housing will be damaged.*

8   Remove and discard the fuel pump O-ring.

Installation

9   Before installing the fuel injection pump, check the pump tappet in the pump body for wear or damage **(see illustration)**.

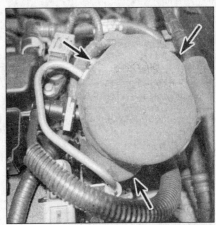

12.3 Spread the sides of the noise insulator apart while pulling up

10   Install a new O-ring on the pump, then apply clean oil to the pump tappet and the O-ring. Install the tappet into the bore.

11   Rotate the engine clockwise until the cam lobe for the fuel injection pump is on the lowest point or Bottom Dead Center (BDC)

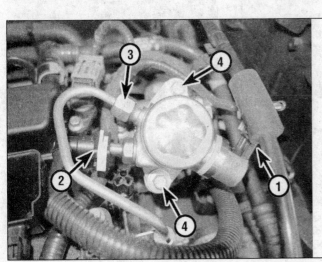

12.4 High-pressure fuel pump details

1. *Electrical connector*
2. *Fuel feed line*
3. *High-pressure fuel line fitting*
4. *Fuel pump mounting bolts*

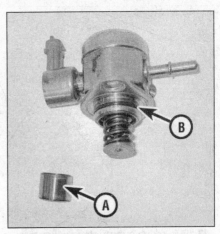

12.9 Check the high-pressure fuel pump tappet for wear (A). Install a new O-ring (B) on the pump

12.11 The cam lobe (and tappet) must be at its lowest point before installing the pump

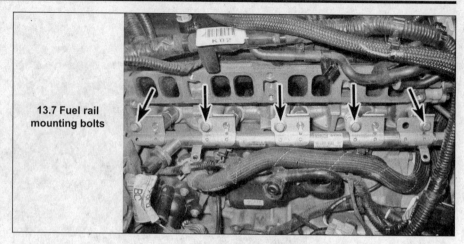

13.7 Fuel rail mounting bolts

(see illustration). The pump tappet will be as low as it can go.

12 Set the pump in the housing, then install the new bolts hand tight.

13 Tighten the bolts in even stages, alternating between the bolts, to the torque listed in this Chapter's Specifications.

14 The remainder of installation is the reverse of removal. Install a new high-pressure fuel line and tighten the fitting nuts to the torque listed in this Chapter's Specifications.

13 Fuel rail and injectors - removal and installation

Warning: *Gasoline is extremely flammable. See* **Fuel system warnings** *in Section 1.*

1 Relieve the fuel system pressure (see Section 3).

2 Disconnect the negative battery cable from the remote ground terminal (see Chapter 5).

3 Remove the intake manifold (see Chapter 2A).

4 Disconnect the high pressure fuel lines

from the fuel pump and fuel rail (see Section 12).

Note: *The manufacturer recommends replacing the high-pressure fuel line anytime it is removed.*

5 Disconnect the electrical connectors for all wiring that shares the harness with the fuel injectors, then disconnect the four fuel injector electrical connectors. Using a trim removal tool, disengage the two pin-type retainers that secure the wiring harness and harness insulator from the fuel rail, then push the harness aside.

6 Clean the area around each injector using compressed air.

7 Remove the fuel rail mounting fasteners **(see illustration)** and discard them, then remove the fuel rail and injectors. Use new fuel rail bolts on installation.

Note: *The fuel injectors may remain in the fuel rails when the rail is removed, but normally they remain in the cylinder heads and require the use of a removal tool.*

8 Remove each fuel injector retaining clip with a pair of needle-nose pliers, then remove the injector from its bore in the fuel rail. Remove and discard the upper injector O-rings. Repeat this procedure for each injector.

Note: *Even if you only removed the fuel rail assembly to replace a single injector or a leak-*

ing O-ring, replace all of the fuel injector retaining clips and O-rings.

9 If any injectors stick in the cylinder head, use special tool #310-206 attached to a slide hammer to remove the injector(s).

10 Remove the old combustion chamber Teflon sealing ring, upper O-ring and support ring from each injector **(see illustration)**.

Caution: *Be extremely careful not to damage the groove for the seal or the rib in the floor of the groove. If you damage the groove or the rib, you must replace the injector.*

11 Before installing the new Teflon seal on each injector, thoroughly clean the groove for the seal and the injector shaft. Remove all combustion residue and varnish with a clean shop rag.

Teflon seal installation using the special tools

12 The manufacturer recommends that you use the special injector tools (310-207, or equivalent) to install the Teflon lower seals on the injectors **(see illustration):** Install the seal assembly cone on the injector, install the special sleeve on the injector and use the sleeve to push on the assembly cone, which pushes the Teflon seal into place on its groove **(see illustration)**. Do NOT use any lubricants to do so.

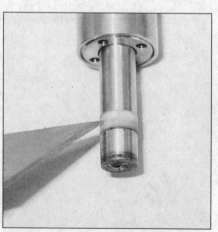

13.10 To remove the Teflon sealing ring, cut it off with a hobby knife (be careful not to scratch the injector groove)

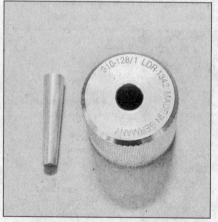

13.12a The special tools recommended for installing and sizing the Teflon seals (typical)

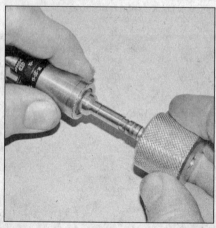

13.12b Slide the seal onto the injector with a rotary motion

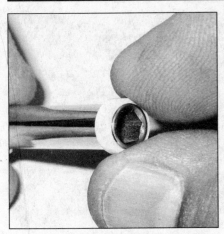

13.15 Slide the new Teflon seal onto the end of a socket that's the same diameter as the end of the fuel injector . . .

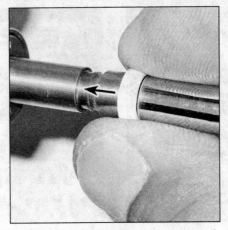

13.16 . . . align the socket with the end of the injector and slide the seal onto the injector and into its mounting groove

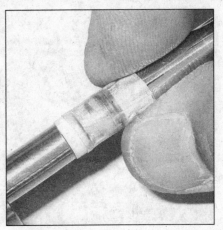

13.17a Use the socket to push a short section of plastic tubing onto the end of the injector and over the new seal . . .

13 Pushing the Teflon seal into place in its groove expands it slightly. The use of a sizing sleeve (tool no. 310-1567, or equivalent) is the preferred method install the seals and then to shrink the seals after they've been installed. Using a clockwise rotating motion of about 180 degrees, install the sleeve onto the injector and over the Teflon seal until the sleeve hits its stop, then carefully turn the sleeve counterclockwise 180 degrees as you pull it off the injector.

Teflon seal installation without special tools

14 If you don't have the special injector tool set, the Teflon seal can be installed using this method: First, find a socket that is equal or very close in diameter to the diameter of the end of the fuel injector.
15 Work the new Teflon seal onto the end of the socket (see illustration).
16 Place the socket against the end of the injector (see illustration) and slide the seal from the socket onto the injector. Do NOT use any lubricants to do so. Continue pushing the seal onto the injector until it seats into its mounting groove.
17 Because the inside diameter of the seal has to be stretched open to fit over the bore of the socket and the injector, its outside diameter is now slightly too large - it is no longer flush with the surface of the injector. It must be shrunk back to its original size. To do so, push a piece of plastic tubing with an interference fit onto the end of the socket; a plastic straw that fits tightly on the injector will work. After pushing the plastic tubing onto the socket about an inch, snip off the rest of the tubing, then use the socket to push the tubing onto the end of the injector (see illustration), sliding it onto the injector until it completely covers the new seal (see illustration). Leave the tubing on for a few hours, then remove it. The seal should now be shrunk back its original outside diameter, or close to it.

13.17b . . . then leave the plastic tubing in place for several hours to compress the new seal

Injector and fuel rail installation

18 Install a new support ring on the top of the injector, then lubricate the new upper O-ring with clean engine oil and install it on the injector. Do not oil the new Teflon seal. Note that the O-ring is installed above the support ring (see illustration).
19 Thoroughly clean the injector bores with a small nylon brush.
20 Insert each injector into its bore in the fuel rail. Install the new retaining clips on the injectors.
21 Install the injectors and fuel rail assembly on the cylinder head. Tighten the fuel rail mounting bolts to the torque listed in this Chapter's Specifications, starting with the center bolt and working outwards.
22 The remainder of installation is the reverse of removal.
23 If removed, install a new fuel rail pressure sensor (see Chapter 6).

13.18 Note that the upper O-ring (1) is installed above the support ring (2)

14 Turbocharger - removal and installation

Warning: *Wait until the engine is completely cool before beginning this procedure.*
Caution: *Do not disassemble the turbocharger or try to adjust the wastegate actuator. The turbocharger or possibly even the engine could be damaged.*
Caution: *Whenever the turbocharger, Charge Air Cooler (CAC) or cooler tubes are removed, always cover any opening to prevent debris from falling in. The system is easily damaged, so carefully clean all openings before reassembling.*

Removal

1 Raise the vehicle and support it securely on jackstands.
2 Remove the catalytic converter (see Chapter 6).
3 Remove the Charge Air Cooler inlet tube and the turbocharger inlet pipe.
4 Drain the cooling system (see Chapter 1).

14.5 Remove the turbocharger heat shield mounting bolts and remove the shield

14.6a Detach the hoses at each end of the coolant pipe

14.6b Disconnect the coolant outlet line from the turbocharger and the engine block

14.7a Remove the oil supply line banjo bolt and detach the line from the turbocharger

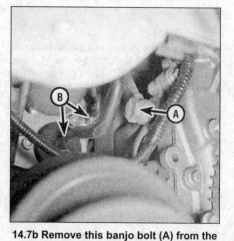

14.7b Remove this banjo bolt (A) from the other end of the oil line. Detach the line from the block, then pull out the filter and install a new one. (B) are coolant lines

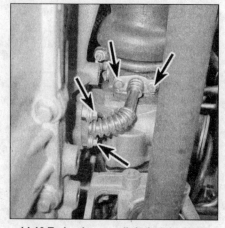

14.10 Turbocharger oil drain tube bolts

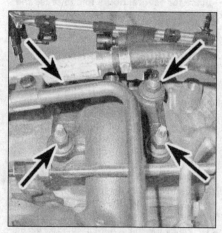

14.11 Remove the turbocharger mounting nuts

Note: *Always replace the linked sealing washers to the banjo bolts and coolant lines.*

7   Remove the oil supply line banjo bolts and discard the sealing washers (**see illustrations**), then pull the inline oil supply filter out of the engine block.

8   Disconnect the vacuum lines and electri-

cal connectors to the turbocharger.

Note: *Early production vehicles are equipped with metal vacuum tubes and later models are equipped with nylon vacuum tubes.*

9   Detach the coolant lines from the right end of the turbocharger (**see illustration 14.6b**).

10   Remove the oil drain tube mounting bolts and drain tube, then discard the gasket and drain tube (**see illustration**).

Note: *The manufacturer requires the oil drain tube be replaced whenever it is removed.*

11   Remove and discard the turbocharger mounting nuts (**see illustration**), then carefully maneuver the turbocharger from the vehicle.

12   Use a stud removal tool (available from most auto parts stores) to remove the turbocharger studs from the cylinder head. Discard the studs.

Installation

13   Install the four new studs in the cylinder head and tighten them to the torque listed in this Chapter's Specifications.

14   Install the turbocharger and tighten the new nuts to the torque listed in this Chapter's Specifications.

5   Remove the turbocharger heat shield mounting bolts and remove the shield (**see illustration**).

6   From above, squeeze and slide back the hose clamps on the coolant line (**see illustration**). From below, remove the coolant outlet line banjo bolt and disconnect the line from the turbocharger (**see illustration**).

15   Install the new oil drain tube and new drain tube gaskets, then install and tighten the bolts to the torque listed in this Chapter's Specifications.

16   Install new oil line sealing washers, oil supply filter and coolant line washers. Tighten the banjo bolts to the torque listed in this Chapter's Specifications.

17   The remainder of installation is the reverse of removal.

18   Refill the cooling system and change the engine oil and filter (see Chapter 1).

15 Charge Air Cooler (CAC) - removal and installation

1   Raise the front of the vehicle and support it securely on jackstands.

2   Remove the engine undershield and the air deflector from beneath the bumper cover.

3   Remove the cooling fan and shroud as described in Chapter 3.

4   Support the radiator and condenser assembly with suitable straps.

5   Unbolt and remove the radiator support panel, as described in Chapter 3.

6   Loosen the hose clamps and remove the inlet and outlet hoses from the CAC

7   Lower the CAC from the vehicle.

8   Installation is the reverse of removal.

16 Fuel Pump Driver Module (FPDM) - removal and installation

Note: *The FPDM is located behind the right-rear C-pillar trim.*

1   Disconnect the negative battery cable from the remote ground terminal (see Chapter 5).

2   Remove the right-rear C-pillar trim panel (see Chapter 11).

3   Disconnect the Fuel Pump Driver Module (FPDM) electrical connector.

4   Pull the FPDM from the sheetmetal (it is adhered with adhesive backing). If necessary, carefully pry it off.

5   Clean the mounting surface of all old adhesive. Peel the backing paper off the new FPDM, set it over the locating studs, then press it firmly into place.

6   Reconnect the electrical connector.

7   The remainder of Installation is the reverse of removal.

Notes

Chapter 5
Engine electrical systems

Contents

Specifications

General
Battery voltage... 12.6 to 12.9 volts
Charging voltage .... 13.5 to 15.0 volts

Torque specifications

	Ft-lbs (unless otherwise indicated)	Nm

Note: *One foot-pound (ft-lb) of torque is equivalent to 12 inch-pounds (in-lbs) of torque. Torque values below approximately 15 ft-lbs are expressed in inch-pounds, because most foot-pound torque wrenches are not accurate at these smaller values.*

	Ft-lbs	Nm
Alternator mounting fasteners		
Upper mounting stud (non-turbo models)	71 in-lbs	8
Mounting nuts or bolts	18	25
Ignition coil mounting bolts	89 in-lbs	10
Starter mounting fasteners		
Mounting bolts	26	35
Support bracket nuts	97 in-lbs	11

1   General information and precautions

General information

Ignition system

1   The electronic ignition system consists of the Crankshaft Position (CKP) sensor, the Camshaft Position (CMP) sensor, the Knock Sensor (KS), the Powertrain Control Module (PCM), the ignition switch, the battery, the individual ignition coils or a coil pack, and the spark plugs. For more information on the CKP, CMP and KS sensors, as well as the PCM, refer to Chapter 6.

Charging system

2   The charging system includes the alternator (with an integral voltage regulator), the Powertrain Control Module (PCM), the Body Control Module (BCM), a charge indicator light on the dash, the battery, a fuse or fusible link and the wiring connecting all of these components. The charging system supplies electrical power for the ignition system, the lights, the radio, etc. The alternator is driven by a drivebelt.

Starting system

3   The starting system consists of the battery, the ignition switch, the starter relay, the Powertrain Control Module (PCM), the Body Control Module (BCM), the Transmission Range (TR) switch, the starter motor and solenoid assembly, and the wiring connecting all of the components.

Precautions

4   Always observe the following precautions when working on the electrical system:

a) *Be extremely careful when servicing engine electrical components. They are easily damaged if checked, connected or handled improperly.*
b) *Never leave the ignition switched on for long periods of time when the engine is not running.*
c) *Never disconnect the battery cables while the engine is running.*
d) *Maintain correct polarity when connecting battery cables from another vehicle during jump starting (see "Booster battery (jump) starting" at the front of this manual).*

e) *Always disconnect the cable from the negative battery terminal before working on the electrical system, but read the battery disconnection procedure first (see Section 3).*

5   It's also a good idea to review the safety-related information regarding the engine electrical systems located in "Saftey First!" at the front of this manual.

2   Troubleshooting

Ignition system

1   If a malfunction occurs in the ignition system, do not immediately assume that any particular part is causing the problem. First, check the following items:

a) *Make sure that the cable clamps at the battery terminals are clean and tight.*
b) *Test the condition of the battery (see Steps 21 through 24). If it doesn't pass all the tests, replace it.*
c) *Check the ignition coil or coil pack connections (see Section 6).*
d) *Check any relevant fuses in the engine compartment fuse and relay box (see Chapter 12). If they're burned, determine the cause and repair the circuit.*

Check

Warning: *Because of the high voltage generated by the ignition system, use extreme care when performing a procedure involving ignition components.*
Note: *Most problems with the ignition system will result in a Diagnostic Trouble Code (DTC) being stored in the Powertrain Control Module (PCM). See Chapter 6 for information on how to extract trouble codes from the PCM.*
Note: *You'll need a spark tester for the following test. Spark testers are available at most auto supply stores.*

2   If the engine turns over but won't start, verify that there is sufficient ignition voltage to fire the spark plugs as follows.

3   On models with a coil-over-plug type ignition system, remove an ignition coil and install the tester between the boot at the lower end of the coil and the spark plug **(see illustration)**. On models with spark plug wires, disconnect a spark plug wire from a spark

plug and install the tester between the spark plug wire boot and the spark plug.
Caution: *Do NOT crank the engine or allow it to run for more than five seconds; running the engine for more than five seconds may set a Diagnostic Trouble Code (DTC) for a cylinder misfire.*

4   Crank the engine and note whether or not the tester flashes.

Models with a coil-over-plug type ignition system

5   If the tester flashes during cranking, the coil is delivering sufficient voltage to the spark plug to fire it. Repeat this test for each cylinder to verify that the other coils are OK.

6   If the tester doesn't flash, remove a coil from another cylinder and swap it for the one being tested. If the tester now flashes, you know that the original coil is bad. If the tester still doesn't flash, the PCM or wiring harness is probably defective. Have the PCM checked out by a dealer service department or other qualified repair shop (testing the PCM is beyond the scope of the do-it-yourselfer because it requires expensive special tools).

7   If the tester flashes during cranking but a misfire code (related to the cylinder being tested) has been stored, the spark plug could be fouled or defective, or the coil could be be malfunctioning under load.

Models with spark plug wires

8   If the tester flashes during cranking, sufficient voltage is reaching the spark plug to fire it.

9   Repeat this test on the remaining cylinders.

10   Proceed on this basis until you have verified that there's a good spark from each spark plug wire. If there is, then you have verified that the coils in the coil pack are functioning correctly and that the spark plug wires are OK.

11   If there is no spark from a spark plug wire, then either the coil is bad, the plug wire is bad or a connection at one end of the plug wire is loose. Assuming that you're using new plug wires or known good wires, then the coil is probably defective. Also inspect the coil pack electrical connector. Make sure that it's clean, tight and in good condition.

12   If all the coils are firing correctly, but the engine misfires, then one or more of the plugs might be fouled. Remove and check the spark plugs or install new ones (see Chapter 1).

13   No further testing of the ignition system is possible without special tools. If the problem persists, have the ignition system tested by a dealer service department or other qualified repair shop.

Charging system

14   If a malfunction occurs in the charging system, do not automatically assume the alternator is causing the problem. First check the following items:

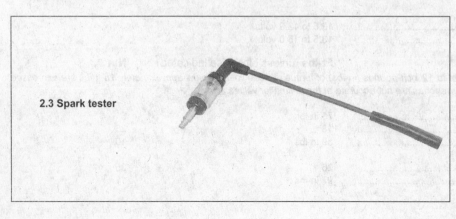

2.3 Spark tester

2.21 To test the open circuit voltage of the battery, touch the negative probe of the voltmeter to the negative terminal and the positive probe to the positive terminal of the battery; a fully charged battery should be at least 12.6 volts

2.23 Connect a battery load tester to the battery and check the battery condition under load following the tool manufacturer's instructions

a) Check the drivebelt tension and condition, as described in Chapter 1. Replace it if it's worn or deteriorated.

b) Make sure the alternator mounting bolts are tight (see Section 7).

c) Inspect the alternator wiring harness and the connectors at the alternator and voltage regulator. They must be in good condition, tight and have no corrosion.

d) Check the fusible link (if equipped) or main fuse in the underhood fuse/relay box. If it is burned, determine the cause, repair the circuit and replace the link or fuse (the vehicle will not start and/or the accessories will not work if the fusible link or main fuse is blown) (see Chapter 12).

e) Start the engine and check the alternator for abnormal noises (a shrieking or squealing sound indicates a bad bearing).

f) Check the battery as described later in this Section. Make sure it's fully charged and in good condition (one bad cell in a battery can cause overcharging by the alternator).

g) Disconnect the battery cables as described in Section 4. Inspect the battery posts and the cable clamps for corrosion. Clean them thoroughly if necessary (see Chapter 1). Reconnect the cables as described in Section 4.

Alternator - check

15 Use a voltmeter to check the battery voltage with the engine off. It should be at least 12.6 volts **(see illustration 2.21)**.

16 Start the engine and check the battery voltage again. It should now be approximately 13.5 to 15 volts.

17 If the voltage reading is more or less than the specified charging voltage, the voltage regulator is probably defective, which will require replacement of the alternator (the voltage regulator is not replaceable separately).

Remove the alternator and have it bench tested (most auto parts stores will do this for you) (see Section 7).

18 The charging system (battery) light on the instrument cluster lights up when the ignition key is turned to ON, but it should go out when the engine starts.

19 If the charging system light stays on after the engine has been started, there is a problem with the charging system. Before replacing the alternator, check the battery condition, alternator belt tension and electrical cable connections.

20 If replacing the alternator doesn't restore voltage to the specified range, have the charging system tested by a dealer service department or other qualified repair shop.

Battery - check

21 Check the battery state of charge. Visually inspect the indicator eye on the top of the battery (if equipped with one); if the indicator eye is black in color, charge the battery as described in Chapter 1. Next perform an open circuit voltage test using a digital voltmeter.
Note: *The battery's surface charge must be removed before accurate voltage measurements can be made. Turn on the high beams for ten seconds, then turn them off and let the vehicle stand for two minutes. With the engine and all accessories Off, touch the negative probe of the voltmeter to the negative terminal of the battery and the positive probe to the positive terminal of the battery* **(see illustration)**. *The battery voltage should be 12.6 volts or slightly above. If the battery is less than the specified voltage, charge the battery before proceeding to the next test. Do not proceed with the battery load test unless the battery charge is correct.*

22 Disconnect the negative battery cable, then the positive cable from the battery.

23 Perform a battery load test. An accurate check of the battery condition can only be performed with a load tester **(see illustration)**. This test evaluates the ability of the battery to

operate the starter and other accessories during periods of high current draw. Connect the load tester to the battery terminals. Load test the battery according to the tool manufacturer's instructions. This tool increases the load demand (current draw) on the battery.

24 Maintain the load on the battery for 15 seconds and observe that the battery voltage does not drop below 9.6 volts. If the battery condition is weak or defective, the tool will indicate this condition immediately.
Note: *Cold temperatures will cause the minimum voltage reading to drop slightly. Follow the chart given in the manufacturer's instructions to compensate for cold climates. Minimum load voltage for freezing temperatures (32 degrees F) should be approximately 9.1 volts.*

Starting system

The starter rotates, but the engine doesn't

25 Remove the starter (see Section 8). Check the overrunning clutch and bench test the starter to make sure the drive mechanism extends fully for proper engagement with the flywheel ring gear. If it doesn't, replace the starter.

26 Check the flywheel ring gear for missing teeth and other damage. With the ignition turned off, rotate the flywheel so you can check the entire ring gear.

The starter is noisy

27 If the solenoid is making a chattering noise, first check the battery (see Steps 21 through 24). If the battery is okay, check the cables and connections.

28 If you hear a grinding, crashing metallic sound when you turn the key to Start, check for loose starter mounting bolts. If they're tight, remove the starter and inspect the teeth on the starter pinion gear and flywheel ring gear. Look for missing or damaged teeth.

29 If the starter sounds fine when you first

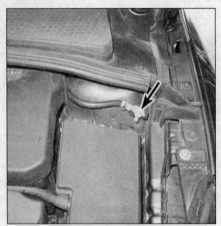

3.3 To cut battery voltage from all of the electrical systems on the vehicle, remove this nut and detach the cable from the stud. Be sure to wrap the cable with a rag or cover it with tape to prevent it from making contact with a grounding point

4.2 Release the clips on the sides of the battery cover, then lift it off

4.5 Detach the battery monitoring sensor from the from the battery tray

turn the key to Start, but then stops rotating the engine and emits a zinging sound, the problem is probably a defective starter drive that's not staying engaged with the ring gear. Replace the starter.

The starter rotates slowly

30   Check the battery (see Steps 21 through 24).
31   If the battery is okay, verify all connections (at the battery, the starter solenoid and motor) are clean, corrosion-free and tight. Make sure the cables aren't frayed or damaged.
32   Check that the starter mounting bolts are tight so it grounds properly. Also check the pinion gear and flywheel ring gear for evidence of a mechanical bind (galling, deformed gear teeth or other damage).

The starter does not rotate at all

33   Check the battery (see Steps 21 through 24).
34   If the battery is okay, verify all connections (at the battery, the starter solenoid and motor) are clean, corrosion-free and tight. Make sure the cables aren't frayed or damaged.
35   Check all of the fuses in the underhood fuse/relay box (see Chapter 12).
36   Check that the starter mounting bolts are tight so it grounds properly.
37   Check for voltage at the starter solenoid "S" terminal when the ignition key is turned to the start position. If voltage is present, replace the starter/solenoid assembly (see Section 8). If no voltage is present, the problem could be the starter relay, the Transmission Range (TR) switch or clutch start switch, or with an electrical connector somewhere in the circuit (see the wiring diagrams). Also, on many modern vehicles, the Powertrain Control Module (PCM) and the Body Control Module (BCM) control the voltage signal to the starter solenoid; on such vehicles a special scan tool is required for diagnosis.

3   Battery - disconnection and reconnection

Caution: *Always disconnect the negative cable from the remote ground terminal FIRST and hook it up LAST or the battery may be shorted by the tool being used to loosen the cable clamps.*
1   Some systems on the vehicle require battery power to be available at all times, either to maintain continuous operation (alarm system, power door locks, etc.), or to maintain control unit memory (radio station presets, Powertrain Control Module and other control units). When the battery is disconnected, the power that maintains these systems is cut. So, before you disconnect the battery, please note that on a vehicle with power door locks, it's a wise precaution to remove the key from the ignition and to keep it with you, so that it does not get locked inside if the power door locks should engage accidentally when the battery is reconnected!
2   *Devices known as "memory-savers" can be used to avoid some of these problems. Precise details vary according to the device used. The typical memory saver is plugged into the cigarette lighter and is connected to a spare battery. Then the vehicle battery can be disconnected from the electrical system. The memory saver will provide sufficient current to maintain audio unit security codes, PCM memory, etc. and will provide power to always hot circuits such as the clock and radio memory circuits.*
Warning: *Some memory savers deliver a considerable amount of current in order to keep vehicle systems operational after the main battery is disconnected. If you're using a memory saver, make sure that the circuit concerned is actually open before servicing it.*
Warning: *If you're going to work near any of the airbag system components, the battery MUST be disconnected and a memory saver must NOT be used. If a memory saver is used, power will be supplied to the airbag, which means that it could accidentally deploy and cause serious personal injury.*

Disconnection

3   To disconnect the battery for service procedures requiring power to be cut from the vehicle, remove the nut securing the negative battery cable to the bracket on the strut tower at the left-rear corner of the engine compartment **(see illustration)**. Wrap the cable end with a plastic bag or shop rag, or cover it with tape, to prevent the cable end from coming into accidental contact with a grounding point (any surrounding metal).

Reconnection

4   After reconnecting the ground cable to the stud and tightening the nut securely, the power window system will have to be initialized. Do this for each window, one at a time:
  a) *Start the engine.*
  b) *Operate the window switch until the window closes completely, then let go of the switch.*
  c) *Operate the window switch in the closed position and hold it there for at least one second.*
  d) *Lower the glass until it is completely open, then release the switch.*
  e) *Raise the glass until the window is completely closed.*
  f) *Verify that the one-touch (up and down) feature functions properly.*

4   Battery and battery tray - removal and installation

1   Disconnect the negative battery cable from the remote ground terminal (see Section 3).
2   Release the clips and remove the forward battery cover **(see illustration)**.
3   Remove the air filter housing (see Chapter 4).
4   Loosen the clamp nut and disconnect the battery positive cable.
5   Slide the battery monitoring sensor up and out of the front of the battery tray, then position it out of the way **(see illustration)**.

4.6 Remove the nuts and lift off the battery hold-down clamp nuts

4.8 Pull the battery forward and up, removing it from the tray

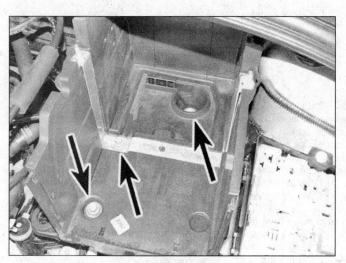

4.9a Remove the bolts . . .

4.9b . . . and lift out the battery tray

Note: *If necessary, unscrew the nuts and detach the cables from the battery monitoring sensor, then remove the sensor completely.*

6   Remove the battery hold-down clamp **(see illustration)**.

7   Slide the battery forward for access to the negative cable clamp, then loosen the nut and detach the cable from the battery terminal.

Note: *If desired, the cable can remain attached to the battery.*

8   Remove the battery from the tray **(see illustration)**.

9   If it's necessary to remove the battery tray, unclip the wiring harness from the side of the tray (if applicable), then remove the mounting bolts. Lift out the battery tray **(see illustrations)**.

10   Installation is the reverse of removal. Initialize the windows as described in Section 3.

Warning: *Do not reconnect the negative battery cable to the remote ground terminal until the battery has been completely reinstalled.*

5   Battery cables - replacement

1   When removing the cables, always disconnect the negative battery cable cable from the remote ground terminal first and hook it up last, or you might accidentally short out the battery with the tool you're using to loosen the cable clamps (see Section 3). Even if you're only replacing the cable for the positive terminal, be sure to disconnect the negative cable from the remote ground terminal first.

2   Trace each of the cables to their opposite ends and disconnect them (also unbolt any routing brackets). Note the routing of each cable before disconnecting it to ensure correct installation.

Note: *If you are replacing the negative cable, remove the battery far enough to access the negative cable clamp (see Section 4).*

3   If you are replacing any of the old cables, take them with you when buying new cables. It is vitally important that you replace the cables with identical parts.

4   Clean the threads of the solenoid or ground connection with a wire brush to remove rust and corrosion. Apply a light coat of battery terminal corrosion inhibitor or petroleum jelly to the threads to prevent future corrosion.

5   Attach the cable to the solenoid or ground connection and tighten the mounting nut/bolt securely. Then route the cables as noted during removal and secure the cables with any mounting brackets.

6   Before connecting a new cable to the battery, make sure that it reaches the battery post without having to be stretched.

7   Connect the cable to the positive battery terminal first, then connect the negative cable to the remote ground terminal (see Section 3).

6.3 Ignition coil details

1   Electrical connector (depress the tab to unlock)
2   Mounting fastener
3   Twist as you pull the coil from the valve cover

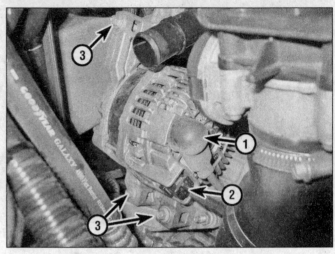

7.7 Alternator mounting details (turbo model shown)

1 B+ terminal		3 Mounting bolts
2 Electrical connector		

6   Ignition coils - replacement

1   Disconnect the negative battery cable from the remote ground terminal (see Section 3).
2   If you're working on a turbocharged model, remove the engine cover by pulling it straight up, then remove the charge air duct that passes over the top of the engine.
3   Disconnect the electrical connector from the ignition coil **(see illustration)**.
4   Remove the mounting fastener from the ignition coil.
5   Grasp the coil firmly, twist it and pull it off the spark plug.
6   Installation is the reverse of removal. Apply a small amount of silicone brake grease or other dielectric compound to the inside of the coil-on-plug boots before installing.

7   Alternator - removal and installation

1   Disconnect the negative battery cable from the remote ground terminal (see Section 3).
2   Loosen the right-front wheel lug nuts. Raise the front of the vehicle and support it securely on jackstands. Remove the wheel.
3   Remove the under-vehicle splash shield and the inner fender splash shield.
4   If you're working on a turbo model, remove the air conditioning compressor drivebelt (see Chapter 1).
5   Rotate the drivebelt tensioner away from the drivebelt, then slip the drivebelt off of the alternator pulley (see Chapter 1).

6   If you're working on a turbo model, disconnect the electrical connector from the air conditioning compressor, then remove the air conditioning compressor mounting bolts (see Chapter 3) and move the compressor out of the way. Support the compressor with wire or rope; don't let it hang by the refrigerant lines.
Warning: Don't disconnect the refrigerant lines.
7   Pull back the protective cover from the alternator's battery terminal, remove the nut and disconnect the battery cable from the alternator **(see illustration)**. Set the battery cable aside. Disconnect the electrical connector from the alternator.
8   Remove the alternator mounting fasteners and remove the alternator from the bottom of the vehicle.
Note: On non-turbo models also remove the stud for the upper mounting nut.
9   If you're replacing the alternator, take the old one with you when purchasing the replacement unit. Make sure that the new/rebuilt unit looks identical to the old alternator. Look at the electrical terminals on the backside of the alternator. They should be the same in number, size and location as the terminals on the old alternator. Finally, look at the identification numbers. They will be stamped into the housing or printed on a tag attached to the housing. Make sure that the ID numbers are the same on both alternators.
10   Many new/rebuilt alternators DO NOT have a pulley installed, so you might have to swap the pulley from the old unit to the new/rebuilt one. When buying an alternator, find out the store's policy regarding pulley swaps. Some stores perform this service free of charge. If your local auto parts store doesn't offer this service, you'll have to purchase a puller for remov-

ing the pulley and do it yourself.
11   Installation is the reverse of removal. On turbo models, if the alternator mounting bracket was removed, install the bracket to the alternator and tighten the fasteners to the torque listed in this Chapter's Specifications. Tighten the alternator mounting fasteners to the torque listed in this Chapter's Specifications.
12   Reconnect the cable to the negative terminal of the battery. Check the charging voltage (see Section 2) to verify that the alternator is operating correctly.

8   Starter motor - removal and installation

1   Disconnect the negative battery cable from the remote ground terminal (see Section 3).

Non-turbocharged models
2   Raise the vehicle and support it securely on jackstands. Remove the under-vehicle splash shield.
3   Disconnect the electrical connector from the oil pressure sending unit (mounted on the oil filter adapter).
4   Remove the nuts and detach the brackets from any interfering wiring harnesses or coolant pipes.
5   Disconnect the starter motor solenoid wire nut and the starter motor battery cable nut, then disconnect both wires from the starter **(see illustration)**.
6   Unscrew the mounting bolts and remove the starter.
7   Installation is the reverse of removal.

Note the following:

a) *Tighten the starter mounting fasteners to the torque listed in this Chapter's Specifications.*

b) *Tighten the wheel lug nuts to the torque listed in the Chapter 1 Specifications.*

Turbocharged models

8   Remove engine cover by pulling it straight up

9   Remove the air filter housing and duct (see Chapter 4).

10   Remove the nuts and detach the starter motor bracket.

11   Disconnect the starter motor solenoid wire nut and the starter motor battery cable nut and disconnect both wires from the starter **(see illustration 8.5)**.

12   Unscrew the mounting bolts and remove the starter.

13   Installation is the reverse of removal. Tighten the starter mounting fasteners to the torque listed in this Chapter's Specifications.

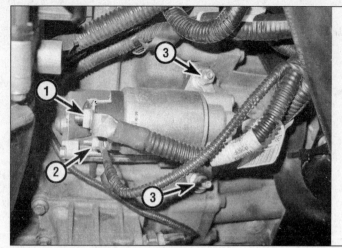

8.5 Starter motor mounting details

1   *Starter motor battery terminal*
2   *Starter solenoid terminal*
3   *Mounting stud-bolts*

Notes

Chapter 6
Emissions and engine control systems

Contents

Specifications

Torque specifications

Note: *One foot-pound (ft-lb) of torque is equivalent to 12 inch-pounds (in-lbs) of torque. Torque values below approximately 15 ft-lbs are expressed in inch-pounds, because most foot-pound torque wrenches are not accurate at these smaller values.*

	Ft-lbs (unless otherwise indicated)	Nm
Cylinder Head Temperature (CHT) sensor (turbo models)	97 in-lbs	11
Fuel Rail Pressure (FRP) sensor		
Step 1	53 in-lbs	6
Step 2	Tighten an additional 5-degrees	
Step 3	Loosen 90-degrees	
Step 4	53 in-lbs	6
Step 5	Tighten an additional 21-degrees	
Knock sensor mounting bolt	15	20
Oxygen sensors	35	47
Oil control solenoid valve bolt	89 in-lbs	10
Transmission Range (TR) sensor mounting bolts	89 in-lbs	10

1 General Information

1   To prevent pollution of the atmosphere from incompletely burned and evaporating gases, and to maintain good driveability and fuel economy, a number of emission control systems are incorporated. They include the:

Catalytic converter

2   A catalytic converter is an emission control device in the exhaust system that reduces certain pollutants in the exhaust gas stream. There are two types of converters: oxidation converters and reduction converters.

3   Oxidation converters contain a monolithic substrate (a ceramic honeycomb) coated with the semi-precious metals platinum and palladium. An oxidation catalyst reduces unburned hydrocarbons (HC) and carbon monoxide (CO) by adding oxygen to the exhaust stream as it passes through the substrate, which, in the presence of high temperature and the catalyst materials, converts the HC and CO to water vapor (H_2O) and carbon dioxide (CO_2).

4   Reduction converters contain a monolithic substrate coated with platinum and rhodium. A reduction catalyst reduces oxides of nitrogen (NOx) by removing oxygen, which in the presence of high temperature and the catalyst material produces nitrogen (N) and carbon dioxide (CO_2).

5   Catalytic converters that combine both types of catalysts in one assembly are known as "three-way catalysts" or TWCs. A TWC can reduce all three pollutants.

Evaporative Emissions Control (EVAP) system

6   The Evaporative Emissions Control (EVAP) system prevents fuel system vapors (which contain unburned hydrocarbons) from escaping into the atmosphere. On warm days, vapors trapped inside the fuel tank expand until the pressure reaches a certain threshold. Then the fuel vapors are routed from the fuel tank through the fuel vapor vent valve and the fuel vapor control valve to the EVAP canister, where they're stored temporarily until the next time the vehicle is operated. When the conditions are right (engine warmed up, vehicle up to speed, moderate or heavy load

on the engine, etc.) the PCM opens the canister purge valve, which allows fuel vapors to be drawn from the canister into the intake manifold. Once in the intake manifold, the fuel vapors mix with incoming air before being drawn through the intake ports into the combustion chambers where they're burned up with the rest of the air/fuel mixture. The EVAP system is complex and virtually impossible to troubleshoot without the right tools and training.

Exhaust Gas Recirculation (EGR) system

7   The EGR system reduces oxides of nitrogen by recirculating exhaust gases from the exhaust manifold, through the EGR valve and intake manifold, then back to the combustion chambers, where it mixes with the incoming air/fuel mixture before being consumed. These recirculated exhaust gases dilute the incoming air/fuel mixture, which cools the combustion chambers, thereby reducing NOx emissions.

8   The EGR system consists of the Powertrain Control Module (PCM), the EGR valve, the EGR valve position sensor and various other information sensors that the PCM uses to determine when to open the EGR valve. The degree to which the EGR valve is opened is referred to as "EGR valve lift." The PCM is programmed to produce the ideal EGR valve lift for varying operating conditions. The EGR valve position sensor, which is an integral part of the EGR valve, detects the amount of EGR valve lift and sends this information to the PCM. The PCM then compares it with the appropriate EGR valve lift for the operating conditions. The PCM increases current flow to the EGR valve to increase valve lift and reduces the current to reduce the amount of lift. If EGR flow is inappropriate to the operating conditions (idle, cold engine, etc.) the PCM simply cuts the current to the EGR valve and the valve closes.

Secondary Air Injection (AIR) system

9   Some models are equipped with a secondary air injection (AIR) system. The secondary air injection system is used to reduce tail-

pipe emissions on initial engine start-up. The system uses an electric motor/pump assembly, relay, vacuum valve/solenoid, air shut-off valve, check valves and tubing to inject fresh air directly into the exhaust manifolds. The fresh air (oxygen) reacts with the exhaust gas in the catalytic converter to reduce HC and CO levels. The air pump and solenoid are controlled by the PCM through the AIR relay. During initial start-up, the PCM energizes the AIR relay, the relay supplies battery voltage to the air pump and the vacuum valve/solenoid, engine vacuum is applied to the air shut-off valve which opens and allows air to flow through the tubing into the exhaust manifolds. The PCM will operate the air pump until closed loop operation is reached (approximately four minutes). During normal operation, the check valves prevent exhaust backflow into the system.

Powertrain Control Module (PCM)

10   The Powertrain Control Module (PCM) is the brain of the engine management system. It also controls a wide variety of other vehicle systems. In order to program the new PCM, the dealer needs the vehicle as well as the new PCM. If you're planning to replace the PCM with a new one, there is no point in trying to do so at home because you won't be able to program it yourself.

Positive Crankcase Ventilation (PCV) system

11   The Positive Crankcase Ventilation (PCV) system reduces hydrocarbon emissions by scavenging crankcase vapors, which are rich in unburned hydrocarbons. A PCV valve or orifice regulates the flow of gases into the intake manifold in proportion to the amount of intake vacuum available.

12   The PCV system generally consists of the fresh air inlet hose, the PCV valve or orifice and the crankcase ventilation hose (or PCV hose). The fresh air inlet hose connects the air intake duct to a pipe on the valve cover. The crankcase ventilation hose (or PCV hose) connects the PCV valve or orifice in the valve cover to the intake manifold.

Information Sensors

Accelerator Pedal Position (APP) sensor - as you press the accelerator pedal, the APP sensor alters its voltage signal to the PCM in proportion to the angle of the pedal, and the PCM commands a motor inside the throttle body to open or close the throttle plate accordingly

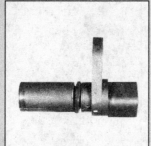

Camshaft Position (CMP) sensor - produces a signal that the PCM uses to identify the number 1 cylinder and to time the firing sequence of the fuel injectors

Crankshaft Position (CKP) sensor - produces a signal that the PCM uses to calculate engine speed and crankshaft position, which enables it to synchronize ignition timing with fuel injector timing, and to detect misfires

Engine Coolant Temperature (ECT) sensor - a thermistor (temperature-sensitive variable resistor) that sends a voltage signal to the PCM, which uses this data to determine the temperature of the engine coolant

Fuel tank pressure sensor - measures the fuel tank pressure and controls fuel tank pressure by signaling the EVAP system to purge the fuel tank vapors when the pressure becomes excessive

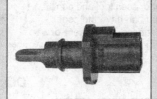

Intake Air Temperature (IAT) sensor - monitors the temperature of the air entering the engine and sends a signal to the PCM to determine injector pulse-width (the duration of each injector's on-time) and to adjust spark timing (to prevent spark knock)

Knock sensor - a piezoelectric crystal that oscillates in proportion to engine vibration which produces a voltage output that is monitored by the PCM. This retards the ignition timing when the oscillation exceeds a certain threshold

Manifold Absolute Pressure (MAP) sensor - monitors the pressure or vacuum inside the intake manifold. The PCM uses this data to determine engine load so that it can alter the ignition advance and fuel enrichment

Mass Air Flow (MAF) sensor - measures the amount of intake air drawn into the engine. It uses a hot-wire sensing element to measure the amount of air entering the engine

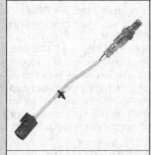

Oxygen sensors - generates a small variable voltage signal in proportion to the difference between the oxygen content in the exhaust stream and the oxygen content in the ambient air. The PCM uses this information to maintain the proper air/fuel ratio. A second oxygen sensor monitors the efficiency of the catalytic converter

Throttle Position (TP) sensor - a potentiometer that generates a voltage signal that varies in relation to the opening angle of the throttle plate inside the throttle body. Works with the PCM and other sensors to calculate injector pulse width (the duration of each injector's on-time)

Photos courtesy of Wells Manufacturing, except APP and MAF sensors.

2.4a Simple code readers are an economical way to extract trouble codes when the CHECK ENGINE light comes on

2.4b Hand-held scan tools like these can extract computer codes and also perform diagnostics

2   On Board Diagnosis (OBD) system

General description

1   All models are equipped with the second generation OBD-II system. This system consists of an on-board computer known as the Powertrain Control Module (PCM), and information sensors, which monitor various functions of the engine and send data to the PCM. This system incorporates a series of diagnostic monitors that detect and identify fuel injection and emissions control system faults and store the information in the computer memory. This system also tests sensors and output actuators, diagnoses drive cycles, freezes data and clears codes.

2   The PCM is the brain of the electronically controlled fuel and emissions system. It receives data from a number of sensors and other electronic components (switches, relays, etc.). Based on the information it receives, the PCM generates output signals to control various relays, solenoids (fuel injectors) and other actuators. The PCM is specifically calibrated to optimize the emissions, fuel economy and driveability of the vehicle.

3   It isn't a good idea to attempt diagnosis or replacement of the PCM or emission control components at home while the vehicle is under warranty. Because of a federally-mandated warranty which covers the emissions system components and because any owner-induced damage to the PCM, the sensors and/or the control devices may void this warranty, take the vehicle to a dealer service department if the PCM or a system component malfunctions.

Scan tool information

4   Because extracting the Diagnostic Trouble Codes (DTCs) from an engine management system is now the first step in troubleshooting many computer-controlled systems and components, a code reader, at the very least, will be required **(see illustration)**. More powerful scan tools can also perform many of the diagnostics once associated with expensive factory scan tools **(see illustration)**. If you're planning to obtain a generic scan tool for your vehicle, make sure that it's compatible with OBD-II systems. If you don't plan to purchase a code reader or scan tool and don't have access to one, you can have the codes extracted by a dealer service department or an independent repair shop.

Note: *Some auto parts stores even provide this service.*

3   Obtaining and clearing Diagnostic Trouble Codes (DTCs)

1   All models covered by this manual are equipped with on-board diagnostics. When the PCM recognizes a malfunction in a monitored emission or engine control system, component or circuit, it turns on the Malfunction Indicator Light (MIL) on the dash. The PCM will continue to display the MIL until the problem is fixed and the Diagnostic Trouble Code (DTC) is cleared from the PCM's memory. You'll need a scan tool to access any DTCs stored in the PCM.

2   Before outputting any DTCs stored in the PCM, thoroughly inspect ALL electrical connectors and hoses. Make sure that all electrical connections are tight, clean and free of corrosion. And make sure that all hoses are correctly connected, fit tightly and are in good condition (no cracks or tears).

Accessing the DTCs

3   The Diagnostic Trouble Codes (DTCs) can only be accessed with a code reader or scan tool. Professional scan tools are expensive, but relatively inexpensive generic code readers or scan tools **(see illustrations 2.4a and 2.4b)** are available at most auto parts stores. Simply plug the connector of the scan tool into the diagnostic connector **(see illustration)**. Then follow the instructions included with the scan tool to extract the DTCs.

4   Once you have outputted all of the stored DTCs, look them up on the accompanying DTC chart.

5   After troubleshooting the source of each DTC, make any necessary repairs or replace the defective component(s).

Clearing the DTCs

6   Clear the DTCs with the code reader or scan tool in accordance with the instructions provided by the tool's manufacturer.

Diagnostic Trouble Codes

7   The accompanying tables are a list of the Diagnostic Trouble Codes (DTCs) that can be accessed by a do-it-yourselfer working at home (there are many, many more DTCs available to professional mechanics with proprietary scan tools and software, but those codes cannot be accessed by a generic scan tool). If, after you have checked and repaired the connectors, wire harness and vacuum hoses (if applicable) for an emission-related system, component or circuit, the problem persists, have the vehicle checked by a dealer service department or other qualified repair shop.

3.3 The Data Link Connector (DLC) is located at the left end of the instrument panel, behind a cover

OBD-II trouble codes

Note: *Not all trouble codes apply to all models.*

Code	Probable cause
P0010	Intake camshaft position actuator, open circuit (Bank 1)
P0011	Intake camshaft position timing over-advanced (Bank 1)
P0012	Intake camshaft position timing, over-retarded (Bank 1)
P0016	Crankshaft position-to-camshaft position correlation (Bank 1)
P0018	Crankshaft position-to-camshaft position correlation (Bank 2)
P0020	Intake camshaft position actuator, open circuit (Bank 2)
P0021	Intake camshaft position timing over-advanced (Bank 2)
P0022	Intake camshaft position timing over-retarded (Bank 2)
P0030	Oxygen sensor heater control circuit (Bank 1, Sensor 1)
P0040	Oxygen sensor signals swapped (Bank 1, Sensor 1/Bank 2, Sensor 1)
P0041	Oxygen sensor signals swapped (Bank 1, Sensor 2/Bank 2, Sensor 2)
P0050	Oxygen sensor heater control circuit (Bank 2, Sensor 1)
P0053	Oxygen sensor heater resistance (Bank 1, Sensor 1)
P0054	Oxygen sensor heater resistance (Bank 1, Sensor 2)
P0055	Oxygen sensor heater resistance (Bank 1, Sensor 3)
P0059	Oxygen sensor heater resistance (Bank 2, Sensor 1)
P0060	Oxygen sensor heater resistance (Bank 2, Sensor 2)
P0068	Manifold Absolute Pressure (MAP) sensor/Mass Air Flow (MAF) sensor-to-throttle position correlation
P0097	Intake Air Temperature (IAT) sensor 2 circuit, low voltage
P0098	Intake Air Temperature (IAT) sensor 2 circuit, high voltage
P0102	Mass or volume air flow A circuit, low voltage
P0103	Mass or volume air flow A circuit, high voltage
P0104	Mass Air Flow (MAF) sensor A circuit, intermittent or erratic signal
P0106	Manifold Absolute Pressure (MAP) sensor circuit, range or performance problem
P0107	Manifold Absolute Pressure (MAP) sensor circuit, low voltage
P0108	Manifold Absolute Pressure (MAP) sensor circuit, high voltage
P0109	Manifold Absolute Pressure (MAP) sensor circuit, intermittent signal
P0111	Intake Air Temperature (IAT) sensor circuit, range or performance problem
P0112	Intake Air Temperature (IAT) sensor circuit, low voltage

OBD-II trouble codes (continued)

Note: *Not all trouble codes apply to all models.*

Code	Probable cause
P0113	Intake Air Temperature (IAT) sensor circuit, high voltage
P0114	Intake Air Temperature (IAT) sensor circuit, intermittent or erratic signal
P0116	Engine Coolant Temperature (ECT) sensor circuit, range or performance problem
P0117	Engine Coolant Temperature (ECT) sensor circuit, low voltage
P0118	Engine Coolant Temperature (ECT) sensor circuit, high voltage
P0119	Engine Coolant Temperature (ECT) sensor circuit, intermittent or erratic signal
P0121	Throttle Position (TP) sensor A circuit, range or performance problem
P0122	Throttle Position (TP) sensor A circuit, low voltage
P0123	Throttle Position (TP) sensor A circuit, high voltage
P0125	Insufficient coolant temperature for closed loop fuel control
P0128	Coolant temperature below coolant thermostat's regulating temperature
P0130	Oxygen sensor circuit malfunction (Bank 1, Sensor 1)
P0132	Oxygen sensor circuit, high voltage (Bank 1, Sensor 1)
P0133	Oxygen sensor circuit, slow response (Bank 1, Sensor 1)
P0134	Oxygen sensor circuit, no activity detected (Bank 1, Sensor 1)
P0135	Oxygen sensor heater circuit malfunction (Bank 1, Sensor 1)
P0138	Oxygen sensor circuit, high voltage (Bank 1, Sensor 2)
P0139	Oxygen sensor circuit, slow response (Bank 1, Sensor 2)
P013A	Oxygen sensor slow response, rich to lean (Bank 1, Sensor 2)
P013C	Oxygen sensor slow response, rich to lean (Bank 2, Sensor 2)
P013E	Oxygen sensor delayed response, rich to lean (Bank 1, Sensor 2)
P0144	Oxygen sensor circuit, high voltage (Bank 1, Sensor 3)
P0147	Oxygen sensor heater circuit malfunction (Bank 1, Sensor 3)
P0148	Fuel delivery error
P014A	Oxygen sensor delayed response, rich to lean (Bank 2, Sensor 2)
P0150	Oxygen sensor circuit malfunction (Bank 2, Sensor 1)
P0152	Oxygen sensor circuit, high voltage (Bank 2, Sensor 1)
P0153	Oxygen sensor circuit, slow response (Bank 2, Sensor 1)
P0154	Oxygen sensor circuit, no activity detected (Bank 2, Sensor 1)

Code	Probable cause
P0155	Oxygen sensor heater circuit malfunction (Bank 2, Sensor 1)
P0158	Oxygen sensor circuit, high voltage (Bank 2, Sensor 2)
P0159	Oxygen sensor circuit, slow response (Bank 2, Sensor 2)
P0161	Oxygen sensor heater circuit malfunction (Bank 2, Sensor 2)
P0171	System too lean (Bank 1)
P0172	System too rich (Bank 1)
P0174	System too lean (Bank 2)
P0175	System too rich (Bank 2)
P0180	Fuel temperature sensor circuit malfunction
P0181	Fuel temperature sensor circuit, range or performance problem
P0182	Fuel temperature sensor circuit, low voltage
P0183	Fuel temperature sensor circuit, high voltage
P0191	Fuel rail pressure sensor circuit, range or performance problem
P0192	Fuel rail pressure sensor circuit, low voltage
P0193	Fuel rail pressure sensor circuit, high voltage
P0196	Engine Oil Temperature (EOT) sensor circuit, range or performance problem
P0197	Engine Oil Temperature (EOT) sensor circuit, low voltage
P0198	Engine Oil Temperature (EOT) sensor circuit, high voltage
P0201	Injector open circuit, cylinder 1
P0202	Injector open circuit, cylinder 2
P0203	Injector open circuit, cylinder 3
P0204	Injector open circuit, cylinder 4
P0217	Engine coolant over-temperature condition
P0218	Transaxle fluid temperature over-temperature condition
P0219	Engine over-speed condition
P0221	Throttle Position (TP) sensor circuit, range or performance problem
P0222	Throttle Position (TP) sensor circuit, low voltage
P0223	Throttle Position (TP) sensor circuit, high voltage
P0230	Fuel pump primary circuit malfunction
P0231	Fuel pump secondary circuit, low voltage
P0232	Fuel pump secondary circuit, high voltage

OBD-II trouble codes (continued)

Note: *Not all trouble codes apply to all models.*

Code	Probable cause
P025A	Fuel pump module control circuit open
P025B	Fuel pump module control circuit range or performance problem
P0297	Vehicle over-speed condition
P0298	Engine oil over-temperature condition
P0300	Random misfire detected
P0301	Cylinder 1 misfire
P0302	Cylinder 2 misfire
P0303	Cylinder 3 misfire
P0304	Cylinder 4 misfire
P0315	Crankshaft position system variation not learned
P0316	Misfire detected on start-up (first 1000 revolutions)
P0320	Ignition/distributor engine speed input circuit
P0325	Knock sensor 1 circuit malfunction (Bank 1)
P0326	Knock sensor 1 circuit, range or performance problem (Bank 1)
P0330	Knock sensor 2 circuit malfunction (Bank 2)
P0331	Knock sensor 2 circuit, range or performance problem (Bank 2)
P0340	Camshaft Position (CMP) sensor circuit malfunction (Bank 1 or single sensor)
P0341	Camshaft Position (CMP) sensor circuit, range or performance problem (Bank 1 or single sensor)
P0344	Camshaft Position (CMP) sensor circuit, intermittent signal (Bank 1 or single sensor)
P0345	Camshaft Position (CMP) sensor circuit malfunction (Bank 2)
P0346	Camshaft Position (CMP) sensor circuit, range or performance problem (Bank 2)
P0349	Camshaft Position (CMP) sensor circuit, intermittent signal (Bank 2)
P0350	Ignition coil primary/secondary circuit malfunction
P0351	Ignition coil A primary/secondary circuit malfunction
P0352	Ignition coil B primary/secondary circuit malfunction
P0353	Ignition coil C primary/secondary circuit malfunction
P0354	Ignition coil D primary/secondary circuit malfunction
P0420	Catalyst system efficiency below threshold (Bank 1)
P0442	Evaporative Emission (EVAP) system, small leak detected

Code	Probable cause
P0443	Evaporative Emission (EVAP) system, purge control valve circuit malfunction
P0446	Evaporative Emission (EVAP) system, vent control circuit malfunction
P0451	Evaporative Emission (EVAP) system, pressure sensor range or performance problem
P0452	Evaporative Emission (EVAP) system, pressure sensor, low voltage
P0453	Evaporative Emission (EVAP) system, pressure sensor, high voltage
P0454	Evaporative Emission (EVAP) system, pressure sensor, intermittent signal
P0455	Evaporative Emission (EVAP) system, gross leak detected/no flow
P0456	Evaporative Emission (EVAP) system, very small leak detected
P0457	Evaporative Emission (EVAP) system, leak detected (fuel cap loose or off)
P0460	Fuel level sensor circuit malfunction
P0461	Fuel level sensor circuit, range or performance problem
P0462	Fuel level sensor circuit, low voltage
P0463	Fuel level sensor circuit, high voltage
P0480	Fan 1 control circuit malfunction
P0481	Fan 2 control circuit malfunction
P0483	Fan performance
P0500	Vehicle Speed Sensor (VSS)
P0503	Vehicle Speed Sensor (VSS), intermittent, erratic or high signal
P050A	Cold start idle air control performance
P050B	Cold start ignition timing performance
P050E	Cold start engine exhaust temperature out of range
P0512	Starter request circuit malfunction
P0528	Fan speed sensor circuit, no signal
P0532	Air conditioning refrigerant pressure sensor circuit, low voltage
P0533	Air conditioning refrigerant pressure sensor circuit, high voltage
P0534	Air conditioning refrigerant charge loss
P0537	Air conditioning evaporator temperature sensor circuit, low voltage
P0538	A/C evaporator temperature sensor circuit, high voltage
P053A	Positive Crankcase Ventilation (PCV) heater control circuit open
P0562	System voltage low
P0563	System voltage high

OBD-II trouble codes (continued)

Note: *Not all trouble codes apply to all models.*

Code	Probable cause
P0571	Brake switch circuit malfunction
P0572	Brake switch circuit, low voltage
P0573	Brake switch circuit, high voltage
P0579	Cruise control multifunction input circuit, ranger or performance problem
P0581	Cruise control multifunction input circuit, high voltage
P0600	Serial communication link
P0601	Powertrain Control Module (PCM), memory checksum error
P0602	Powertrain Control Module (PCM) programming error
P0603	Powertrain Control Module (PCM), Keep Alive Memory (KAM) error
P0604	Powertrain Control Module (PCM), Random Access Memory (RAM) error
P0605	Powertrain Control Module (PCM), Read Only Memory (ROM) error
P0606	Powertrain Control Module (PCM) processor
P0607	Powertrain Control Module (PCM) performance
P060A	Internal control module monitoring processor performance
P060B	Internal control module analog/digital processing performance
P060C	Internal control module main processor performance
P060D	Internal control module accelerator pedal position performance
P0610	Powertrain Control Module (PCM) options error
P061B	Internal control module torque calculation performance
P061C	Internal control module engine rpm performance
P061D	Internal control module engine air mass performance
P061F	Internal control module throttle actuator controller performance
P0620	Alternator control circuit malfunction
P0622	Alternator field terminal, circuit malfunction
P0625	Alternator field terminal, low circuit voltage
P0626	Alternator field terminal, high circuit voltage
P0627	Fuel pump, open control circuit
P062C	Internal control module vehicle speed performance
P062F	Internal control module EEPROM error

Code	Probable cause
P0642	Sensor reference voltage (VREF) circuit below VREF minimum voltage
P0643	Sensor reference voltage (VREF) circuit, high voltage
P0645	Air conditioning clutch relay control circuit malfunction
P064D	Internal control module oxygen sensor processor performance (Bank 1)
P064E	Internal control module oxygen sensor processor performance (Bank 2)
P0657	Actuator supply voltage, open circuit
P065B	Alternator control circuit range or performance problem
P0685	Powertrain Control Module (PCM) power relay control circuit open
P0689	Powertrain Control Module (PCM) power relay sense circuit, low voltage
P0690	Powertrain Control Module (PCM) power relay sense circuit, high voltage
P06B8	Internal control module Non-volatile random access memory (NVRAM) error
P0703	Brake switch input circuit malfunction
P0704	Clutch switch input circuit malfunction
P0705	Transmission Range (TR) sensor circuit (PRNDL) input problem
P0706	Transmission Range (TR) sensor circuit, range or performance problem
P0707	Transmission Range (TR) sensor circuit, low voltage
P0708	Transmission range sensor circuit, high voltage
P0711	Transmission fluid temperature sensor circuit, range or performance problem
P0712	Transmission fluid temperature sensor circuit, low input
P0713	Transmission fluid temperature sensor circuit, high input
P0715	Input/turbine speed sensor circuit malfunction
P0716	Input/turbine speed sensor circuit, range or performance problem
P0717	Input/turbine speed sensor circuit, no signal
P0720	Output Shaft Speed (OSS) sensor circuit malfunction
P0721	Output Shaft Speed (OSS) sensor circuit, range or performance problem
P0722	No signal from Output Shaft Speed (OSS) sensor
P0723	Output Shaft Speed (OSS) sensor circuit, intermittent signal
P0729	Gear 6 incorrect ratio
P072C	Stuck in Gear 1
P072E	Stuck in Gear 3
P072F	Stuck in Gear 4

OBD-II trouble codes (continued)

Note: *Not all trouble codes apply to all models.*

Code	Probable cause
P0730	Incorrect gear ratio
P0731	Incorrect gear ratio, first gear
P0732	Incorrect gear ratio, second gear
P0733	Incorrect gear ratio, third gear
P0734	Incorrect gear ratio, fourth gear
P0735	Incorrect gear ratio, fifth gear
P0736	Incorrect gear ratio, reverse gear
P0745	Pressure control solenoid malfunction
P0748	Pressure control solenoid malfunction
P0750	Shift solenoid A, performance problem
P0751	Shift solenoid A, performance problem or stuck in Off position
P0752	Shift solenoid A, stuck in On position
P0753	Shift solenoid A, electrical problem
P0755	Shift solenoid B, performance problem
P0756	Shift solenoid B, performance problem or stuck in Off position
P0757	Shift solenoid B, stuck in On position
P0758	Shift solenoid B, electrical problem
P0760	Shift solenoid C, performance problem
P0761	Shift solenoid C, performance problem or stuck in Off position
P0762	Shift solenoid C, stuck in On position
P0763	Shift solenoid C, electrical problem
P0765	Shift solenoid D, performance problem
P0765	Shift solenoid E, performance problem
P0766	Shift solenoid D, performance problem or stuck in Off position
P0767	Shift solenoid D, stuck in On position
P0768	Shift solenoid D, electrical problem
P0771	Shift solenoid E, performance problem or stuck in Off position
P0772	Shift solenoid E, stuck in On position
P0773	Shift solenoid E, electrical problem

Code	Probable cause
P0774	Shift solenoid E, intermittent electrical problem
P0777	Pressure control solenoid "B" stuck On
P0778	Pressure control solenoid "B" electrical
P0780	Shift malfunction
P0791	Intermediate shaft speed sensor circuit malfunction
P0812	Reverse input circuit malfunction
P0815	Upshift switch circuit malfunction
P0816	Downshift switch circuit malfunction
P0817	Starter disable circuit malfunction
P0830	Clutch pedal switch circuit malfunction
P0840	Transmission fluid pressure sensor circuit malfunction
P0841	Transmission fluid pressure sensor/switch "A" circuit range/performance problem
P0850	Park/neutral switch input circuit malfunction
P0882	Transmission control module (TCM) power input signal low
P0894	Transmission component slipping
P0960	Pressure control (PC) solenoid A - control circuit open
P0961	Pressure control (PC) solenoid A - control circuit range/performance problem
P0962	Pressure control (PC) solenoid A - control circuit low
P0963	Pressure control (PC) solenoid A - control circuit high
P0973	Shift solenoid (SS) A - control circuit low
P0974	Shift solenoid (SS) A - control circuit high
P0976	Shift solenoid (SS) B - control circuit low
P0977	Shift solenoid (SS) B - control circuit high
P0978	Shift solenoid (SS) C - control circuit range/performance problem
P0979	Shift solenoid (SS) C - control circuit low
P0980	Shift solenoid (SS) C - control circuit high
P0981	Shift solenoid (SS) D - control circuit range/performance problem
P0982	Shift solenoid (SS) D - control circuit low
P0983	Shift solenoid (SS) D - control circuit high
P0984	Shift solenoid (SS) E - control circuit range/performance problem
P0985	Shift solenoid (SS) E - control circuit low

OBD-II trouble codes (continued)

Note: *Not all trouble codes apply to all models.*

Code	Probable cause
P0986	Shift solenoid (SS) E - control circuit high
P0997	Shift solenoid (SS) F - control circuit range/performance problem
P0998	Shift solenoid (SS) F - control circuit low
P0999	Shift solenoid (SS) F - control circuit high

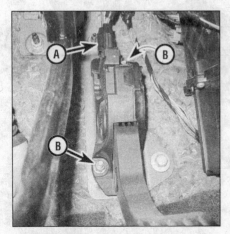

4.1 APP sensor electrical connector (A)
and mounting nuts (B)

5.2 The intake CMP
sensor (A) and the
exhaust CMP sensor
(B) are located on the
top of the valve cover

4   Accelerator Pedal Position (APP) sensor - replacement

Note: *Replacing the APP sensor is difficult. The APP sensor is located at the upper end of the accelerator pedal assembly, between the brake pedal assembly and the housing for the heater core and air conditioning evaporator.*

1   Disconnect the electrical connector from the upper end of the APP sensor assembly **(see illustration)**.
2   Remove the accelerator pedal/APP sensor assembly mounting nuts and remove the assembly.
3   Installation is the reverse of removal.

5   Camshaft Position (CMP) sensor - replacement

Note: *The CMP sensors are located at the top corners of the valve cover, above the left end of the intake and exhaust camshafts.*

1   Disconnect the negative battery cable from the remote ground terminal (see Chapter 5).
2   Disconnect the CMP sensor electrical connector **(see illustration)**.
3   Remove the CMP sensor mounting bolt and remove the sensor from the valve cover.
4   Inspect the condition of the CMP sensor O-ring. If it's cracked, torn or deteriorated, replace it.
5   Installation is the reverse of removal.

6   Crankshaft Position (CKP) sensor - removal and installation

Note: *Replacing the CKP sensor might set a Diagnostic Trouble Code (DTC). If it does, and you have a generic scan tool that can clear codes, erase the code and see if it reappears. If it does, drive the vehicle to a dealer service department or other properly equipped repair shop to perform a Misfire Monitor Neutral Profile Correction procedure with a factory scan tool.*

Removal

Note: *The CKP sensor is located at the lower rear corner of the timing chain cover, behind the crankshaft pulley.*

1   Disconnect the negative battery cable from the remote ground terminal (see Chapter 5).
2   Loosen the right-front wheel lug nuts, then raise the front of the vehicle and support it securely on jackstands. Remove the wheel and the wheel arch liner (see Chapter 11).
3   Put the No. 1 cylinder at Top Dead Center (TDC) (see Chapter 2A).
4   Disconnect the electrical connector from the CKP sensor **(see illustration)**.
5   Unscrew the CKP sensor mounting bolts and remove the sensor.

Installation

Note: *If you're installing a new CKP sensor, the new sensor comes with a special alignment jig (303-1521) that, according to the manufacturer, is available only with a new sensor. However, you might be able to find an*

6.4 CKP sensor details:

1   *Electrical connector*   3   *CKP sensor*
2   *Mounting bolts*

7.3 The CHT sensor is located on the back side of the cylinder head (turbo models only)

aftermarket tool that does the same thing. If you removed the CKP sensor simply to access some other component, like the timing chain, use the alternate method of aligning the CKP sensor included here.

6   Install the CKP sensor but don't tighten the sensor mounting bolts.

7   Align the sensor with the special alignment jig in accordance with the tool manufacturer's instructions. With the alignment jig in place, tighten the CKP sensor bolts securely, then remove the alignment jig.

8   Remove the crankshaft pulley bolt that you installed in Step 6, then remove the special timing tool and install the cylinder block plug (see Chapter 2A). Installation is otherwise the reverse of removal.

7   Cylinder Head Temperature (CHT) sensor - replacement

Warning: *Wait until the engine has cooled completely before beginning this procedure.*
Note: *This procedure applies to turbocharged models only.*
Note: *The CHT is located on the back side of the cylinder head, towards the middle.*

1   Disconnect the negative battery cable from the remote ground terminal (see Chapter 5).

2   Remove the engine cover by pulling it straight up, then remove the charge air duct that passes over the top of the engine.

3   Pull back the weather cover from the CHT sensor electrical connector and disconnect the connector **(see illustration)**.

4   Unscrew the CHT sensor from the cylinder head. Discard the sensor. It cannot be reused once removed.

5   Installation is the reverse of removal. When installing the CHT sensor, be sure to tighten it to the torque listed in this Chapter's Specifications.

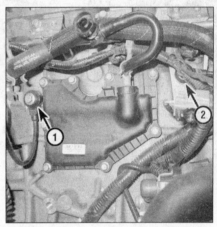

8.2 ECT sensor location (difficult to see in this photo)

8   Engine Coolant Temperature (ECT) sensor - replacement

Warning: *Wait until the engine has cooled completely before beginning this procedure.*
Note: *The ECT sensor is used on non-turbocharged models only.*

1   Drain the engine coolant (see Chapter 1).

2   Disconnect the electrical connector from the ECT sensor **(see illustration)**.

3   To remove the ECT sensor, remove the retaining clip and pull it out of the coolant passage.

4   Remove and inspect the sensor O-ring. If it's cut, torn, damaged or otherwise deteriorated, replace it.

5   To install the ECT sensor, apply clean engine coolant to the O-ring, insert the sensor into the coolant passage, then push it inwards and install the retaining clip in its groove.

6   Refill the cooling system (see Chapter 1).

9.4 Knock sensor details (2.0L engine)

1   *Right-hand knock sensor - must be installed with the wire end of the sensor pointing towards the 6 o'clock position*
2   *Left-hand knock sensor - must be installed with the wire end pointing towards the 3 o'clock position*

9   Knock sensor (KS) - replacement

Note: *The knock sensors are located on the front side of the block, behind the intake manifold.*

1   Disconnect the negative battery cable from the remote ground terminal (see Chapter 5).

2   Remove the intake manifold (see Chapter 2A).

3   Note the routing of the wiring and the position of the sensor, then disconnect the electrical connector from the knock sensor.

4   Remove the knock sensor bolt and remove the knock sensor **(see illustration)**.

5   Installation is the reverse of removal. Tighten the knock sensor bolt to the torque listed in this Chapter's Specifications.

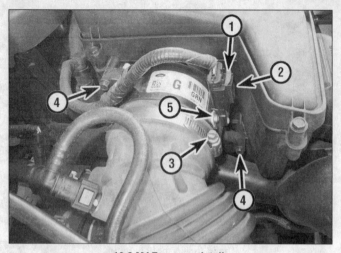

10.2 MAF sensor details

12.3 Location of the Fuel Rail Pressure (FRP) sensor (non-turbo model shown, turbo model similar)

1   *Electrical connector lock (slide up)*
2   *Electrical connector retaining tab (push, then unplug connector)*
3   *Air intake duct clamp*
4   *Air duct outlet fitting screws*
5   *MAF sensor screw (other screw not shown)*

10   Mass Air Flow (MAF) sensor (non-turbo models) - replacement

1   Loosen the clamp and detach the air intake duct from the air filter housing.
2   Disconnect the electrical connector from the MAF sensor **(see illustration)**.
3   Remove the screws and pull the air duct outlet fitting from the air filter housing.
4   Remove the MAF sensor mounting screws and detach the sensor from the air duct outlet fitting.
5   Installation is the reverse of removal.

11   Turbocharger Boost Pressure (TBP) and Charge Air Cooler Temperature (CACT) sensor - replacement

Note: *The TBP/CACT sensor is located on the right-side of the Charge Air Cooler duct fitting.*
1   Disconnect the electrical connector from the sensor.
2   Remove the sensor mounting screw and pull the sensor from the Charge Air Cooler.
3   Installation is the reverse of the removal procedure.

12   Fuel Rail Pressure (FRP) sensor - replacement

1   Relieve the fuel system pressure (see Chapter 4).
2   Disconnect the negative battery cable from the remote ground terminal (see Chapter 5).
3   Disconnect the FRP sensor electrical connector **(see illustration)**.

4   Unscrew and remove the FRP sensor.
Note: *Depending on your selection of tools, you can make more working room by removing the drivebelt and the drivebelt tensioner (see Chapter 1).*
5   Installation is the reverse of removal; tighten the sensor to the torque listed in this Chapter's Specifications.

13   Oxygen sensors - replacement

Note: *Because it is installed in the exhaust manifold or pipe, both of which contract when cool, an oxygen sensor might be very difficult to loosen when the engine is cold. Rather than risk damage to the sensor or its mounting threads, start and run the engine for a minute or two, then shut it off. Be careful not to burn yourself during the following procedure.*
1   Be particularly careful when servicing an oxygen sensor:

a)   *Oxygen sensors have a permanently attached pigtail and an electrical connector that cannot be removed. Damaging or removing the pigtail or electrical connector will render the sensor useless.*
b)   *Keep grease, dirt and other contaminants away from the electrical connector and the louvered end of the sensor.*
c)   *Do not use cleaning solvents of any kind on an oxygen sensor.*
d)   *Oxygen sensors are extremely delicate. Do not drop a sensor or handle it roughly.*
e)   *Make sure that the silicone boot on the sensor is installed in the correct position. Otherwise, it might melt and it might prevent the sensor from operating correctly.*
2   Disconnect the negative battery cable from the remote ground terminal (see Chapter 5).

3   If you're removing the downstream oxygen sensor on a turbocharged model, remove the engine cover by pulling it straight up, then remove the charge air duct that passes over the top of the engine.
4   If you're removing the upstream sensor on a turbocharged model, remove the battery and the battery tray (see Chapter 5).
5   To access the downstream sensor on all models, or the upstream sensor on turbocharged models, raise the front of the vehicle and place it securely on jackstands. Remove the under-vehicle splash shield.

Upstream oxygen sensor

Note: *The upstream sensor is installed in the upper part of the integral exhaust manifold/catalytic converter assembly.*
6   Locate the upstream oxygen sensor **(see illustration)**, then trace the sensor's electrical lead to its electrical connector and disconnect the connector. Disengage any harness clips.

13.6 Upstream oxygen sensor location (non-turbo model)

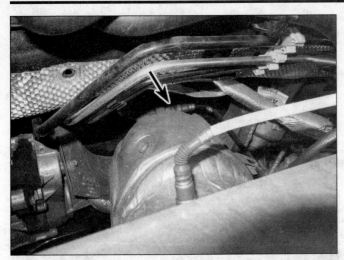

13.11 Downstream oxygen sensor location, seen from above (non-turbo model)

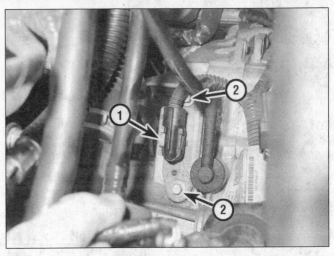

15.2 TR sensor details

1   Electrical connector (pull up the lock then push in the tab
    to release)
2   Mounting bolts

7   Using a wrench or an oxygen sensor socket, unscrew the upstream oxygen sensor.
8   If you're going to install the old sensor, apply anti-seize compound to the threads of the sensor to facilitate future removal. If you're going to install a new oxygen sensor, it's not necessary to apply anti-seize compound to the threads; the threads on new sensors already have anti-seize compound on them.
9   Installation is the reverse of removal. Tighten the oxygen sensor to the torque listed in this Chapter's Specifications.

Downstream oxygen sensor

Note: The downstream oxygen sensor is located in the exhaust pipe, just past the catalytic converter. It is also known as the "catalyst monitor sensor."
10   Locate the downstream oxygen sensor, then trace the lead up to the electrical connector and disconnect the connector. Disengage any harness clips.
11   Using a wrench or an oxygen sensor socket, unscrew the downstream oxygen sensor **(see illustration)**.
12   If you're going to install the old sensor, apply anti-seize compound to the threads of the sensor to facilitate future removal. If you're going to install a new oxygen sensor, it's not necessary to apply anti-seize compound to the threads. The threads on new sensors already have anti-seize compound on them.
13   Installation is the reverse of removal. Tighten the oxygen sensor to the torque listed in this Chapter's Specificaitons.

14   Throttle Position (TP) sensor - replacement

The TP sensor is an integral component of the electronic throttle body, and is not sepa-

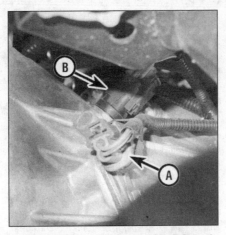

16.2 Locations of the Input Shaft Speed sensor (A) and Output Shaft Speed sensor (B)

rately serviceable. If you need to replace the TP sensor you must replace the throttle body (see Chapter 4).

15   Transmission Range (TR) sensor - removal and installation

Note: The TR sensor is located on the top of the transaxle, near the rear, just to the left of the coolant hose outlet.

Removal
1   Place the shift lever in DRIVE.
2   Disconnect the electrical connector from the TR sensor **(see illustration)**.
3   Remove the TR sensor mounting bolts and remove the sensor.

Installation
4   Clean the TR sensor mounting surface

on the transaxle.
5   Position the TR sensor on the transaxle and install the mounting bolts, then tighten the bolts to the torque listed in this Chapter's Specifications.
6   Reconnect the electrical connector.
7   Adjust the shift cable (see Chapter 7B).
8   Verify that the engine will only start in PARK or NEUTRAL. If it does, test drive the vehicle and check for proper operation.
Note: It may be necessary to have the Transmission Control Module (TCM) adaptive learning function programmed by a dealer service department or other properly equipped repair shop if driveability is not acceptable or the Check Engine light comes on.

16   Transaxle speed sensors - replacement

1   Loosen the left-front wheel lug nuts, then raise the vehicle and support it securely on jackstands. Remove the wheel and the under-vehicle splash shield.

Input Shaft Speed (ISS) sensor
Note: There are two input shaft speed sensors; ISS A and ISS B. Both are located on the left-rear side of the transaxle. ISS A is the lower sensor and ISS B is the upper sensor.
2   Disconnect the electrical connector from the ISS sensor **(see illustration)**.
3   Remove the mounting bolt and remove the ISS sensor from the transaxle case.
4   Remove and discard the old ISS sensor O-ring.
5   Installation is the reverse of removal, noting the following:
a) Install a new O-ring on the ISS sensor.
b) Tighten the wheel lug nuts to the torque listed in the Chapter 1 Specifications.

16.6 Location of the OSS sensor

19.2 The EVAP canister purge valve is located between the left end of the engine and the battery

Output Shaft Speed (OSS) sensor

Note: *The OSS sensor is located on the differential housing portion of the transaxle, behind the right driveaxle inner CV joint.*

6   Pull back the heat-shielding boot and disconnect the electrical connector from the OSS sensor **(see illustration)**.

7   Remove the mounting bolt and remove the OSS sensor from the transaxle case.

8   Remove and discard the old OSS sensor O-ring.

9   Installation is the reverse of removal, noting the following:

a) *Install a new O-ring on the OSS sensor.*

b) *Tighten the wheel lug nuts to the torque listed in the Chapter 1 Specifications.*

17 Powertrain Control Module (PCM) - removal and installation

Caution: *To avoid electrostatic discharge damage to the PCM, handle the PCM only by its case. Do not touch the electrical terminals during removal and installation. If available, ground yourself to the vehicle with an anti-static ground strap, available at computer supply stores.*

Note: *This procedure applies only to disconnecting, removing and installing the PCM that is already installed in your vehicle. If the PCM is defective and has to be replaced, it must be programmed with new software and calibrations. This procedure requires the use of Vehicle Communication Module (VCM) and Integrated Diagnostic System (IDS) software with appropriate hardware, or equivalent scan tool, so you WILL NOT BE ABLE TO REPLACE THE PCM AT HOME.*

1   Disconnect the negative battery cable from the remote ground terminal (see Chapter 5).

2   Loosen the left-front wheel lug nuts, then raise the vehicle and support it securely on jackstands. Remove the wheel arch liner (see Chapter 11).

3   The PCM is located at the front of the wheel well. Remove the screws and detach the PCM cover.

4   Disconnect the electrical connectors from the PCM.

5   Remove the PCM mounting bolts and remove the PCM.

Note: *The PCM might be retained by shear bolts (to prevent theft). If so, drill down the center of each bolt and unscrew the bolt using a screw extractor.*

6   Installation is the reverse of removal, note the following:

a) *If shear bolts are used, tighten them until the heads break off.*

b) *Tighten the wheel lug nuts to the torque listed in the Chapter 1 Specifications.*

18 Catalytic converter - replacement

Non-turbocharged models

1   On these models, the catalytic converter is an integral component of the exhaust manifold and cannot be serviced separately (see Chapter 2A).

Turbocharged models

2   Disconnect the negative battery cable from the remote ground terminal (see Chapter 5).

3   Remove the engine cover by pulling it straight up, then remove the charge air duct that passes over the top of the engine.

4   Raise the vehicle and support it securely on jackstands.

5   Locate the downstream oxygen sensor on the upper central part of the catalyst, trace the sensor to its electrical connector and disconnect it. Unscrew and remove the downstream oxygen sensor/catalyst sensor from the catalyst (see Section 13).

6   Raise the vehicle and support it securely on jackstands.

7   Remove any brackets or crossmembers near the converter that would interfere with removal.

8   Attach splints on each side of the exhaust flexible section (two wooden strips secured by cable ties will suffice) to prevent excessive bending.

9   Loosen the fasteners on the clamp that secures the front end of the catalyst to the turbocharger. If the threads are damaged or rusted, apply some penetrant to the threads and wait the amount of time specified by the rust penetrant manufacturer before loosening them.

10   Remove the nuts and bolts that secure the flange at the rear end of the catalyst to the exhaust pipe. If the threads are damaged or rusted, apply some penetrant to the threads and wait the amount of time specified by the rust penetrant manufacturer before loosening them.

11   Remove the catalytic converter.

12   Remove and discard the old gasket between the turbocharger and the catalytic converter

13   Installation is the reverse of removal. Use a new gasket and fasteners. Apply anti-seize compound to the fasteners and tighten them securely.

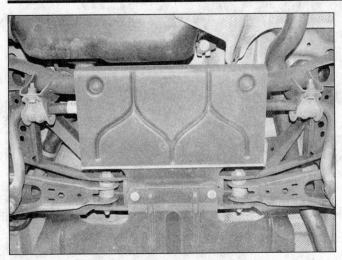

19.8a Remove the protective cover . . .

19.8b . . . to access the canister, which is attached to the rear subframe

19.9 Disconnect the electrical connector and hoses from the canister

19.10 Remove the screws and detach the canister from the subframe

19 Evaporative Emissions Control (EVAP) system - component replacement

EVAP canister purge valve

1 Disconnect the negative battery cable from the remote ground terminal (see Chapter 5).
2 Disconnect the electrical connector from the canister purge valve **(see illustration)**.
3 Follow the line from each side of the canister purge valve and quick-connect fittings (the lines are permanently attached to the valve) (see Chapter 4 for information on quick-connect fittings).
4 Slide the purge valve from its mounting bracket.

5 Installation is the reverse of removal.

EVAP canister

6 Disconnect the negative battery cable from the remote ground terminal (see Chapter 5).
7 Raise the rear of the vehicle and support it securely on jackstands.
8 The canister is located under the rear of the vehicle, attached to the rear subframe **(see illustrations)**.
9 Disconnect the electrical connector and the EVAP hose quick-connect fittings **(see illustration)**.
10 Remove the mounting fasteners that secure the canister and remove the canister **(see illustration)**.
11 Installation is the reverse of removal.

EVAP canister vent solenoid

Note: *The EVAP canister vent solenoid is mounted on the EVAP canister.*
12 Remove the EVAP canister (see Steps 6 through 10).
13 Rotate the canister vent solenoid counterclockwise and pull it from the canister.
14 Installation is the reverse of removal.

20 Crankcase vent oil separator - removal and installation

Note: *The PCV valve is an integral part of the crankcase vent oil separator, which is located on the front side of the engine block.*
1 Remove the intake manifold (see Chapter 2A), then detach the hose from the vent oil separator.

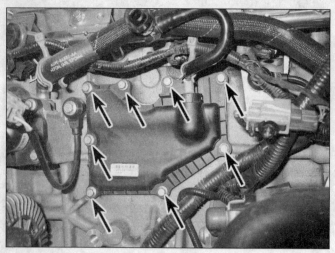

20.2 Location of the crankcase vent oil separator bolts

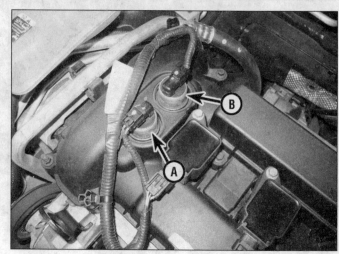

21.2 Location of the intake VCT oil control solenoid (A) and the exhaust VCT oil control solenoid (B)

2   Remove the oil vent separator mounting bolts **(see illustration)** and gasket.
3   Clean the engine block and install a new gasket to the separator.
4   Installation is the reverse of removal.

21   Variable Camshaft Timing (VCT) oil control solenoid - description and replacement

Description
1   The VCT system controls valve timing to increase engine torque in the low and mid-speed range and to increase horsepower in the high-speed range.
2   The VCT system consists of the PCM-controlled oil control solenoids, which are mounted on top of the cylinder head, and the VCT actuators, which are mounted on the front end of the camshafts **(see illustration)**.
3   The PCM-controlled oil control solenoids varies the oil pressure in the VCT actuators, which continuously varies the timing of both camshafts.

Replacement
4   Remove the valve cover (see Chapter 2A).
5   Remove the mounting bolt and pull the VCT oil control solenoid from the cylinder head.
6   Installation is the reverse of removal. Tighten the VCT bolt to the torque listed in this Chapter's Specifications.

Chapter 7 Part A
Manual transaxle

Contents

Specifications

General

Transaxle type	Five or six forward speeds, one reverse. Synchromesh on all forward gears. Shift linkage operated by twin cables
Fluid type and capacity:	See Chapter 1

Final drive ratios

Torque specifications

Note: *One foot-pound (ft-lb) of torque is equivalent to 12 inch-pounds (in-lbs) of torque. Torque values below approximately 15 ft-lbs are expressed in inch-pounds, because most foot-pound torque wrenches are not accurate at these smaller values.*

	Ft-lbs (unless otherwise indicated)	Nm
Transaxle left-hand mounting lower section	59	80
Transaxle left-hand mounting upper section		
Center bolt*	109	148
Four outer nuts	35	47
Transaxle rear mounting bracket (to transaxle)		
Five-speed models	35	47
Six-speed models		
Upper mounting fasteners	35	47
Lower mounting fastener	63	85
Transaxle rear mounting bracket (to subframe)	92	125
Transaxle-to-engine bolts	35	47

* Do not re-use

2.5 Pry out the locking insert to unlock the selector cable

3.4a Carefully pry off the cable ends...

1   General Information

1   The vehicles covered by this manual are equipped with either a 5-speed automatic or a 5- or 6-speed manual transaxle. This Chapter contains information on the manual transaxle. Service procedures for the automatic transaxle are contained in Chapter 7B.
2   The transaxle is contained in a cast-aluminum alloy casing bolted to the engine's left-hand end, and consists of the gearbox and final drive differential. The transaxle unit type is stamped on a plate attached to the transaxle.

Transaxle overhaul

3   Because of the complexity of the assembly, possible unavailability of replacement parts and special tools necessary, internal repair procedures for the transaxle are not recommended for the home mechanic. The bulk of the information in this Chapter is devoted to removal and installation procedures.

2   Shift cables – adjustment

1   If you're working on a six-speed manual transaxle, remove the battery and battery tray (see Chapter 5).
2   If you're working on a five-speed manual transaxle, remove the air intake duct (see Chapter 4).
3   Inside the car, apply the parking brake, then move the shift lever to Neutral.
4   Only the selector cable is to be adjusted during this procedure – this is the cable which comes to the lowest point on the front of the transaxle.
5   Unlock the selector cable by prying out the locking insert on the end of the selector cable **(see illustration)**.
6   Inside the car, move the shift lever to fourth gear position.

3.4b ... release the outer part of the cable by pulling back on the spring-loaded collar, then remove the cable from the bracket

7   Reinsert the locking insert on the end of the selector cable.
8   The remainder of installation is the reverse of removal.
9   Start the engine, keeping the clutch pedal depressed, and check for correct gear selection.

3   Shift cables – removal and installation

1   If you're working on a six-speed manual transaxle, remove the battery and battery tray (see Chapter 5)
2   If you're working on a five-speed manual transaxle, remove the air intake duct (see Chapter 4).
3   Apply the parking brake, then raise the front of the vehicle and support it securely on jackstands. Remove the engine undershield.
4   At the transaxle, remove the cables from the shift lever arms, then disconnect the cables from the support bracket **(see illustrations)**.

5   Under the vehicle, remove the washer-type fasteners, and slide the exhaust heat shield rearwards.
6   Unclip the cables from the vehicle body underside.
7   Remove the center console as described in Chapter 11.
8   Pry off the selector cable and press the release button on the shift cable **(see illustrations)**.
9   Disconnect the cables from the shift lever housing by pulling back on the spring loaded collars, then pulling the cables from the housing **(see illustration)**.
10   Fold back the carpet and insulation material under the center part of the instrument panel for access to the selector cable floor grommet. Remove the two fasteners and release the grommet from the floor **(see illustration)**.
11   Pass the cables up through the floor.
12   Installation is the reverse of removal. Use new clips when reconnecting the cables, and adjust the cables as described in Section 2.

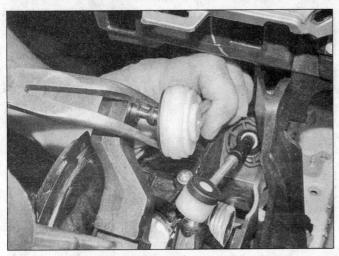

3.8a Pry off the selector cable…

3.8b …and release the shift cable

3.9 Release the outer cables

3.10 Remove the fasteners to release the grommet – shown with the heater removed for clarity

4   Driveaxle oil seals – replacement

1   Oil leaks frequently occur due to wear or deterioration of the driveshaft oil seals. Replacement of these seals is relatively easy, since the repairs can be performed without removing the transaxle from the vehicle.

Driveshaft oil seals

2   The driveaxle oil seals are located at the sides of the transaxle, where the driveaxles enter the transaxle. If leakage at the seal is suspected, raise the vehicle and support it securely on jackstands. If the seal is leaking, oil will be found on the side of the transaxle below the driveaxle.

3   Refer to Chapter 8 and remove the appropriate driveaxle.

4   Using a large screwdriver or seal removal tool, carefully pry the oil seal out of the transaxle casing, taking care not to damage the transaxle casing (see illustration).

4.4 A special oil seal removal tool can be used to pry the driveaxle oil seal from the transaxle

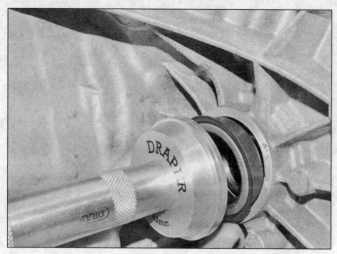

4.7 Drive the oil seal into place using a socket, or as shown here a special seal installation tool

5.7 Remove the clutch hydraulic fluid line

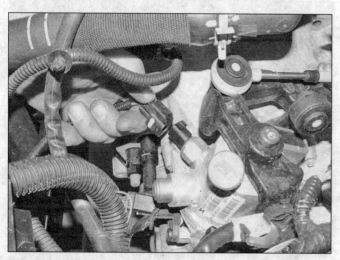

5.9a Disconnect the vehicle speed sensor electrical connector ...

5.9b ...then disconnect the wiring harness from the top of the transaxle

5   Wipe clean the oil seal seating in the transaxle casing.

6   Dip the new oil seal in clean oil, then press it a little way into the casing by hand, making sure that it is square to its seating.

7   Using a large socket or seal installation tool, carefully drive the oil seal fully into the casing until it contacts the seating surface **(see illustration)**.

8   Install the driveaxle (see Chapter 8).

5   Transaxle – removal and installation

Removal

1   Drain the transmission fluid (see Chapter 1).

2   Pull up and remove the engine cover.

3   Remove the air filter and inlet duct as described in Chapter 4.

4   Remove the battery and battery tray (see Chapter 5).

5   Remove the battery tray (see Chapter 5).

6   Make sure that the shift lever is in neutral. Taking adequate precautions against brake fluid spillage, pull out the securing clip, then pull the pipe fitting out of the clutch release cylinder at the top of the transaxle. Plug or tape over the pipe end to avoid losing fluid and to prevent dirt entry.

7   Unclip the release cylinder fluid pipe from the support bracket **(see illustration)**, and move it clear of the transaxle.

8   Disconnect the shift cables from the transmission as described in Section 3.

9   Disconnect the electrical connector

for the vehicle speed sensor, unclip the wiring harness cable(s), and disconnect the transaxle ground **(see illustrations)**.

10   Attach an engine support fixture to the lifting hook at the transaxle end of the engine. If no hook is provided, use a bolt of the proper size and thread pitch to attach the support fixture chain to a hole at the end of the cylinder head.

Note: *Engine support fixtures can be obtained at most equipment rental yards and some auto parts stores.*

11   Loosen the front wheel driveaxle/hub nuts and the wheel lug nuts, raise the front of the vehicle and support it securely on jackstands. Remove the wheels.

12   Remove the engine undershield.

13   Remove both driveshafts from the transaxle (see Chapter 8).

5.9c Remove the ground harness

5.14 Remove the exhaust/catalytic converter support bracket

5.22 Remove the central bolt

5.23 Remove the mounting bracket

14   If equipped, remove the exhaust/catalytic converter support bracket from above the rear engine mount **(see illustration)**.

15   Remove the starter motor (see Chapter 5).

16   Separate the exhaust pipe at the front subframe. Attach splints to each side of the exhaust flexible section (two wooden strips secured by cable ties will suffice) to prevent excessive bending. Discard the exhaust gaskets and use new ones during installation.

17   Make alignment marks between the engine and transaxle to help with alignment during installation, then unbolt and remove the rear engine mounting/torque strap from the rear of the transaxle bell housing.

18   Work around the transaxle bell housing and move the remaining hoses and wiring harness to one side.

19   Secure the coolant hoses with cable ties as required.

20   Support the transaxle with a jack - preferably a transmission jack made for this pur-pose (available at most tool rental yards). Safety chains will help steady the transaxle on the jack.

21   Remove the 2 upper transaxle-to-engine retaining bolts.

22   With the engine securely supported, unscrew and remove the central left-hand mounting bolt **(see illustration)**.

23   Remove three further nuts/bolts, and remove the lower section of the engine left-hand mounting bracket **(see illustration)**.

24   Taking care that nothing which is still attached to the engine is placed under strain, lower the transaxle so that it will clear the left-hand chassis leg.

25   Remove the lower transaxle-to-engine bolts. The bell housing bolts are of different lengths, so note their positions carefully for installation.

26   Check that, apart from the remaining bell housing bolts, there is nothing prevent-ing the transaxle from being removed. Make sure that any wiring or hoses lying on top of

the transaxle are not going to get caught up and stretched as the transaxle is lowered.

27   Unscrew the remaining bell housing bolts. If the transaxle does not separate on its own, it must be rocked from side-to-side, to free it from the locating dowels. As the transaxle is withdrawn from the engine, make sure its weight is supported at all times – the transaxle input shaft (or the clutch) may other-wise be damaged as it is withdrawn through the clutch assembly bolted to the engine fly-wheel.

28   Keeping the transaxle steady, carefully lower it down and remove it from under the car.

29   The clutch components can now be inspected, and replaced if necessary (see Chapter 8).

Installation

30   If removed, install the clutch components (see Chapter 8). Also ensure that the engine-to-transaxle adapter plates (if equipped) are

in position on the engine.

31 Lightly oil the splines of the transaxle input shaft. Take care not to apply too much or the clutch plates may become contaminated.

32 With the transaxle secured to the transmission jack as on removal, raise it into position, then carefully slide it onto the engine while engaging the input shaft with the clutch driven plate splines. If marks were made between the transaxle and engine on removal, these can be used as a guide to correct alignment.

33 Do not use excessive force to install the transaxle – if the input shaft does not slide into place easily, readjust the angle of the transaxle so that it is level, and/or turn the input shaft so that the splines engage properly with the plate. If problems are still experienced, check that the clutch driveplate is correctly centered (see Chapter 8).

34 Once the transaxle is successfully mated to the engine, insert as many of the flange bolts as possible, and tighten them progressively to draw the transaxle fully onto the locating dowels.

35 Install the lower section of the engine left-hand mounting, and tighten the nuts to the torque listed in this Chapter's Specifications.

36 Raise the transaxle into position, then install the upper section of the engine left-hand mounting. Tighten the nuts to the torque listed in this Chapter's Specifications, noting that the center nut is tightened considerably more than the four outer ones.

37 Install the remaining transaxle-to-engine bolts, and tighten all of them to the torque listed in this Chapter's Specifications.

38 Install the engine/transaxle rear mounting to the subframe, and tighten the through-bolts to the specified torque.

39 Once the engine/transaxle mountings have been installed, the engine support fixture can be removed.

40 The remainder of installation is the reverse of removal, noting the following points:

a) *Install the starter motor as described in Chapter 5.*

b) *Install the driveaxles as described in Chapter 8.*

c) *Use new exhaust gaskets and tighten the exhaust fasteners to the torque listed in the Chapter 4 Specifications.*

d) *Refill the transmission fluid (see Chapter 1).*

e) *Adjust the shift cables as described in Section 2.*

6　Manual transaxle overhaul - general information

Overhauling a manual transaxle is a difficult job for the do-it-yourselfer. It involves the disassembly and reassembly of many small parts. Numerous clearances must be precisely measured and, if necessary, changed with select-fit spacers and snap-rings. As a result, if transaxle problems arise, it can be removed and installed by a competent do-it-yourselfer, but overhaul should be left to a transmission repair shop. Rebuilt transaxles may be available - check with your dealer parts department and auto parts stores. At any rate, the time and money involved in an overhaul is almost sure to exceed the cost of a rebuilt unit.

Chapter 7 Part B
Automatic transaxle

Contents

Specifications

General

Fluid type and capacity .... See Chapter 1

Torque specifications

Note: *One foot-pound (ft-lb) of torque is equivalent to 12 inch-pounds (in-lbs) of torque. Torque values below approximately 15 ft-lbs are expressed in inch-pounds, because most foot-pound torque wrenches are not accurate at these smaller values.*

	Ft-lbs (unless otherwise indicated)	Nm
Clutchplate-to-driveplate fasteners	18	24
Transaxle-to-engine bolts	35	47
Transaxle mounting bolts		
Upper mount	109	148
Lower mount		
Mount bracket-to-subframe bolt	92	125
Mount through-bolt	59	80
Mount-to-transaxle	59	80

1   General information

1   All information on the automatic transaxle is included in this Chapter. Information for the manual transaxle can be found in Chapter 7A.

2   Because of the complexity of the automatic transaxles and the specialized equipment necessary to perform most service operations, this Chapter contains only those procedures related to general diagnosis, adjustment and removal and installation.

3   If the transaxle requires major repair work, it should be left to a dealer service department or an automotive or transmission repair shop. Once properly diagnosed you can, however, remove and install the transaxle yourself and save the expense, even if the repair work is done by a transmission shop.

2   Diagnosis - general

1   Automatic transaxle malfunctions may be caused by five general conditions:
   a) *Poor engine performance*
   b) *Improper adjustments*
   c) *Hydraulic malfunctions*
   d) *Mechanical malfunctions*
   e) *Malfunctions in the Powertrain Control Module (PCM) or its signal network*

2   Diagnosis of these problems should always begin with a check of the easily repaired items: fluid level and condition (see Chapter 1), shift cable adjustment and shift lever installation. Next, perform a road test to determine if the problem has been corrected or if more diagnosis is necessary. If the problem persists after the preliminary tests and corrections are completed, additional diag-

nosis should be performed by a dealer service department or other qualified transmission repair shop. On modern electronically-controlled automatic transaxles, a scan tool is helpful in retrieving trouble codes relating to the transaxle. Refer to "Troubleshooting" at the front of this manual for information on troubleshooting and symptoms of transaxle problems.

Preliminary checks

3   Drive the vehicle to warm the transaxle to normal operating temperature.

4   Check the fluid level as described in Chapter 1 :
   a) *If the fluid level is unusually low, add enough fluid to bring the level within the designated area of the dipstick, then check for external leaks (see following).*

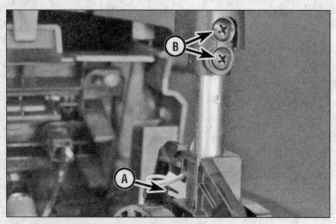

3.2 Shift lever electrical connector (A) and mounting screws (B)

3.6 Pry the cable end from the ballstud on the shifter

b) *If the fluid level is abnormally high, drain off the excess, then check the drained fluid for contamination by coolant. The presence of engine coolant in the automatic transmission fluid indicates that a failure has occurred in the internal radiator oil cooler walls that separate the coolant from the transmission fluid (see Chapter 3).*

c) *If the fluid is foaming, drain it and refill the transaxle, then check for coolant in the fluid, or a high fluid level.*

5   Check to see if any trouble codes are stored in the Powertrain Control Module (PCM) (see Chapter 6).

Note: *If the engine is malfunctioning, do not proceed with the preliminary checks until it has been repaired and runs normally.*

6   Check and adjust the shift cable, if necessary (see Section 4).

7   If hard shifting is experienced, inspect the shift cable under the steering column and at the manual lever on the transaxle (see Section 4).

Fluid leak diagnosis

8   Most fluid leaks are easy to locate visually. Repair usually consists of replacing a seal or gasket. If a leak is difficult to find, the following procedure may help.

9   Identify the fluid. Make sure it's transmission fluid and not engine oil or brake fluid (automatic transmission fluid is a deep red color).

10   Try to pinpoint the source of the leak. Drive the vehicle several miles, then park it over a large sheet of cardboard. After a minute or two, you should be able to locate the leak by determining the source of the fluid dripping onto the cardboard.

11   Make a careful visual inspection of the suspected component and the area immediately around it. Pay particular attention to gasket mating surfaces. A mirror is often helpful for finding leaks in areas that are hard to see.

12   If the leak still cannot be found, clean the suspected area thoroughly with a degreaser or solvent, then dry it thoroughly.

13   Drive the vehicle for several miles at normal operating temperature and varying

speeds. After driving the vehicle, visually inspect the suspected component again.

14   Once the leak has been located, the cause must be determined before it can be properly repaired. If a gasket is replaced but the sealing flange is bent, the new gasket will not stop the leak. The bent flange must be straightened.

15   Before attempting to repair a leak, check to make sure that the following conditions are corrected or they may cause another leak.

Note: *Some of the following conditions cannot be fixed without highly specialized tools and expertise. Such problems must be referred to a qualified transmission shop or a dealer service department.*

Gasket leaks

16   Check the pan periodically. Make sure the bolts are tightened to the torque listed in this Chapter's Specifications , no bolts are missing, the gasket is in good condition and the pan is flat (dents in the pan may indicate damage to the valve body inside).

17   If the pan gasket is leaking, the fluid level or the fluid pressure may be too high, the vent may be plugged, the pan bolts may be too tight, the pan sealing flange may be warped, the sealing surface of the transaxle housing may be damaged, the gasket may be damaged or the transaxle casting may be cracked or porous. If sealant instead of gasket material has been used to form a seal between the pan and the transaxle housing, it may be the wrong type of sealant.

Seal leaks

18   If a transaxle seal is leaking, the fluid level or pressure may be too high, the vent may be plugged, the seal bore may be damaged, the seal itself may be damaged or improperly installed, the surface of the shaft protruding through the seal may be damaged or a loose bearing may be causing excessive shaft movement.

19   Make sure the dipstick tube seal is in good condition and the tube is properly seated. Periodically check the area around the sensors for leakage. If transmission fluid is evident, check the seals for damage.

Case leaks

20   If the case itself appears to be leaking, the casting is porous and will have to be repaired or replaced.

21   Make sure the oil cooler hose fittings are tight and in good condition.

Fluid comes out vent pipe or fill tube

22   If this condition occurs the possible causes are: the transaxle is overfilled; there is coolant in the fluid; the case is porous; the dipstick is incorrect; the vent is plugged or the drain-back holes are plugged.

---

3   Shift lever - replacement

Warning: *These models are equipped with a Supplemental Restraint System (SRS), more commonly known as airbags. Always disable the airbag system before working in the vicinity of any airbag system component to avoid the possibility of accidental deployment of the airbag(s), which could cause personal injury (see Chapter 12).*

Warning: *Do not use a memory saving device to preserve the PCM or radio memory when working on or near airbag system components.*

Floor shifter

Shift knob

1   Remove the upper shift lever bezel (see Chapter 11).

2   Pull up the shift knob boot and disconnect the electrical connector. Remove the two screws and pull the knob off the shaft **(see illustration)**.

3   Installation is the reverse of removal.

Shift lever assembly

4   Disconnect the negative battery cable from the remote ground terminal (see Chapter 5). Wait at least five minutes before proceeding.

5   Remove the floor console and center trim covers as needed to access the shift lever assembly components (see Chapter 11).

6   Use a trim tool to pry the cable end from the ballstud on the shifter **(see illustration)**.

3.7 Pry the tabs forward to release the cable retainer from the console

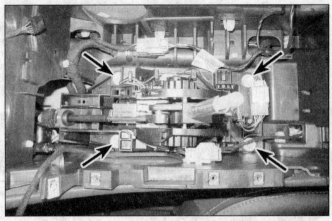

3.9 Remove the shift lever assembly bolts to remove the shifter

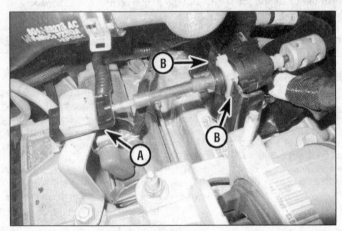

4.11 Remove the cable end from the ballstud on the shift control lever (A), then depress the tabs (B) and slide the cable housing out of the bracket

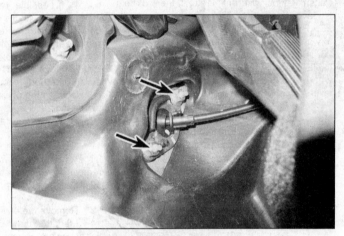

4.14 Shift cable grommet plate nuts

7   Release the tabs on the sides of the shift cable and detach it from the console **(see illustration)**.
8   Disconnect the electrical connector and wire harness clips. Remove the carpet retainers from both sides of the shift lever assembly.
9   Remove the shifter base bolts and remove the shift lever assembly from the vehicle **(see illustration)**.
10   Installation is the reverse of removal.
11   Check the shift cable adjustment (see Section 4) and adjust as necessary. Ensure the vehicle starts in Park and Neutral, and the back-up lights illuminate when in Reverse.

4   Shift cable - replacement and adjustment

Warning: *The models covered by this manual are equipped with Supplemental Restraint Systems (SRS), more commonly known as airbags. Always disarm the airbag system before working in the vicinity of any airbag sys-*tem component to avoid the possibility of accidental deployment of the airbag, which could cause personal injury (see Chapter 12).*
Warning: *Do not use a memory saving device to preserve the PCM or radio memory when working on or near airbag system components.*

Replacement

1   If the vehicle has just been driven, wait several hours to allow the engine to cool down before beginning this procedure. Disconnect both the negative and positive cables from the battery (see Chapter 5). Wait at least five minutes before proceeding.
2   Place the shifter in Neutral.
3   Raise the vehicle on a hoist, or raise the front of the vehicle and support it securely on jackstands.
4   Remove the air filter housing (see Chapter 4).
5   Remove the center console and trim to access the shift cable and disconnect the cable from the shift lever (see Chapter 11).

6   Remove the driver's side knee bolster (see Chapter 11).
7   Use a trim tool to pry the cable eye from the ballstud on the shifter (see Section 3).
8   Release the tabs on the sides of the shift cable and detach it from the console (see Section 3).
9   Remove the two instrument panel brace bolts at the floor, then slide the cable under the brace and remove it.
10   Remove the insulation from the floor area under the center of the instrument panel and remove the fasteners securing the transaxle cable plate/grommet.
11   To disconnect the shift cable at the transaxle control lever, remove the cable end from the lever ballstud **(see illustration)**.
12   Squeeze the retaining tab(s) and detach the cable housing from the mounting bracket on the transaxle **(see illustration 4.11)**.
13   Disconnect any cable retainers along the length of the cable.
14   Remove the grommet plate nuts from the floorpan studs below the HVAC housing **(see illustration)**.

15   Pull the shift cable through the floor from the inside.

Note: *The grommet is integral to the cable assembly.*

16   Installation is the reverse of removal. Adjust the new cable after installation (see following).

Adjustment

Note: *The transaxle end of the shift cable is equipped with an adjuster mechanism.*

17   Set the parking brake, then disconnect the negative battery cable from the remote ground terminal (see Chapter 5).

18   Remove the air filter housing (see Chapter 4).

19   Place the shifter in Drive.

20   Remove the cable from the shift lever ballstud **(see illustration 4.11)**.

21   Manually move the shift arm at the transaxle clockwise until it stops, then rotate the lever counterclockwise one click.

22   Pry the lock tabs out and slide the lock forward to release **(see illustration)**.

23   Slide the shift lever cable end until the cable is aligned with the control lever.

24   Reconnect the cable end to the manual lever ballstud, with the lock still released.

25   Slide back the lock on the adjuster.

Note: *Make sure the adjuster is locked and the cable is securely seated onto the ball stud.*

26   Install any remaining components, then apply the parking brake, start the engine (verify that it only starts in Park and Neutral), and shift into each range to verify the adjustment is correct and the back-up lights illuminate when in Reverse. If you have have any doubts whatsoever about the shift mechanism effectiveness, a special scan tool will be required to preform a transmission range sensor adaptive learning procedure. Have the vehicle towed to a dealer service department or other qualified repair shop.

---

5   Automatic transaxle - removal and installation

Warning: *Wait until the engine is completely cool before beginning this procedure.*

Removal

1   Loosen the front wheel lug nuts. Place the vehicle on a hoist or raise and support the front of the vehicle on jackstands. Remove the wheels. Have an assistant depress the brake pedal, then loosen the driveaxle/hub nuts.

2   Drain the transaxle fluid into a suitable container for recycling (see Chapter 1).

3   Drain the cooling system (see Chapter 1).

4   Remove the cowl cover (see Chapter 11).

5   Remove the battery and battery tray (see Chapter 5).

6   Remove the air filter housing and duct (see Chapter 4), then remove the housing bracket bolts and bracket. Remove the throttle body intake hose.

7   Disconnect the shift cable from the shift lever and housing from the bracket (see Section 4). If possible, remove the bracket from the transaxle with the cable attached.

8   Disconnect the ground straps and remove the bolts holding the electrical harness to the transaxle.

9   Remove the PCV hose and disconnect the throttle body vacuum lines. Remove the bolt securing the power steering hose bracket to the engine.

10   Remove the starter motor (see Chapter 5).

11   Remove the bolt and disconnect the large ground cable from the transaxle, then remove the bolt from the bellhousing.

12   Remove the upper transaxle-to-engine bolts.

13   Remove the driveaxles (see Chapter 8).

14   Mark the relationship of the cutchplate to the driveplate. Remove the clutchplate mounting nuts.

15   Remove the lower transaxle mount (see Section 8).

16   Attach an engine support fixture to the lifting hook at the transaxle end of the engine. If no hook is provided, use a bolt of the proper size and thread pitch to attach the support fixture chain to a hole at the end of the cylinder head.

17   Remove the transaxle upper mount from the engine (see Section 8).

18   Support the transaxle with a jack - preferably a transmission jack made for this purpose (available at most tool rental yards). Safety chains will help steady the transaxle on the jack.

19   Remove the remaining bolts securing the transaxle to the engine.

20   Move the transaxle away from the engine to disengage it from the engine block dowel pins. Carefully lower the transmission jack to the floor and remove the transaxle. Ensure the torque converter is secure in the transaxle and does not fall out. Transfer the transaxle components to the new transaxle before installation.

Installation

21   Installation is the reverse of removal, noting the following:

a)   *As the torque converter is reinstalled, ensure that the drive tangs at the center of the torque converter hub engage with the recesses in the automatic transaxle fluid pump inner gear. This can be confirmed by turning the torque converter while pushing it towards the transaxle. If it isn't fully engaged, it will clunk into place.*

b)   *When installing the transaxle, make sure the matchmarks you made on the clutchplate and driveplate line up. Install the transaxle-to-engine mounting bolts and tighten to the torque listed in this Chapter's Specifications.*

c)   *Install all of the clutchplate-to-driveplate fasteners before tightening any of them.*

d)   *Tighten the clutchplate-to-driveplate fasteners to the torque listed in this Chapter's Specifications.*

e)   *Tighten the transaxle mounting bolts to the torque listed in this Chapter's Specifications.*

f)   *Tighten the subframe mounting bolts to the torque listed in the Chapter 10 Specifications.*

g)   *Tighten the driveaxle/hub nuts to the torque listed in the Chapter 8 Specifications.*

h)   *Tighten the wheel lug nuts to the torque listed in the Chapter 1 Specifications.*

i)   *Fill the transaxle with the correct type and amount of automatic transmission fluid (see Chapter 1).*

j)   *Adjust the shift cable (see Section 4).*

---

6   Automatic transaxle overhaul - general information

1   In the event of a problem occurring, it will be necessary to establish whether the fault is electrical, mechanical or hydraulic in nature, before repair work can be contemplated. Diagnosis requires detailed knowledge of the transaxle's operation and construction, as well as access to specialized test equipment, and so is deemed to be beyond the scope of this manual. It is therefore essential that problems with the automatic transaxle are referred to a dealer service department or other qualified

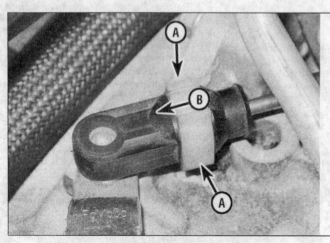

4.22 Pry the lock tabs out (A) then slide the lock forward (B) to release

repair facility for assessment.

2   Note that a faulty transaxle should not be removed before the vehicle has been diagnosed by a knowledgeable technician equipped with the proper tools, as trouble-shooting must be performed with the transaxle installed in the vehicle.

7   Driveaxle oil seals - replacement

1   Oil leaks frequently occur due to wear of the driveaxle oil seals. Replacement of these seals is relatively easy, since the repair can be performed without removing the transaxle from the vehicle.

2   Driveaxle oil seals are located at the sides of the transaxle, where the driveaxles are attached. If leakage at the seal is suspected, raise the vehicle and support it securely on jackstands. If the seal is leak-ing, lubricant will be found on the sides of the transaxle, below the seals.

3   Remove the driveaxles (see Chapter 8).

4   Use a screwdriver or prybar to carefully pry the oil seal out of the transaxle bore.

5   If the oil seal cannot be removed with a screwdriver or prybar, a special oil seal removal tool (available at auto parts stores) will be required.

6   Using a large section of pipe or a large deep socket (slightly smaller than the outside diameter of the seal) as a drift, install the new oil seal. Drive it into the bore squarely and

make sure it's completely seated. Coat the seal lip with transaxle lubricant.

7   Install the driveaxle(s). Be careful not to damage the lip of the new seal with the inboard splines of the driveaxle.

8   Transaxle mount - replacement

1   Insert a large screwdriver or prybar between the mount and the transaxle and pry up/down (upper mount) or left/right (lower mount).

2   The transaxle should not move exces-sively away from the mount. If it does, replace the mount.

Lower mount

3   Raise the front of the vehicle and sup-port it securely on jackstands.

4   Remove the transaxle mount-to-sub-frame and mount-to-transaxle case mounting bolts, and remove the mount.

5   Installation is the reverse of removal. Tighten the mounting bolts to the torque listed in this Chapter's Specifications.

Note: *Install all of the mount fasteners before tightening any of them.*

Upper mount

6   Remove the air filter housing (see Chap-ter 4).

7   Remove the battery and battery tray (see Chapter 5).

8.8 Transaxle upper mount mounting bolt

8   Supporting the transaxle with a floor jack or engine support, remove the support mounting bolt, then remove the mount **(see illustration)**. It may be necessary to raise the transaxle slightly to provide enough clearance to remove the mount.

9   Remove the remaining mount bolts.

10   Installation is the reverse of removal. Tighten the mounting bolts to the torque listed in this Chapter's Specifications.

Note: *Install all of the mount fasteners before tightening any of them.*

Notes

Chapter 8
Clutch and driveaxles

Contents

Specifications

General

Clutch type	Single dry plate, diaphragm spring, hydraulic actuation
Clutch fluid type	See Chapter 1
Clutch disc warpage limit	0.008 inch (0.2 mm)

Torque specifications

Note: *One foot-pound (ft-lb) of torque is equivalent to 12 inch-pounds (in-lbs) of torque. Torque values below approximately 15 ft-lbs are expressed in inch-pounds, because most foot-pound torque wrenches are not accurate at these smaller values.*

	Ft-lbs (unless otherwise indicated)	Nm
Pressure plate retaining bolts	21	28
Release bearing and release cylinder mounting bolts	97 in-lbs	11
Driveaxle/hub nut*		
Step 1	60	80
Step 2	Tighten an additional 90-degrees	
Intermediate shaft support bearing nuts*		
Step 1 (lower nut)	44 in-lbs	5
Step 2 (upper nut)	18	25
Step 3 (lower nut)	18	25
Wheel lug nuts	see Chapter 1	

* Use new fasteners during installation

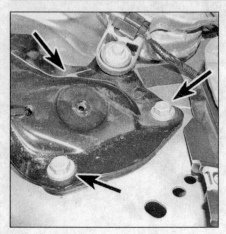

2.4 Remove the bolts from the suspension brace

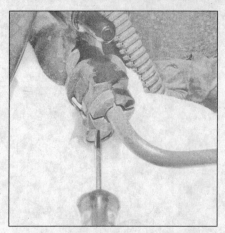

2.5a Pry down the clip and pull the pressure line from the clutch master cylinder

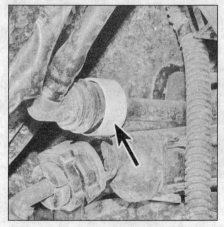

2.5b Pull back the collar and disconnect the fluid supply pipe

1   General Information

Clutch

1   A single dry plate diaphragm spring clutch is used on all manual transaxle models. The clutch is hydraulically operated via a master and release cylinder. All models have an internally mounted release cylinder and release bearing combined into one unit.

2   The main components of the clutch are the pressure plate, the driven plate (sometimes called the friction plate or disc) and the release bearing. The pressure plate is bolted to the flywheel, with the driven plate sandwiched between them. The center of the driven plate carries female splines which mate with the splines on the transaxle input shaft. The release bearing acts on the diaphragm spring fingers of the pressure plate.

3   When the engine is running and the clutch pedal is released, the diaphragm spring clamps the pressure plate, driven plate and flywheel firmly together. Drive is transmitted through the friction surfaces of the flywheel and pressure plate to the linings of the driven plate, and on to the transaxle input shaft.

4   The release cylinder is incorporated into the release bearing – when the release cylinder operates, the release bearing moves against the diaphragm spring fingers. As the spring pressure on the pressure plate is relieved, the flywheel and pressure plate spin without moving the driven plate. As the pedal is released, spring pressure is restored and the drive is gradually taken up.

5   The clutch hydraulic system consists of a master cylinder, a release cylinder and the associated pipes and hoses. The fluid reservoir is shared with the brake master cylinder.

Driveaxles

6   Drive is transmitted from the differential to the front wheels by means of two solid-steel, equal-length driveaxles equipped with constant velocity (CV) joints at their inner and outer ends. Due to the position of the transaxle, an intermediate shaft and support bearing are incorporated into the right-hand driveaxle assembly.

7   A ball-and-cage type CV joint is fitted to the outer end of each driveaxle. The joint has an outer member, which is splined at its outer end to accept the wheel hub, and is threaded so that it can be fastened to the hub by a large bolt. The joint contains six balls within a cage, which engage with the inner member. The complete assembly is protected by a flexible boot secured to the driveaxle and joint outer member.

8   At the inner end, the driveaxle incorporates a tripod type CV joint, containing needle roller bearings and cups. On the left-hand side, the driveaxle inner CV joint engages directly with the differential side gear. On the right-hand side, the inner joint is integral with the intermediate shaft, the inner end of which engages with the other differential side gear. As on the outer joints, a flexible boot secured to the driveaxle and CV joint outer member protects the complete assembly.

2   Clutch pedal – removal and installation

Warning: *Brake fluid is poisonous; wash it off immediately and thoroughly in the case of skin contact, and seek immediate medical advice if any fluid is swallowed or gets into the eyes. Certain types of brake fluid is flammable, and may ignite when allowed into contact with hot components; when servicing any hydraulic system, it is safest to assume that the fluid IS flammable, and to take precautions against the risk of fire as though it is petrol that is being handled. Brake fluid is also an effective paint stripper, and will attack some plastics; if any is spilled, it should be washed off immediately, using copious quantities of clean water. Finally, it is hygroscopic (it absorbs moisture from the air) – old fluid may be contaminated and unfit for further use. When adding or replacing fluid, always use the recommended type, and ensure that it comes from a freshly opened sealed container.*

Removal

1   Remove the battery and battery tray (see Chapter 5). Using a suction gun or baster, remove as much fluid from the reservoir as possible.

Warning: *If a baster is used, never again use it for the preparation of food.*

2   Remove the lower dash panel as described in Chapter 11.

3   Remove the pinch bolt and separate the steering column intermediate shaft from the steering gear input shaft (see Chapter 10).

4   Remove the wiper arms, windshield cowl panel and wiper motors (see Chapter 12), then remove the strut brace from the suspension towers **(see illustration)**. With the brace removed, temporarily reinstall the bolts to the suspension towers.

5   Depress the release buttons/pry out the clip and disconnect the pressure line from the clutch master cylinder connection at the engine compartment firewall, then disconnect the fluid supply hose from the master cylinder **(see illustrations)**.

Caution: *Be prepared for fluid spillage – wipe up any spills immediately – the fluid could damage paint.*

6   Disconnect the clutch pedal position sensor wiring plug **(see illustration)**.

7   Remove the retaining nuts and maneuver the clutch pedal out of place, complete with the bracket and master cylinder **(see illustration)**.

8   To separate the master cylinder from the pedal bracket, begin by squeezing the sides of the retaining clip and pull the pushrod from the pedal **(see illustration)**.

9   Rotate the master cylinder 60-degrees clockwise and pull it from the bracket **(see illustration)**.

2.6 Disconnect the electrical connector from the clutch pedal position sensor

2.7 Unscrew the nuts and remove the pedal/master cylinder assembly

2.8 Squeeze the sides of the clip and pull the pushrod from the pedal

Installation

10   Install by reversing the removal operations. Note the following points:
   a) *Tighten all fasteners securely.*
   b) *Replace the seal between the master cylinder and the firewall if necessary.*
   c) *Bleed the clutch hydraulic system as described in Section 5.*
   d) *Check the operation of the clutch before installing the lower dash panel (see Chapter 11)*

3   Clutch master cylinder – removal and installation

Note: *No repair or overhaul of the cylinder is possible. In the event of a hydraulic system fault, or any sign of visible fluid leakage on or around the master cylinder or clutch pedal, the unit should be replaced.*

   Removal and installation of the master cylinder is included in the pedal removal and installation procedure (see Section 2).

4   Clutch release cylinder – removal and installation

Warning: *Refer to the* **Warning** *at the beginning of Section 2 before proceeding.*
Note: *Release cylinder internal components are not available separately, and no repair or overhaul of the cylinder is possible. In the event of a hydraulic system fault, or any sign of fluid leakage, the unit should be replaced.*

Removal

1   Remove the transaxle as described in Chapter 7A. The internal release cylinder cannot be removed with the transaxle in place.
2   Release the rubber seal from the transaxle.
3   Remove the mounting bolts securing the cylinder and release bearing assembly to the transaxle **(see illustration)**. Remove the

2.9 Rotate the master cylinder 60-degrees clockwise and pull it from the bracket

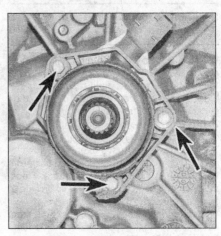

4.3 Release cylinder mounting bolts

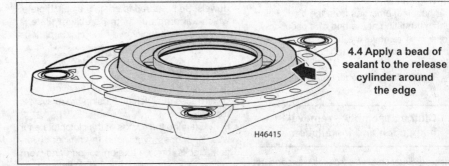

4.4 Apply a bead of sealant to the release cylinder around the edge

H46415

assembly, feeding the fluid pipe in through the transaxle aperture.

Installation

4   Ensure the release bearing cylinder and transaxle casing mating surfaces are clean. Apply a bead of sealant to the rear of the bearing/cylinder as shown **(see illustration)**.
5   Lubricate the inner lips of the seal with a little multi-purpose grease, then position the release bearing cylinder on the input shaft, and tighten the bolts to the torque listed in this Chapter's Specifications. Take care not

to damage the seal lips with the input shaft splines – wrap tape around the splines prior to installing the cylinder.
6   Install the rubber seal around the hydraulic lines, ensuring it is correctly positioned.
7   The remainder of installation is a reversal of removal, noting the following points:
   a) *Install the transaxle as described in Chapter 7A.*
   b) *Remove the tape from the input shaft splines.*
   c) *Bleed the clutch hydraulic system (see Section 5).*

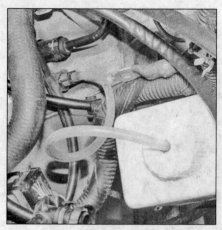

5.3 Connect the hose to the bleed fitting on the top of the transaxle housing

6.3a Remove the pressure plate retaining bolts

6.3b Using a home-made tool to lock the flywheel

5   Clutch hydraulic system – bleeding

Warning: *Refer to the* **Warning** *at the beginning of Section 2 before proceeding.*

1   Top-up the brake fluid reservoir on the brake master cylinder with fresh clean fluid of the specified type (see Chapter 1).
2   Remove the air filter housing as described in Chapter 4.
3   Remove the dust cover, and push a length of clear hose over the bleed fitting on the release cylinder **(see illustration)**. Place the other end of the hose in a jar containing a small amount of brake fluid.
4   Loosen the bleed fitting half a turn, then have an assistant depress the clutch pedal. Tighten the bleed fitting when the pedal is depressed. Have the assistant release the pedal, then loosen the bleed screw again.
5   Repeat the process until clean fluid, free of air bubbles, emerges from the bleed fitting. Tighten the fitting at the end of a pedal down-stroke, and remove the hose and jar. Reinstall the dust cover and air filter housing (see Chapter 4).
6   Top-up the brake fluid reservoir.

6   Clutch assembly – removal, inspection and installation

Warning: *Dust created by clutch wear and deposited on the clutch components is a health hazard. DO NOT blow it out with compressed air or inhale any of it. DO NOT use gasoline or petroleum-based solvents to clean off the dust. Brake system cleaner should be used to flush the dust into a drain pan. After the clutch components are wiped clean with a rag, dispose of the contaminated rag and the cleaner in a sealed, marked container.*

Removal

1   Access to the clutch may be gained in one of two ways. Either the engine/transaxle

assembly can be removed as described in Chapter 2B, and the transaxle then separated from the engine, or the engine may be left in the car and the transaxle removed independently as described in Chapter 7A.
2   Having separated the transaxle from the engine, check if there are any marks identifying the relation of the pressure plate to the flywheel. If not, make your own marks using a dab of paint or a scribe. These marks will be used if the original pressure plate is reinstalled, and will help to maintain the balance of the unit. A new pressure plate may be installed in any position allowed by the locating dowels.
3   Unscrew the pressure plate retaining bolts, working in a diagonal sequence, and loosening the bolts only a turn at a time. If necessary, the flywheel may be held stationary using a home-made locking tool **(see illustrations)**.
4   Ease the pressure plate off its locating dowels. Be prepared to catch the clutch plate, which will drop out as the pressure plate is removed. Note which way the clutch plate is oriented.

Inspection

5   With the clutch assembly removed, wash off all traces of clutch dust using brake system cleaner.
6   Examine the linings of the clutch plate for wear and loose rivets, and the rim for distortion, cracks, broken torsion springs and worn splines. The surface of the friction linings may be highly glazed, but, as long as the friction material pattern can be clearly seen, this is satisfactory.
7   If there is any sign of oil contamination, indicated by a continuous or patchy, shiny black discolouration, the plate must be replaced and the source of the contamination traced and rectified. This will be either a leaking crankshaft oil seal or transmission input shaft oil seal – or both.
8   The clutch plate must also be replaced if the lining thickness has worn down to, or just above, the level of the rivet heads. Given the

amount of work necessary to gain access to the clutch plate, it's a good idea to install a new plate regardless of the old one's condition.
9   Check the machined faces of the flywheel and pressure plate. If either is grooved, or heavily scored, replacement is necessary. Providing the damage is not too serious, the flywheel can be removed as described in Chapter 2A, and taken to an automotive machine shop for refacing.
10   The pressure plate must be replaced if any cracks are apparent, if the diaphragm spring is damaged or its pressure suspect, or if there is excessive warpage of the pressure plate face.
11   With the transaxle removed, check the condition of the clutch release bearing, as described in Section 7.

Installation

12   It is advisable to install the clutch assembly with clean hands, and to wipe down the pressure plate and flywheel faces with brake system cleaner before assembly begins.
13   Install an appropriate clutch alignment tool into the hole at the end of the crankshaft. The tool must be a sliding fit in the crankshaft hole and the clutch plate splines. These tools are available at most auto parts stores.
14   Place the clutch plate in position as noted on removal. Note that the new clutch plate will be marked to indicate which side faces the flywheel **(see illustrations)**.
15   Place the pressure plate over the dowels. Intall the retaining bolts and tighten them finger-tight so that the clutch plate is gripped lightly, but can still be moved.
16   Center the clutch disc by ensuring the alignment tool extends through the splined hub and into the hole in the end of the crankshaft. Wiggle the tool up, down or side-to-side as needed to center the disc. Tighten the pressure plate-to-flywheel bolts a little at a time, working in a criss-cross pattern to prevent distorting the cover. After all of the bolts are snug, tighten them to the torque listed in this Chapter's Specifications. Remove the alignment tool.

6.14a The clutch driven plate should be marked to indicate which side faces the transaxle or flywheel

6.14b Position the clutch plate using a clutch aligning tool

8.3 On some models you can pry out the center cap and loosen the diveaxle/hub nut

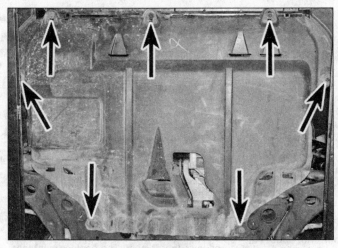

8.4 Unscrew the bolts and remove the splash shield

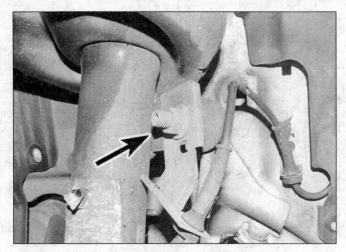

8.8 Remove the brake hose mounting bolt

17   The engine and/or transaxle can now be reinstalled by referring to the appropriate Chapters of this manual.

7   Clutch release bearing – removal, inspection and installation

Removal

1   Access to the clutch release bearing may be gained in one of two ways. Either the engine/transaxle assembly can be removed as described in Chapter 2B, and the transaxle then separated from the engine, or the engine may be left in the car and the transaxle removed independently as described in Chapter 7A.

2   The release bearing and release cylinder are combined into one unit, and cannot be separated. Refer to the release cylinder removal procedure in Section 4.

Inspection

3   Check the bearing for smoothness of operation, and replace it if there is any rough-ness or harshness as the bearing is spun. It is a good idea to replace the bearing as a matter of course during clutch replacement, regardless of its apparent condition, considering the amount of work necessary to gain access to it.

Installation

4   Refer to Section 4.

8   Driveaxles – removal and installation

Removal

1   Firmly apply the parking brake and chock the rear wheels. When the driveaxle/hub nut is to be loosened (or tightened), it is preferable to do so with the car resting on its wheels. If the car is jacked up, this places a high load on the jack, and the car could slip off.

2   If the car has steel wheels, remove the wheel trim on the side being worked on – the driveaxle/hub nut can then be loosened with the wheel on the ground. On models with alloy wheels, remove the center cap from the wheel to access the driveaxle/hub nut – if a suitable socket is available. The other option is to remove the wheel on the side being worked on, and to install the temporary spare – this wheel allows easy access to the driveaxle/hub nut

3   With an assistant firmly depressing the brake pedal, loosen the driveaxle/hub nut using a socket and a long breaker bar **(see illustration)**.

4   Loosen the front wheel lug nuts, then raise the front of the vehicle and support it securely on jackstands. Remove the wheel, then remove the under-vehicle splash shield **(see illustration)**.

5   Remove the driveaxle/hub nut. Discard the nut – a new one must be installed.

6   Tap the end of the driveshaft into the wheel hub slightly.

7   Remove the bolt/nut and detach the headlight leveling sensor bracket from the lower arm (where applicable).

8   Unbolt the flexible brake hose from the suspension strut **(see illustration)**.

8.10a Push the control arm downwards, pull the hub carrier outwards, and withdraw the driveshaft

8.10b If necessary, use a drive hub remover to push the driveaxle out of the hub splines

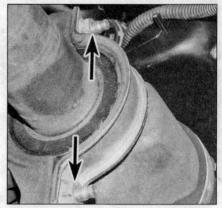

8.12 Unscrew the two nuts and remove the intermediate bearing cap

9.3 Cut the boot retaining clamps

9.7 Pack the outer CV joint with about half the grease supplied

9   Detach the control arm balljoint from the steering knuckle (see Chapter 10).

10   Swivel the suspension strut and steering knuckle assembly outwards, and withdraw the driveaxle CV joint from the hub splines. If the splines stick, use a hub flange remover to push the driveaxle out of the hub splines **(see illustrations)**.

11   If removing the left-hand driveaxle, free the inner CV joint from the transaxle by prying between the edge of the joint and the transaxle case with a large screwdriver or pry-bar. Take care not to damage the transaxle oil seal or the inner CV joint boot.

12   If removing the right-hand driveaxle, unscrew the two nuts and remove the cap from the intermediate shaft support bearing **(see illustration)**. Dispose of the cap and nuts – new ones must be installed. Pull the intermediate shaft out of the transaxle and remove the driveaxle assembly.

Caution: *Do not pull the outer shaft from the intermediate shaft – the coupling will separate.*

Installation

13   Installation is a reversal of removal, but observe the following points.

a) *Prior to installation, remove all traces of rust, oil and dirt from the splines of the outer CV joint, and lubricate the splines of the inner joint with wheel bearing grease.*

b) *Apply a little grease to the driveaxle seal lips in the transaxle case.*

c) *If working on the left-hand driveaxle, ensure that the inner CV joint is pushed fully into the transaxle, so that the retaining clip locks into place in the differential gear.*

d) *Always use a new driveaxle/hub nut.*

e) *Install the same wheel that was used for loosening the driveaxle/hub nut, then lower the car to the ground.*

f) *Tighten all nuts and bolts to the specified torque (see Chapters 8 and 9 for brake and suspension component torque specifications). When tightening the driveaxle/hub nut, first tighten it to the torque listed in this Chapter's Specifications, then further, through the specified angle, using an angle-tightening gauge.*

g) *The manufacturer specifies that when installing the right-hand driveaxle, the intermediate shaft bearing cap and nuts must be replaced with new ones, then*

tighten to the torque listed in this Chapter's Specifications

h) *Where applicable, install the alloy wheel on completion. Tighten the wheel lug nuts to the torque listed in the Chapter 1 Specifications.*

9   Outer constant velocity (CV) joint boot – replacement

1   Disassemble the inner constant velocity joint as described in Section 10.

2   On models with a vibration damper, after removing the inner CV joint, measure and note the distance from the end of the shaft to the edge of the damper. The damper must then be pressed from the shaft, the outer joint boot replaced, and the damper pressed back into its original position using the dimensions previously noted. If access to a hydraulic press is not available, most automotive machine shops would be prepared to carry out this task for a modest fee.

3   Cut off the boot retaining clamps, then slide the boot down the shaft to expose the outer constant velocity joint **(see illustration)**.

Caution: *Do not disassemble the outer CV joint.*

4   Scoop out as much grease as possible from the joint.

5   Inspect the ball tracks on the inner and outer members. If the tracks have widened, the balls will no longer be a tight fit. At the same time, check the ball cage windows for wear or cracking between the windows. If the joints appear worn, complete replacement of the joint may be the only option – check with a dealer or other parts supplier.

6   If the joint is in satisfactory condition, obtain a repair kit.

7   Pack the joint with the half of the grease supplied, working it well into the ball tracks **(see illustration)**.

8   Slide the clamps and boot onto the shaft.

9.10a Locate the outer clamp on the boot. . .

9.10b. . . then, using a special pair of crimping pliers. . .

9.10c. . . remove any slack in the clamp

9   Apply the remaining grease to the joint and the inside of the boot.

10   Locate the outer lip of the boot in the groove on the outer joint housing, then install the retaining clamp. Remove any slack in the clamp by carefully compressing the raised section using a special pair of crimping pliers **(see illustrations)**.

Note: *Ensure no grease is on the surfaces between the boot and the joint housing.*

11   Use a small screwdriver to lift the inner lip of the boot, allowing the air pressure inside the boot to equalize, then install the inner clip to the boot **(see illustration)**.

12   Where applicable, press the damper into its original position.

13   Reassemble the inner constant velocity joint as described in Section 10.

10   Inner constant velocity (CV) joint boot – replacement

1   Remove the driveaxle(s) as described in Section 8.

2   Cut through the metal clamps and slide the boot from the inner CV joint.

3   Clean out some of the grease from the joint, then make alignment marks between the housing and the shaft to aid in reassembly **(see illustration)**.

4   Carefully pull the housing from the tripod, twisting the housing so the tripod rollers come out one at a time. If necessary, use a soft-faced hammer or mallet to tap the housing off.

5   Clean the grease from the tripod and housing.

6   Remove the snap-ring, and carefully drive the tripod from the end of the shaft **(see illustrations)**. Discard the snap-ring; a new one (supplied in the repair kit) must be installed. Remove the boot if still on the shaft.

9.11 Lift the inner edge of the boot to equalize the air pressure inside

10.3 Make alignment marks between the shaft and housing

10.6a Remove the snap-ring from the end of the shaft. . .

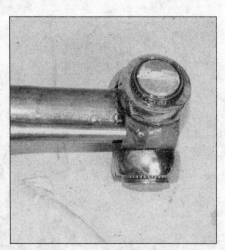

10.6b. . . then carefully drive the tripod from the shaft

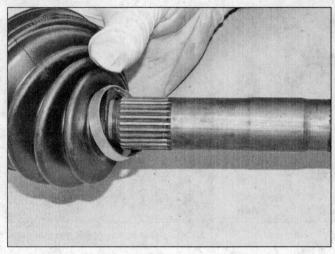

10.7 Slide the new boot and smaller diameter clamp onto the shaft

10.8a Install the tripod with the beveled edge towards the shaft. . .

10.8b. . . then install the new snap-ring

10.11 The smaller diameter of the boot must locate over the groove in the shaft

10.12 Equalize the air pressure before tightening the boot clamp

7　Slide the new boot onto the shaft along with the smaller clamp (see illustration).

8　Reinstall the tripod with the beveled edge towards the driveaxle, and drive it fully into place, until the new snap-ring can be installed (see illustrations).

9　Lubricate the tripod rollers with some of the grease supplied in the boot kit, then fill the housing and boot with the remainder of the grease.

10　Reinstall the housing to the tripod, tapping it gently into place using a soft-hammer or mallet if necessary.

11　Slide the new boot into place, ensuring the smaller diameter of the boot locates over the grooves in the shaft (see illustration).

12　Install the new retaining clamps (see illustration).

13   Install the new retaining clip to the end of the shaft **(see illustration)**.

11   Intermediate shaft support bearing – removal and installation

1   If the bearing is suspect it can be replaced. Note however that a driveaxle with a faulty bearing will normally have covered a high mileage. It may be more cost effective to replace the complete driveaxle with a reconditioned assembly as the constant velocity joints are likely to be worn anyway.

2   Remove the outer CV joint as described in Section 9. The bearing must be pressed from the shaft using a hydraulic press. If access to a hydraulic press in not available, most automotive machine shops would be prepared to carry out this task for a modest fee.

3   Press the replacement bearing into position and then install a new outer CV joint boot as described in Section 9.

10.13 The retaining clip on the end of the shaft must be replaced

Notes

Chapter 9
Brakes

Contents

Specifications

Front brakes
Disc minimum thickness	Cast into disc
Maximum disc thickness variation	0.0008 inch (0.020 mm)
Maximum disc/hub run-out (installed)	0.003 inch (0.076 mm)
Brake pad friction material minimum thickness	See Chapter 1

Rear drum brakes
Drum diameter (maximum)	Cast into drum
Brake shoe friction material minimum thickness	See Chapter 1

Rear disc brakes
Disc minimum thickness	Cast into disc
Maximum disc thickness variation	0.0009 inch (0.023 mm)
Maximum disc/hub runout (installed)	0.004 inch (0.1 mm)
Brake pad friction material minimum thickness	See Chapter 1

Torque specifications
Note: *One foot-pound (ft-lb) of torque is equivalent to 12 inch-pounds (in-lbs) of torque. Torque values below approximately 15 ft-lbs are expressed in inch-pounds, because most foot-pound torque wrenches are not accurate at these smaller values.*

	Ft-lbs (unless otherwise indicated)	Nm
ABS wheel sensor securing bolts	42 in-lbs	4.5
Front brake disc backing plate	22	30
Front caliper guide bolts	21	28
Front caliper mounting bracket bolts	129	175
Master cylinder-to-power brake booster nuts*	18	24
Power brake booster mounting nuts*	18	24
Brake vacuum pump nuts	89 in-lbs	10
Rear caliper bracket	52	71
Rear caliper guide bolts	21	28
Rear wheel cylinder bolts	105 in-lbs	12
Wheel lug nuts	See Chapter 1	
Suspension strut brace bolts*	See Chapter 10	

* Use new fasteners

1 General information

1 The braking system is of diagonally-split, dual-circuit design, with ventilated discs at the front, and drum or disc brakes (according to model) at the rear. The front calipers are of single sliding piston design, and (on models so equipped) the rear calipers are of a single-piston floating design. The rear drum brakes are of the leading and trailing shoe type, and are self-adjusting during regular operation. The rear brake shoe linings are of different thicknesses in order to allow for the different proportional rates of wear.

Hydraulic system

2 The hydraulic system consists of two separate circuits. The master cylinder has separate reservoirs for the two circuits, and, in the event of a leak or failure in one hydraulic circuit, the other circuit will remain operative. The Anti-lock Brake System (ABS) hydraulic control unit is installed between the master cylinder and the four brake units at each wheel.

Power brake booster

3 On non-turbocharged models, the power brake booster uses engine manifold vacuum to boost the effort applied by the driver at the brake pedal and transmits this increased effort to the master cylinder pistons. On turbocharged models, a camshaft-driven vacuum pump is used to supply vacuum to the power brake booster.

Parking brake

4 The parking brake is cable-operated, and acts on the rear brakes. On rear drum brake models, the cables operate on the rear trailing brake shoe operating levers; on rear disc brake models, they operate on levers on the rear calipers. The lever incorporates an automatic adjuster, which will adjust the cable when the parking brake is operated several times.

Service

5 After completing any operation involving disassembly of any part of the brake system, always test drive the vehicle to check for proper braking performance before resuming normal driving. When testing the brakes, perform the tests on a clean, dry, flat surface. Conditions other than these can lead to inaccurate test results.

6 Test the brakes at various speeds with both light and heavy pedal pressure. The vehicle should stop evenly without pulling to one side or the other. Tire pressure and condition, vehicle load and wheel alignment are factors which also affect braking performance.

Precautions

7 There are some general cautions and warnings involving the brake system on this vehicle:

a) *Use only brake fluid conforming to the specification listed in Chapter 1.*

b) *The brake pads contain fibers which are hazardous to your health if inhaled. Whenever you work on brake system components, clean all parts with brake system cleaner. Do not allow the fine dust to become airborne. Also, wear an approved filtering mask.*

c) *Safety should be paramount whenever any servicing of the brake components is performed. Do not use parts or fasteners which are not in perfect condition, and be sure that all clearances and torque specifications are adhered to. If you are at all unsure about a certain procedure, seek professional advice. Upon completion of any brake system work, test the brakes carefully in a controlled area before putting the vehicle into normal service. If a problem is suspected in the brake system, don't drive the vehicle until it's fixed.*

8 The Anti-lock Braking System (ABS) uses the basic conventional brake system, together with an ABS hydraulic unit installed between the master cylinder and the four brake units at each wheel. The hydraulic unit consists of a hydraulic actuator, an ABS brake pressure pump, and an ABS module. Braking at each of the four wheels is controlled by separate solenoid valves in the hydraulic actuator. If wheel lock-up is detected by one of the wheel sensors, when the vehicle speed is above 3 mph, the valve opens; releasing pressure to the relevant brake until the wheel regains a rotational speed corresponding to the speed of the vehicle. The cycle can be repeated many times a second. In the event of a fault in the ABS system, the conventional braking system is not affected. Diagnosis of a fault in the ABS system requires the use of special equipment, and this work should therefore be left to a dealer or other qualified repair shop. The wheel speed sensor signal rings are built-into the oil seals of the wheel bearings.

9 On models so equipped, the traction control systems are integrated with the ABS, and use the same wheel sensors. The hydraulic control unit has additional solenoid valves incorporated to enable control of the wheel brake pressure. The system is only active at speeds up to 53 mph – when the system is active the warning light on the instrument panel illuminates to warn the driver. This uses controlled braking of the spinning driving wheel when the grip at the driven wheels are different. The spinning wheel is braked by the ABS system, transferring a greater proportion of the engine torque through the differential to the other wheel, which increases the use of the available traction control.

10 Some models are equipped with an Electronic Stability Program (ESP). This system supports the vehicle's stability and steering through a combination of ABS and traction control operations. There is a switch on the center console, so that if required the system can be switched off. This will then illuminate the warning light on the instrument panel, to inform the driver that the ESP is not in operation. The stability of the vehicle is measured by Yaw rate and Accelerometer sensors, which sense the movement of the vehicle about its vertical axis, and also lateral acceleration. **Note:** *When servicing any part of the system, work carefully and methodically; also observe scrupulous cleanliness when overhauling any part of the hydraulic system. Always replace components in axle sets (where applicable) if in doubt about their condition, and use only genuine manufacturer parts, or at least those of known good quality. Pay special attention to the Warnings and Cautions given in this Section and at relevant points in this Chapter concerning the dangers of brake dust and hydraulic fluid.*

2 Front brake pads – replacement

Warning: *Disc brake pads must be replaced on both front or both rear wheels at the same time - never replace the pads on only one wheel. Also, the dust created by the brake system is harmful to your health. Never blow it out with compressed air and don't inhale any of it. An approved filtering mask should be worn when working on the brakes. Do not, under any circumstances, use petroleum-based solvents to clean brake parts. Use brake system cleaner only!*

1 Apply the parking brake, then loosen the front wheel lug nuts. Raise the front of the vehicle and support it securely on jackstands. Remove both front wheels and wash the brake assemblies with brake system cleaner **(see illustration)**.

2 Follow the accompanying photos **(see illustrations 2.2a through 2.2p)** for the actual pad pad replacement procedure. Be sure to stay in order and read the caption under each illustration, and note the following points:

a) *Work on one brake assembly at a time, using the assembled brake for reference if necessary.*

2.1 Always wash the brakes with brake system cleaner before disassembling anything

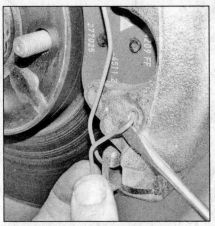

2.2a Use a flat-bladed screwdriver to carefully pry off the caliper retaining spring

2.2b Pry out the rubber caps. . .

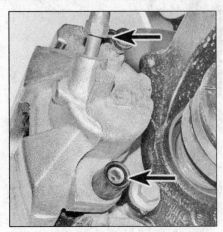

2.2c. . . and use an Allen key to unscrew the caliper guide bolts

2.2d Slide the caliper and inner pad from the disc

2.2e Pull the inner brake pad from the caliper piston. . .

2.2f. . . and lift the outer pad from the caliper bracket

2.2g Push the piston back into the caliper using a piston retraction tool or C-clamp

2.2h Clean the pad mounting surfaces with a wire brush

2.2i Measure the thickness of the pad's friction material. If it's 1/16-inch (1.5 mm) or less, replace all the front pads

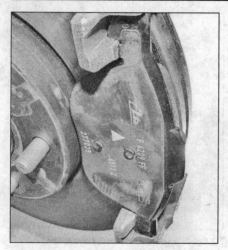

2.2j Install the outer pad to the caliper mounting bracket. . .

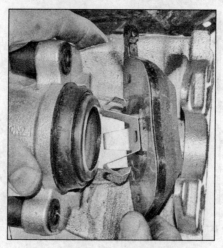

2.2k. . . then install the inner pad to the caliper piston

2.2l Slide the caliper and inner pad over the disc and outer pad

2.2m Install the caliper guide bolts and tighten them to the torque listed in this Chapter's Specifications

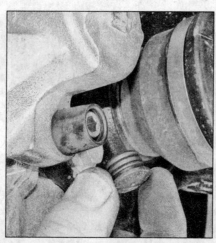

2.2n Press the rubber caps into position

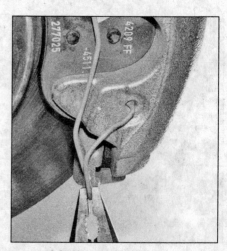

2.2o Use a pair of pliers. . .

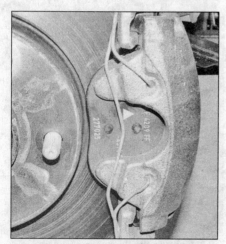

2.2p. . . to reinstall the caliper retaining spring, making sure it seats properly

b) New pads may have an adhesive foil on the backing plates. Remove this foil prior to installation.

c) Thoroughly clean the caliper guide surfaces, and apply a little high-temperature brake grease to them. Be careful not to get any grease onto the brake pads or discs during installation.

d) When pushing the caliper piston back to accommodate new pads, keep a close eye on the fluid level in the reservoir, removing fluid as necessary.

3   Depress the brake pedal repeatedly until the pads are pressed into firm contact with the brake disc, and normal (non-assisted) pedal pressure is restored.

4   Repeat the above procedure on the remaining front brake caliper.

5   Reinstall the wheels, then lower the vehicle to the ground and tighten the lug nuts to the torque listed in the Chapter 1 Specifications.

6   Check the brake fluid level as described

in Chapter 1.
Caution: *New pads will not give full braking efficiency until they have bedded-in. Be prepared for this, and avoid hard braking for the first hundred miles or so after pad replacement.*

3   Front brake caliper – removal and installation

Warning: *Refer to the precautions at the beginning of Section 1 before proceeding.*

Removal

1   Apply the parking brake, then loosen the front wheel lug nuts. Raise the front of the vehicle and support it securely on jackstands. Remove the wheel.

2   Install a brake hose clamp to the flexible hose leading to the caliper (**see illustration**).

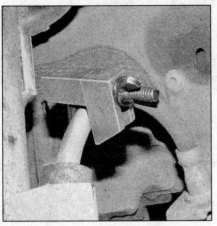

3.2 Use a hose clamp on the flexible hoses

3.3 Loosen the brake hose fitting

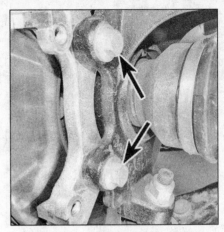

3.6 Caliper mounting bracket bolts

4.2 Suspend the caliper from the spring using wire

4.4 Measure the thickness of the disc using a micrometer

4.5 To check disc runout, mount a dial indicator as shown and rotate the disc

This will minimize brake fluid loss during this procedure.

3   Break loose the fitting on the caliper end of the flexible brake hose **(see illustration)**. Once loosened, do not try to unscrew the hose at this stage.

4   Remove the brake pads as described in Section 2.

5   Support the caliper in one hand, and prevent the hydraulic hose from turning with the other hand. Unscrew the caliper from the hose, making sure that the hose is not twisted unduly or strained. Once the caliper is detached, plug the open hydraulic unions in the caliper and hose, to keep out dust and dirt.

6   If required, the caliper mounting bracket can be unbolted from the steering knuckle **(see illustration)**.

Installation

7   If removed, reinstall the caliper mounting bracket and tighten the bolts to the torque listed in this Chapter's Specifications.

8   Reinstall the brake pads as described in Section 2, but screw the caliper onto the flexible hose as far as possible before reinstalling it to the caliper bracket.

9   Once the caliper has been installed,

tighten the brake hose fitting, ensuring the hose is not kinked/twisted.

10   Bleed the brake circuit according to the procedure given in Section 14, remembering to remove the brake hose clamp from the flexible hose. Make sure there are no leaks from the hose connections. Test the brakes carefully before returning the vehicle to normal service.

4   Front brake disc – inspection, removal and installation

Note: *To prevent uneven braking, BOTH front brake discs must be replaced or resurfaced at the same time.*

Inspection

1   Apply the parking brake, then loosen the front wheel lug nuts. Raise the front of the vehicle and support it securely on jackstands. Remove the wheel.

2   Remove the front brake caliper (see Section 3) and remove the two caliper mounting bracket bolts (see Section 3). Do not disconnect the flexible hose from the caliper. Sus-

pend the caliper out of the way with a piece of wire, taking care to avoid straining the flexible hose **(see illustration)**.

3   Temporarily reinstall two of the wheel lug nuts to diagonally opposite studs, with the flat sides of the nuts against the disc. Tighten the nuts progressively, to hold the disc firmly.

4   Scrape any corrosion from the disc. Rotate the disc, and examine it for deep scoring, grooving or cracks. Using a micrometer, measure the thickness of the disc in several places **(see illustration)**. The minimum thickness is stamped on the disc hub. Light wear and scoring is normal, but if excessive, the disc should be removed, and either resurfaced by an automotive machine shop, or replaced. If resurfacing is undertaken, the minimum thickness must be maintained. Obviously, if the disc is cracked, it must be replaced.

5   Using a dial indicator, check that the disc run-out 3/8-inch (10 mm) from the outer edge does not exceed the limit listed in this Chapter's Specifications. To do this, install the dial indicator and rotate the disc, noting the variation in measurement as the disc is rotated **(see illustration)**. The difference between the minimum and maximum measurements recorded is the disc run-out.

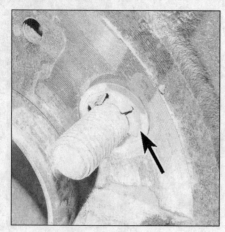

5.2a Pry off the clip

5.2b Use two 8 mm bolts to force the drum from the hub

6.3 Clean the components with brake system cleaner

6   If the run-out is greater than the specified amount, check for variations of the disc thickness as follows. Mark the disc at eight positions 45° apart. Using a micrometer, measure the disc thickness at the eight positions, 15 mm in from the outer edge. If the variation between the minimum and maximum readings is greater than the amount listed in this Chapter's Specifications, the disc should be replaced.

7   The hub face run-out can also be checked in a similar way. First remove the disc (see Steps 8 through 10), install the dial indicator, then slowly rotate the hub and check that the run-out does not exceed the amount listed in this Chapter's Specifications. If the hub face run-out is excessive, this should be corrected by replacing the hub bearings (see Chapter 10) before rechecking the disc run-out.

Removal

8   With the wheel, caliper and bracket removed, remove the wheel nuts which were temporarily reinstalled.

9   Mark the disc in relation to the hub, if the same one is to be reinstalled.

10   Remove the washer/retaining clip(s) (if equipped), and remove the disc from the wheel studs.

Installation

11   Make sure that the disc and hub mating surfaces are clean, then install the disc over the wheel studs. Align the previously-made marks if the original disc is being reinstalled. It is not necessary to reinstall the washers/retaining clips.

12   Reinstall the caliper mounting bracket and caliper (see Section 3).

13   Reinstall the wheels, then lower the vehicle to the ground and tighten the lug nuts to the torque listed in the Chapter 1 Specifications.

14   Test the brakes carefully before returning the vehicle to normal service.

5   Rear brake drum – removal, inspection and installation

Warning: *Brake drums must be replaced on BOTH rear wheels at the same time – never replace the drums on only one wheel, as uneven braking may result. Also, the dust created by wear of the shoes is a health hazard. Never blow it out with compressed air, and don't inhale any of it. An approved filtering mask should be worn when working on the brakes. DO NOT use petroleum-based solvents to clean brake parts; use brake system cleaner only.*

Removal

1   Chock the front wheels, release the parking brake and engage 1st gear (or Park). Loosen the rear wheel lug nuts, raise the rear of the vehicle and support it securely on jackstands. Remove the wheel.

2   Pry off the spring clip (if equipped), and pull the drum from the hub. If the drum is stuck, use two 8.0 mm bolts screwed into the threaded holes provided, then evenly tighten the bolts and draw the drum from place **(see illustrations)**. If the brake drum still won't come off, loosen the parking brake cable as described in Section 22 and try again.

3   With the brake drum removed, clean the dust from the drum, brake shoes, wheel cylinder and backing plate using brake system cleaner. Take care not to inhale the dust.

Inspection

4   Clean the inside surfaces of the brake drum, then examine the internal friction surface for signs of scoring or cracks. If it is cracked, deeply scored, or has worn to a diameter greater than the maximum cast into the drum, then it should be replaced, together with the drum on the other side.

Warning: *Resurfacing of the brake drum is not recommended.*

Installation

5   Installation is the reverse of removal. Adjust the parking brake as described in Section 21.

6   Test the brakes carefully before returning the vehicle to normal service.

6   Rear brake shoes – replacement

Warning: *Drum brake shoes must be replaced on BOTH rear wheels at the same time – never replace the shoes on only one wheel, as uneven braking may result. Also, the dust created by wear of the shoes is a health hazard. Never blow it out with compressed air, and don't inhale any of it. An approved filtering mask should be worn when working on the brakes. DO NOT use petroleum-based solvents to clean brake parts; use brake system cleaner only.*

1   Chock the front wheels, release the parking brake and engage 1st gear (or make sure the shifter is in Park). Loosen the rear wheel lug nuts, raise the rear of the vehicle and support it securely on jackstands. Remove the rear wheels. Work on one brake assembly at a time, using the assembled brake for reference if necessary.

2   Remove the rear brake drum as described in Section 5.

3   Note the installed position of the springs and the brake shoes, then clean the components with brake system cleaner and allow to dry **(see illustration)**; position a drain pan beneath the brake to catch the cleaner and residue.

4   Remove the two shoe hold-down springs; use a pair of pliers to depress the ends so that they can be withdrawn off the pins. If required, remove the hold-down pins from the backing plate **(see illustration)**. Note that on some models, it's not possible to remove the rearmost hold-down pin with the backing plate in place.

5   Disconnect the top ends of the shoes

6.4 Depress the hold-down spring, and slide it from under the head of the pin

6.5 Pull the top end of the shoe assembly outwards from the wheel cylinder

6.7a Pull the bottom end of the shoes from the anchor. . .

6.7b. . . then pivot the whole brake shoe assembly outwards

6.8 Pull the spring back and disengage the parking brake lever cable end fitting from the lever on the shoe

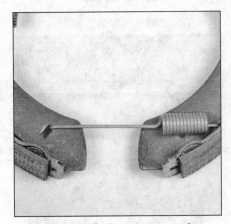

6.9 Unhook the lower return spring

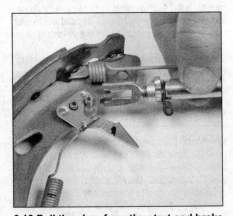

6.10 Pull the shoe from the strut and brake shoe adjuster

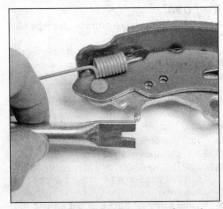

6.11a Pull the adjustment strut from the trailing shoe. . .

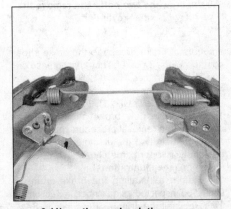

6.11b. . . then unhook the upper return spring

from the wheel cylinder, taking care not to damage the rubber boots **(see illustration)**.

6 To prevent the wheel cylinder pistons from being accidentally ejected, wrap a suitable elastic band or wire length-wise over the cylinder/pistons. DO NOT press the brake pedal while the shoes are removed.

7 Pull the bottom end of the brake shoes from the bottom anchor **(see illustrations)**. Use pliers or an adjustable wrench over the edge of the shoe to pry it away, if required.

8 Pull the parking brake cable spring back from the operating lever on the rear of the trailing shoe. Unhook the cable end from the cut-out in the lever, and remove the brake shoes **(see illustration)**.

9 Working on a clean bench, move the bottom ends of the brake shoes together and unhook the lower return spring from the shoes, noting the location holes **(see illustration)**.

10 Pull the leading shoe from the strut and brake shoe adjuster **(see illustration)**.

11 Pull the adjustment strut to release it from the trailing brake shoe, then unhook the upper return spring from the shoes, noting the location holes **(see illustrations)**. The manufacturer recommends that the upper return spring be replaced.

12 If the wheel cylinder shows signs of fluid leakage, or if there is any reason to suspect it of being defective, replace it as described in Section 7.

13 Clean the backing plate, and apply small

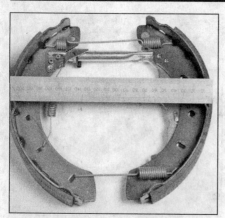

6.15a Set the adjustment strut so the diameter of the shoe assembly is 8-31/32 inches (228 mm)

6.15b When reassembled, the top of the assembly should look like this. . .

6.15c. . . and the lower end should look like this

7.5 Unscrew the two bolts and remove the wheel cylinder

amounts of brake grease to the brake shoe contact points. Be careful not to get grease on any friction surfaces.

14   Lubricate the sliding components of the brake shoe adjuster with a little brake grease.

15   Install the new brake shoes using a reversal of the removal procedure, but set the adjustment strut so the diameter of the shoe assembly is approximately 8-31/32 inches (228 mm) **(see illustrations)**.

16   Before reinstalling the brake drum, it should be inspected as described in Section 5.

17   Reinstall the drum as described in Section 5. Install the wheel and install the lug nuts finger tight.

18   Lower the vehicle to the ground, and tighten the wheel lug nuts to the torque listed in this Chapter's Specifications.

19   Depress the brake pedal several times, in order to operate the self-adjusting mechanism and set the shoes at their normal operating position.

20   Make several forward and reverse stops, and operate the parking brake fully two or three times. If necessary, adjust the parking brake as required (see Section 21). Give

the vehicle a road test, to make sure that the brakes are functioning correctly, and to bed-in the new shoes to the contours of the drum. Remember that the new shoes will not give full braking efficiency until they have bedded-in.

7   Rear wheel cylinder – removal and installation

Note: *No service parts are available for the wheel cylinders. Bear in mind that if the brake shoes have been contaminated by fluid leaking from the wheel cylinder, they must be replaced. The shoes on BOTH sides of the vehicle must be replaced, even if they are only contaminated on one side.*

Removal

1   Remove the brake drum as described in Section 5.

2   Minimize fluid loss either by removing the master cylinder reservoir cap, then tightening it down onto a piece of plastic wrap to obtain an airtight seal, or by using a brake hose clamp to clamp the flexible hose at the nearest convenient point to the wheel cylinder.

3   Pull the brake shoes apart at their top ends, so that they are just clear of the wheel cylinder. The automatic adjuster will hold the shoes in this position so that the cylinder can be withdrawn.

4   Wipe away all traces of dirt around the hydraulic fitting at the rear of the wheel cylinder, then remove the rear brake hose (see Section 13).

5   Unscrew the two bolts securing the wheel cylinder to the backing plate **(see illustration)**.

6   Remove the wheel cylinder from the backing plate so that it is clear of the brake shoes.

Installation

7   Wipe clean the backing plate and remove the plug from the end of the hydraulic

line. Install the cylinder onto the backing plate and screw in the hydraulic fitting nut by hand, being careful not to cross-thread it.

8   Tighten the rear wheel cylinder mounting bolts to the torque listed in this Chapter's Specifications, then tighten the hydraulic union nut.

9   Retract the automatic brake adjuster mechanism, so that the brake shoes engage with the pistons of the wheel cylinder. To do this, pry the shoes apart slightly, turn the automatic adjuster to its minimum position, and release the shoes.

10   Remove the clamp from the flexible brake hose, or the plastic wrap from the master cylinder (as applicable).

11   Install the brake drum (see Section 5).

12   Bleed the hydraulic system as described in Section 14. Providing suitable precautions were taken to minimize loss of fluid, it should only be necessary to bleed the relevant rear brake.

13   Test the brakes carefully before returning the vehicle to normal service.

8   Rear brake pads – replacement

Warning: *Disc brake pads must be replaced on both front or both rear wheels at the same time - never replace the pads on only one wheel. Also, the dust created by the brake system is harmful to your health. Never blow it out with compressed air and don't inhale any of it. An approved filtering mask should be worn when working on the brakes. Do not, under any circumstances, use petroleum-based solvents to clean brake parts. Use brake system cleaner only!*

1   Chock the front wheels, loosen the rear wheel nuts, then raise the rear of the vehicle and support it on jackstands. Remove the rear wheels.

2   With the parking brake lever fully released, follow the accompanying photos **(see illustrations 8.2a through 8.2u)** for the actual pad replacement procedure. Be sure to stay in order and read the caption under each

illustration, and note the following points:

a) If re-installing the original pads, ensure they are returned to their original positions.

b) Thoroughly clean the caliper guide surfaces and guide bolts. When installing the guide bolts, tighten them to the torque listed in this Chapter's Specifications.

c) If new pads are to be installed, use a piston retraction tool to push the piston back and twist it clockwise at the same time – keep an eye on the fluid level in the reservoir while retracting the piston.

3 Depress the brake pedal repeatedly until the pads are pressed into firm contact with the brake disc, and normal (non-assisted) pedal pressure is restored.

4 Repeat the above procedure on the remaining brake caliper.

5 If necessary, adjust the parking brake as described in Section 21.

6 Reinstall the wheels, lower the vehicle to the ground and tighten the lug nuts to the torque listed in the Chapter 1 Specifications.

7 Check the hydraulic fluid level as described in Chapter 1.

Caution: New pads will not give full braking efficiency until they have bedded-in. Be prepared for this, and avoid hard braking for the first hundred miles or so after pad replacement.

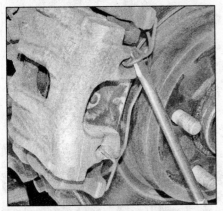

8.2a Pry away the retaining spring

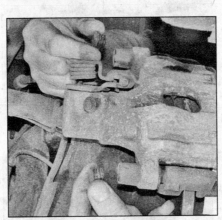

8.2b Pull out the rubber caps. . .

8.2c. . . and use a 7 mm Allen key or bit to unscrew the guide bolts

8.2d Unclip the brake hose from the bracket

8.2e Lift away the caliper. . .

8.2f. . . and suspend it from the suspension using cable ties or wire

8.2g Remove the outer brake pad. . .

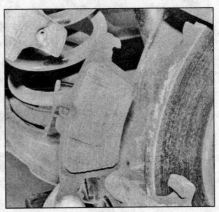

8.2h. . . and the inner pad

8.2i Measure the thickness of the pad friction material

8.2j Use a wire brush to clean the caliper mounting bracket

8.2k Note that the inner pad has an anti-rattle spring

8.2l Apply a little high-temperature anti-seize grease to the rear of the pad. . .

8.2m. . . and the areas where the pad backing plate contacts the mounting bracket

8.2n Install the inner pad (friction material side against the disc). . .

8.2o. . . followed by the outer pad

8.2p If new pads have been installed, use a retraction tool to rotate the caliper piston clockwise, while at the same time pushing it into the caliper

8.2q Install the caliper over the pads. . .

8.2r. . . then install and tighten the guide bolts to the torque listed in this Chapter's specifications

8.2s Reinstall the rubber caps

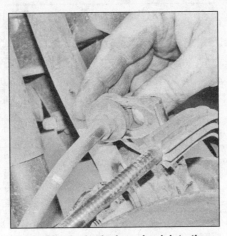

8.2t Clip the brake hose back into the bracket

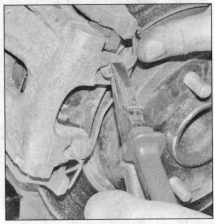

8.2u Use pliers to reinstall the caliper retaining spring

9 Rear brake caliper – removal and installation

Removal

1   Chock the front wheels, loosen the rear wheel lug nuts, then raise the rear of the vehicle and support it on jackstands. Remove the rear wheels.

2   Install a brake hose clamp to the flexible hose leading to the caliper (see illustration 3.2). This will minimize brake fluid loss during subsequent operations.

3   Break loose (but do not try to unscrew) the fitting on the caliper end of the flexible hose.

4   Unclip the parking brake inner cable fitting from the lever on the caliper, then detach the outer cable from the bracket (see illustration).

5   Pull out the dust caps, remove the guide bolts and lift the caliper from the disc. If necessary, unbolt the caliper mounting bracket from the hub carrier (see illustration).

6   Unscrew the caliper from the brake hose, making sure that the hose is not twisted or strained. Plug the open hydraulic fitting to keep dust and dirt out.

Installation

7   Reinstall the caliper (and mounting bracket, if it was removed) by reversing the removal procedure. Refer to Section 22 when reconnecting the parking brake cable. Remove the clamp from the brake hose then carefully thread it to the caliper and tighten it (see Section 13). Tighten the mounting bolts to the torque listed in this Chapter's Specifications, and tighten the wheel lug nuts to the torque listed in the Chapter 1 Specifications.

8   Bleed the brake circuit according to the procedure given in Section 14. Make sure there are no leaks from the hose connections.

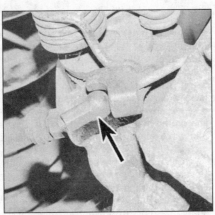

9.4 Unclip the cable end fitting from the caliper lever

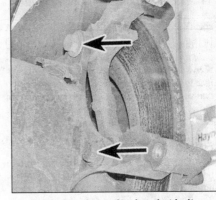

9.5 Caliper mounting bracket bolts

Test the brakes carefully before returning the vehicle to normal service.

10 Rear brake disc and backing plate – inspection, removal and installation

1   Remove the rear caliper and pads (see Sections 8 and 9).

2   Unbolt the caliper mounting bracket from the hub carrier (see illustration 9.5), then mark the disc in relation to the hub (if the same one is to be reinstalled).

3   Remove the retaining clip from the wheel stud (if equipped), and withdraw the disc over the wheel studs (see illustration).

4   If the backing plate must be removed, remove the hub and wheel bearing assembly (see Chapter 10), then remove the backing plate.

5   Procedures for inspection of the rear brake discs are the same as the front brake discs (see Section 4).

6   Installation is a reversal of removal.

10.3 Pull the rear brake disc over the wheel studs

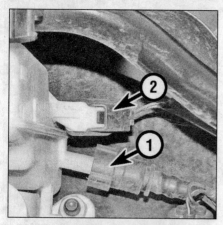

11.4 Depress the release button on the other side of the of the connector (1), and disconnect the clutch fluid supply hose, then disconnect the level warning sensor wiring plug (2)

11.7 Unscrew the brake line fittings

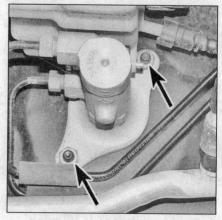

11.8 Master cylinder retaining nuts

11   Master cylinder – removal and installation

Warning: *Brake fluid can harm your eyes and damage painted surfaces, so use extreme caution when handling or pouring it. Do not use brake fluid that has been standing open or is more than one year old. Brake fluid absorbs moisture from the air. Excess moisture can cause a dangerous loss of braking effectiveness.*

Removal

1   Deplete the vacuum in the power brake booster by depressing the brake pedal a few times with the engine switched off.
2   Remove the battery and the battery tray (see Chapter 5).
3   Loosen the front wheel lug nuts, then raise the front of the vehicle and support it securely on jackstands. Remove the front wheels. Loosen the bleeder screws from both front brake calipers, attach a rubber hose to the bleeder screws, and place the other end of the hose in suitable containers. Operate the brake pedal until the fluid level is down to the base of the reservoir.
4   Depress the release button and detach the clutch master cylinder fluid supply hose from the side of the brake fluid reservoir (**see illustration**). Plug the openings to prevent contamination.
5   Disconnect the wiring plug from the fluid level sensor on the side of the reservoir.
6   Identify the locations of each brake line on the master cylinder, then place rags beneath the master cylinder to catch spilled brake fluid.
7   Clean around the brake line fitting nuts. Unscrew the nuts and disconnect the brake lines from the master cylinder (**see illustration**). If the nuts are tight, a flare-nut wrench should be used to prevent rounding-off the corners of the fittings. Cap the end of the pipes and the master cylinder to prevent any contamination.
8   Unscrew the master cylinder securing nuts, and remove the master cylinder from the studs on the power brake booster (**see illustration**). Discard the nuts – new ones must be used during installation.
9   Remove the gasket/seal from the master cylinder.

10   If the master cylinder is faulty, it must be replaced. At the time of writing, no overhaul kits were available.

Bleeding prior to installation

11   Bench bleed the new master cylinder before installing it. Mount the master cylinder in a vise, with the jaws of the vise clamping on the mounting flange.
12   Attach a pair of master cylinder bleeder tubes to the outlet ports of the master cylinder (**see illustration**).
13   Fill the reservoir with brake fluid of the recommended type (see Chapter 1).
14   Slowly push the pistons into the master cylinder (a large Phillips screwdriver can be used for this) - air will be expelled from the pressure chambers and into the reservoir. Because the tubes are submerged in fluid, air can't be drawn back into the master cylinder when you release the pistons.
15   Repeat the procedure until no more air bubbles are present.
16   Remove the bleed tubes, one at a time, and install plugs in the open ports to prevent fluid leakage and air from entering. Install the reservoir cap.

Installation

17   Installation is the reversel of removal procedure, noting the following points:
   a) Clean the contact surfaces of the master cylinder and booster, and locate a new gasket on the master cylinder.
   b) Install and tighten new nuts to the torque listed in this Chapter's Specifications.
   c) Carefully insert the brake pipes in the apertures in the master cylinder, then tighten the fitting nuts. Make sure that the nuts enter their threads correctly.
   d) Fill the reservoir with fresh brake fluid.
   e) Bleed the brake hydraulic system as described in Section 14.
   f) Test the brakes carefully before returning the vehicle to normal service.

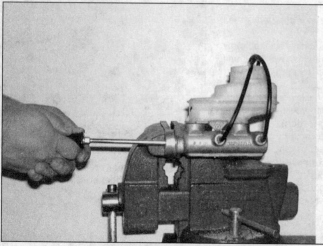

11.12 The best way to bleed air from the master cylinder before installing it on the vehicle is with a pair of bleeder tubes that direct brake fluid into the reservoir during bleeding

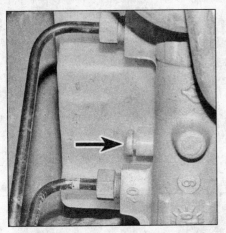

11.20 Pull out the reservoir retaining pin (viewed from underneath)

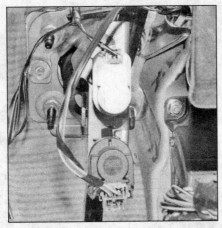

12.4 Disconnect the electrical connectors from the brake pedal switches

12.5 Pry out and discard the booster pushrod pin

Brake fluid reservoir removal and installation

18 Perform Steps 1 through 7 of this Section.

19 Disconnect the wiring plug from the fluid level sensor on the side of the reservoir.

20 Remove the retaining pin and detach the reservoir from the master cylinder (see illustration).

21 Installation is the reverse of removal. Use new seals and lubricate them with the brake fluid listed in the Chapter 1 Specifications.

12 Brake pedal – removal and installation

1 Working inside the vehicle, move the driver's seat fully to the rear, to allow maximum working area.

2 Remove the driver's side lower dash panel as described in Chapter 11.

3 Remove the accelerator pedal as described in Chapter 4.

4 Disconnect the electrical connectors to the brake pedal switches. Remove the switches by turning them, then pulling them out of the pedal bracket (see illustration).

5 Pry out the pin securing the brake booster pushrod to the pedal (see illustration). Discard the pin – a new one must be installed.

6 Loosen the retaining nuts on the pedal bracket assembly (see illustration).

7 Maneuver the pedal assembly rearwards and down from under the instrument panel. No further disassembly of the pedal is recommended.

8 Installation is the reversel of removal. Install a new brake booster pushrod pin.

9 Reinstall the brake pedal switches as described in Section 20.

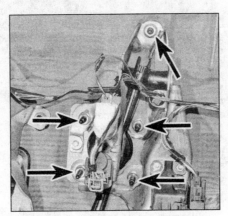

12.6 Brake pedal bracket assembly retaining nuts

13 Hydraulic lines and hoses – inspection, removal and installation

Warning: *Brake fluid can harm your eyes and damage painted surfaces, so use extreme caution when handling or pouring it. Do not use brake fluid that has been standing open or is more than one year old. Brake fluid absorbs moisture from the air. Excess moisture can cause a dangerous loss of braking effectiveness.*

Inspection

1 Raise the vehicle, and support it securely on jackstands, making sure the vehicle is level.

2 Check for signs of leakage at the pipe fittings, then examine the flexible hoses for signs of cracking, chafing and fraying.

3 The brake lines should be examined carefully for signs of dents, corrosion or other damage. Corrosion should be scraped off, and if the depth of pitting is significant, the lines should be replaced. This is particularly likely

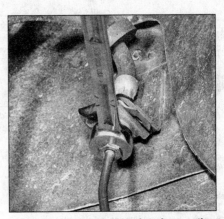

13.7 Use a flare-nut wrench to loosen the fitting nuts

in those areas underneath the vehicle body where the lines are exposed and unprotected.

4 Replace any defective brake lines and/or hoses.

Removal

5 If a section of brake line or hose is to be removed, loss of brake fluid can be reduced by unscrewing the filler cap, and completely sealing the top of the reservoir with plastic wrap or adhesive tape.

6 To remove a section of brake line, hold the adjoining hose fitting nut with a wrench to prevent it from turning, then unscrew the fitting nut at the end of the pipe. Repeat the procedure at the other end of the line, then release the line by pulling out the clips attaching it to the body.

7 Where the fitting nuts are exposed to the full force of the weather, they can sometimes be quite tight. If an open-ended wrench is used, rounding of the corners on the nuts is not uncommon, and for this reason, it is preferable to use a flare-nut wrench (see illustration). If such a wrench is not available, self-

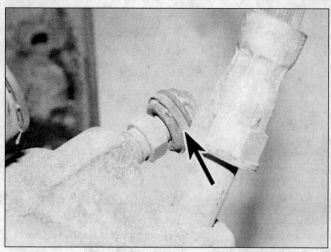

14.7a Remove the dust cap from the bleed screw

14.7b Connect the hose and open the bleed screw

locking pliers may be used as a last resort; these may well damage the nuts, but if the pipe is to be replaced, this does not matter.

8   To further minimize the loss of fluid when disconnecting a flexible brake hose from a rigid line, clamp the hose as near as possible to the line to be detached, using a brake hose clamp or a pair of self-locking pliers with protected jaws.

9   To remove a flexible hose, first clean the ends of the hose and the surrounding area, then unscrew the fitting nuts from the hose ends. Remove the spring clip, and withdraw the hose from the serrated mounting in the support bracket. Where applicable, unscrew the hose from the caliper.

10   Brake lines supplied with flared ends and fitting nuts can be obtained individually or in sets from dealer parts departments or accessory shops. The line is then bent to shape, using the old line as a guide. Be careful not to kink or crimp the line when bending it; ideally, a proper pipe-bending tool should be used.

Installation

11   Installation is the reversel of removal. Make sure that all brake lines are securely supported in their clips, and ensure that the hoses are not kinked. Check also that the hoses are clear of all suspension components and underbody fittings, and will remain clear during movement of the suspension and steering.

12   Bleed the hydraulic system as described in Section 14.

14   Brake hydraulic system – bleeding

Warning: *Brake fluid can harm your eyes and damage painted surfaces, so use extreme caution when handling or pouring it. Do not use brake*

fluid that has been standing open or is more than one year old. Brake fluid absorbs moisture from the air. Excess moisture can cause a dangerous loss of braking effectiveness.

Note: *On models with Electronic Stability Control (ESC), if air enters the ABS valve block, special diagnostic equipment will be required to successfully bleed the brakes.*

1   If the master cylinder has been disconnected and reconnected, then the complete system (all circuits) must be bled of air. If a component of one circuit has been disturbed, then only that particular circuit needs to be bled.

2   Bleeding should begin on the furthest brake from the master cylinder, followed by the next one until the brake nearest to the master cylinder is bled last.

3   There are a variety of do-it-yourself one-man brake bleeding kits available from auto parts stores, and it is recommended that one of these kits be used wherever possible, as they greatly simplify the brake bleeding operation. Follow the kit manufacturer's instructions in conjunction with the following procedure. If a pressure-bleeding kit is obtained, then it will not be necessary to depress the brake pedal in the following procedure.

4   During the bleeding operation, do not allow the brake fluid level in the reservoir to drop below the minimum mark. If the level is allowed to fall so far that air is drawn in, the whole procedure will have to be started again from scratch. Only use new fluid for topping-up, preferably from a freshly opened container. Never re-use fluid bled from the system.

5   Before starting, check that all rigid lines and flexible hoses are in good condition, and that all hydraulic fittings are tight. Take great care not to allow brake fluid to come into contact with the vehicle's paint, otherwise the finish will be seriously damaged. Wash off any

spilled fluid immediately with cold water.

6   If a brake bleeding kit is not being used, gather together a clean jar, a length of plastic or rubber tubing which is a tight fit over the bleeder screw, and a new container of the specified brake fluid. The help of an assistant will also be required.

7   Clean the area around the bleeder screw on the rear brake unit to be bled (it is important that no dirt be allowed to enter the hydraulic system), and remove the dust cap. Connect one end of the tubing to the bleeder screw, and immerse the other end in the jar **(see illustrations)**. The jar should be filled with sufficient brake fluid to keep the end of the tube submerged.

8   Open the bleed screw by half a turn, and have the assistant depress the brake pedal to the floor. Tighten the bleed screw at the end of the down stroke, then have the assistant release the pedal. Continue this procedure until clean brake fluid, free from air bubbles, can be seen flowing into the jar. Finally tighten the bleed screw with the pedal in the fully depressed position.

9   Remove the tube and install the dust cap. Top-up the master cylinder reservoir if necessary, then repeat the procedure on the opposite rear brake.

10   Repeat the procedure on the front brake furthest from the master cylinder, followed by the brake nearest to the master cylinder.

11   Check the feel of the brake pedal – it should be firm. If it is spongy, there is still some air in the system, and the bleeding procedure should be repeated.

12   When bleeding is complete, top-up the master cylinder reservoir and reinstall the cap.

13   Check the clutch operation on completion; it may be necessary to bleed the clutch hydraulic system as described in Chapter 8.

15.6 Disconnect the electrical connector

16.5 The vacuum check valve is located in the pipe between the intake manifold and the booster

18.4 Front ABS sensor mounting bolt

15   Power brake booster – check, removal and installation

Check

1   To test the operation of the booster, depress the brake pedal four or five times to dissipate the vacuum, then start the engine while keeping the brake depressed. As the engine starts, there should be a noticeable give in the brake pedal as vacuum builds-up. Allow the engine to run for at least two minutes, and then switch it off. If the brake pedal is now depressed again, it should be possible to hear a hiss from the booster when the pedal is depressed. After four or five applications, no further hissing should be heard, and the pedal should feel harder.
2   Before assuming that a problem exists in the booster itself, inspect the check valve as described in Section 16.

Removal

3   Remove the suspension strut brace. Reinstall the fasteners temporarily back in the suspension strut.
4   Remove the master cylinder (see Section 11), then unclip the brake lines from the firewall.
5   Carefully pry the vacuum line from the brake booster.
6   Disconnect the electrical connector from the brake vacuum sensor **(see illustration)** and the ABS brake pedal travel sensor.
7   Raise the front of the vehicle and support it securely on jackstands, then remove the engine undershield.
8   Remove the driver's side lower dash panel as described in Chapter 11.
9   Disconnect the electrical connectors, then remove the brake pedal position switch and the brake light switch from the bracket. Rotate the position switch counterclockwise, and the light switch clockwise. Do not move the brake pedal during this procedure.
10   Carefully pry the pin from the booster actuator rod **(see illustration 12.6)**. Discard the pin – a new one must be installed.
11   Remove the four nuts securing the servo to the firewall/pedal bracket and maneuver it

from the engine compartment.
12   Note that the booster unit cannot be disassembled for repair or overhaul and, if faulty, must be replaced.

Installation

13   Installation is the reverse of removal, noting the following points:
  a) Compress the actuator rod into the brake booster before installing.
  b) Make sure the gasket is correctly positioned on the booster.
  c) Install new bolts to the suspension tower and the brake pedal assembly.
  d) Tighten the suspension strut brace bolts to the torque listed in the Chapter 10 Specifications.
  e) Test the brakes carefully before returning the vehicle to normal service.

16   Power brake booster vacuum hose and check valve – removal, check and installation

Note: *The check valve is supplied complete with the brake booster vacuum hose.*

Removal

1   With the engine switched off, depress the brake pedal four or five times, to dissipate any remaining vacuum from the booster.
2   Disconnect the vacuum hose adapter at the booster by pulling it free from the rubber grommet. If necessary, pry it free using a screwdriver with its blade inserted under the flange.
3   Detach the vacuum hose from the intake manifold connection, pressing in the collar to disengage the tabs, then withdrawing the collar slowly.
4   If the hose or the fixings are damaged or in poor condition, they must be replaced.

Check

5   Examine the check valve **(see illustration)** for damage and signs of deterioration, and replace it if necessary. The valve may be tested by blowing through its connecting

hoses in both directions. It should only be possible to blow from the booster end towards the intake manifold end.

Installation

6   Installation is the reversel of removal. If installing a new check valve, ensure that it is installed in the proper direction.

17   ABS hydraulic unit – removal and installation

Replacement of the ABS unit assembly requires access to specialist diagnostic and testing equipment in order to purge air from the system, initialize and program the control module. Consequently, this task must be performed by a dealer service department or other properly equipped repair shop.

18   ABS wheel sensor – check, removal and installation

Check

1   Checking of the sensors is done either by substitution for a known good unit, or scanning the ABS ECU for stored fault codes, using a special scan tool used by dealer service departments or other properly equipped repair shops.

Removal

Note: *Clean around the electrical connectors, the sensors and surrounding areas to keep dirt and debris from damaging the sensors and wheel bearings.*

Front wheel sensor

2   Apply the parking brake and loosen the front wheel lug nuts. Raise the front of the vehicle and support it securely on jackstands. Remove the wheel.
3   Disconnect the sensor electrical connector.
4   Unscrew the sensor mounting bolt from the steering knuckle and remove the sensor **(see illustration)**. Withdraw the O-ring seal.

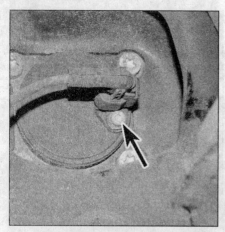

18.7 Rear ABS sensor retaining bolt (disc brake model shown)

20.3 Disconnect the electrical connector

20.4 Turn the switch counterclockwise and remove it from the bracket

21.3 Disconnect the parking brake warning light switch

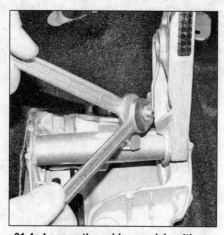

21.4a Loosen the cable - models with no armrest shown ...

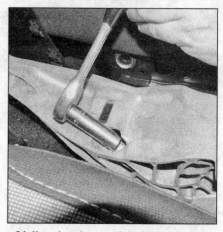

21.4b ... here's a model with an armrest

Rear wheel sensor

5   Chock the front wheels, engage 1st gear (or Park), then loosen the rear wheel lug nuts. Raise the rear of the vehicle and support it securely on jackstands. Remove the wheel.

6   Disconnect the sensor electrical connector.

7   Unscrew the sensor mounting bolt and remove the sensor **(see illustration)**. Withdraw the O-ring seal.

Installation

8   Installation is the reversal of removal. Install a new O-ring seal to the hub carrier (not the sensor). Tighten the ABS wheel sensor securing bolt to the torque listed in this Chapter's Specifications.

19   Traction control system – general information

1   The Traction control system is an expanded version of the ABS system. It is integrated with the ABS, and uses the same

wheel sensors. It also uses the hydraulic control unit, which incorporates additional internal solenoid valves.

2   Remove the wheel sensors, (see Section 18) .

3   Replacement of the ABS unit requires access to specialized diagnostic and testing equipment in order to purge air from the system, initialize and program the control unit. Consequently, we recommend this task be performed by a dealer service department or other qualified repair shop.

20   Brake light switch – removal and installation

1   Disconnect the negative battery cable from the remote ground terminal (see Chapter 5).

2   Remove the driver's side lower dash panel as described in Chapter 11.

3   Disconnect the wiring connector from the brake light switch **(see illustration)**.

4   Rotate the switch counterclockwise and withdraw it from the pedal bracket **(see illus-**

tration). Do not depress the brake pedal during the removal or installation procedure – the pedal must be at rest.

5   Installation is the reversal of removal.

Note: *If both switches have been removed, the brake pedal position switch must be installed before the brake light switch (see Section 15).*

21   Parking brake lever – removal, installation and adjustment

Removal

1   Chock the front wheels and engage 1st gear (or Park).

2   Remove the center console as described in Chapter 11.

3   Disconnect the electrical connector from the parking brake warning switch **(see illustration)**.

4   Loosen the locknut, then remove the parking brake adjusting nut **(see illustrations)**.

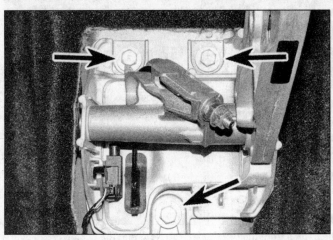

21.5 Parking brake lever mounting bolts. Models without an armrest shown, models with an armrest are similar

21.11 Insert a 0.003-inch (0.7 mm) feeler gauge between the caliper lever and the abutment (stop)

21.15 Insert a 0.080-inch (2.0 mm) feeler gauge between the lever end stop and the side of the shoe

22.4 Remove the air deflector panel at each side

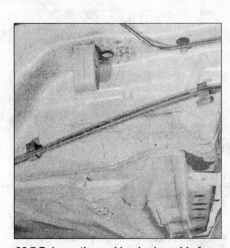

22.7 Release the parking brake cable from the retaining clips

5   Unscrew the mounting bolts securing the parking brake lever to the floor (**see illustration**).
6   Remove the parking brake handle.

Installation and adjustment

7   Installation is the reverse of removal, ensuring the cable retaining tab is positioned away from the cable.
8   When installing the lever, it will be necessary to adjust the mechanism as follows.
Note: *The parking brake should only be adjusted when the brakes are cool.*
9   Tighten the cable adjustment nut finger-tight, then raise the parking brake lever 12 notches.
10   Fully release the parking brake, then loosen the adjustment nut to the end of the threads.

Disc brake models

11   Insert a 0.003-inch (0.08 mm) feeler gauge between the parking brake lever and the caliper abutment on both sides (**see illustration**).

12   With the help of an assistant, tighten the adjustment nut until movement is observed on one of the caliper parking brake levers.
13   Remove the feeler gauges from both sides, then check that the wheels rotate freely with no excess friction or drag caused by the brake. Tighten the adjustment locknut.

Drum brake models

14   Remove the brake drums as described in Section 5.
15   Ensure the parking brake lever is fully released, then insert a 0.080-inch (2.0 mm) feeler gauge between the parking brake lever end stop and the rear brake shoe on each side (**see illustration**).
16   With the help of an assistant, tighten the cable adjustment nut until movement is observed on one of the parking brake levers.
17   Remove the feeler gauges, and install the brake drums as described in Section 5.
18   Check that the wheels rotate freely with no excess friction or drag caused by the brake. Tighten the cable locknut.

22   Parking brake cables – removal and installation

Removal

1   Starting at the rear, pry up and remove the boot/trim around the parking brake lever.
2   Move the locknut to the end of the cable and loosen the parking brake adjustment nut to the end of the threads.
3   Chock the front wheels and engage 1st gear (or Park). Loosen the wheel lug nuts on the relevant rear wheel, then raise the rear of the vehicle and support it securely on jackstands. Fully release the parking brake lever.
4   Release the fasteners and remove the air deflector panel on each side (**see illustration**).
5   Remove the exhaust system as described in Chapter 4.
6   Unscrew the fasteners and remove the front and center exhaust heat shields.
7   Remove the relevant rear wheel and unclip the parking brake outer cable from its retaining clips (**see illustration**).

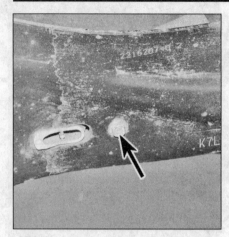

22.8 Unscrew the bolt securing the cable guide to the tie-bar

22.10a Disconnect the cables from the equalizer bracket

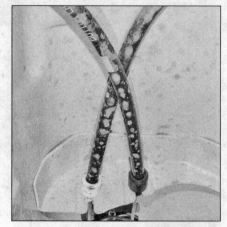

22.10b Note that the cables cross over when installed correctly

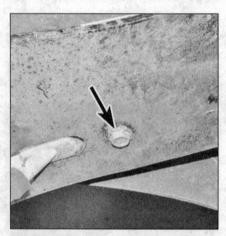

22.11 Remove the bolt securing the parking brake cable to the trailing arm

23.2 Squeeze the sides of the connector and detach the vacuum hose from the brake booster pump

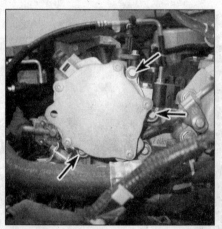

23.3 Brake booster vacuum pump bolts

Disc brake models

8   Unbolt the cable guide from the arm on both sides (**see illustration**).
9   Use a pair of pliers to detach the parking brake cable inner fitting from the lever on each caliper (**see illustration 9.4**).
10   Detach each outer cable from the bracket on the vehicle underbody, then disengage them from the equalizer bracket (**see illustrations**). Note that the left-hand cable has a black sleeve, and the right-hand cable has a white sleeve.

Drum brake models

11   Unbolt the outer cable guide from the trailing arm on both sides (**see illustration**).
12   Unclip the parking brake cable from the arm on both sides. Pull the cable through the trailing arm on both sides.
13   Unclip the cable from the support hangers. Note that there are marks on the cable outer sleeve to indicate the clip positions.
14   Rotate each cable 90-degrees and detach them from the equalizer, then depress the clips and pull the outer cables from the bracket (**see illustrations 22.10a and**

22.10b). Withdraw the cables from beneath the vehicle. Note that the left-hand cable has a black sleeve, while the right-hand cable has a white sleeve.

Installation

15   Installation is the reversal of removal, noting the following points:
a) *Make sure that the cable end fittings are correctly located.*
b) *Adjust the cable as described in Section 21.*
c) *Check the operation of the parking brake. Make sure that both wheels are locked, then free to turn, as the parking brake is operated then released.*

---

23   Brake booster vacuum pump - removal and installation

---

1   Remove the air intake duct (see Chapter 4).
2   Detach the vacuum hose from the fitting on the pump (**see illustration**).

3   Remove the mounting bolts and detach the pump from the cylinder head (**see illustration**).
4   Check the condition of the pump O-ring; if it's in good condition, it can be re-used.
5   Installation is the reverse of removal. Be sure to align the pump with the slot on the camshaft, and tighten the bolts to the torque listed in this Chapter's Specifications.

---

24   Anti-lock Brake System (ABS)/ Traction Control System (TCS)/ Electronic Stability Control (ESC) - general information

---

Anti-lock Brake System

1   The anti-lock braking system (ABS) uses the basic conventional brake system, together with an ABS hydraulic unit fitted between the master cylinder and the four brake units at each wheel. The hydraulic unit consists of a hydraulic actuator, an ABS brake pressure pump, and an ABS module. Braking at each

of the four wheels is controlled by separate solenoid valves in the hydraulic actuator. If wheel lock-up is detected by one of the wheel sensors, the valve opens; releasing pressure to the relevant brake until the wheel regains a rotational speed corresponding to the speed of the vehicle. The cycle can be repeated many times a second. In the event of a fault in the ABS system, the conventional braking system is not affected.

Traction Control System (TCS)

2 The traction control system is integrated with the ABS, and uses the same wheel sensors. The hydraulic control unit has additional solenoid valves incorporated to enable control of the wheel brake pressure. The system is only active at speeds up to 53 mph – when the system is active the warning light on the instrument panel illuminates to warn the driver. This uses controlled braking of the spinning driving wheel when the grip at the driven wheels are different. The spinning wheel is braked by the ABS system, transferring a greater proportion of the engine torque through the differential to the other wheel, which increases the use of the available traction control.

Electronic Stability Control (ESC)

3 This system supports the vehicle's stability and steering through a combination of ABS and traction control operations. There is a switch on the center console, so that if required the system can be switched off. This will then illuminate the warning light on the instrument panel, to inform the driver that the ESC is not in operation. The stability of the vehicle is measured by Yaw rate and Accelerometer sensors, which sense the movement of the vehicle about its vertical axis, and also lateral acceleration.

Diagnosis and repair

4 If a dashboard warning light comes on and stays on while the vehicle is in operation, the ABS system requires attention. Although special electronic ABS diagnostic testing tools are necessary to properly diagnose the system, you can perform a few preliminary checks before taking the vehicle to a dealer service department.

a) Check the brake fluid level in the reservoir.
b) Check the electrical connectors at the hydraulic control unit.
c) Check the fuses.
d) Follow the wiring harness to each wheel and verify that all connections are secure and that the wiring is undamaged.

25 Troubleshooting

PROBABLE CAUSE	CORRECTIVE ACTION

No brakes - pedal travels to floor

1 Low fluid level	1 and 2 Low fluid level and air in the system are symptoms of another problem - a leak somewhere in the hydraulic system. Locate and repair the leak
2 Air in system	
3 Defective seals in master cylinder	3 Replace master cylinder
4 Fluid overheated and vaporized due to heavy braking	4 Bleed hydraulic system (temporary fix). Replace brake fluid (proper fix)

Brake pedal slowly travels to floor under braking or at a stop

1 Defective seals in master cylinder	1 Replace master cylinder
2 Leak in a hose, line, caliper or wheel cylinder	2 Locate and repair leak
3 Air in hydraulic system	3 Bleed the system, inspect system for a leak

Brake pedal feels spongy when depressed

1 Air in hydraulic system	1 Bleed the system, inspect system for a leak
2 Master cylinder or power booster loose	2 Tighten fasteners
3 Brake fluid overheated (beginning to boil)	3 Bleed the system (temporary fix). Replace the brake fluid (proper fix)
4 Deteriorated brake hoses (ballooning under pressure)	4 Inspect hoses, replace as necessary (it's a good idea to replace all of them if one hose shows signs of deterioration)

Troubleshooting (continued)

PROBABLE CAUSE

CORRECTIVE ACTION

Brake pedal feels hard when depressed and/or excessive effort required to stop vehicle

1 Power booster faulty	1 Replace booster
2 Engine not producing sufficient vacuum, or hose to booster clogged, collapsed or cracked	2 Check vacuum to booster with a vacuum gauge. Replace hose if cracked or clogged, repair engine if vacuum is extremely low
3 Brake linings contaminated by grease or brake fluid	3 Locate and repair source of contamination, replace brake pads or shoes
4 Brake linings glazed	4 Replace brake pads or shoes, check discs and drums for glazing, service as necessary
5 Caliper piston(s) or wheel cylinder(s) binding or frozen	5 Replace calipers or wheel cylinders
6 Brakes wet	6 Apply pedal to boil-off water (this should only be a momentary problem)
7 Kinked, clogged or internally split brake hose or line	7 Inspect lines and hoses, replace as necessary

Excessive brake pedal travel (but will pump up)

1 Drum brakes out of adjustment	1 Adjust brakes
2 Air in hydraulic system	2 Bleed system, inspect system for a leak

Excessive brake pedal travel (but will not pump up)

1 Master cylinder pushrod misadjusted	1 Adjust pushrod
2 Master cylinder seals defective	2 Replace master cylinder
3 Brake linings worn out	3 Inspect brakes, replace pads and/or shoes
4 Hydraulic system leak	4 Locate and repair leak

Brake pedal doesn't return

1 Brake pedal binding	1 Inspect pivot bushing and pushrod, repair or lubricate
2 Defective master cylinder	2 Replace master cylinder

Brake pedal pulsates during brake application

1 Brake drums out-of-round	1 Have drums machined by an automotive machine shop
2 Excessive brake disc runout or disc surfaces out-of-parallel	2 Have discs machined by an automotive machine shop
3 Loose or worn wheel bearings	3 Adjust or replace wheel bearings
4 Loose lug nuts	4 Tighten lug nuts

Brakes slow to release

1 Malfunctioning power booster	1 Replace booster
2 Pedal linkage binding	2 Inspect pedal pivot bushing and pushrod, repair/lubricate
3 Malfunctioning proportioning valve	3 Replace proportioning valve
4 Sticking caliper or wheel cylinder	4 Repair or replace calipers or wheel cylinders
5 Kinked or internally split brake hose	5 Locate and replace faulty brake hose

Brakes grab (one or more wheels)

1 Grease or brake fluid on brake lining	1 Locate and repair cause of contamination, replace lining
2 Brake lining glazed	2 Replace lining, deglaze disc or drum

PROBABLE CAUSE

CORRECTIVE ACTION

Vehicle pulls to one side during braking

PROBABLE CAUSE	CORRECTIVE ACTION
1 Grease or brake fluid on brake lining	1 Locate and repair cause of contamination, replace lining
2 Brake lining glazed	2 Deglaze or replace lining, deglaze disc or drum
3 Restricted brake line or hose	3 Repair line or replace hose
4 Tire pressures incorrect	4 Adjust tire pressures
5 Caliper or wheel cylinder sticking	5 Repair or replace calipers or wheel cylinders
6 Wheels out of alignment	6 Have wheels aligned
7 Weak suspension spring	7 Replace springs
8 Weak or broken shock absorber	8 Replace shock absorbers

Brakes drag (indicated by sluggish engine performance or wheels being very hot after driving)

PROBABLE CAUSE	CORRECTIVE ACTION
1 Brake pedal pushrod incorrectly adjusted	1 Adjust pushrod
2 Master cylinder pushrod (between booster and master cylinder) incorrectly adjusted	2 Adjust pushrod
3 Obstructed compensating port in master cylinder	3 Replace master cylinder
4 Master cylinder piston seized in bore	4 Replace master cylinder
5 Contaminated fluid causing swollen seals throughout system	5 Flush system, replace all hydraulic components
6 Clogged brake lines or internally split brake hose(s)	6 Flush hydraulic system, replace defective hose(s)
7 Sticking caliper(s) or wheel cylinder(s)	7 Replace calipers or wheel cylinders
8 Parking brake not releasing	8 Inspect parking brake linkage and parking brake mechanism, repair as required
9 Improper shoe-to-drum clearance	9 Adjust brake shoes
10 Faulty proportioning valve	10 Replace proportioning valve

Brakes fade (due to excessive heat)

PROBABLE CAUSE	CORRECTIVE ACTION
1 Brake linings excessively worn or glazed	1 Deglaze or replace brake pads and/or shoes
2 Excessive use of brakes	2 Downshift into a lower gear, maintain a constant slower speed (going down hills)
3 Vehicle overloaded	3 Reduce load
4 Brake drums or discs worn too thin	4 Measure drum diameter and disc thickness, replace drums or discs as required
5 Contaminated brake fluid	5 Flush system, replace fluid
6 Brakes drag	6 Repair cause of dragging brakes
7 Driver resting left foot on brake pedal	7 Don't ride the brakes

Brakes noisy (high-pitched squeal)

PROBABLE CAUSE	CORRECTIVE ACTION
1 Glazed lining	1 Deglaze or replace lining
2 Contaminated lining (brake fluid, grease, etc.)	2 Repair source of contamination, replace linings
3 Weak or broken brake shoe hold-down or return spring	3 Replace springs
4 Rivets securing lining to shoe or backing plate loose	4 Replace shoes or pads
5 Excessive dust buildup on brake linings	5 Wash brakes off with brake system cleaner
6 Brake drums worn too thin	6 Measure diameter of drums, replace if necessary
7 Wear indicator on disc brake pads contacting disc	7 Replace brake pads
8 Anti-squeal shims missing or installed improperly	8 Install shims correctly

Troubleshooting (continued)

PROBABLE CAUSE	CORRECTIVE ACTION

Brakes noisy (scraping sound)

1 Brake pads or shoes worn out; rivets, backing plate or brake shoe metal contacting disc or drum	1 Replace linings, have discs and/or drums machined (or replace)

Brakes chatter

1 Worn brake lining	1 Inspect brakes, replace shoes or pads as necessary
2 Glazed or scored discs or drums	2 Deglaze discs or drums with sandpaper (if glazing is severe, machining will be required)
3 Drums or discs heat checked	3 Check discs and/or drums for hard spots, heat checking, etc. Have discs/ drums machined or replace them
4 Disc runout or drum out-of-round excessive	4 Measure disc runout and/or drum out-of-round, have discs or drums machined or replace them
5 Loose or worn wheel bearings	5 Adjust or replace wheel bearings
6 Loose or bent brake backing plate (drum brakes)	6 Tighten or replace backing plate
7 Grooves worn in discs or drums	7 Have discs or drums machined, if within limits (if not, replace them)
8 Brake linings contaminated (brake fluid, grease, etc.)	8 Locate and repair source of contamination, replace pads or shoes
9 Excessive dust buildup on linings	9 Wash brakes with brake system cleaner
10 Surface finish on discs or drums too rough after machining (especially on vehicles with sliding calipers)	10 Have discs or drums properly machined
11 Brake pads or shoes glazed	11 Deglaze or replace brake pads or shoes

Brake pads or shoes click

1 Shoe support pads on brake backing plate grooved or excessively worn	1 Replace brake backing plate
2 Brake pads loose in caliper	2 Loose pad retainers or anti-rattle clips
3 Also see items listed under Brakes chatter	

Brakes make groaning noise at end of stop

1 Brake pads and/or shoes worn out	1 Replace pads and/or shoes
2 Brake linings contaminated (brake fluid, grease, etc.)	2 Locate and repair cause of contamination, replace brake pads or shoes
3 Brake linings glazed	3 Deglaze or replace brake pads or shoes
4 Excessive dust buildup on linings	4 Wash brakes with brake system cleaner
5 Scored or heat-checked discs or drums	5 Inspect discs/drums, have machined if within limits (if not, replace discs or drums)
6 Broken or missing brake shoe attaching hardware	6 Inspect drum brakes, replace missing hardware

Rear brakes lock up under light brake application

1 Tire pressures too high	1 Adjust tire pressures
2 Tires excessively worn	2 Replace tires
3 Defective proportioning valve	3 Replace proportioning valve

PROBABLE CAUSE	CORRECTIVE ACTION

Brake warning light on instrument panel comes on (or stays on)

1 Low fluid level in master cylinder reservoir (reservoirs with fluid level sensor)	1 Add fluid, inspect system for leak, check the thickness of the brake pads and shoes
2 Failure in one half of the hydraulic system	2 Inspect hydraulic system for a leak
3 Piston in pressure differential warning valve not centered	3 Center piston by bleeding one circuit or the other (close bleeder valve as soon as the light goes out)
4 Defective pressure differential valve or warning switch	4 Replace valve or switch
5 Air in the hydraulic system	5 Bleed the system, check for leaks
6 Brake pads worn out (vehicles with electric wear sensors - small probes that fit into the brake pads and ground out on the disc when the pads get thin)	6 Replace brake pads (and sensors)

Brakes do not self adjust

Disc brakes

1 Defective caliper piston seals	1 Replace calipers. Also, possible contaminated fluid causing soft or swollen seals (flush system and fill with new fluid if in doubt)
2 Corroded caliper piston(s)	2 Same as above

Drum brakes

1 Adjuster screw frozen	1 Remove adjuster, disassemble, clean and lubricate with high-temperature grease
2 Adjuster lever does not contact star wheel or is binding	2 Inspect drum brakes, assemble correctly or clean or replace parts as required
3 Adjusters mixed up (installed on wrong wheels after brake job)	3 Reassemble correctly
4 Adjuster cable broken or installed incorrectly (cable-type adjusters)	4 Install new cable or assemble correctly

Rapid brake lining wear

1 Driver resting left foot on brake pedal	1 Don't ride the brakes
2 Surface finish on discs or drums too rough	2 Have discs or drums properly machined
3 Also see Brakes drag	

Notes

Chapter 10
Suspension and steering

Contents

Specifications

Torque specifications

Note: *One foot-pound (ft-lb) of torque is equivalent to 12 inch-pounds (in-lbs) of torque. Torque values below approximately 15 ft-lbs are expressed in inch-pounds, because most foot-pound torque wrenches are not accurate at these smaller values.*

Front suspension

	Ft-lbs (unless otherwise indicated)	Nm
Stabilizer bar clamp bolts/nuts*		
Stage 1	85	115
Stage 2	Tighten an additional 90 degrees	
Stabilizer bar link nuts*	46	62
Balljoint-to-control arm pinch bolt/nut*	61	83
Control arm to subframe		
Rear bolts/nuts*		
Stage 1	85	115
Stage 2	Tighten an additional 90 degrees	
Front bolt*		
Stage 1	111	150
Stage 2	Tighten an additional 90 degrees	
Driveaxle/hub nut*	See Chapter 8	
Lower torque rod bolts (engine side)		
Stage 1	35	47
Stage 2	Loosen 360 degrees	
Stage 3	46	62
Subframe front and rear mounting bolts*		
Front	85	115
Rear		
Stage 1	103	140
Stage 2	Tighten an additional 180 degrees	
Rear mounting brackets	177 in-lbs	20
Suspension strut piston nut*	41	56
Suspension strut-to-steering knuckle pinch bolt*		
Stage 1	59	80
Stage 2	Tighten an additional 180 degrees	
Suspension strut upper mounting bolts*	26	35

* Do not re-use

Torque specifications

Ft-lbs (unless otherwise indicated)   **Nm**

Note: *One foot-pound (ft-lb) of torque is equivalent to 12 inch-pounds (in-lbs) of torque. Torque values below approximately 15 ft-lbs are expressed in inch-pounds, because most foot-pound torque wrenches are not accurate at these smaller values.*

Rear suspension

	Ft-lbs	Nm
Stabilizer bar link-to-rear lower control arms	35	48
Stabilizer bar link-to-stabilizer bar nuts*	81	110
Stabilizer bar-to-subframe bolts*	44	60
Trailing arm-to-chassis bolts*	129	175
Rear lower control arm-to-rear knuckle*	85	115
Rear lower control arm-to-subframe*	66	90
Front lower control arm bolts*	85	115
Upper control arm bolts*	85	115
Rear hub and bearing assembly bolts*	81	110
Shock absorber lower mounting bolt*	85	115
Shock absorber upper mount nut*	18	25
Shock absorber upper mounting bolts*	18	25
Subframe bolts*	85	115

Steering

	Ft-lbs	Nm
Steering column mounting bolts*	21	28
Steering gear mounting bolts*		
Stage 1	81	110
Stage 2	Loosen one full turn	
Stage 3	41	56
Stage 4	Tighten an additional 180 degrees	
Steering wheel bolt	35	48
Steering shaft universal joint pinch-bolt*	21	28
Tie-rod end balljoint nuts*	35	48
Tie-rod end locknuts	66	90
Wheel lug nuts	See Chapter 1	

* Do not re-use

1.1 Front suspension

1	Strut/coil spring assembly	5	Stabilizer bar	8	Steering gear boot
2	Steering knuckle	6	Tie-rod end	9	Control arm rear bushing
3	Balljoint	7	Tie-rod	10	Stabilizer bar link
4	Control arm				

1   General information

1   The independent front suspension is of the MacPherson strut type, incorporating coil springs and integral telescopic shock absorbers. The struts are located by transverse control arms, which are attached to the front subframe via rubber bushings at their inner ends and incorporate a balljoint at their outer ends. The steering knuckles, which carry the hub bearings, brake calipers and the hub/disc assemblies, are bolted to the MacPherson struts, and connected to the control arms through the balljoints. All models are equipped with a front stabilizer bar, which is attached to the subframe and to the MacPherson struts via links **(see illustration)**.

2   The rear suspension is of the fully independent, multi-link type, consisting of an upper control arm and two lower control arm mounted via rubber bushings to the trailing arm/rear knuckle and rear subframe. The trailing arm is attached to the vehicle body

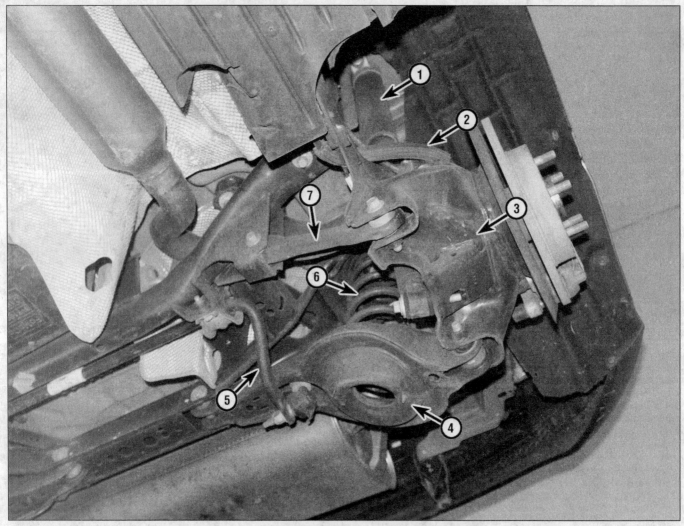

1.2 Rear suspension

1   Shock absorber
2   Upper control arm
3   Rear knuckle

4   Lower control arm (rear)
5   Stabilizer bar

6   Coil spring
7   Lower control arm (front)

at the front end and incorporates the knuckle at the rear. The assembly is located laterally by a pair of lower control arms on each side. Coil springs are installed between the rear lower control arm and the subframe. Separate hydraulic telescopic shock absorbers are installed between the rear knuckle and the vehicle body **(see illustration)**.

3   A power-assisted rack-and-pinion steering gear is standard equipment. Power assistance is derived from an electric motor mounted on the steering gear.

---

2   Steering knuckle and hub and bearing assembly – removal, bearing replacement and installation

---

Note: *The hub bearing is a sealed, pre-adjusted and pre-lubricated, double-row ball type, and is intended to last the car's entire service life without maintenance or attention. The hub flange and bearing are serviced as a complete assembly, and these components cannot be disassembled or replaced individually.*

Removal

1   Loosen the wheel lug nuts and the drive-axle/hub nut (see Chapter 8), then raise the vehicle and support it securely on jackstands. Remove the wheel.

2   Remove the under-vehicle splash shield.

3   Remove the front brake disc (see Chapter 9). If necessary, also remove the brake backing plate.

4   Remove the ABS wheel speed sensor from the steering knuckle (see Chapter 9).

5   Disconnect the tie-rod end from the steering knuckle (see Section 17).

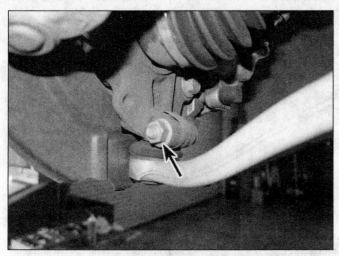

2.6 Remove the balljoint pinch bolt/nut and separate the control arm from the steering knuckle (use a prybar if necessary)

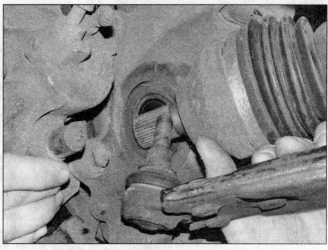

2.8 Lever the control arm downwards, pull the hub carrier outwards, and withdraw the end of the driveshaft from the hub flange

2.9a Remove the pinch bolt

2.9b With the bolt removed, spread the knuckle slightly using a large screwdriver. . .

6   Remove the balljoint pinch bolt nut and bolt **(see illustration)**.

7   If necessary, use a prybar to pry the control arm downwards to separate the balljoint from the steering knuckle. Take care not to damage the balljoint boot during and after disconnection.

8   Swivel the steering knuckle outwards and withdraw the driveaxle stub shaft from the hub **(see illustration)**.

9   Remove the pinch bolt securing the steering knuckle to the strut body **(see illustration)**. Discard the fastener; a new one must be used for installation. Insert a flat-bladed tool into the gap and very slightly spread the hub carrier where it clamps onto the lower end of the strut. Tap the knuckle downwards from the strut at the same time **(see illustrations)**.

2.9c. . . then gently tap the knuckle downwards from the strut

2.10a Using the special tool to support the knuckle, press the hub flange and bearing out. . .

2.10b. . . then assemble the special tool around the new bearing/flange assembly

2.10c Position the knuckle over the new bearing, and the special tool in place on the knuckle. . .

2.10d. . . then press the knuckle. . .

2.10e. . . fully onto the bearing

3.4a Remove the screws. . .

Bearing replacement

10   The hub and bearing must be removed from the knuckle as an assembly. Due to the design of the assembly, we found it impossible to press the new hub/bearing into the knuckle without using manufacturer special tool No 204-348 (see illustrations). The bearing will be destroyed by removal and cannot be re-used.

Installation

11   Prior to installation, remove all traces of thread locking compound, rust, oil and dirt from the splines and threads of the driveaxle stub shaft and the bearing housing mating surface on the knuckle.
12   The remainder of installation is the reverse of removal, but observe the following points:
a) Ensure that the hub and brake disc mating faces are spotlessly clean, and reinstall the disc with the orientation marks aligned.

b) A new strut-to-steering knuckle pinch bolt must be used.
c) A new driveaxle retaining nut must be used.
d) Ensure that the ABS sensor, and the sensor location in the hub carrier, are perfectly clean before installing.
e) Tighten all nuts and bolts to the torque values listed in this Chapter's Specifications. See Chapter 9 for brake component torque settings.

3   Strut/coil spring assembly (front) – removal and installation

1   Loosen the front wheel lug nuts, raise the front of the vehicle and support it securely on jackstands. Remove the wheel.
2   Pull up and remove the engine cover.
3   Remove the wiper arms as described in Chapter 12.
4   Release the screws and fasteners and

remove the upper cowl panel (see illustrations).
5   Release the lower cowl panel from the rain channels at each end, then unbolt and remove the panel (see illustration).
6   Remove the nut securing the stabilizer bar link to the suspension strut. Use an Allen wrench to counterhold the balljoint shank (see illustration). A new nut will be required.
7   Unbolt the brake hose from the bracket on the suspension strut.
8   Detach the steering knuckle from the strut body (see Section 2).
9   Remove the strut upper mounting bolts (see illustration). Dispose of the bolts – they must be replaced. Have an assistant support the strut assembly.
10   Maneuver the strut out from underneath the wheel well.
11   Installation is the reverse of removal. Tighten all nuts and bolts to the torque listed in this Chapter's Specifications.

3.4b. . . and the fasteners

3.4c Remove the panel

3.5 Remove the lower panel

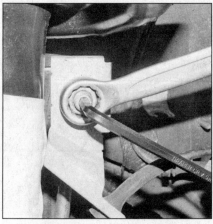

3.6 Use an Allen wrench to counterhold the stabilizer bar link balljoint nut

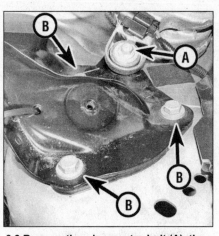

3.9 Remove the wiper motor bolt (A), then the strut upper mounting bolts (B)

4.2 Hold the strut piston rod with an Allen key, and loosen the retaining nut

4   Strut/coil spring assembly (front) – disassembly, inspection and reassembly

Warning: *Before attempting to disassemble the suspension strut, a coil spring compressor must be obtained. Adjustable coil spring compressors which can be positively secured to the spring coils are readily available, and are recommended for this operation. Any attempt to disassemble the strut without such a tool is likely to result in damage or personal injury.*

Disassembly

1   Remove the strut as described in Section 3.

2   Loosen the strut mounting nut 1/2-turn, while holding the protruding portion of the piston rod with an Allen wrench **(see illustration)**. Do not remove the nut at this stage.

3   Install the spring compressors to the coil springs, then tighten the compressors until the load is taken off the spring seats **(see illustration)**.

4   Remove the piston nut, then make alignment marks where the ends of the spring contact the upper and lower seats **(see illustration)**. Discard the nut – a new one must be used.

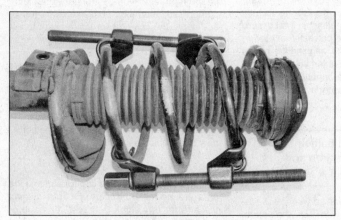

4.3 Install the compressors to the springs

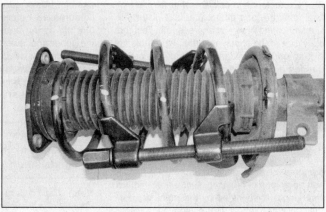

4.4 Make alignment marks between the spring and seats

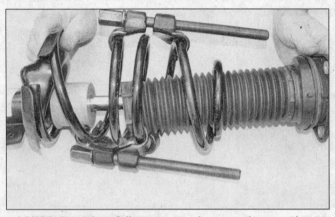

4.5 With the springs fully compressed, remove the mount/seat, bump stop and boot, followed by the spring

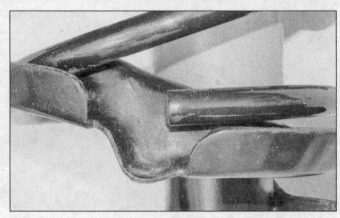

4.11a Ensure the spring ends are correctly located in their seats

4.11b Tighten the new piston rod nut to the specified torque

5.5a Control arm rear mounting bolts. . .

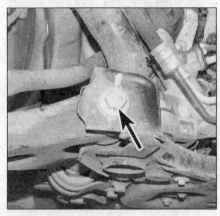

5.5b. . . and front pivot bolt

5   Remove the upper mount/spring seat, bump stop and boot, followed by the spring **(see illustration)**. Do not attempt to separate the spring seat from the mount or the bearing balls will fall out.

Inspection

6   With the strut assembly now completely disassembled, examine all the components for wear, damage or deformation. Replace any of the components as necessary.

7   Examine the shock absorber for signs of fluid leakage, and check the strut piston for signs of pitting along its entire length. Test the operation of the shock absorber, while holding it in an upright position, by moving the piston through a full stroke and then through short strokes of 50 to 100 mm. In both cases, the resistance felt should be smooth and continuous. If the resistance is jerky, or uneven, or if there is any visible sign of wear or damage, replacement is necessary.

8   If any doubt exists about the condition of the coil spring, gradually release the spring compressor and check the spring for distortion and signs of cracking. Since no minimum free length is specified by the manufacturer, the only way to check the tension of the spring is to compare it to a new component. Replace

the spring if it is damaged or distorted, or if there is any doubt as to its condition.

9   Inspect all other components for signs of damage or deterioration, and replace any that are suspect.

10   If a new strut body is being installed, hold it vertically and pump the piston a few times to prime it.

Reassembly

11   Reassembly is the reverse of disassembly, but ensure that the spring is fully compressed before installing it. Make sure that the spring ends are correctly located in the upper and lower seats, aligning the marks made on removal, then tighten the new piston retaining nut and strut mounting bolts to the torque listed in this Chapter's Specifications **(see illustrations)**.

---

5   Control arm and balljoint (front) – removal, inspection and installation

---

Note: *The balljoint is not serviceable separately. If the balljoint is worn out, the control arm must be replaced.*

Removal

1   Loosen the wheel lug nuts, then raise the vehicle and support it securely on jackstands. Remove the wheel.

2   Remove the under-vehicle splash shield.

3   Remove the nut and pinch bolt and separate the control arm balljoint from the steering knuckle (see Section 2).

4   The air conditioning compressor must be moved to gain access to the forward bolt on the right hand side control arm. Unbolt the compressor mounting bolts (see Chapter 3) and move the compressor just enough to get access to the bolt. Support the compressor so there is no strain on the lines or fittings.

Warning: *Do not detach the refrigerant lines from the air conditioning compressor.*

5   Remove the two bolts securing the control arm rear mount and the front pivot bolt and maneuver the control arm from under the vehicle **(see illustrations)**. Discard the bolts - new ones must be installed.

Inspection

6   Thoroughly clean the control arm and the area around the control arm mounts. Inspect the arm for any signs of cracks, damage or distortion, and carefully check the inner pivot

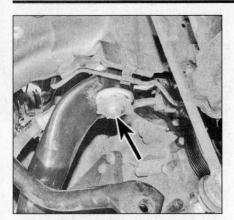

6.10 Loosen the subframe front mounting bolt about six turns

6.11 Remove the subframe rear mounting bolts

6.13 Stabilizer bar clamp bolts

bushings for signs of swelling, cracks or deterioration of the rubber.

7   If either bushing requires replacement, the work should be entrusted to an automotive machine shop. A hydraulic press and suitable spacers are required to remove and install the bushings and a setting gauge is needed for accurate positioning of the bushings in the arm.

Installation

8   Locate the arm on the subframe, and starting at the rear, install the new mounting bolts. Fully tighten the rear bolts to the torque listed in this Chapter's Specifications.

9   Connect the balljoint to the control arm, then install the pinch bolt and nut, tightening the nut to the torque listed in this Chapter's Specifications.

10   Raise the control arm with a floor jack to simulate normal ride height, then tighten the pivot bolt to the torque listed in this Chapter's Specifications.

11   The remainder of installation is the reverse of removal. Have the front wheel alignment checked and, if necessary, adjusted.

6   Stabilizer bar (front) – removal and installation

Removal

1   Loosen the front wheel lug nuts, raise the front of the vehicle and support it securely on jackstands. Remove the wheel.

2   Detach the control arm balljoints from the steering knuckles (see Section 2).

3   With the front wheels pointing straight ahead, remove the steering column lower universal joint pinch-bolt (see Section 14). Discard the bolt – a new one must be installed.

4   Detach the stabilizer bar links from the bar **(see illustration 3.6)**.

5   Detach the tie-rod ends from the steering knuckles (see Section 17).

6   Remove the bolt at the lower rear of the engine securing the lower torque rod to the bracket on the transaxle/engine.

6.14 The stabilizer bar bushings are split to facilitate replacement, and are shaped to fit the bar profile

7   Attach splints on each side of the exhaust flexible section (two wooden strips secured by cable tie will suffice) to prevent excessive bending, then remove the bolts/nuts securing the center exhaust section to the front section.

8   Unhook the exhaust hangers at the front.

9   Support the rear of the subframe with a floor jack (positioned in the center).

10   Unscrew the subframe front mounting bolts approximately six turns **(see illustration)**. Note that new subframe front mounting bolts will be required for installation.

11   Remove the bolts securing the rear mounting brackets to the subframe and vehicle body, and remove the washers **(see illustration)**. Note that new subframe mounting bolts will be required for installation.

12   Carefully lower the jack and allow the subframe to drop slightly at the rear, so that the stabilizer bar clamp bolts are accessible.

13   Remove the bolts securing the stabilizer bar clamps to the subframe, and maneuver the stabilizer bar out from under the car **(see illustration)**. Discard the bolts - new ones must be installed.

14   Examine the stabilizer bar for signs of damage or distortion, and the connecting links

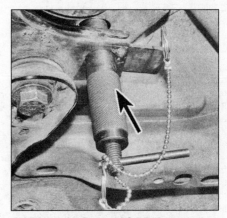

6.17 Align the front subframe by inserting aligning tools through the holes in the subframe into the corresponding holes in the vehicle body

and mounting bushings for signs of deterioration of the rubber. The bushings are split along their length and must be installed in their original positions **(see illustration)**.

Installation

15   Maneuver the stabilizer bar into position on the subframe. Install the new clamp bolts and tighten them to the torque listed in this Chapter's Specifications.

16   Raise the subframe at the rear, install the rear mounting brackets to the body, and tighten the bolts hand-tight only at this stage.

17   The alignment of the subframe must be checked by inserting round tools that can be inserted through the holes in the side members. Special tools (part No 205-880) may be available. Alternatively, you can use two lengths of wooden dowel, 20 mm in diameter, and approximately 150 mm in length **(see illustration)**.

18   With the subframe correctly aligned, install new front subframe mounting bolts, and tighten all subframe bolts to the torque listed in this Chapter's Specifications.

19   The remainder of installation is the reverse of removal. Have the front wheel alignment checked and, if necessary, adjusted.

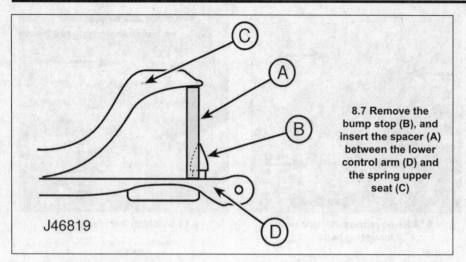

8.7 Remove the bump stop (B), and insert the spacer (A) between the lower control arm (D) and the spring upper seat (C)

J46819

7   Hub and bearing assembly (rear) – replacement

1   The rear hub bearings cannot be replaced separately, and are supplied with the rear hub as a complete assembly.
2   Remove the brake disc or drum (as applicable) as described in Chapter 9.
3   Unscrew the bolt and remove the ABS wheel speed sensor from the knuckle.
4   Remove the mounting bolts and detach the bearing assembly from the knuckle.
5   Install the new assembly to the knuckle, then insert and tighten the bolts to the torque listed in this Chapter's Specifications.
6   Install the ABS wheel speed sensor and brake disc or drum as described in Chapter 9.

8   Rear knuckle/trailing arm – removal and installation

Removal

1   Remove the rear hub as described in Section 7. On models with disc brakes, unbolt and remove the disc shield.
2   Remove the bolt securing the parking brake cable retaining clip to the trailing arm, then unhook the cable from the connecting sleeve. Pull the cable through the trailing arm/rear knuckle.
3   Unclip the brake hose from the knuckle.
4   Unclip the parking brake cable from the knuckle.
5   Release the ABS wheel speed sensor wiring harness from the clips on the trailing arm.
6   Remove the coil spring as described in Section 10.
7   Fabricate a spacer 1.5-inch (38 mm) in diameter, and 7-inches (178 mm) (all models except Focus ST), or 6-1/2 inches (164 mm) long (Focus ST models). Unscrew the suspension bump stop, insert the spacer between the lower control arm and the coil spring upper seat, then raise the lower arm with a floor jack until the spacer is lightly trapped **(see illustration)**. Ensure the spacer is vertical.
8   Remove the fasteners and remove the air baffle plate **(see illustration)**.
9   Remove the retaining bolt and withdraw the ABS wheel sensor from the hub carrier/lateral link. Do not disconnect the wheel sensor wiring plug.
10   Remove the bolts securing the upper control arm and front lower control arm to the knuckle **(see illustrations 11.3 and 11.5b)**.
11   Remove the bolt and detach the rear lower control arm from the knuckle **(see illustration 11.7a)**.
12   Remove the trailing arm-to-chassis bolts and remove the arm/knuckle assembly **(see illustration)**.
13   Replacement of the bushing at the front of the trailing arm requires the use of special tools and a hydraulic press. Therefore it is recommended that this task be entrusted to an automotive machine shop.

Installation

14   Place the trailing arm into position and tighten the front mounting bolts to the torque listed in this Chapter's Specifications.
15   Install the ABS wheel speed sensor wiring harness clips to the arms.
16   Position the parking brake cable and install the cable retaining clip.
17   Reconnect the upper control arm and lower control arms, but don't tighten the bolts yet.
18   Ensure the fabricated spacer is still in place between the rear lower control arm and the spring seat **(see illustration 8.7)**.
19   Tighten the upper control arm and lower control arm bolts to the torque values listed in this Chapter's Specifications. Remove the spacer and reinstall the bump stop.
20   The remainder of installation is the reverse of removal. Have the rear wheel alignment checked and, if necessary, adjusted.

9   Shock absorber (rear) – removal and installation

1   Block the front wheels. Loosen the rear wheel lug nuts, then raise the rear of the vehicle and support it securely on jackstands. Remove the wheels.
2   Place a floor jack under the rear lower control arm and raise the suspension a little to take the load off the shock absorber.
3   Remove the shock absorber upper mounting bolts **(see illustration)**.

8.8 Remove the air baffle plate

8.12 Trailing arm/rear knuckle front mounting bolts

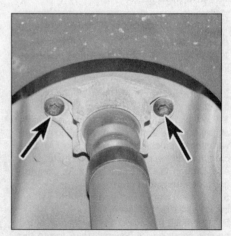

9.3 Shock absorber upper mounting bolts

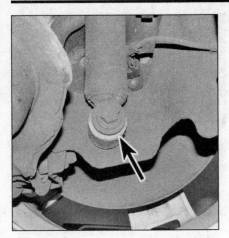

9.4 Shock absorber lower mounting bolt

9.5 Shock absorber upper mount nut

10.5 Remove the rear springs using spring compressors

4   Remove the lower mounting bolt and pull the shock absorber from the rear knuckle **(see illustration)**.
5   If required, unscrew the nut and pull the upper mount from the shock absorber **(see illustration)**.
6   Installation is the reversel of removal, tightening all nuts and bolts to the torque values listed in this Chapter's Specifications.

10   Coil spring (rear) – removal and installation

Removal

1   Block the front wheels. Loosen the rear wheel lug nuts, then raise the rear of the vehicle and support it securely on jackstands. Remove the wheels.
2   Remove the nut securing the stabilizer bar link to the lower control arm **(see illustration 12.2)**.
3   Place a floor jack under the rear lower control arm and raise the suspension a little to take the load off the shock absorber.
4   Remove the shock absorber lower

mounting bolt.
5   Attach spring compressors to the spring and compress the spring **(see illustration)**.
6   Slowly lower the floor jack, and remove the spring.
7   Examine all the components for wear or damage, and replace as necessary.

Installation

8   Reinstall the rubber seats to the control arm and spring, ensuring the ends of the spring locate correctly **(see illustrations)**.
9   Install the compressed spring onto the seat in the lower control arm. Rotate the spring until the spring engages correctly in the control arm grooves.
10   Raise the control arm with the floor jack, and guide the upper end of the spring into its recess in the body.
11   Reinstall the shock absorber lower mounting bolt finger tight at this time. Raise the control arm with the floor jack to simulate normal ride height, then tighten the shock absorber lower mounting bolt to the torque listed in this Chapter's Specifications.
12   Release and remove the spring compressor.

13   The remainder of installation is the reverse of removal.

11   Control arms (rear) – removal and installation

Removal

1   Block the front wheels. Loosen the rear wheel lug nuts, then raise the rear of the vehicle and support it securely on jackstands. Remove the wheel.

Front lower control arm

2   Support the lower rear control arm with a floor jack placed under the spring seat. Raise the arm slighly.
3   Remove the outer and inner bolts, then remove the control arm **(see illustration)**. Note that the arm is marked FRONT on one side.

Upper control arm

4   Support the upper rear control arm with a floor jack placed under the spring seat. Raise the arm slighly.

10.8a The on the underside of the seat must locate in the hole in the arm

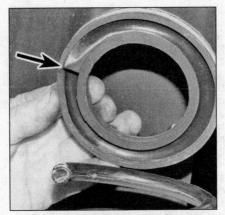

10.8b The end of the spring must fit against the stop in the rubber seat

11.3 Front lower control arm mounting bolts

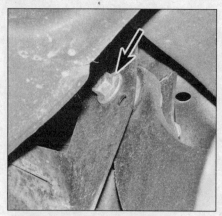

11.5a Upper control arm inner bolt. . .

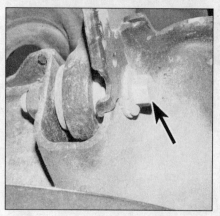

11.5b. . . and outer bolt

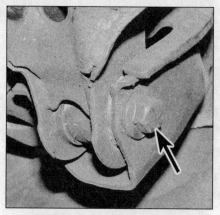

11.7a Remove the lower control arm outer bolt. . .

11.7b. . . then mark the position of the eccentric washer and remove the bolt

12.2 Rear stabilizer bar-to-link nut (A) and link-to-control arm nut (B)

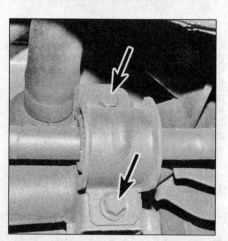

12.3 Remove the bolts securing the stabilizer bar clamps

5   Remove the outer and inner bolts, then remove the control arm **(see illustrations)**.

Rear lower control arm
6   Remove the coil spring as described in Section 10.
7   Mark the position of the inner bolt eccentric washer in relation to the subframe, then remove the inner and outer control arm bolts and remove the control arm **(see illustrations)**.
8   Examine the condition of the metal-elastic bushings in the control arm. If replacement is necessary, the bushings must be pressed from the arm and new ones pressed into place. This necessitates the use of a hydraulic press and the necessary adapters. Entrust this task to an automotive machine shop or other qualified repair facility.

Installation
9   Installation is the reverse of removal, noting the following points:
a) Align the concentric washer with the marks made during removal.
b) Tighten all fasteners to the torque values listed in this Chapter's Specifications, using a little thread-locking compound.
c) Before tightening any control arm mounting bolts, raise the rear lower control arm

with a floor jack to simulate normal ride height.

---

12   Stabilizer bar (rear) – removal and installation

Removal
1   Block the front wheels. Loosen the rear wheel lug nuts, then raise the rear of the vehicle and support it securely on jackstands. Remove the wheel.
2   Remove the nuts securing the outer ends of the stabilizer bar to the links **(see illustration)**. Discard the nuts; new ones must be used during installation.
3   Remove the bolts securing the stabilizer bar clamps to the subframe, and remove the stabilizer bar from under the vehicle **(see illustration)**. Discard the fasteners; new ones must be installed during installation.
4   Examine the stabilizer bar for signs of damage or distortion, and the bushings for signs of deterioration of the rubber. The bushings are split along their length and must be installed in their original positions.

Installation
5   Position the stabilizer bar, then install new bolts to secure the clamps to the subframe. Tighten the bolts to the torque listed in this Chapter's Specifications.
6   Connect the stabilizer bar links and install new nuts. Tighten the nuts to the torque listed in this Chapter's Specifications.
7   The remainder of installation is the reverse of removal.

---

13   Steering wheel – removal and installation

Warning: *These models are equipped with a Supplemental Restraint System (SRS), more commonly known as airbags. Always disable the airbag system before working in the vicinity of any airbag system component to avoid the possibility of accidental deployment of the airbag(s), which could cause personal injury (see Chapter 12).*
Warning: *Do not use a memory saving device to preserve the PCM or radio memory when working on or near airbag system components.*

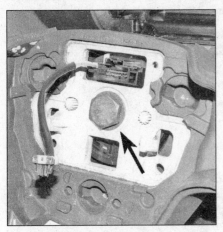

13.4 Steering wheel retaining bolt

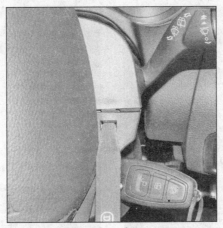

14.4 Release the clip securing the column upper shroud to the lower shroud

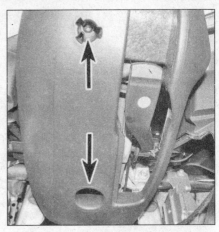

14.5 Remove the screws securing the column lower shroud

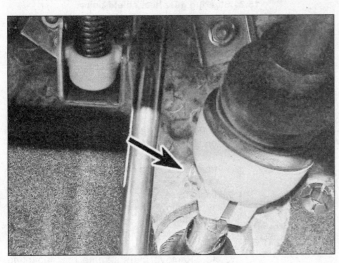

14.8 Steering column lower pinch-bolt

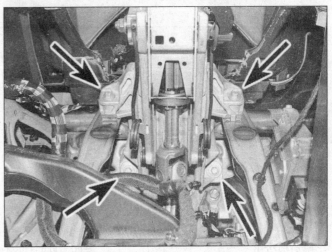

14.9 Steering column mounting bolts

Removal

1   Drive the car forwards, and park it with the front wheels in the straight-ahead position.

2   Remove the driver's airbag as described in Chapter 12. Secure the clockspring in place using tape to prevent any rotation.

3   Disconnect the electrical connector at the top of the steering wheel aperture.

4   Remove the steering wheel retaining bolt **(see illustration)**.

5   Make alignment marks between the steering wheel hub and the column shaft (if none exist), then lift the steering wheel off the column shaft and feed the wiring and plastic strip through the hole in the wheel. Place a piece of tape over the clockspring unit to keep it aligned.

Installation

6   Ensure that the front wheels are still in the straight-ahead position.

7   Check the airbag clockspring is still aligned. Refer to Chapter 12 if necessary. Remove the securing tape.

8   Feed the wiring through the hole in the steering wheel, then engage the wheel with the steering column shaft. Ensure that the marks made on removal are aligned, and that the pegs on the clockspring engage with the recesses on the steering wheel hub.

9   Reinstall the steering wheel retaining bolt and tighten it to the torque listed in this Chapter's Specifications.

10   Reinstall the airbag unit to the steering wheel as described in Chapter 12.

---

14   Steering column – removal and installation

Removal

1   Disconnect the negative battery cable from the remote ground terminal (see Chapter 5).

2   Fully extend and lower the steering column.

3   Remove the lower dash panel on the driver's side (see Chapter 11).

4   Turn the steering wheel for access, then release the retaining clips and remove the

steering column upper shroud **(see illustration)**. Turn the steering wheel back to the straight-ahead position.

5   Unscrew the two retaining screws and remove the steering column lower shroud **(see illustration)**. Release the steering column locking lever to remove the shroud completely.

6   Remove the steering wheel as described in Section 13.

7   Noting their positions and routing, disconnect the various column wiring plugs and release the harness retaining clips.

8   Remove the steering column lower pinch-bolt and pull the joint upwards from the pinion **(see illustration)**. Ensure the column adjustment lever is released before detaching the joint from the pinion. Discard the pinch-bolt; a new one must be installed.

9   Remove the four retaining bolts and maneuver the column from the vehicle **(see illustration)**. Discard the bolts; new ones must be installed.

10   If required, drill out the security bolts and remove the steering lock from the column. No further disassembly of the column is recommended.

15.15 Disconnect the electrical connectors

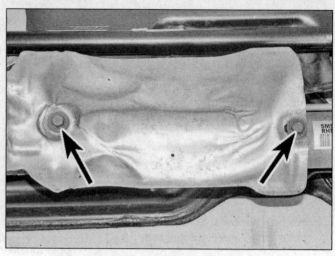

15.21 Steering gear heat shield bolts

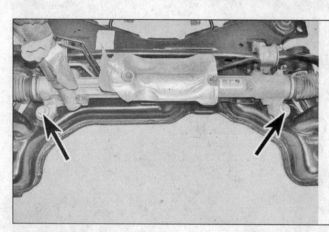

15.22 Steering gear retaining bolts

Installation

11   Installation is the reverse of removal, noting the following points:

a) *Lubricate universal joint splines with grease before engaging the steering column.*

b) *When installing the new column retaining bolts, the shortest bolts are installed nearest to the firewall.*

c) *Use a new universal joint pinch-bolt.*

d) *Tighten the fasteners to the torque listed in this Chapter's Specifications.*

e) *If the steering lock was removed, tighten the new security bolts until their heads snap off.*

f) *If the steering column has been rotated, or the front wheels turned from straight-ahead, center the airbag clockspring as described in Chapter 12.*

15   Steering gear – removal and installation

Removal

1   Drive the car forwards and park it with the steering wheels in the straight-ahead position. Remove the ignition key to lock the steering in this position.

2   Disconnect the negative battery cable from the remote ground terminal (see Chapter 5).

3   Remove the lower dash panel on the driver's side.

4   Remove the steering column pinch bolt and pull the joint upwards from the pinion (**see illustration 14.8**). Ensure the column adjustment lever is released before detaching the joint from the pinion. Discard the pinch bolt; a new one must be installed.

5   Loosen the front wheel lug nuts, raise the front of the vehicle and support it securely on jackstands. Remove the wheel.

6   Remove the engine undershield.

7   Remove the bolt securing the headlight leveling sensor bracket to the lower control arm (where applicable).

8   On some models, disconnect the steering angle sensor wiring plug (located at the steering column pinion in the engine compartment).

9   Attach splints to each side of the exhaust flexible section (two wooden strips secured by cable tie will suffice) to prevent excessive bending, then remove the bolts/nuts securing the center exhaust section to the front section.

10   Unhook the exhaust hangers at the front.

11   Separate the control arm balljoint from the steering knuckle (see Section 2).

12   Detach the stabilizer bar links from the bar (see Section 6).

13   Separate the tie-rod ends from the steering knuckles (see Section 17).

14   Remove the bolt at the lower rear of the engine securing the lower torque rod to the bracket on the transaxle/engine.

15   Disconnect the electrical connectors from the steering gear (**see illustration**).

16   Support the rear of the subframe with a floor jack.

17   Remove and discard the subframe front mounting bolts (**see illustration 6.10**). New subframe front mounting bolts will be required for installation.

18   Remove the subframe rear mounting bolts and washers (**see illustration 6.11**). Note that new subframe mounting bolts will be required for installation.

19   Carefully lower the jack and subframe.

20   Unscrew the bolts and remove the stabilizer bar (see illustration 6.13). Discard the bolts – new ones must be installed.

21   Remove the steering gear heat shield (**see illustration**).

22   Remove the retaining bolts and lift the steering gear from the subframe (**see illustration**).

Installation

23   Guide the steering gear into position and tighten the bolts to the torque listed in this Chapter's Specifications.

24   Install the steering gear heat shield and tighten the bolts securely.

25   Install the stabilizer bar to the subframe and tighten the new bolts to the torque listed in this Chapter's Specifications.

26   Ensure the steering gear firewall seal is in place, then raise the subframe into position.

27   Install the subframe rear mounting brackets to the body, then insert the new front and rear subframe mounting bolts. Only hand tighten them at this stage.

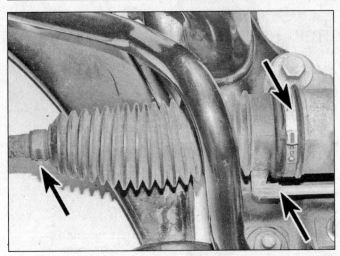

16.2 Steering boot clamps and breather hose - shown with the steerng gear removed for clarity

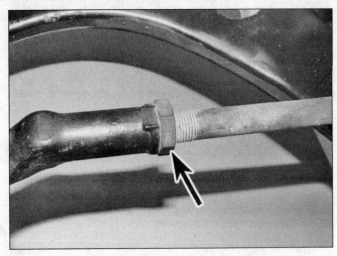

17.2 Loosen the tie-rod end locknut

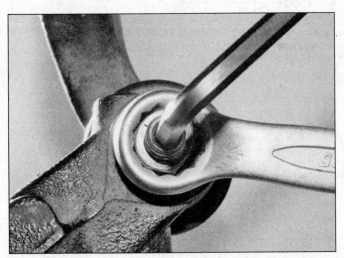

17.3a Use an Allen wrench to counterhold the tie-rod end balljoint shank

17.3b Use a separator tool to detach the tie-rod end from the steering knuckle

28   The alignment of the subframe must be checked by inserting round tools though the holes in the side members. Special tools (part No 205-880) may be available. Alternatively, using two lengths of wooden dowel, 20 mm in diameter, and approximately 150 mm in length **(see illustration 6.17)**.

29   With the subframe correctly aligned, tighten all subframe bolts to the torque listed in this Chapter's Specifications.

30   Engage the steering shaft universal joint with the pinion shaft.

31   Install the new universal joint pinch bolt and tighten it to the torque listed in this Chapter's Specifications.

32   The remainder of installation is the reverse of removal, noting the following points:

a) Tighten all fasteners to the torque listed in this Chapter's Specifications.

b) Have the wheel alignment checked and, if necessary, adjusted.

16   Steering gear boots – replacement

1   Remove the tie-rod end on the side concerned as described in Section 17. Unscrew the locknut from the tie-rod.

2   Release the two clamps and peel off the boot. Disconnect the breather hose as the boot is withdrawn **(see illustration)**

3   Clean out any dirt and grit from the inner end of the tie-rod and (when accessible) the steering gear.

4   Wrap electrical tape around the tie-rod threads to protect the new boot while installing.

5   Install the tie-rod end locknut.

6   Reinstall the tie-rod end as described in Section 17.

17   Tie-rod end – removal and installation

Removal

1   Loosen the front wheel lug nuts, raise the front of the vehicle and support it securely on jackstands. Remove the wheel.

2   Counterhold the tie-rod end with a wrench and loosen the tie-rod end locknut by 1/2-turn **(see illustration)**. If the locknut is now left in this position, it will act as a further guide for installation.

3   Unscrew the tie-rod end balljoint nut a few turns, using an Allen key to counterhold the balljoint shank. Separate the balljoint from the steering knuckle arm with a balljoint separator, then remove the nut and disengage the balljoint from the arm **(see illustrations)**.

4   Unscrew the tie-rod end from the tie-

rod, counting the number of turns needed to remove it. Make a note of the number of turns, so that the toe-in can be reset (or at least approximated) on installation.

Installation

5   Screw the tie-rod end onto the tie-rod by the same number of turns noted during removal.
6   Engage the balljoint in the steering arm. Install a new nut and tighten it to the torque listed in this Chapter's Specifications.
7   Counterhold the tie-rod end and tighten the locknut to the torque listed in this Chapter's Specifications.
8   Install the wheel and lug nuts, lower the car and tighten the lug nuts to the torque listed in the Chapter 1 Specifications.
9   Have the wheel alignment checked and, if necessary, adjusted.

18   Wheels and tires - general information

1   All vehicles covered by this manual are equipped with metric-sized fiberglass or steel belted radial tires **(see illustration)**. Use of other size or type of tires may affect the ride and handling of the vehicle. Don't mix different types of tires, such as radials and bias belted, on the same vehicle as handling may be seriously affected. It's recommended that tires be replaced in pairs on the same axle, but if only one tire is being replaced, be sure it's the same size, structure and tread design as the other.
2   Because tire pressure has a substantial effect on handling and wear, the pressure on all tires should be checked at least once a month or before any extended trips (see Chapter 1).
3   Wheels must be replaced if they are bent, dented, leak air, have elongated bolt holes, are heavily rusted, out of vertical symmetry or if the lug nuts won't stay tight. Wheel repairs that use welding or peening are not recommended.
4   Tire and wheel balance is important in the overall handling, braking and performance of the vehicle. Unbalanced wheels can adversely affect handling and ride characteristics as well as tire life. Whenever a tire is installed on a wheel, the tire and wheel should be balanced by a shop with the proper equipment.

19   Wheel alignment - general information

1   A wheel alignment refers to the adjustments made to the wheels so they are in proper angular relationship to the suspension and the ground. Wheels that are out of proper alignment not only affect vehicle control, but also increase tire wear. The front end angles normally measured are camber, caster and

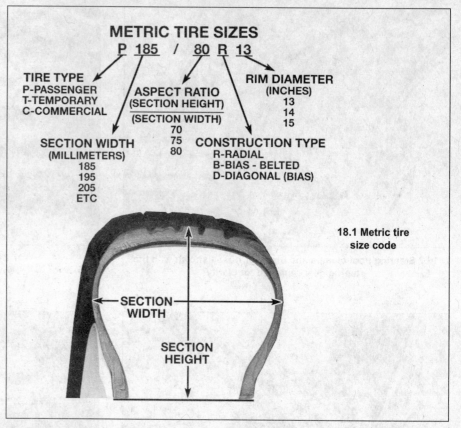

18.1 Metric tire size code

toe-in **(see illustration)**. Camber and caster are preset at the factory on the vehicles covered by this manual; toe-in is the only adjustable angle on these vehicles (however, camber and caster are usually measured to check for bent or worn suspension parts). Toe-in and camber are both adjustable at the rear.
2   Getting the proper wheel alignment is an exacting process, one in which complicated and expensive machines are necessary to perform the job properly. Because of this, you should have a technician with the proper equipment perform these tasks. We will, however, use this space to give you a basic idea of what is involved with a wheel alignment so you can better understand the process and deal intelligently with the shop that does the work.
3   Toe-in is the turning in of the wheels. The purpose of a toe specification is to ensure parallel rolling of the wheels. In a vehicle with zero toe-in, the distance between the front edges of the wheels will be the same as the distance between the rear edges of the wheels. The actual amount of toe-in is normally only a fraction of an inch. Incorrect toe-in will cause the tires to wear improperly by making them scrub against the road surface.
4   Camber is the tilting of the wheels from vertical when viewed from one end of the vehicle. When the wheels tilt out at the top, the camber is said to be positive (+). When the wheels tilt in at the top the camber is negative (-). The amount of tilt is measured in degrees from vertical and this measurement is called the camber angle. This angle affects the

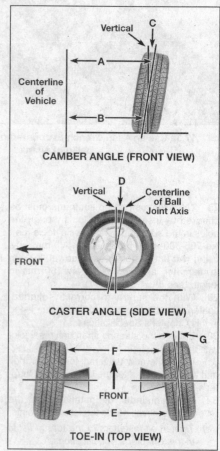

19.1 Camber, caster and toe-in angles

amount of tire tread which contacts the road and compensates for changes in the suspension geometry when the vehicle is cornering or traveling over an undulating surface.

5   Caster is the tilting of the front steering axis from the vertical. A tilt toward the rear is positive caster and a tilt toward the front is negative caster.

20 Front subframe – removal and installation

The front subframe removal and installation procedure is described within the steering gear removal and installation procedure, as described in Section 15. If the subframe is to be removed as part of another procedure, the steering gear and stabilizer bar can be left in place on the subframe.

Notes

Chapter 11
Body

Contents

Specifications

Torque specifications

Note: *One foot-pound (ft-lb) of torque is equivalent to 12 inch-pounds (in-lbs) of torque. Torque values below approximately 15 ft-lbs are expressed in inch-pounds, because most foot-pound torque wrenches are not accurate at these smaller values.*

	Ft-lbs (unless otherwise indicated)	Nm
Crossmember A-pillar bolts	30	40
Crossmember bolts	18	24
Front seat mounting bolts	26	35
Heater box-to-crossmember bolts	84 in-lbs	10
Passenger's airbag module lower support bracket		
Bolts	72 in-lbs	9
Nuts	60 in-lbs	7
Rear seat cushion bolts	18	24
Rear seat backrest catch retaining bolts	17	23
Rear seat hinge	18	24
Seat belt mounting nuts and bolts		
Front inertia reel bolt	26	35
Front lower anchorage	26	35
Front seat belt buckle stake	35	47
Front seat bolts shoulder height adjuster	26	35
Front upper anchorage	26	35
Rear belt buckle stalks	41	56
Rear center inertia reel	35	47
Rear center lower anchorage	41	56
Rear outer inertia reel	35	47
Rear outer lower anchorage	30	40
Wheel lug nuts	See Chapter 1	

1   General information

Warning: *The models covered by this manual are equipped with Supplemental Restraint Systems (SRS), more commonly known as airbags. Always disable the airbag system before working in the vicinity of any airbag system components to avoid the possibility of accidental deployment of the airbags, which could cause personal injury (see Chapter 12).*

1   Certain body components are particularly vulnerable to accident damage and can be unbolted and repaired or replaced. Among these parts are the hood, doors, tailgate, liftgate, bumpers and front fenders.

2   Only general body maintenance practices and body panel repair procedures within the scope of the do-it-yourselfer are included in this Chapter.

Make sure the damaged area is perfectly clean and rust free. If the touch-up kit has a wire brush, use it to clean the scratch or chip. Or use fine steel wool wrapped around the end of a pencil. Clean the scratched or chipped surface only, not the good paint surrounding it. Rinse the area with water and allow it to dry thoroughly

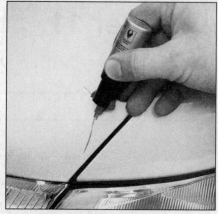

Thoroughly mix the paint, then apply a small amount with the touch-up kit brush or a very fine artist's brush. Brush in one direction as you fill the scratch area. Do not build up the paint higher than the surrounding paint

2   Repairing minor paint scratches

No matter how hard you try to keep your vehicle looking like new, it will inevitably be scratched, chipped or dented at some point. If the metal is actually dented, seek the advice of a professional. But you can fix minor scratches and chips yourself. Buy a touch-up paint kit from a dealer service department or an auto parts store. To ensure that you get the right color, you'll need to have the specific make, model and year of your vehicle and, ideally, the paint code, which is located on a special metal plate under the hood or in the door jamb.

3   Body repair - minor damage

Plastic body panels

1   The following repair procedures are for minor scratches and gouges. Repair of more serious damage should be left to a dealer service department or qualified auto body shop. Below is a list of the equipment and materials necessary to perform the following repair procedures on plastic body panels.

Wax, grease and silicone removing solvent
Cloth-backed body tape
Sanding discs
Drill motor with three-inch disc holder
Hand sanding block
Rubber squeegees
Sandpaper
Non-porous mixing palette
Wood paddle or putty knife
Curved-tooth body file
Flexible parts repair material

Flexible panels (bumper trim)

2   Remove the damaged panel, if necessary or desirable. In most cases, repairs can be carried out with the panel installed.

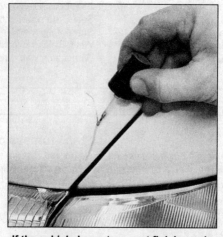

If the vehicle has a two-coat finish, apply the clear coat after the color coat has dried

3   Clean the area(s) to be repaired with a wax, grease and silicone removing solvent applied with a water-dampened cloth.
4   If the damage is structural, that is, if it extends through the panel, clean the backside of the panel area to be repaired as well. Wipe dry.
5   Sand the rear surface about 1-1/2 inches beyond the break.
6   Cut two pieces of fiberglass cloth large enough to overlap the break by about 1-1/2 inches. Cut only to the required length.
7   Mix the adhesive from the repair kit according to the instructions included with the kit, and apply a layer of the mixture approximately 1/8-inch thick on the backside of the panel. Overlap the break by at least 1-1/2 inches.
8   Apply one piece of fiberglass cloth to the adhesive and cover the cloth with additional adhesive. Apply a second piece of fiberglass cloth to the adhesive and immediately cover the cloth with additional adhesive in sufficient quantity to fill the weave.

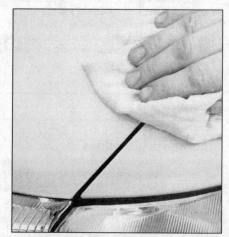

Wait a few days for the paint to dry thoroughly, then rub out the repainted area with a polishing compound to blend the new paint with the surrounding area. When you're happy with your work, wash and polish the area

9   Allow the repair to cure for 20 to 30 minutes at 60-degrees to 80-degrees F.
10   If necessary, trim the excess repair material at the edge.
11   Remove all of the paint film over and around the area(s) to be repaired. The repair material should not overlap the painted surface.
12   With a drill motor and a sanding disc (or a rotary file), cut a "V" along the break line approximately 1/2-inch wide. Remove all dust and loose particles from the repair area.
13   Mix and apply the repair material. Apply a light coat first over the damaged area; then continue applying material until it reaches a level slightly higher than the surrounding finish.
14   Cure the mixture for 20 to 30 minutes at 60-degrees to 80-degrees F.
15   Roughly establish the contour of the area being repaired with a body file. If low areas or

pits remain, mix and apply additional adhesive.

16   Block sand the damaged area with sandpaper to establish the actual contour of the surrounding surface.

17   If desired, the repaired area can be temporarily protected with several light coats of primer. Because of the special paints and techniques required for flexible body panels, it is recommended that the vehicle be taken to a paint shop for completion of the body repair.

Steel body panels

Repair of dents

18   When repairing dents, the first job is to pull the dent out until the affected area is as close as possible to its original shape. There is no point in trying to restore the original shape completely as the metal in the damaged area will have stretched on impact and cannot be restored to its original contours. It is better to bring the level of the dent up to a point that is about 1/8-inch below the level of the surrounding metal. In cases where the dent is very shallow, it is not worth trying to pull it out at all.

19   If the backside of the dent is accessible, it can be hammered out gently from behind using a soft-face hammer. While doing this, hold a block of wood firmly against the opposite side of the metal to absorb the hammer blows and prevent the metal from being stretched.

20   If the dent is in a section of the body which has double layers, or some other factor makes it inaccessible from behind, a different technique is required. Drill several small holes through the metal inside the damaged area, particularly in the deeper sections. Screw long, self-tapping screws into the holes just enough for them to get a good grip in the metal. Now pulling on the protruding heads of the screws with locking pliers can pull out the dent.

21   The next stage of repair is the removal of paint from the damaged area and from an inch or so of the surrounding metal. This is easily done with a wire brush or sanding disk in a drill motor, although it can be done just as effectively by hand with sandpaper. To complete the preparation for filling, score the surface of the bare metal with a screwdriver or the tang of a file or drill small holes in the affected area. This will provide a good grip for the filler material. To complete the repair, see the Section on filling and painting.

Repair of rust holes or gashes

22   Remove all paint from the affected area and from an inch or so of the surrounding metal using a sanding disk or wire brush mounted in a drill motor. If these are not available, a few sheets of sandpaper will do the job just as effectively.

23   With the paint removed, you will be able to determine the severity of the corrosion and decide whether to replace the whole panel, if possible, or repair the affected area. New body panels are not as expensive as most people think and it is often quicker to install a new panel than to repair large areas of rust.

24   Remove all trim pieces from the affected area except those which will act as a guide to the original shape of the damaged body, such as headlight shells, etc. Using metal snips or a hacksaw blade, remove all loose metal and any other metal that is badly affected by rust. Hammer the edges of the hole in to create a slight depression for the filler material.

25   Wire-brush the affected area to remove the powdery rust from the surface of the metal. If the back of the rusted area is accessible, treat it with rust inhibiting paint.

26   Before filling is done, block the hole in some way. This can be done with sheet metal riveted or screwed into place, or by stuffing the hole with wire mesh.

27   Once the hole is blocked off, the affected area can be filled and painted. See the following subsection on filling and painting.

Filling and painting

28   Many types of body fillers are available, but generally speaking, body repair kits which contain filler paste and a tube of resin hardener are best for this type of repair work. A wide, flexible plastic or nylon applicator will be necessary for imparting a smooth and contoured finish to the surface of the filler material. Mix up a small amount of filler on a clean piece of wood or cardboard (use the hardener sparingly). Follow the manufacturer's instructions on the package, otherwise the filler will set incorrectly.

29   Using the applicator, apply the filler paste to the prepared area. Draw the applicator across the surface of the filler to achieve the desired contour and to level the filler surface. As soon as a contour that approximates the original one is achieved, stop working the paste. If you continue, the paste will begin to stick to the applicator. Continue to add thin layers of paste at 20-minute intervals until the level of the filler is just above the surrounding metal.

30   Once the filler has hardened, the excess can be removed with a body file. From then on, progressively finer grades of sandpaper should be used, starting with a 180-grit paper and finishing with 600-grit wet-or-dry paper. Always wrap the sandpaper around a flat rubber or wooden block, otherwise the surface of the filler will not be completely flat. During the sanding of the filler surface, the wet-or-dry paper should be periodically rinsed in water. This will ensure that a very smooth finish is produced in the final stage.

31   At this point, the repair area should be surrounded by a ring of bare metal, which in turn should be encircled by the finely feathered edge of good paint. Rinse the repair area with clean water until all of the dust produced by the sanding operation is gone.

32   Spray the entire area with a light coat of primer. This will reveal any imperfections in the surface of the filler. Repair the imperfections with fresh filler paste or glaze filler and once more smooth the surface with sandpaper. Repeat this spray-and-repair procedure until you are satisfied that the surface of the filler and the feathered edge of the paint are perfect. Rinse the area with clean water and allow it to dry completely.

33   The repair area is now ready for painting. Spray painting must be carried out in a warm, dry, windless and dust free atmosphere. These conditions can be created if you have access to a large indoor work area, but if you are forced to work in the open, you will have to pick the day very carefully. If you are working indoors, dousing the floor in the work area with water will help settle the dust that would otherwise be in the air. If the repair area is confined to one body panel, mask off the surrounding panels. This will help minimize the effects of a slight mismatch in paint color. Trim pieces such as chrome strips, door handles, etc., will also need to be masked off or removed. Use masking tape and several thickness of newspaper for the masking operations.

34   Before spraying, shake the paint can thoroughly, then spray a test area until the spray painting technique is mastered. Cover the repair area with a thick coat of primer. The thickness should be built up using several thin layers of primer rather than one thick one. Using 600-grit wet-or-dry sandpaper, rub down the surface of the primer until it is very smooth. While doing this, the work area should be thoroughly rinsed with water and the wet-or-dry sandpaper periodically rinsed as well. Allow the primer to dry before spraying additional coats.

35   Spray on the top coat, again building up the thickness by using several thin layers of paint. Begin spraying in the center of the repair area and then, using a circular motion, work out until the whole repair area and about two inches of the surrounding original paint is covered. Remove all masking material 10 to 15 minutes after spraying on the final coat of paint. Allow the new paint at least two weeks to harden, then use a very fine rubbing compound to blend the edges of the new paint into the existing paint. Finally, apply a coat of wax

4   Body repair - major damage

1   Major damage must be repaired by an auto body shop specifically equipped to perform body and frame repairs. These shops have the specialized equipment required to do the job properly.

2   If the damage is extensive, the frame must be checked for proper alignment or the vehicle's handling characteristics may be adversely affected and other components may wear at an accelerated rate.

3   Due to the fact that all of the major body components (hood, fenders, etc.) are separate and replaceable units, any seriously damaged components should be replaced rather than repaired. Sometimes the components can be found in a wrecking yard that specializes in used vehicle components, often at considerable savings over the cost of new parts.

These photos illustrate a method of repairing simple dents. They are intended to supplement *Body repair - minor damage* in this Chapter and should not be used as the sole instructions for body repair on these vehicles.

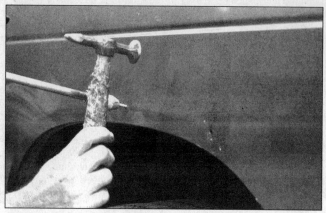

1   If you can't access the backside of the body panel to hammer out the dent, pull it out with a slide-hammer-type dent puller. Tap with a hammer near the edge of the dent to help 'pop' the metal back to its original shape, about 1/8-inch below the surface of the surrounding metal

2   Using coarse-grit sandpaper, remove the paint down to the bare metal. Clean the repair area with wax/silicone remover.

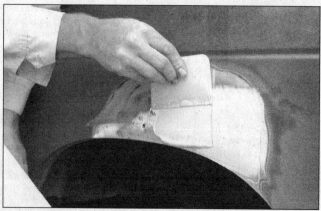

3   Following label instructions, mix up a batch of plastic filler and hardener, then quickly press it into the metal with a plastic applicator. Work the filler until it matches the original contour and is slightly above the surrounding metal

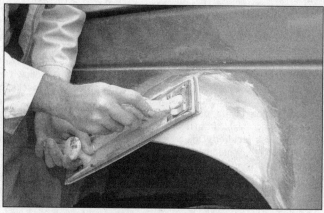

4   Let the filler harden until you can just dent it with your fingernail. File, then sand the filler down until it's smooth and even. Work down to finer grits of sandpaper - always using a board or block - ending up with 360 or 400 grit

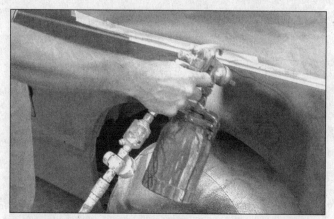

5   When the area is smooth to the touch, clean the area and mask around it. Apply several layers of primer to the area. A professional-type spray gun is being used here, but aerosol spray primer works fine

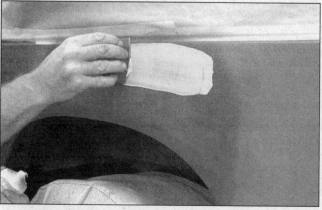

6   Fill imperfections or scratches with glazing compound. Sand with 360 or 400-grit and re-spray. Finish sand the primer with 600 grit, clean thoroughly, then apply the finish coat. Don't attempt to rub out or wax the repair area until the paint has dried completely (at least two weeks)

5   Fastener and trim removal

1   There is a variety of plastic fasteners used to hold trim panels, splash shields and other parts in place in addition to typical screws, nuts and bolts. Once you are familiar with them, they can usually be removed without too much difficulty.

2   The proper tools and approach can prevent added time and expense to a project by minimizing the number of broken fasteners and/or parts.

3   Trim panels are typically made of plastic and their flexibility can help during removal. The key to their removal is to use a tool to pry the panel near its retainers to release it without damaging surrounding areas or breaking-off any retainers. The retainers will usually snap out of their designated slot or hole after force is applied to them. Stiff plastic tools designed for prying on trim panels are available at most auto parts stores **(see illustration)**. Tools that are tapered and wrapped in protective tape, such as a screwdriver or small pry tool, are also very effective when used with care.

6   Bumper covers – removal and installation

Front bumper cover removal

1   Apply the handbrake, jack up the front of the vehicle and support it on jackstands. Undo the fasteners and remove the engine undershield.

2   Still working from below, remove the air deflector from the base of the bumper cover, then disconnect the electrical connectors from the front fog lights and headlight washer system (where equipped).

3   Remove both front headlights as described in Chapter 12.

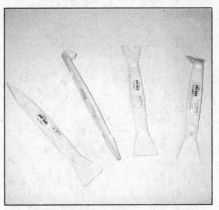

5.3 These small plastic pry tools are ideal for prying off trim panels

Fasteners

This tool is designed to remove special fasteners. A small pry tool used for removing nails will also work well in place of this tool

A Phillips head screwdriver can be used to release the center portion, but light pressure must be used because the plastic is easily damaged. Once the center is up, the fastener can easily be pried from its hole

Here is a view with the center portion fully released. Install the fastener as shown, then press the center in to set it

This fastener is used for exterior panels and shields. The center portion must be pried up to release the fastener. Install the fastener with the center up, then press the center in to set it

This type of fastener is used commonly for interior panels. Use a small blunt tool to press the small pin at the center in to release it . . .

. . . the pin will stay with the fastener in the released position

Reset the fastener for installation by moving the pin out. Install the fastener, then press the pin flush with the fastener to set it

This fastener is used for exterior and interior panels. It has no moving parts. Simply pry the fastener from its hole like the claw of a hammer removes a nail. Without a tool that can get under the top of the fastener, it can be very difficult to remove

6.5 Disconnect the cable from the handle

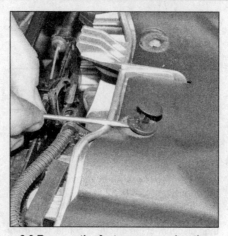
6.6 Remove the fasteners securing the radiator cover

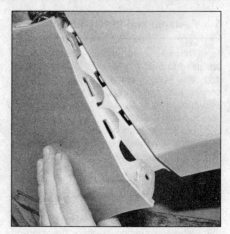
6.8 Remove the bumper from the front fender

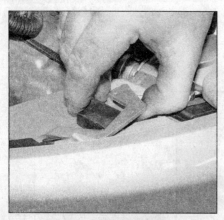
6.9 Detach the locking tabs

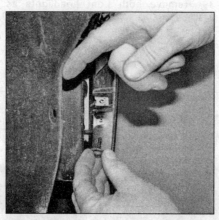
6.12 Remove the hidden screw

6.14 Remove the fasteners

4   On models equipped with a headlight washer system, pull the washer cover forward and unclip it from the washer jet assembly.
5   Remove the hood safety catch release handle. This is held in place by 6 locking tabs. Partially lift the handle to release each tab in turn. Alternatively, disconnect the cable from the handle **(see illustration)**.

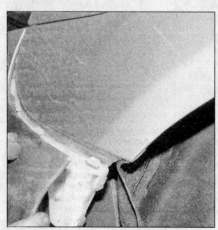
6.16 Remove the bumper cover from the rear fender

6   On the radiator cover remove the fasteners by prying up the center of the push fastener **(see illustration)**. Loosen, but at this stage do not remove the torx screws in the headlight housings – 1 screw per side.
7   Working in each wheel well, remove the fasteners that secure the front edge of the fender liner to the bumper cover.
8   Work both ends of the bumper cover free from the front fender **(see illustration)**. Note that reaching through the headlight opening and looseneing the bolts that hold the bumper support bracket in place makes removal of the bumper cover from the fender easier.
9   Remove the previously loosened torx head screw and unhook the bumper from the locking tabs in each headlight opening **(see illustration)**. With the aid of an assistant, remove the bumper cover.

Rear bumper cover removal

Hatchback models
10   Block the front wheels, raise the rear of the vehicle and support it securely on jackstands. Open up the liftgate.
11   Remove both rear taillight housings as described in Chapter 12.
12   Undo the 2 bolts on each side securing

the mudflap to the bumper cover. Remove the single screw from the fender liner, then peel back the fender liner to expose a hidden screw **(see illustration)**. Remove the screw.
13   From below, disconnect the electrical connector from the parking assistance sensors (if equipped).
14   Remove the 2 fasteners from the bottom of the bumper cover **(see illustration)**.
15   Undo the bolt from each side in the liftgate opening.
16   Release the bumper cover edges from the wheel arches and the rear fenders **(see illustration)**. With the aid of an assistant, remove the bumper cover.

Sedan models
17   Block the front wheels, raise the rear of the vehicle and support it securely on jackstands .
18   Remove the fasteners and retaining clips from each side and remove the mudflaps.
19   On both sides, partially fold back the fender liner to access the hidden bolt. Remove the bolt.
20   From below, disconnect the electrical connector from the rear parking assistance sensors (if equipped) **(see illustration)**.
21   Remove the plastic expanding rivets

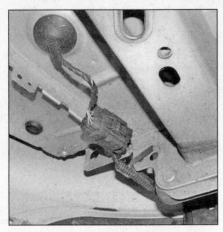

6.20 Disconnect the parking assistance sensor electrical connecter

7.5 Disconnect the electrical connecter

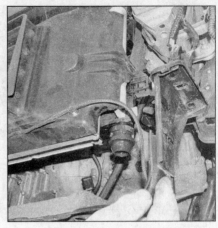

7.6 Remove the support panel

from the bottom of the bumper cover.

22   Remove the 4 bolts from the tailgate opening. With the aid of an assistant, release the bumper cover edges from the rear wing. Remove the bumper cover.

23   If required, drill out the rivets (5 mm drill bit) and remove the bumper cover support panel.

All models

24   If required, the parking distance sensors can be removed from the bumper cover, by depressing the retaining tangs and withdrawing the sensor.

Installation

25   Installation is the reverse of removal. Make sure that, where applicable, the bumper cover guides are located correctly. Check all electrical components that have been disconnected. If equipped, verify the headlight washer system is correctly installed.

---

7   Active shutter grille – removal and installation

---

1   All models feature a motorized grille, installed behind the radiator/condenser assembly and in front of the cooling fan. The opening and closing of the slats in the grille is controlled by the Power Control Module (PCM). The position of the slats is calculated from various parameters including vehicle speed, ambient temperature and AC compressor operation. The default position is open. The PCM will open and shut the grille slats at engine start to calibrate the position of the slats. A single stepper motor is used to control the slats in the grille.

2   Block the rear wheels, raise the front of the vehicle and support it securely on jackstands.

3   Remove the engine undershield and the air deflector from below the bumper cover.

4   Remove the bumper cover as described in Section 6.

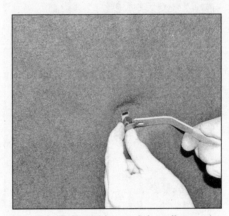

8.1a Release the retaining clips…

5   Disconnect the electrical connectors from the grille stepper motor and unclip the loom from the chassis leg **(see illustration)**.

6   Support the radiator and AC condenser assembly with suitable straps and then remove the lower support panel **(see illustration)**.

7   Partially lower the radiator assembly, checking carefully that no strain is placed on the AC condenser connections. Pivot the radiator assembly towards the engine and lift up the grille to free it from the retaining clips. Lower the grille from the radiator assembly.

8   If required, the stepper motor and grille slats can be removed on the bench.

9   Installation is the reverse of removal.

---

8   Hood – removal, installation and adjustment

Removal

1   Open the hood, and support it in the open position using the stay. Release the clips and remove the hood insulation panel **(see illustrations)**.

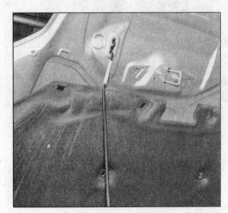

8.1b …and remove the insulation panel

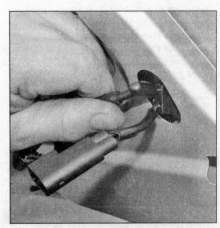

8.2 Disconnect the washer jets

2   Disconnect the windshield washer hoses from the bottom of the jets, and unclip them from the hood **(see illustration)**.

3   Disconnect the windshield washer electrical connector from the bottom of the jets, and unclip the loom from the hood.

4   To assist in correctly realigning the

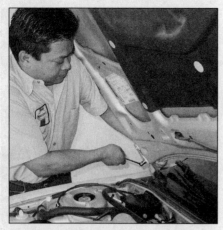

8.5 Support the hood with your shoulder while removing the hood bolts

9.1 Disconnect the switch electrical connector

9.3 Remove the bolts

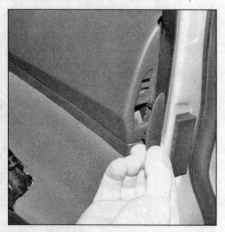

10.2a Remove the cover...

10.2b ...then remove the screw

10.3a Remove the reflector...

hood when installing it, mark the outline of the hinges with a soft pencil. Loosen the two hinge retaining nuts on each side.

5   With the help of an assistant, unscrew the four nuts, release the stay, and lift the hood from the vehicle **(see illustration)**.

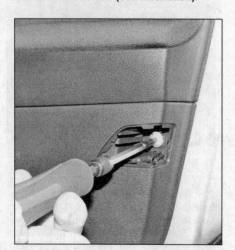

10.3b ...then remove the screw

Installation and adjustment

6   Installation is the reverse of removal, noting the following points:

a) *Position the hood hinges within the outline marks made during removal, but if necessary, alter its position to provide a uniform gap all around.*

b) *Adjust the front height by repositioning the lock (see Section 9) and turning the rubber buffers on the engine compartment front cross panel up or down to support the hood.*

9   Hood latch – removal, installation and adjustment

Removal

1   Open the hood and disconnect the electrical connector from the hood open warning switch **(see illustration)**.

2   Unclip the coolant pipe from the lock.

3   Make alignment marks between the lock and panel, then undo the 2 bolts securing the lock assembly **(see illustration)**.

Installation and adjustment

4   Installation is the reverse of removal, starting by positioning the lock as noted before removal.

5   If the front of the hood is not level with the front fenders, the lock may be moved up or down within the mounting holes. After making an adjustment, raise or lower the rubber buffers to support the hood correctly.

10   Door trim panel – removal and installation

1   Disconnect the negative battery cable from the remote ground terminal (see Chapter 5).

Front door

2   Use a plastic type trim tool to remove the small trim piece from the end of the panel. Remove the now exposed screw **(see illustrations)**.

3   At the rear edge of the panel, remove the door ajar reflector and remove the screw **(see illustrations)**.

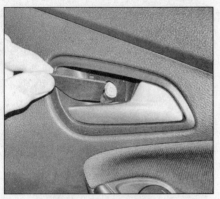

10.4 Remove the cover and now exposed screw

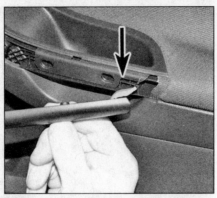

10.5 Note the hooked end of the trim piece

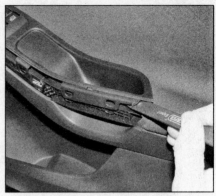

10.6a Carefully pry up the panel...

10.6b ...and disconnect the electrical connector

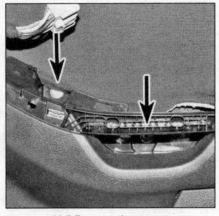

10.7 Remove the screws

10.11a Release the spring clip

4   Remove the cover from the center of the door release handle, then remove the now exposed screw **(see illustration)**.

5   Using a plastic trim tool, carefully pry free the trim piece from around the door switch panel. Work the upper end free first, then lift out the lower end **(see illustration)**.

6   Carefully pry up the switch panel, then disconnect the electrical connector as the panel is removed **(see illustrations)**.

7   Remove the screws from behind the switch panel **(see illustration)**.

8   At the top of the door, pry free the audio system tweeter panel. Disconnect the electrical connector as the panel is removed.

9   Working around the outer edge, use a forked trim release tool to release the retaining clips securing the trim panel.

10   Lift the panel slightly to release it. Disconnect the cable from the release handle **(see illustration 10.15)** and unclip the wiring loom from the panel as it is removed.

Rear door

11   On models with manual windows, use a suitable tool to release the spring clip **(see illustrations)**. Alternatively the spring clip can be released using a cloth dragged around the handle. Remove the washer.

12   Pry free the door pull handle trim piece. On models with power windows, disconnect the electrical connector as the handle is removed **(see illustrations)**.

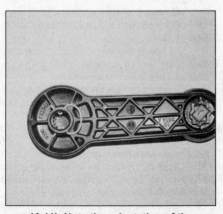

10.11b Note the orientation of the spring clip

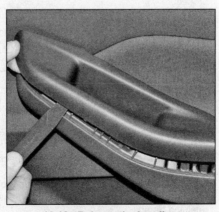

10.12a Release the handle...

10.12b ...and, on models with power windows, disconnect the electrical connector

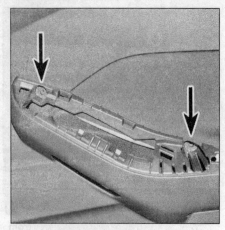

10.13 Remove the screws

10.14 Remove the cover

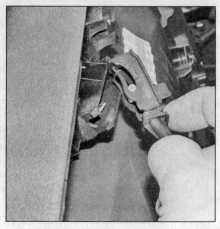

10.15 Disconnect the door release cable

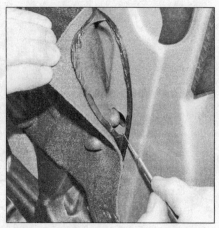

11.2 Carefully peel off the watershield

11.4 Release the glass clamp

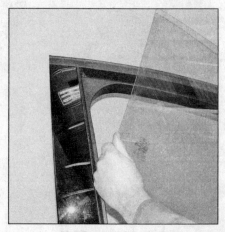

11.5 Remove the glass

13   Remove the now exposed Torx head screws **(see illustration)**.
14   Use a plastic trim tool to remove the screw cover from the door release handle **(see illustration)**. Remove the now exposed screw.
15   Working around the outer edge of the

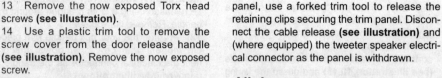

11.10 Remove the upper trim panel

panel, use a forked trim tool to release the retaining clips securing the trim panel. Disconnect the cable release **(see illustration)** and (where equipped) the tweeter speaker electrical connector as the panel is withdrawn.

All doors
16   Installation is the reverse of the removal procedure.

---

11   Door window glass – removal and installation

Removal
Front door
1   Remove the door trim panel as described in Section 10.
2   Use a sharp knife to carefully peel back the watershield **(see illustration)**.
3   Connect the power window switch panel and lower the window to access the glass retaining clamps.
4   Use a suitable screwdriver or punch and

release the glass clamps **(see illustration)**.
5   With the glass free from the clamps, push the glass up and remove it from the outside of the door **(see illustration)**. The aid of an assistant is recommended here.

Rear door
6   Remove the door trim panel as described in Section 10.
7   Remove the door watershield by carefully cutting through the sealant **(see illustration 11.2)**.
8   On power window models, connect the switch, on manual windows install the winder handle. Fully lower the window.
9   Carefully remove the outer weather strip. Protect the door paint work with masking tape if necessary.
10   Carefully pry free and remove the 2 sections of the trim panel from around the upper door frame **(see illustration)**.
11   Carefully pry free the inner weather strip and then pull up and remove the rear rubber seal from the glass guide channel.
12   At the rear edge of the door remove the outer trim panel. It is held in place by 3 screws **(see illustration)**.

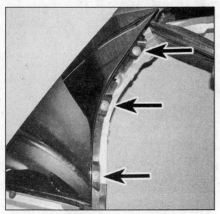

11.12 Remove the screws

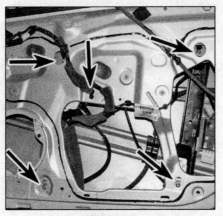

12.3a Loosen the screws...

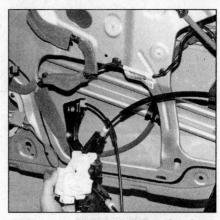

12.3b ...then work the regulator free from the door frame

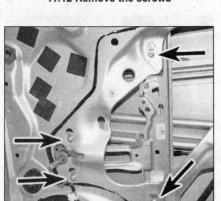

12.6 The regulator mounting screws

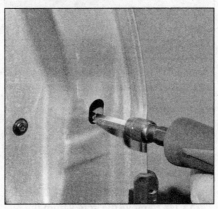

13.2 Loosen the screw

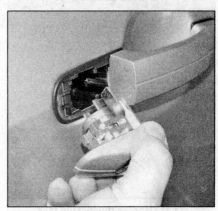

13.3 Remove the smaller section of the handle

13   Lower the window to access the glass retaining clamp.

14   Use a suitable screwdriver and release the glass clamp.

15   With the glass free from the clamps, push the glass up and remove it from the outside. The aid of an assistant is recommended here.

Installation

16   Installation is the reverse of removal, but note the following:

a) *Make sure that the glass is correctly located in the clamp.*

b) *Start the vehicle and initialize the window by fully lowering the appropriate window and holding the switch in the down position for a few seconds. Fully raise the window and hold the switch in the up position for several seconds.*

c) *Repeat the above procedure once more.*

12   Door window regulator – removal and installation

Removal

Front door

1   Follow the procedure for glass removal in

Section 11, but do not fully remove the glass, simply tape it in the up position using strong adhesive tape.

2   Remove the front door speaker (see Chapter 12), reach through the opening and disconnect the electrical connector. Unclip the wiring loom from the cable clip below the motor.

3   Release the cable guide clip from the regulator and loosen (but do not remove) the five retaining screws. Work the guide channels and motor free from the key hole slots and remove the channels, cables and motor as a single item **(see illustrations)**.

4   If required the motor can now be removed from the regulator.

Rear door

5   Follow the procedure for glass removal in Section 11, but do not remove any of the door frame upper trim panels or fully remove the glass. Tape the glass in the fully closed position using strong adhesive tape.

6   If equipped, disconnect the electrical connector from the motor and loosen (but do not remove) the 4 regulator mounting bolts **(see illustration)**.

7   Work the regulator free from the key hole slots and remove it from the vehicle.

Installation

8   Installation is the reverse of removal, but

note the following:

a) *Make sure that the glass is correctly located in the clamps.*

b) *Start the vehicle and initialize the window by fully lowering the appropriate window and holding the switch in the down position for a few seconds. Fully raise the window and hold the switch in the up position for several seconds.*

c) *Repeat the above procedure once more.*

13   Door handle and lock components – removal and installation

Removal

Front exterior handle

1   Pry out the rubber grommet from the end of the door adjacent to the exterior handle.

2   Working through the opening, loosen the handle retaining bolt approximately 22 turns **(see illustration)**.

3   If equipped, carefully pull the trim and lock cylinder from the door **(see illustration)**. On all other handles, remove the trim at the rear of the handle (where the lock cylinder would be on conventional systems).

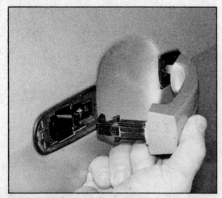

13.4 Remove the main section of the exterior handle

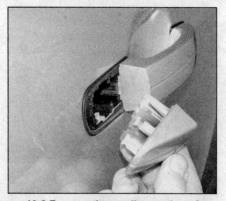

13.8 Remove the smaller section of the handle

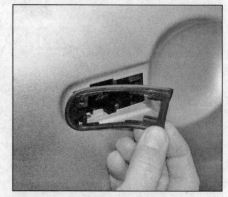

13.9 Recover the seals

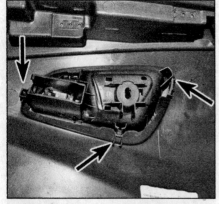

13.11 Depress the locking tabs

13.14a Remove the screw from the door skin ...

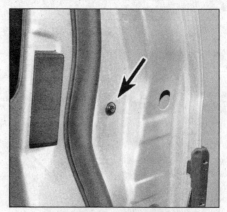

13.14b ... and from the doors edge

13.15a Remove the cover...

13.15b ...and the screws

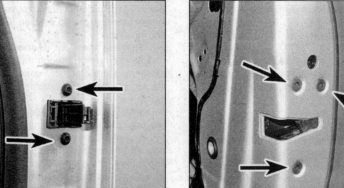

13.16a Remove the screws ...

4   Pull the exterior handle rearwards, and remove it from the door **(see illustration)**.
5   Remove the seals between the handle and the door skin.

Rear exterior handle

6   Pry out the rubber grommet from the end of the door adjacent to the exterior handle.
7   Working through the opening, loosen the handle retaining bolt approximately 7 turns **(see illustration 13.2)**.
8   Pull the trim at the rear of the handle outwards **(see illustration)**.
9   Pull the exterior handle rearwards, and

remove it from the door. Remove the seals between the handle and the door skin **(see illustration)**.

Interior handle

10   Remove the door inner trim panel as described in Section 10.
11   Detach the door release handle from the door trim panel by depressing the locking tabs and removing the handle **(see illustration)**.

Front latch

12   Remove the window regulator as described in Section 12.
13   Remove the exterior handle as described

in this Section.
14   Unclip the inner section of the door handle assembly from the door skin and remove the single upper screw from the doors edge **(see illustrations)**.
15   On models equipped with door edge protectors, unclip the door edge protector and remove the operating rod cover from the edge protector. Remove the 2 screws and push the edge protector inside the door frame **(see illustrations)**.
16   Remove the 3 main bolts from the latch and remove the complete assembly from the door frame **(see illustrations)**. Disconnect the electrical connector as the latch is removed.

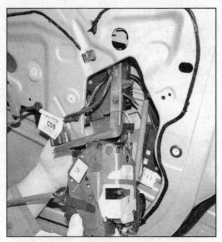

13.16b ...and remove the assembly from
the door

13.21a Remove the cover...

13.21b ... and the snap-ring

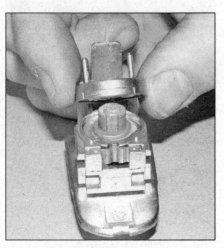

13.21c Remove the cover...

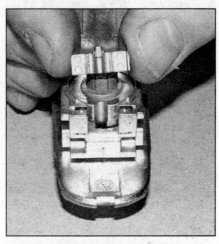

13.21d ...and slide out the locking plate

13.21e Drill out the locking pin
cover...

17   If the latch assembly is to be replaced,
disconnect the interior release cable from the
latch.

Lock cylinder

18   Pry out the rubber grommet from the end
of the door adjacent to the exterior handle.
19   Working through the opening, loosen the
handle retaining bolt approximately 22 turns
(see illustration 13.2).
20   Pull the trim and lock cylinder from the
door **(see illustration 13.3)**.
21   The key barrel can now be removed
from the housing by prying off the snap-ring,
the barrel cover and the locking plate. Using a
4mm drill bit, partially drill out the locking pin
housing and drive out the locking pin with a
2mm punch **(see illustrations)**. Remove the
cylinder while covering the tumblers with one
hand. Immediately insert the key to lock the
tumblers in place.

**13.21f ...then drive
out the locking pin**

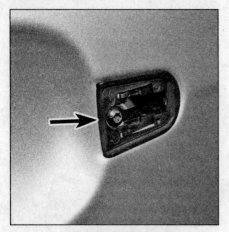

13.23 Remove the screw

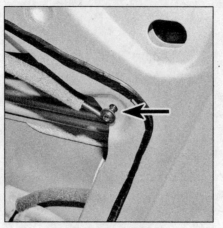

13.24 Remove the screw

13.25 Disconnect the wiring plug

14.3 Disconnect the electrical connector

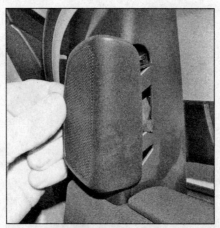

15.1a Remove the cover...

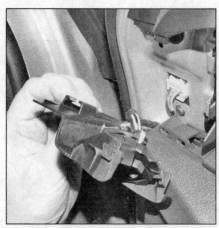

15.1b ...and then the speaker panel

Rear latch

22   Remove the door interior panel and the door watershield as described in Sections 10 and 11.

23   Remove the exterior handle as described in this Section. Remove the screw and then unclip the inner section of the door handle assembly from the door skin **(see illustration)**.

24   Release the cable clip from the inner handle cable and remove the single screw from the latch **(see illustration)**.

25   Remove the 3 mounting bolts for the latch and partially remove the latch, so that the electrical connector can be disconnected **(see illustration)**. Remove the latch from the door frame.

26   If required, the inner release cable, the outer handle cable and the glass guide channel can now be removed from the latch assembly.

Installation

27 Installation is the reverse of removal.

14   Door – removal and installation

Removal

1   Disconnect the negative battery cable from the remote ground terminal (see Chapter 5).

2   Using a Torx key, unscrew and remove the door stop strut mounting bolt from the door pillar.

3   Pry out the rubber boot, and disconnect the wiring block connector **(see illustration)**.

4   Position a jack under the door. The head of the jack should be covered with a suitable material to avoid damage to the door.

5   Have an assistant support the door, then undo the retaining bolts in the top and bottom hinge pins.

6   Carefully lift the door from the hinges, and with the aid of the jack (and an assistant) remove the door from the vehicle.

Installation

7   Installation is the reverse of removal,

but check that the door lock passes over the striker centrally. If necessary, reposition the striker.

15   Exterior mirror and glass – removal and installation

Removal

Mirror

1   Unclip the trim panel from the front of the window opening over the tweeter speaker and remove it . Remove the tweeter and disconnect the electrical connector **(see illustrations)**.

2   Disconnect the electrical connector and remove the grommet **(see illustrations)**.

3   Unscrew the mirror mounting screws **(see illustration)**, then release the clip and withdraw the mirror from the outside of the door. Recover the mirror seal as the wiring/cable is being drawn through the rubber grommet.

15.2a Disconnect the electrical connector ...

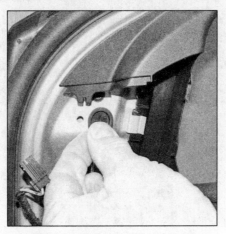

15.2b ...and remove the grommet

15.3 Remove the mounting screws

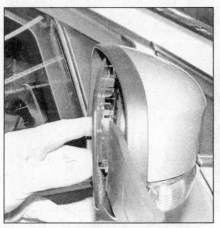

15.4 Pry the glass from the housing

15.5 Disconnect the electrical connectors

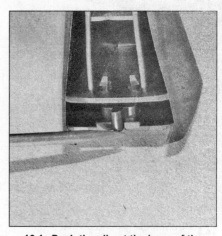

16.1a Push the clip at the base of the mirror rearwards, and slide it up from the windshield mounting

16.1b Mirror retaining clip – viewed from the front face of the mirror base

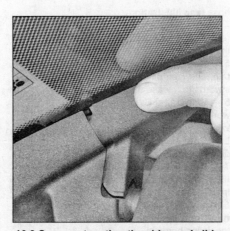

16.3 Squeeze together the sides and slide up the upper cover

Installation

6   Installation is the reverse of removal.

16   Interior mirror – removal and installation

Basic mirror

1   Press the retaining clip away from the windshield, then slide the mirror up from the base (**see illustrations**).
2   Installation is the reverse of removal.

Auto-dimming mirror

3   Squeeze together the sides, and slide up the mirror base upper cover (**see illustration**).
4   Pull apart the top edges and slide down

Mirror glass

4   Pull the outer edge of the glass rearwards, insert a broad plastic trim tool behind the glass, and gently pry the glass from the

housing (**see illustration**).
5   Withdraw the mirror glass and disconnect the electrical connectors for the heated mirrors (**see illustration**).

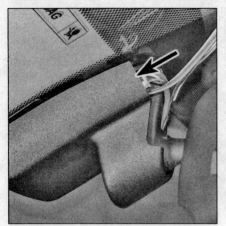

16.4 Pull apart the top edges and slide down the lower cover

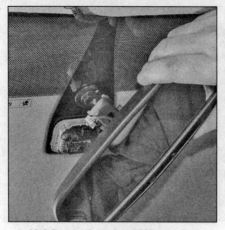

16.6 Rotate the mirror 60° counter-clockwise to release it

17.3 Disconnect the washer hose

17.7 Unbolt the ground connections

17.8 Pry the grommet free

17.11 Unclip the liftgate struts

the mirror base lower cover **(see illustration)**.

5   Disconnect the mirror electrical connector (if equipped).

6   Rotate the mirror base 60° counterclockwise and detach it from the mounting **(see illustration)**.

7   Installation is the reverse of removal procedure.

17 Liftgate/trunk lid – removal and installation

Liftgate

Removal

1   Disconnect the negative battery cable from the remote ground terminal (see Chapter 5).

2   Remove the liftgate trim panels as described in Section 26.

3   Remove the high mounted brake light (see Chapter 12) and disconnect the washer

hose **(see illustration)**.

4   Remove the retaining bolts in the handle recesses, then pull the trim panel away from the liftgate to release the retaining clips.

5   Carefully unclip the upper central liftgate trim, and then pull the rear window side trims inwards to release the clips.

6   With all the liftgate trim panels removed, work around the liftgate and disconnect the various wiring harness electrical connectors. Label the electrical connectors as they are disconnected.

7   Unbolt the ground connections **(see illustration)** and unclip the wiring harness from the multiple cable clips.

8   Pry the rubber grommet **(see illustration)** from the liftgate opening, and pull out the wiring harness.

9   Mark the position of the liftgate hinge and loosen, but do not remove, the hinge bolts.

10   Have an assistant support the liftgate in its open position.

11   Using a small screwdriver, pry off the clip securing the struts to the liftgate **(see illustration)**. Pull the sockets from the ball-studs, and

move the struts downwards.

12   Unscrew and remove the hinge bolts (two on each side) from the liftgate **(see illustration)**. Remove the liftgate from the body, taking care not to damage the paintwork.

Installation

13   Installation is the reverse of removal. Use the alignment marks made during removal to initially position the liftgate. Check that the liftgate is located centrally in the body opening, and that the striker enters the lock centrally. If necessary, loosen the mounting nuts and reposition the liftgate as required.

Trunk lid

Removal

Note: *The trunk lid is heavy and awkward to remove, so have a helper handy to assist you.*

14   Carefully pry out the trunk lid trim panel pin-type fasteners, then remove the trunk lid trim panel.

15   Inside the luggage compartment, disconnect the electrical connector for the trunk lid

17.12 Remove the hinge bolts

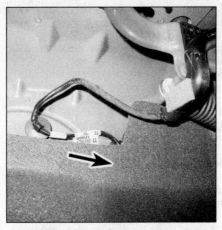

17.15 The harness electrical connector is located behind this panel

17.16 Disengage the clips securing the wiring harness

17.18 Insert a 10mm punch into the alignment hole to align the hinge to the trunk lid

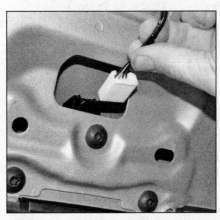

19.2 Disconnect the electrical connector

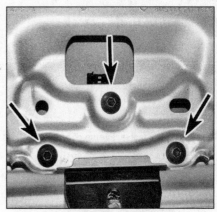

19.3 Remove the bolts

wiring harness **(see illustration)**.
16   Disengage the wiring harness clips and set the wiring harness aside **(see illustration)**.
17   With an assistant helping you support the trunk lid, remove the fasteners from the trunk lid hinges and remove the trunk lid.

Installation
18   With an assistant helping you support the trunk lid, align the hinge to the lid by inserting a 10mm punch into the alignment hole, then install the mounting fasteners **(see illustration)**.
19   The remainder of installation is the reverse of removal.

18   Liftgate/trunk lid support struts – removal and installation

1   Have an assistant support the tailgate or trunk lid in its open position.
2   Pry off the upper spring clip securing the strut to the liftgate or trunk lid. Pull the socket from the ball-stud **(see illustration 17.11)**.

3   Similarly pry off the bottom clip, and pull the socket from the ball-stud. Remove the strut.
4   Installation is the reverse of removal, making sure that the strut is installed the same way up as when it was removed.

19   Liftgate/trunk lid lock components – replacement

Liftgate models

Latch
1   Remove the liftgate interior trim panel as described in Section 26.
2   Disconnect the electrical connector from the liftgate latch assembly **(see illustration)**.
3   Remove the bolts securing the latch, then remove the latch assembly **(see illustration)**.

Release switch
4   Remove the liftgate interior trim panel as described in Section 26.
5   Unbolt the switch mounting bolts from

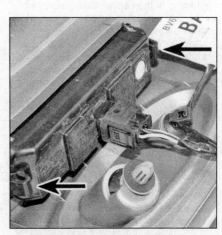

19.7 Depress the locking tabs

the liftgate (6 in total). On Sedan models, disconnect the electrical connectors. Remove the panel complete with the switch.
6   Disconnect the electrical connector from the switch.
7   Depress the locking tabs and remove the switch **(see illustration)**.
8   Installation is the reverse of removal.

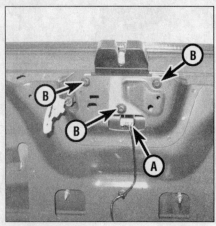

19.10 Disconnect the electrical connector (A), then remove the mounting fasteners (B)

Trunk lid models - latch

9   Carefully pry out the trunk lid trim panel pin-type fasteners, then remove the trunk lid trim panel.
10   Disconnect the electrical connector, then remove the fasteners securing the latch **(see illustration)**.
11   Remove the latch from the vehicle.
12   Installation is the reverse of removal.

20 Central locking system – testing, reprogramming, removal and installation

Testing/reprogramming

1   Testing of the central locking/alarm system can only be carried out using a manufacturer IDS diagnostic tester.
2   Prior to reprogramming a remote locking transmitter, ensure the vehicle battery is fully-charged, and the alarm is not armed or triggered. Fasten all seat belts, and close all doors.

3   Turn the ignition switch from position I to position II four times within 6 seconds, then turn it to position 0 (off).
4   A chime will be heard to indicate that the learning mode has begun.
5   Within 10 seconds of the previous step, press any button on the remote transmitter until a further chime is heard. This indicates the process has been successful. Turn the ignition switch to position II to exit the learning mode.

Removal

Body Control Module (BCM)

Note: *If the BCM is to be replaced, the unit settings must be saved prior to removal, then initialized using the Manufacturer diagnostic tester.*

6   Removal and installation of the BCM is described in Chapter 12, Section 26.

Keyless entry system module

Note: *If the module is to be replaced, the unit settings must be saved prior to removal, then initialized using the manufacturer diagnostic tester.*

7   Disconnect the negative battery cable from the remote ground terminal (see Chapter 5).
8   Remove the left-hand luggage compartment side panel, C-pillar panel and parcel shelf support as described in Chapter 12, Section 26
9   Remove the 2 retaining bolts, and remove the module. Disconnect the electrical connectors as the module is withdrawn.

Door motors

10   The door lock motors are integral with the locks. Refer to Section 13.

Liftgate motor

11   The trunk lid/liftgate motors are integral with the locks. Refer to Section 19.

Installation

12   In all cases, installation is the reverse of the removal procedure.

21 Windshield and fixed windows – removal and installation

The windshield and rear window on all models are bonded in place with special mastic, as are the rear side windows. Special tools are required to cut free the old units and install new ones; special cleaning solutions and primer are also required. It is therefore recommended that this work is entrusted to a factory dealer or windshield replacement specialist.

22 Body side-trim moldings and adhesive emblems – removal and installation

Removal

1   Body side trims and moldings are attached either by retaining clips or adhesive bonding. On bonded moldings, insert a length of strong cord (fishing line is ideal) behind the molding or emblem concerned. With a sawing action, break the adhesive bond between the molding or emblem and the panel.
2   Thoroughly clean all traces of adhesive from the panel using an adhesive remover, and allow the location to dry.
3   On moldings with retaining clips, unclip the moldings from the panel, taking care not to damage the paintwork.

Installation

4   Peel back the protective paper from the rear face of the new molding or emblem. Carefully fit it into position on the panel concerned, but take care not to touch the adhesive. When in position, apply hand pressure to the molding/emblem for a short period, to ensure maximum adhesion to the panel.
5   Replace any broken retaining clips before installing trims or moldings.

23 Sunroof – general information and adjustment

Glass panel

1   Slide back the sun blind, and set the glass panel in the closed position.
2   Pull the panel guide arm covers inwards and remove them **(see illustration)**.
3   Remove the 2 retaining bolts from each side, then lift the sunroof glass panel out from the vehicle.
4   When installing, adjust the position of the rear edge of the panel so that it is flush with the roof, then tighten the bolts.
5   The remainder of installation is the reverse of removal.

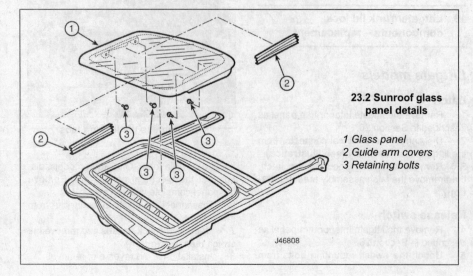

23.2 Sunroof glass panel details

1 Glass panel
2 Guide arm covers
3 Retaining bolts

J46808

24.2 Remove the bolt and disconnect the electrical connector

24.3 Remove the front bolts

24.9 Release the catch and lift the outer end of the backrest

Sun blind

6   Remove the glass panel as described in Steps 1 to 3.
7   Close the sun blind, then remove the bolts on each side securing the blind.
8   Remove the blind from the vehicle.
9   Installation is the reverse of removal.

Sunroof mechanism and motor

10   Removal of the sunroof mechanism and/or motor involves removal of the headliner. This is a complex task, which requires patience and dexterity, and is considered to be beyond the scope of a DIYer. Consequently, we recommend this task be entrusted to a factory dealer or upholstery specialist.

Adjustment

11   The sunroof should operate freely, without sticking or binding, as it is opened and closed. When in the closed position, check that the panel is flush with the surrounding roof panel.
12   If adjustment is required, slide back the sun blind, but leave the glass panel in the closed position.
13   Loosen the rear securing bolts (one on each side). Adjust the glass panel up or down, so that it is flush at its back edge with the roof panel.
14   Loosen the front securing bolts (one on each side). Adjust the glass panel up or down, so that it is flush at its front edge with the roof panel.
15   Retighten the four securing bolts.
16   Check the roof seal for wind noise and water leaks.

Drain tubes

17   There are four drain tubes, one located in each corner of the sunroof opening.
18   To remove any obstruction insert a length of suitable nylon wire down through the tubes. If the obstruction cannot be cleared, access the drain tubes as follows:
19   The front drain tubes go down the front A-pillars; remove the lower trim panel to gain access to the drain tube (see Section 26).

24.10 Pull the backrest from the pivot to disengage the mounting pin

20   The rear drain tubes go down the C-pillars (Hatchback) or D-pillars (Sedan); remove the rear side trims to gain access (see Section 26).

24   Seats – removal and installation

Warning: *The models covered by this manual are equipped with Supplemental Restraint Systems (SRS), more commonly known as airbags. Always disable the airbag system before working in the vicinity of any airbag system components to avoid the possibility of accidental deployment of the airbags, which could cause personal injury (see Chapter 12).*

Removal

Front seat

1   Disconnect the negative battery cable from the remote ground terminal (see Chapter 5).
Warning: *Before proceeding, wait a minimum of 5 minutes, as a precaution against accidental firing of the airbag unit or seat belt pretensioner. This period ensures that any residual electrical energy is dissipated.*
2   Push the seat fully rearward and undo the security bolt from the electrical connector **(see illustration)**. Disconnect the electrical connector.

3   Remove the front seat mounting bolts **(see illustration)**.
4   Move the seat fully forward and remove the 2 rear bolts.
5   To ease removal, depress the locking clip and remove the seat headrest, and then with the help of an assistant, remove the seat from the vehicle. Note that the seat is extremely heavy.

Rear seat cushion

6   Unclip the plastic trim from the hinges at the front of each seat cushion.
7   Unscrew and remove the Torx mounting bolts from the hinges and then withdraw the seat cushion from inside the vehicle.

Rear seat backrest

8   Fold the rear seat cushion forwards (if not already removed). Unbolt and remove the center seatbelt and latch. Disconnect the electrical connector (where equipped). Fold the backrest forward.
9   Use a screwdriver to force rearwards the locking catch, and lift the outer end of the backrest from the hinge **(see illustration)**.
10   Pull the backrest from the center pivot to disengage the mounting pin **(see illustration)**. If necessary, undo the seat belt stalk mounting bolt and remove the backrest from the vehicle.

Installation

11   Installation is the reverse of removal. Tighten the mounting bolts to the torque listed in this Chapter's Specifications.

25   Seat belts – removal and installation

Warning: *The models covered by this manual are equipped with Supplemental Restraint Systems (SRS), more commonly known as airbags. Always disable the airbag system before working in the vicinity of any airbag system components to avoid the possibility of accidental deployment of the airbags, which could cause personal injury (see Chapter 12).*

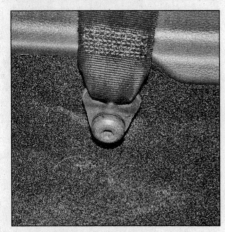

25.2 Remove the lower bolt

25.3 Remove the upper mounting bolt

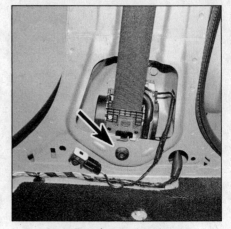

25.4a Remove the inertia reel mounting bolt …

25.4b …and disconnect the electrical connector

25.7a Remove the lower mounting…

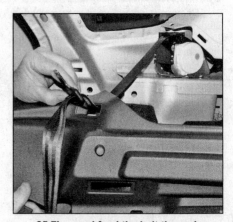

25.7b …and feed the belt through the panel

Warning: *Be careful when handling the seat belt tensioning device, it contains a small explosive charge (pyrotechnic device) similar to the one used to deploy the airbag(s). Clearly, injury could be caused if these are released in an uncontrolled fashion. Once fired, the tensioner cannot be reset, and must be replaced. Note also that seat belts and associated components which have been subject to impact loads must be replaced.*

Removal

Front seat belt

1   Disconnect the negative battery cable from the remote ground terminal (see Chapter 5).
Warning: *Before proceeding, wait a minimum of 5 minutes, as a precaution against accidental firing of the seat belt tensioner. This period ensures that any residual electrical energy is dissipated.*
Warning: *There is a potential risk of the seat belt tensioning device firing during removal, so it should be handled carefully. Once removed, treat it with care – do not use chemicals on or near it, and do not expose it to high temperatures, or it may detonate.*

2   Remove the lower mounting bolt **(see illustration)** and remove the B-pillar trim panel as described in Section 26.
3   Remove the seat belt upper anchorage bolt from the height adjuster **(see illustration)**.
4   Unscrew the mounting bolt, and lift the seat belt reel unit to remove it from the base of the pillar. Disconnect the electrical connector as the reel is removed **(see illustrations)**.
5   If required, the seat belt shoulder strap height adjuster can now be removed.

Rear side seat belt

6   Remove the C-pillar, shelf support panel (part of the C-pillar panel) and where necessary, the smaller D-pillar panel as described in Section 26.
7   Unbolt the lower mounting and feed the belt through the C-pillar/shelf support panel **(see illustrations)**.
8   Remove the mounting bolt securing the seat belt reel **(see illustration)**.

Rear center seat belt

9   The center rear seat belt reel is attached to the rear seat backrest. Remove the backrest as described in Section 24.

10   Do not allow the seatbelt webbing to fully retract. To avoid this, fit a suitable clip around the webbing above the plastic belt stop rivet.
11   Use a screwdriver to pry up the backrest release button surround trim, releasing the clips. When installing the trim, align the notch with the slot **(see illustrations)**.
12   Push down the backrest padding and use a screwdriver to depress the clip on the

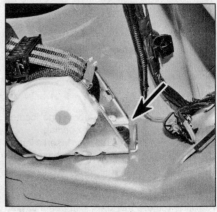

25.8 Remove the bolt

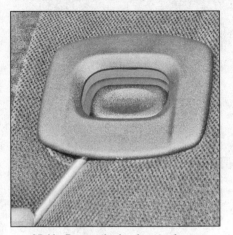

25.11a Pry up the backrest release button surround

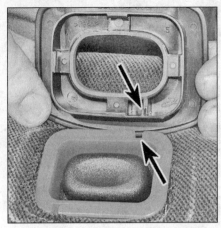

25.11b Align the notch with the slot

25.12a Push-in the clip and pull the headrest guide tube from the backrest

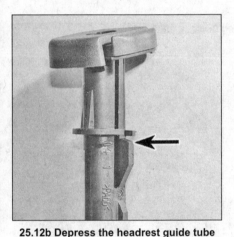

25.12b Depress the headrest guide tube clip – shown with the tube removed

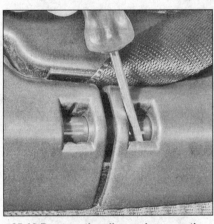

25.13 Depress the clips and remove the belt guide trim

25.14 Pry out the beading securing the top part of the backrest fabric

side of the headrest guide tubes **(see illustrations)**. Pull the guide tubes from the backrest.

13   Depress the clips and remove the seat belt guide trim from the top of the backrest **(see illustration)**. Feed the seat belt through the slot in the trim.

14   Gently pry out the beading securing the top half of the backrest seat fabric **(see illustration)**.

15   Carefully pull the seat foam padding from the top part of the backrest **(see illustrations)**.

16   Peel away the top part of the backrest

fabric covering, which is glued in place **(see illustration)**.

17   Remove the Torx bolt and remove the seat belt reel from the seat backrest. Feed the seat belt through the seat backrest bracket as the reel is withdrawn.

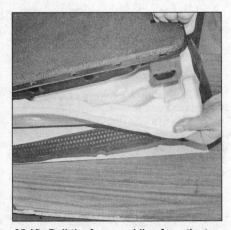

25.15a Pull the foam padding from the top part of the backrest . . .

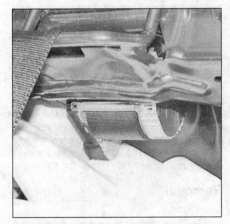

25.15b . . . to access the inertia seat belt reel

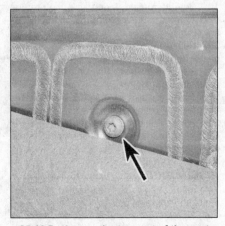

25.16 Peel away the top part of the seat backrest fabric to expose the inertia reel retaining bolt

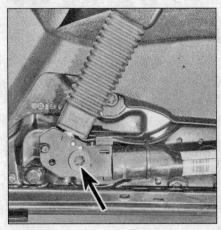

25.18 Seat belt pretensioner retaining bolt

25.23 The rear seatbelts stalks

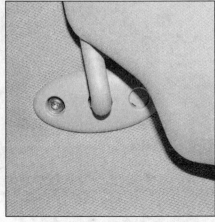

26.1 Remove the screws

26.3 Pry up the cover

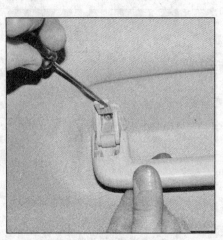

26.4 Pry up the covers

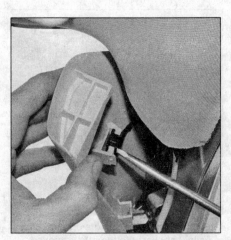

26.6a Pry the panel free…

Seat belt stalks

18   The front seat belt stalks are bolted to the seat frame (see illustration) and can be removed after removing the front seat as described in Section 24.

19   Note its routing, then unclip the pretensioner wiring harness from the underside of the seat.

20   Unclip the pretensioner electrical connector from the seat frame.

21   Remove the Torx bolt and remove the pretensioner/stalk.

22   The rear stalks are bolted to the floor. Tip the rear seat cushion forward.

23   Where equipped, disconnect the electrical connector and unbolt the appropriate stalk (see illustration).

Installation

24   Installation is the reverse of removal, noting the following points:

a) *Tighten the mounting nuts and bolts to the torque listed in this Chapter's Specifications.*

b) *Make sure the seat belt reel locating dowel is correctly positioned.*

c) *Install the spacers in their correct position.*

26   Interior trim panels – removal and installation

Note: *This section covers the removal and installation of the interior trim panels. It may be necessary to remove an overlapping trim before you can remove the one required. For more information on trim removal, look at the relevant Chapters and Sections, where the trims may need to be removed to carry out any other procedures (eg, to remove the steering column you will need to remove the shrouds).*

Removal

Sunvisor

1   Remove the screw covers, unscrew the mounting bolts and remove the visor (see illustration).

2   Disconnect the electrical connector for the vanity mirror light, where equipped.

3   Pry up the cover, unscrew the inner bracket mounting bolts, and remove the bracket (see illustration).

Passenger grab handle

4   Pry up the covers, then unscrew the mounting bolts and remove the grab handle (see illustration).

A-pillar trim

5   Pull the rubber weatherstrip away from the area adjacent to the pillar.

6   Starting at the top, carefully pull the A-pillar trim inwards to release the retaining clips (see illustrations). Note that it is quite likely that some of the clips will be damaged during the removal procedure.

B-pillar trim

7   Pull the rubber weatherstrip from the rear door opening adjacent to the B-pillar trim.

8   Pry up the front and rear sill door step panels (see illustration).

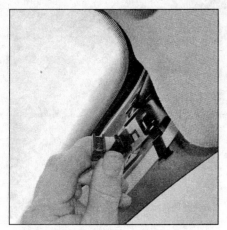

26.6b ...account for the upper trim clip...

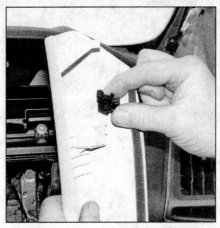

26.6c ...and transfer it to the panel

26.8 Pull up the door step panels

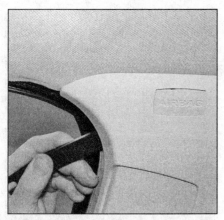

26.9a Slide a thin trim tool behind
the panel...

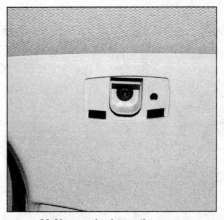

26.9b ...and release the cover

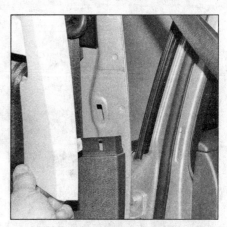

26.11 Remove the upper section of
the panel

9   Pry out the cover and undo the screw at the top of the B-pillar trim upper section **(see illustrations)**.
10   Unscrew the seat belt mounting bolt from its lower anchorage point.
11   Carefully pull the upper B-pillar trim from the pillar **(see illustration)**.
12   Feed the seatbelt webbing through the

panel as it is removed.
13   Pry free the lower section of the B-pillar trim panel **(see illustration)**.

C-pillar trim

Hatchback models

14   Remove the rear parcel shelf and then fold the rear seat back forwards.

15   Remove the rear seat back as described in Section 24.
16   Pull the rubber weatherstrip from the tailgate opening adjacent to the C-pillar.
17   Remove the trim clip and then pull up the rear door step panel **(see illustration)**.
18   Pry down the panel from above the rear side window glass and then remove the cover

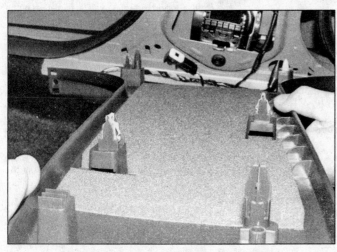

26.13 Note the position of the retaining clips

26.17 Remove the panel

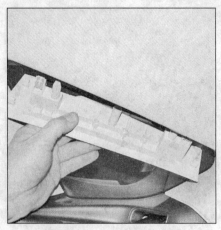

26.18a Remove the roof panel

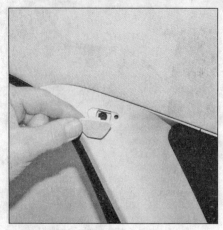

26.18b Remove the cover and remove the screw…

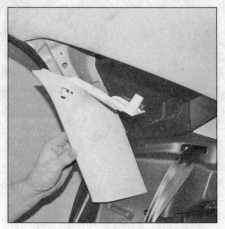

26.18c …and pry the panel free

26.20 Remove the shelf support panel

26.21 Remove the C-pillar trim panel

26.34 Release the upper shroud

from the upper section of the C-pillar panel. Remove the bolt and then remove the panel **(see illustrations)**.

19   Unbolt the rear seat belt mounting from beneath the seat cushion.

20   Locate and remove the 2 screws from the parcel shelf support panel **(see illustration)**.

26.35 Remove the screws

Feed the seat belt through the panel as it is removed and then disconnect the electrical connector from the lamp as the panel is removed.

21   Remove the 2 trim clips and then pull the main section of the C-pillar trim downwards and inwards to release the retaining clips **(see illustration)**.

Sedan models

22   Fold the rear seat backrest cushion forwards.

23   Pull the rubber weatherstrip from the door opening adjacent to the C-pillar.

24   Remove the cover from the upper section of the trim by inserting a thin plastic trim tool from the rear of the panel. Remove the now exposed bolt.

25   Pull the C-pillar trim inwards to release the retaining clips.

D-pillar trim

Hatchback models

26   Remove the parcel shelf and the shelf support panel as described above.

27   Pull the rubber weatherstrip from the rear of the D-pillar and then pry the trim panel from the pillar.

Sedan models

28   Tilt the rear seat backrest forwards, then remove the C-pillar trim as described in this Section.

29   Pull the rubber weatherstrip from the tailgate opening adjacent to the D-pillar

30   Undo the 2 screws and pull the parcel shelf support panel inwards to release the retaining clips.

31   Disconnect the electrical connectors from the load area lamp and the 12 volt power outlet as the panel is removed.

32   Pull the D-pillar trim forwards and downwards to release it.

Steering column shrouds

33   Fully extend and lower the column.

34   To release the upper shroud from the lower shroud, turn the steering wheel 90°, insert a thin screwdriver into a hole at each side of the column **(see illustration)**. Lift the upper shroud from the column and unclip it from the bottom of the instrument panel.

35   Raise the steering column. Undo the 2 securing bolts from the lower shroud, and remove from the column **(see illustration)**.

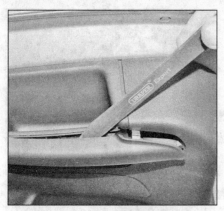

26.44a Remove the handle cover

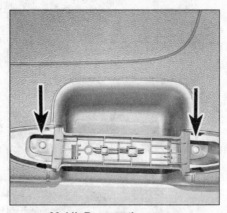

26.44b Remove the screws

26.45 Remove the main panel

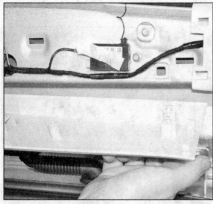

26.46 Remove the upper trim panel

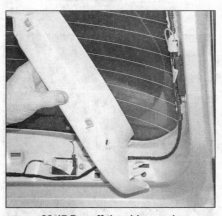

26.47 Pry off the side panels

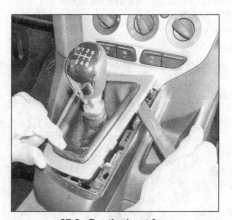

27.2a Pry the boot free

27.2b Unscrew the shift lever nob…

27.2c …and lift off the boot

44   Open the liftgate and remove the covers from the pull handles. Remove the now exposed screws **(see illustrations)**.
45   Pry free the main panel section **(see illustration)**.
46   Use a suitable plastic trim tool and release the upper trim panel **(see illustration)**.
47   With the upper and lower panels removed the side sections can now be pried off **(see illustration)**.

Installation
48   Installation is the reverse of removal. Replace any damaged fasteners.

---

27   Center console – removal and installation

Removal
1   Removal is considerably easier if both front seats are removed (see Section 24).

Models without an armrest
2   Starting at the rear, unclip the shift lever boot and trim panel. The boot can be left on the shift lever, or alternatively unscrew the shift lever knob and remove the boot completely **(see illustrations)**.

Luggage area side panel
Note: *The procedure is the same for both Hatchback and Sedan models.*

36   Remove the parcel shelf and the luggage compartment floor covering.
37   Pull up the rear seat cushion and then remove the rear seat backrest (see Section 24).
38   Remove the C-pillar trim as described previously in this Section.
39   Remove the parcel shelf support panel – as described above, then pry up and remove the rear door step scuff panel.
40   Pull the rubber weatherstrip from the tailgate opening.
41   Remove the trim clips and then pry up the tailgate slam panel trim panel.
42   Pull the panel free and disconnect the power outlet electrical connector.

Liftgate trim panel
43   On both the Hatchback and Sedan models, removal of the liftgate trim panels is similar.

27.3a Remove the cover…

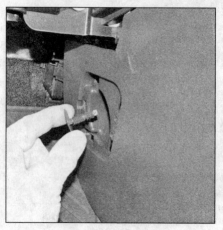

27.3b …the trim clip…

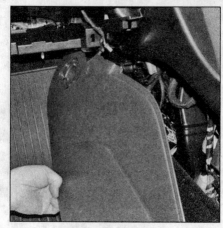

27.3c …and the panel

27.4a Remove the screw

27.4b Pull down the panel

27.5 Pry off the side panel

3   On the side of the console, remove the cover at the front edge of the panel. Remove the now exposed trim clip. A new one may be required for installation as the trim clip is difficult to remove without damaging it. Pry free the rear edge of the side panel and then remove the panel (see illustrations). Note that removal is considerably easier if the glovebox is removed first (see Section 29).

4   Remove the right-hand facia end panel, then remove the single screw from the end of the facia. Pull down the storage compartment and the trim panel from beneath the steering column (see illustrations).

5   Remove the cover and the trim clip from the right-hand side panel. Pry off the panel (see illustration).

6   Pry off the handbrake lever surround panel (see illustration).

7   Remove the screws and release the shift lever boot trim support panel (see illustrations).

8   On the side of the console, remove the upper trim panel (see illustration).

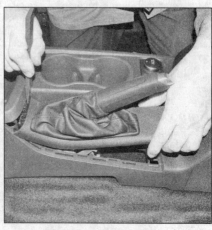

27.6 Pry the panel free

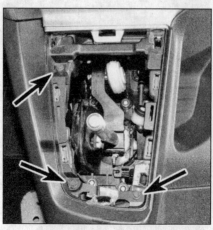

27.7a Remove the screw…

27.7b …and release the panel

27.8 Remove the panel

27.9 Remove the bolts at the rear

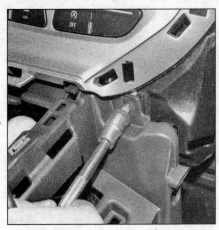

27.10a Remove the front mounting bolts

27.10b Disconnect the
electrical connectors...

27.10c ...and remove the console from
the vehicle

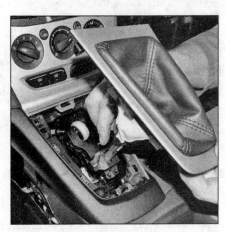

27.12 Lift off the boot

9   If the front seats have not been removed, then move both seats fully rearwards and remove the bolts at the rear of the console **(see illustration)**.

10   Remove the 2 bolts from the front of the console and then lift up the console. Disconnect the electrical connectors from the side of the console and then remove the console from the vehicle **(see illustrations)**.

11   Installation is the reverse of the removal procedure.

Models with an armrest

12   Unscrew the shift lever knob and then pry free the boot trim panel. Lift the boot over the shift lever **(see illustration)**, disconnect the link rod (some models only) and then remove the boot. Unplug the electrical con-

nector (automatic transmission models only).

13   With the handbrake fully engaged use a plastic trim tool and pry off the trim panel from the handbrake lever **(see illustration)**.

14   Pry off the left and right-hand side panels **(see illustration)** and then remove the left-hand upper side panel.

15   If not already done so, either remove both front seats (see Section 24) or move

27.13 Remove the handbrake trim panel

27.14 Removing the side panel

27.16a Remove the bolts

27.16b Disconnect the electrical connectors and…

27.16c …remove the console

29.1 Remove the facia end panel

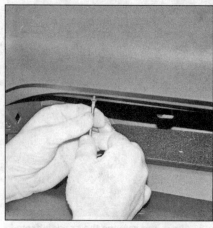

29.3 Remove the upper mounting screws

29.5 Remove the glovebox

them fully rearwards. Remove the bolts at the rear of the console.

16   Remove the 2 bolts from the front of the console and then lift up the console. Disconnect the electrical connectors from the side of the console and then remove the console from the vehicle **(see illustrations)**.

Installation

17   Installation is the reverse of removal, but it is advisable to interlock all the trim panels before finally clipping them back into position. This is especially true on vehicles fitted with an armrest.

28 Overhead console – removal and installation

1   Open the storage compartment and remove the combined switch and light panel. Disconnect the wiring plugs as the panel is removed.

2   Pry free the outer trim panel. Disconnect the electrical connector as the panel is removed.

3   If required the main mounting panel

can now be removed. Unclip the wiring harness and then remove the 2 mounting bolts. Remove the panel from the vehicle.

4   Installation is the reverse of the removal procedure.

29 Glovebox – removal and installation

1   Pry off the facia end panel **(see illustration)**.

2   Release the two clips and remove the trim panel from below the glovebox.

3   Open the glovebox and remove the 2 upper mounting screws **(see illustration)**.

4   Remove the screw from the facia end panel and then remove the 2 lower mounting screws. Note that the lower fixing screws are difficult to locate.

5   Partially remove the glovebox, disconnect the electrical connector from the right-hand side of the glovebox and then fully remove the glovebox **(see illustration)**.

6   Installation is the reverse of the removal procedure, making sure that the glovebox is located correctly before tightening the bolts.

30 Instrument panel and crossmember – removal and installation

Warning: *Wait until the engine is completely cool before beginning this procedure.*

Warning: *Models covered by this manual are equipped with a Supplemental Restraint System (SRS), more commonly known as airbags. Always disable the airbag system before working in the vicinity of any airbag system component to avoid the possibility of accidental deployment of the airbag, which could cause personal injury (see Chapter 12).*

Warning: *The air conditioning system is under high pressure. DO NOT loosen any fittings or remove any components until after the system has been discharged. Air conditioning refrigerant must be properly discharged into an EPA-approved container at a dealer service department or an automotive air conditioning repair facility. Always wear eye protection when disconnecting air conditioning system fittings.*

Note: *This is a difficult procedure for the home mechanic. There are many hidden fasteners, difficult angles to work in and many electrical connectors to tag and disconnect/connect. We*

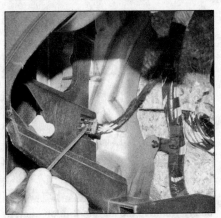

30.4 Unclip the PAD switch wiring harness

30.7 Release the wiring harness clips

30.16 Disconnect the diagnostic socket

30.19 The instrument panel bolts

30.21 Disconnect the solar sensor electrical connector

recommend that this procedure be done only by an experienced do-it-yourselfer

Note: *During removal of the instrument panel, make careful notes of how each piece comes off, where it fits in relation to other pieces and what holds it in place. If you note how each part is installed before removing it, getting the instrument panel back together again will be much easier.*

Instrument panel

1 Have the air conditioning system refrigerant discharged and recovered by an air conditioning technician.

2 Disconnect the negative battery cable from the remote ground terminal (see Chapter 5). Drain the cooling system (see Chapter 1).

3 Remove the center console as described in Section 27.

Note: *Though not absolutely necessary, access to the center console, steering column and instrument panel will be greatly improved if both front seats are removed first (see Section 24).*

4 Remove the glovebox (see Section 29) and then unbolt the passenger side airbag from the crossmember. Disconnect the electrical connectors from the passenger airbag

and the passenger airbag deactivation (PAD) switch **(see illustration)**.

5 Working below the glovebox, remove the single bolt and remove the duct pipe.

6 Remove the heater/climate control panel as described in Chapter 3 and the audio unit as described in Chapter 12.

7 Disconnect the wiring harness from the clips directly behind the now removed heater/audio control panel **(see illustration)**.

8 Where equipped, remove the keyless entry control unit. Note the routing of the wiring harness and disconnect it from the retaining clips.

9 Remove the driver's side lower dash panel.

10 Fully extend and lower the steering column and then remove the upper and lower column shrouds (Section 26).

11 Disconnect the wiring harness and electrical connectors from the steering column.

12 With the aid of an assistant, unbolt and remove the complete steering column assembly as described in Chapter 10.

13 Remove the instrument cluster as described in Chapter 12.

14 If equipped, disconnect the electrical connector from the stop/start switch.

15 Disconnect the electrical connector from the main light switch and remove the switch

(see Chapter 12).

16 Working in the drivers side footwell, disconnect the electrical connector(s) from the pedal assembly and disconnect the diagnostic socket **(see illustration)**. Remove the single bolt and release the air distribution ducting.

17 Remove both A-pillar trims (see Section 26). Check that all the wiring harness retaining clips have been released from the instrument panel.

18 Remove the lower mounting bolts from the instrument panel. There are 3 on the passenger's side, 3 on the driver's side and 2 directly in front of the shift lever.

19 Remove the 2 bolts from the instrument panel opening **(see illustration)** and the single bolt from the information display/heater control opening.

20 Mark the position of the instrument panel in relation to the crossmember and the A-pillars.

21 With the aid of an assistant remove the bolts from the end of the instrument panel (1 at each end) and partially remove the instrument panel by pulling it forward. Disconnect the electrical connector from the sunlight (solar) sensor **(see illustration)**, then remove the instrument panel from the vehicle.

22 Installation is the reverse of removal. On completion, check the operation of all electrical components.

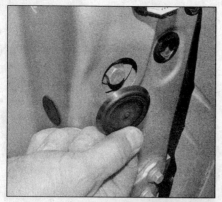

30.26a Remove the plug...

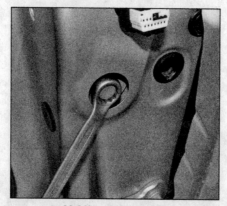

30.26b ...and the bolt

30.27a Remove the air distribution ducts...

30.27b ...and the support bracket

30.29 Remove the bolts (uppers shown)

30.30 Remove the bolts

30.32a Remove the handle...

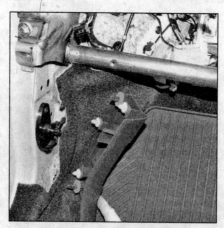

30.32b ...and the panel

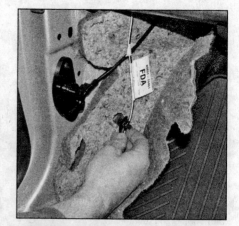

30.32c Disconnect the wiring harness

Crossmember

Removal

23 Remove the instrument panel as described above.

24 Remove the wiper arms and the cowl cover as described in Chapter 12. Disconnect the drain tube as the panel is removed.

25 Remove both front doors (see Section 14).

26 Remove the mounting bolts from both A-pillars (see illustrations).

27 At the transmission tunnel, remove the air distribution ducts and then remove the support brackets from each side of the transmission tunnel (see illustrations).

28 Remove the 4 lower bolts from the lower section of the heater box. Remove the lower section from the vehicle.

29 Unbolt the heater box from the crossmember (4 bolts) (see illustration).

30 Working under the hood remove the 2 bolts from the firewall (see illustration).

31 Disconnect the wiring harness from the crossmember as required. Note the position and layout of the wiring harness and label it as required in order to aid installation.

32 Remove the hood release handle and the scuff panel from the base of the A-pillar. Fold back the carpet and remove the ground

30.33a Disconnect the electrical connectors from the BCM...

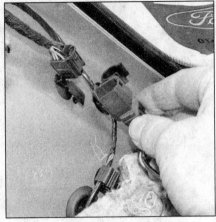

30.33b ...and the A-pillar

30.34 Mark the position on the crossmember

30.37 The adjuster must contact the A-pillar

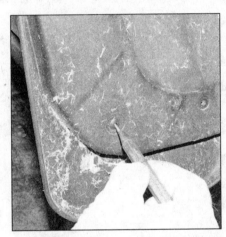

31.2 Push in the center pin to release the clip

31.3 Remove the screws

31.4 Remove the liner

connections from the sill **(see illustrations)**. Repeat the procedure on the drivers side.

33   Disconnect the electrical connectors from the Body Control Module (BCM) and from the A-pillar **(see illustrations)**.

34   Mark the position of the crossmember in relation to the A-pillars **(see illustration)**.

35   Remove the 4 bolts. With the aid of an assistant, remove the crossmember from the vehicle.

Installation

36   Before installing the crossmember, fully unwind, and then turn back one revolution the tolerance adjusters at both ends of the crossmember.

37   Install the crossmember, ensuring that the tolerance adjuster are in contact with the A-pillars **(see illustration)** and that the previously made marks all line up correctly.

38   Installation is the reverse of removal. Tighten all fasteners to the torque listed in this Chapter's Specifications.

31   Wheel arch liner – removal and installation

Removal

Front

1   Apply the parking brake. Loosen the wheel lug nuts. Raise the front of the vehicle and support it securely on jackstands. Remove the front wheel

2   Remove the mudflap (if equipped). These are held in place with clips and screws **(see illustration)**.

3   Unscrew the screws securing the liner to the inner wheel arch panel **(see illustration)**.

4   Remove the bolts and clips securing the liner to the outer edge of the wheel arch and bumper. Withdraw the liner from under the vehicle **(see illustration)**.

Rear

5   Chock the front wheels. If the wheel is to be removed (to improve access), loosen the wheel lug nuts. Raise the rear of the vehicle and support it securely on jackstands. Remove the rear wheel.

6   Remove the mudflap (if equipped) **(see illustration)**.

7   Undo the bolts securing the liner to the outer edge of the wheel arch and bumper.

8   Remove the clips securing the liner to the inner wheel arch, and withdraw the liner from under the vehicle.

Installation

9   Installation is the reverse of removal. If the wheels were removed, tighten the wheel lug nuts to the torque listed in the Chapter 1 Specifications .

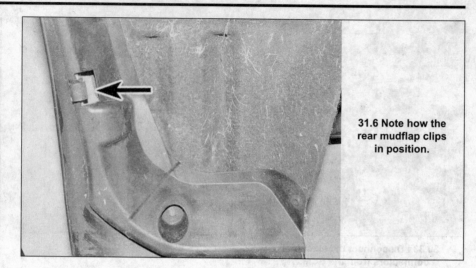

31.6 Note how the rear mudflap clips in position.

Chapter 12
Chassis electrical system

Contents

1 General information

1   The electrical system is a 12-volt, negative ground type. Power for the lights and all electrical accessories is supplied by a lead/acid-type battery that is charged by the alternator.
2   This Chapter covers repair and service procedures for the various electrical components not associated with the engine. Information on the battery, alternator, ignition system and starter motor can be found in.
3   It should be noted that when portions of the electrical system are serviced, the negative cable should be disconnected from the battery to prevent electrical shorts and/or fires.

2 Electrical troubleshooting - general information

1   A typical electrical circuit consists of an electrical component, any switches, relays, motors, fuses, fusible links or circuit breakers related to that component and the wiring and connectors that link the component to both the battery and the chassis. To help you pinpoint an electrical circuit problem, wiring diagrams are in.
2   Before tackling any troublesome electrical circuit, it would be wise to understand the basics of electrical theory and how a circuit in an automobile is connected. Knowing how any system works before attempting repairs will greatly reduced the possibility of replacing unneeded components. A good place to start is to study the appropriate wiring diagrams to get a complete understanding of what makes up that individual circuit. Trouble spots, for instance, can often be narrowed down by noting if other components related to the circuit are operating properly. Taking it step by step and following the guidelines provided will reduce your time in diagnosing electrical issues.
3   Electrical problems usually stem from simple causes, such as loose or corroded connections, worn or chafed wiring, a blown fuse, a melted fusible link, or faulty components. Visually inspect the condition of all fuses, wires and connections in a problem cir-

cuit before troubleshooting the circuit. Be sure to check not only the positive signals but the negative signals as well. Faulty grounds, or weak ground connections are a leading factor in system failures.

4   If test equipment and instruments are going to be utilized, be sure you understand how to use the equipment properly before attempting a repair. A bad diagnostic routine can start with bad equipment or the lack of proper use of the equipment. Use the wiring diagrams to plan ahead of time where you will make the necessary connections in order to accurately pinpoint your test connections as well as were the possible trouble could be.

5   The basic tools needed for electrical troubleshooting include a multi-meter that is capable of reading DC and AC voltage, Ohms (resistance), and Amps, a test light, jumper wires with alligator clips at each end, a jumper wire preferably with a circuit breaker incorporated, and a few sharp pins (straight pins work well) which can be used to bypass electrical components **(see illustrations)**. Before attempting to locate a problem with test instruments, use the wiring diagram(s) to decide where to make the connections.

Voltage checks

Note: *Keep in mind that some circuits receive voltage only when the ignition key is in the Accessory or Run position.*

6   Voltage checks should be performed if a circuit is not functioning properly. Connect one lead of a circuit tester to either the negative battery terminal or a known good ground. Always check your test light before checking the actual circuit you're working on to be sure it is making good contact with the negative and the positive leads. Connect the other lead to a connector in the circuit being tested, preferably nearest to the battery or fuse **(see illustration)**. If the bulb of the tester lights, voltage is present, which means that the part of the circuit between the connector and the battery is problem free. Continue checking the rest of the circuit in the same fashion. When

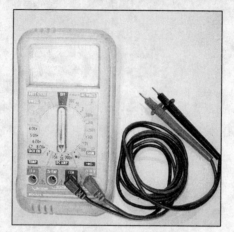

2.5a The most useful tool for electrical troubleshooting is a digital multimeter that can check volts, amps, and test continuity

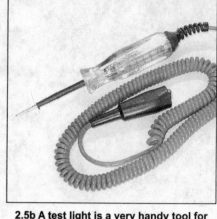

2.5b A test light is a very handy tool for checking voltage

you reach a point at which no voltage is present, the problem lies between that point and the last test point with voltage. Most of the time the problem can be traced to a loose connection.

Finding a short

7   A short occurs when the path of electricity takes a route to ground that it was not designed for. This is usually associated with a blown fuse or melted fusible link. One method of finding shorts in a circuit is to remove the fuse and connect a test light or voltmeter in place of the fuse terminals. A fuse terminal has two connections. One is the supplied voltage to the fuse while the other is the send lead to that circuit. There should be no readable voltage at those two connectors because they should be of the same potential. Moving the wiring harness from side-to-side while watching the test light may also allow you to find any chaffed wiring that might have blown the fuse originally. If the bulb is on, there is a negative and a positive potential at the fuse connection. When the light is on, there is a

short to ground somewhere in that area, probably where the insulation has rubbed through. The same test can be performed on each component in the circuit, or on a switch.

Ground check

8   Perform a ground test to check whether a component is properly grounded. Disconnect the battery and connect one lead of a continuity tester or multimeter (set to the ohms scale), to a known good ground. Connect the other lead to the wire or ground connection being tested. If the resistance is low (less than 5 ohms), the ground is good. If the bulb on a self-powered test light does not go on, the ground is bad. A more accurate method is the voltage drop test. Place the positive side of your multimeter on the positive post of the battery, then place the negative side on the chassis. Note the reading, then move the negative lead to the suspected bad ground area, such as the engine (which should have the same grounded leads to it). Take another reading. The two readings should be exactly the same.

2.6 In use, a test light's lead is clipped to a known ground, then the pointed probe can test connectors, wires or electrical sockets - if the bulb lights, the circuit being tested has battery voltage

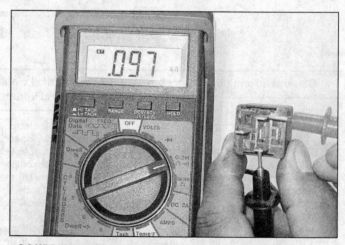

2.9 With the multimeter set to the ohm scale, resistance can be checked across two terminals - when checking for continuity, a low reading indicates continuity; a high reading or infinity indicates diminished or lack of continuity.

3.1a The main fuse/relay panel is in the engine compartment; disengage the locking tabs and remove the cover for access to the fuses and relays

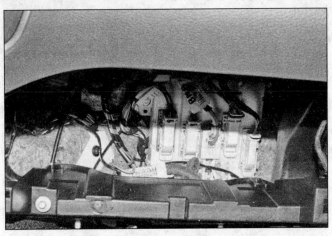

3.1b The interior fuse/relay panel is located under a cover on the right side, just below and behind the glove box area

Continuity check

9   A continuity check is done to determine if there are any breaks in a circuit - if it is passing electricity properly. With the circuit off (no power in the circuit), a self-powered continuity tester or multimeter can be used to check the circuit. Connect the test leads to both ends of the circuit (or to the power end and a good ground), and if the test light comes on the circuit is passing current properly **(see illustration)**. If the resistance is low (less than 5 ohms), there is continuity; if the reading is 10,000 ohms or higher, there is a break somewhere in the circuit. The same procedure can be used to test a switch, by connecting the continuity tester to the switch terminals. With the switch turned On, the test light should come on (or low resistance should be indicated on a meter).
Caution: *Always check your multimeter before hooking it up to any circuit so that you know you are on the right scale. If there is voltage present on a lead, and you are trying to measure resistance, you can do permanent damage to your meter if it is set on the wrong scale.*

Finding an open circuit

10   When diagnosing for possible open circuits, it is often difficult to locate them by sight because the connectors hide oxidation or terminal misalignment. Merely wiggling a connector on a sensor or in the wiring harness may correct the open circuit condition. Remember this when an open circuit is indicated when troubleshooting a circuit. Intermittent problems may also be caused by oxidized or loose connections.

11   Electrical troubleshooting is simple if you keep in mind that all electrical circuits are basically electricity running from the battery, through the wires, switches, relays, fuses and fusible links to each electrical component (light bulb, motor, etc.) and to ground, from which it is passed back to the battery. Any electrical problem is an interruption in the flow of electricity to and from the battery.

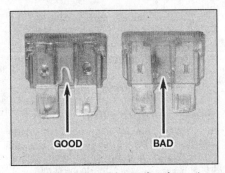

3.4 When a fuse blows, the element between the terminals melts

Finding a battery drain

Note: *Before attempting to find a drain, test the battery to be sure the battery itself is not the cause (see Chapter 5).*

12   Battery drain is any electrical load that is present when it shouldn't be, which will cause the battery to have insufficient amperage/voltage to restart the vehicle. Today's vehicles have what is referred to as parasitic battery drain. This is a normal process that occurs with all newer vehicles. Each of the different computer based systems in the vehicle have a certain amount of constant current required to maintain enough electricity to restart. The required voltage is very small - so small, a standard test light or volt meter will not pick up the signal correctly. An amperage meter in line with the battery negative post and negative clamp is recommended to read the amount of current being passed to the vehicle. A reading of less than 0.02 to 0.04 amps indicates a lack of battery drain. Anything above that would indicate something has been left on, or one of the computer based systems is still activated.

13   Modules all have a sleep mode; this varies with each module or system. Some will carry out their functions shortly after the last door is closed or when the key is turned off. Delay systems such as dome light entry and exit are a good example of a module cycling through the sleep mode. When the light comes on, it's awake, and when it goes out a few seconds later, it's asleep.

14   Finding a battery drain can be quite challenging. If you are hesitant in trying to locate the drain, take your vehicle to your local dealer or qualified independent shop that specializes in electrical repairs.

3   Fuses, fusible links and circuit breakers - general information

Fuses

1   The electrical circuits of the vehicle are protected by a combination of fuses, circuit breakers and fusible links. The main fuse/relay panel is in the engine compartment **(see illustration)**, while the interior fuse/relay panel is located on the right side, below the glove box area **(see illustration)**. The covers have a legend on the underside to identify the fuses and relays.

2   Each of the fuses is designed to protect a specific circuit, and the various circuits are identified on the fuse panel itself.

3   Several sizes of fuses are employed in the fuse blocks. There are small, medium and large sizes of the same design, all with the same blade terminal design. The medium and large fuses can be removed with your fingers, but the small fuses require the use of pliers or the small plastic fuse-puller tool found in most fuse boxes.

4   If an electrical component fails, always check the fuse first. The best way to check the fuses is with a test light. Check for power at the exposed terminal tips of each fuse. If power is present at one side of the fuse but not the other, the fuse is blown. A blown fuse can also be identified by visually inspecting it **(see illustration)**.

5   Be sure to replace blown fuses with the correct type. Fuses (of the same physical

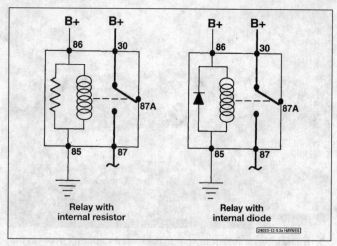

4.2a Typical ISO relay designs, terminal numbering and circuit connections

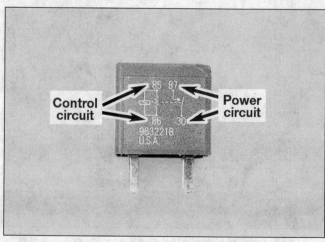

4.2b Most relays are marked on the outside to easily identify the control circuit and power circuit - this one is of the four-terminal type

size) of different ratings may be physically interchangeable, but only fuses of the proper rating should be used. Replacing a fuse with one of a higher or lower value than specified is not recommended. Each electrical circuit needs a specific amount of protection. The amperage value of each fuse is molded into the top of the fuse body.

6   If the replacement fuse immediately fails, don't replace it again until the cause of the problem is isolated and corrected. In most cases, this will be a short circuit in the wiring caused by a broken or deteriorated wire.

Fusible links

7   Some circuits are protected by fusible links. The links are used in circuits that are not ordinarily fused, such as the alternator circuit.

8   On this particular vehicle, the alternator circuit (main lead - large red wire) runs from the battery, to the underhood fuse box, then to an inline 200 amp fusible link. Voltage is present at all times on this lead.

Circuit breakers

9   Circuit breakers protect certain circuits, such as the power windows and power seats. Depending on the vehicle's accessories, there may be two 25-amp circuit breakers for the door locks and one 30-amp circuit breaker for the power seats, located in the interior fuse/relay box under the left rear seat.

10   Because the circuit breakers reset automatically, an electrical overload in a circuit-breaker-protected system will cause the circuit to fail momentarily, then come back on. If the circuit does not come back on, check it immediately.

Caution: *If there is a short in the circuit breaker wiring, the metal casing of the breaker may be extremely hot. Use caution when removing the breaker.*

11   With the voltmeter negative lead on a good chassis ground, touch each end prong of the circuit breaker with the positive meter probe. There should be battery voltage at each end. If there is battery voltage only at one

end, the circuit breaker must be replaced.

---

4   Relays - general information and testing

General information

1   Several electrical accessories in the vehicle, such as the fuel injection system, horns, starter, and fog lamps use relays to transmit the electrical signal to the component. Relays use a low-current circuit (the control circuit) to open and close a high-current circuit (the power circuit). If the relay is defective, that component will not operate properly. Most relays are mounted in the engine compartment and interior fuse/relay boxes. If a faulty relay is suspected, it can be removed and tested using the procedure below or by a dealer service department or a repair shop. Defective relays must be replaced as a unit.

Testing

2   Most of the relays used in these vehicles are of a type often called ISO relays, which refers to the International Standards Organization. The terminals of ISO relays are numbered to indicate their usual circuit connections and functions. There are two basic layouts of terminals on the relays used in these vehicles **(see illustrations)**.

3   Refer to the wiring diagram in this manual for the circuit to determine the proper connections for the relay you're testing. If you can't determine the correct connection from the wiring diagrams, however, you may be able to determine the test connections from the information that follows.

4   Two of the terminals are the relay control circuit and connect to the relay coil. The other relay terminals are the power circuit. When the relay is energized, the coil creates a magnetic field that closes the larger contacts of the power circuit to provide power to the circuit loads.

5   Terminals 85 and 86 are normally the control circuit. If the relay contains a diode, terminal 86 must be connected to battery positive (B+) voltage and terminal 85 to ground. If the relay contains a resistor, terminals 85 and 86 can be connected in either direction with respect to B+ and ground.

6   Terminal 30 is normally connected to the battery voltage (B+) source for the circuit loads. Terminal 87 is connected to the ground side of the circuit, either directly or through a load. If the relay has several alternate terminals for load or ground connections, they usually are numbered 87A, 87B, 87C, and so on.

7   Use an ohmmeter to check continuity through the relay control coil.

a)   *Connect the meter according to the polarity shown in illustration 4.2a for one check; then reverse the ohmmeter leads and check continuity in the other direction.*

b)   *If the relay contains a resistor, resistance should be indicated on the meter, and should be the same value with the ohmmeter in either direction.*

c)   *If the relay contains a diode, resistance should be higher with the ohmmeter in the forward polarity direction than with the meter leads reversed.*

d)   *If the ohmmeter shows infinite resistance in both directions, replace the relay.*

8   Remove the relay from the vehicle and use the ohmmeter to check for continuity between the relay power circuit terminals. There should be no continuity between terminal 30 and 87 with the relay de-energized.

9   Connect a fused jumper wire to terminal 86 and the positive battery terminal. Connect another jumper wire between terminal 85 and ground. When the connections are made, the relay should click.

10   With the jumper wires connected, check for continuity between the power circuit terminals. Now, there should be continuity between terminals 30 and 87.

11   If the relay fails any of the above tests, replace it.

5 Electrical connectors - general information

1   Most electrical connections on these vehicles are made with multiwire plastic connectors. The mating halves of many connectors are secured with locking clips molded into the plastic connector shells. The mating halves of some large connectors, such as some of those under the instrument panel, are held together by a bolt through the center of the connector.

2   To separate a connector with locking clips, use a small screwdriver to pry the clips apart carefully, then separate the connector halves. Pull only on the shell, never pull on the wiring harness, as you may damage the individual wires and terminals inside the connectors. Look at the connector closely before trying to separate the halves. Often the locking clips are engaged in a way that is not immediately clear. Additionally, many connectors have more than one set of clips.

3   Each pair of connector terminals has a male half and a female half. When you look at the end view of a connector in a diagram, be sure to understand whether the view shows the harness side or the component side of the connector. Connector halves are mirror images of each other, and a terminal shown on the right side end-view of one half will be on the left side end-view of the other half.

4   It is often necessary to take circuit voltage measurements with a connector connected. Whenever possible, carefully insert a small straight pin (not your meter probe) into the rear of the connector shell to contact the terminal inside, then clip your meter lead to the pin. This kind of connection is called backprobing. When inserting a test probe into a terminal, be careful not to distort the terminal opening. Doing so can lead to a poor connection and corrosion at that terminal later. Using the small straight pin instead of a meter probe results in less chance of deforming the terminal connector.

Electrical connectors

Most electrical connectors have a single release tab that you depress to release the connector

Some electrical connectors have a retaining tab which must be pried up to free the connector

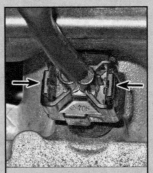

Some connectors have two release tabs that you must squeeze to release the connector

Some connectors use wire retainers that you squeeze to release the connector

Critical connectors often employ a sliding lock (1) that you must pull out before you can depress the release tab (2)

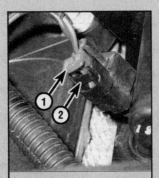

Here's another sliding-lock style connector, with the lock (1) and the release tab (2) on the side of the connector

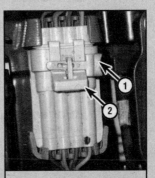

On some connectors the lock (1) must be pulled out to the side and removed before you can lift the release tab (2)

Some critical connectors, like the multi-pin connectors at the Powertrain Control Module employ pivoting locks that must be flipped open

6.3 Disconnect the electrical connector

6.7a Remove the cover...

6.7b ...and disconnect the combined electrical connector and bulb retainer

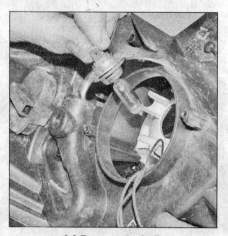

6.8 Remove the bulb

6.11 Remove the bulb complete with the bulb holder

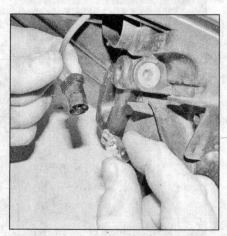

6.12 Remove the bulb from the bulb holder

6   Exterior light bulbs – replacement

Note: *This section does not cover bulb replacement on models equipped with Xenon (HID) headlights; refer to Section 9 for replacement details.*

1   Whenever a bulb is replaced, note the following points:

a) *Remember that if the light has just been in use, the bulb may be extremely hot.*

b) *Do not touch the bulb glass with the fingers, as the small deposits can cause the bulb to cloud over.*

c) *Always check the bulb contacts and holder, ensuring that there is clean metal-to-metal contact. Clean off any corrosion or dirt before installing a new bulb.*

d) *Wherever bayonet-type bulbs are installed, ensure that the live contacts bear firmly against the bulb contact.*

e) *Always ensure that the new bulb is of the correct rating and that it is completely clean before installing it.*

Halogen high beam

Warning: *For information regarding Xenon*

lights, see Section 9.

2   Remove the headlight housing as described in Section 8.

3   Remove the cover and disconnect the combined locking/electrical connector **(see illustration)**.

4   Note the orientation of the bulb, then remove it.

5   Install the new bulb using a reversal of the removal procedure.

Halogen low beam

Warning: *For information regarding Xenon lights, see Section 9.*

6   Remove the headlight housing as described in Section 8.

7   Remove the cover and disconnect the combined locking/electrical connector **(see illustrations)**.

8   Note the orientation of the bulb and remove it **(see illustration)**.

9   Install the new bulb using a reversal of the removal procedure.

Sidelight

Note: *On models equipped with Xenon (HID) headlights, the sidelights are LED type bulbs.*

These are not replaceable. If they are faulty, the entire headlight assembly must be replaced.

10   Remove the headlight housing as described in Section 8, then remove the cover from the rear of the headlight.

11   Remove the bulb holder complete with the bulb **(see illustration)**. Note that this is difficult to access and it may prove easier to remove the bulb and holder with a pair of long nose pliers.

12   Remove the bulb from the bulb holder **(see illustration)**.

13   Install the new bulb using a reversal of the removal procedure.

Front turn signal

14   Remove the headlight housing as described in Section 8.

15   Turn the headlight upside down to access the bulb cover. Remove the bulb cover.

16   Rotate the bulb holder counterclockwise and pull it from the headlight **(see illustration)**.

17   Depress and twist the bulb to remove it from the bulb holder.

18   Install the new bulb using a reversal of the removal procedure.

6.16 Remove the bulb and bulb holder

6.21 Remove the integrated bulb and bulb holder

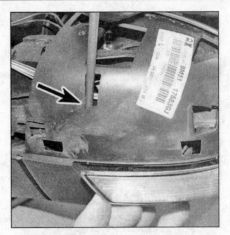

6.26a Insert a suitable screwdriver and release the housing

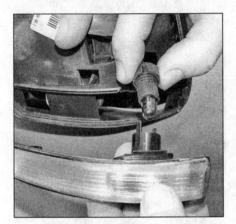

6.26b Remove the bulb holder…

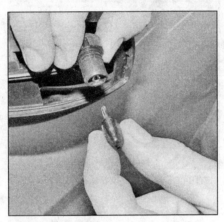

6.26c …then pull the capless bulb from the bulb holder

6.27 The bulb is also accessible with the mirror glass removed

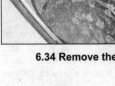

6.34 Remove the bulb holder

Front foglight

19   Access to the front foglight bulbs can be gained from above, by removing the head-light, or from below by jacking up the vehicle.
20   If working from below, remove the engine undershield, the intermediate panel and the air deflector from below the bumper cover (see Chapter 11).
21   Rotate the bulbholder counterclockwise and pull it from the foglight **(see illustration)**. Note that the bulb is integral with the bulb-holder.

22   Disconnect the electrical connector from the bulb holder.
23   Install the new bulb using a reversal of the removal procedure.

Side turn signal

24   The side turn signal is located in the door mirror.
25   Access is possible by either removing the mirror glass, or by removing the upper mirror cover (see Chapter 11).
26   Remove the cover, depress the locking tab and remove the light. Remove the bulb holder from the light and then remove the bulb **(see illustrations)**.
27   Alternatively, remove the mirror glass (see Chapter 11) and remove the bulb **(see illustration)**.
28   Installation is the reverse of removal.

Approach light

29   Remove the exterior mirror glass as described in Chapter 11.
30   Release the clip and remove the lens from the mirror housing.
31   Pull the wedge-type bulb from the bulb-holder.
32   Install the new bulb using a reversal of the removal procedure.

Taillight

Note: *On models equipped with Xenon head-lights, the sidelights are LED type bulbs. These are not replaceable. If they are faulty the entire lamp must be replaced (see Section 9).*

Hatchback models

33   Remove the taillight housing as described in Section 8.
34   Rotate the bulbholder counterclockwise and pull it from the housing **(see illustration)**.
35   Where a bayonet type bulb is installed, push and twist the bulb counterclockwise to remove it. Where a capless bulb is installed, pull the bulb straight out from the bulb holder.
36   Installation is the reverse of removal.

Sedan models

37   Remove the taillight housing as described in Section 8.
38   Remove the bolts and remove the bulb-holder.
39   Press and twist the relevant bulb coun-terclockwise and withdraw it from the bulb-holder.
40   Installation is the reversal of the removal procedure.

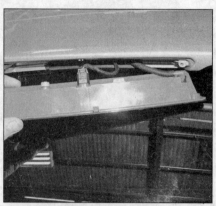

6.47 Remove the light

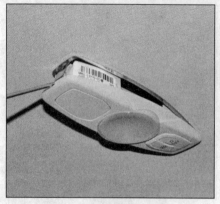

7.2a Pry the light free

7.2b Remove the bulb holder...

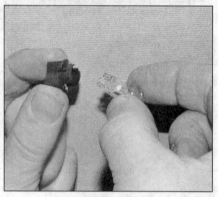

7.2c ...and remove the bulb from the bulb holder

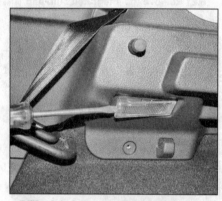

7.10a Carefully pry off the lamp lens...

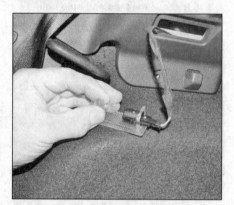

7.10b ...and remove the bulb

Rear foglight

41 Remove the relevant light unit as described in Section 8.

42 Rotate the relevant bulbholder countet-rclockwise and pull it from the light.

43 Push and twist the bulb counterclockwise, and pull it from the bulbholder.

44 Installation is the reverse of removal.

License plate light

45 The license plate light uses LED type bulbs. If a fault develops with the light the complete assembly (including the liftgate release switch) must be replaced.

46 To replace the light, remove the liftgate handle as described in Chapter 11.

High-mounted brake light

Note: *The high-mounted brake light uses LED type bulbs. If a problem develops with the light, the entire assembly must be replaced.*

47 Remove the screws and remove the light assembly **(see illustration)**.

48 Installation is the reverse of removal.

---

7   Interior light bulbs – replacement

1 Whenever a bulb is replaced, note the following points:

a) *Remember that if the light has just been in use, the bulb may be extremely hot.*

b) *Always check the bulb contacts and holder, ensuring that there is clean metal-to-metal contact between the bulb and its live and ground. Clean off any corrosion or dirt before installing a new bulb.*

c) *Wherever bayonet-type bulbs are installed, ensure that the live contact(s) bear firmly against the bulb contact.*

d) *Always ensure that the new bulb is of the correct rating and that it is completely clean before installing it.*

e) *Some vehicles feature LED type bulbs. If these fail the entire assembly will require replacement.*

Interior lights

2 Pry out the light, ensuring that the metal frame stays fixed to the headliner. Remove the bulb holder and pull the capless style bulb from the holder. **(see illustrations)**.

3 Install a new bulb using a reversal of removal procedure.

Glovebox

4 Remove the glovebox as described in Chapter 11.

5 Disconnect the electrical connector.

6 Work the white locking clip free (see Section 5).

7 Pull the wedge-type bulb from its holder.

8 Install the new bulb using a reversal of the removal procedure.

Footwell lights/ luggage area light

9 The footwell lights and the luggage area lights are identical.

10 Reach under the instrument panel (or open the liftgate) and pry off the lens. Pull the wedge-type capless bulb from the holder **(see illustrations)**.

11 Install the new bulb using a reversal of the removal procedure.

Instrument cluster bulbs

12 It is not possible to install the instrument cluster bulbs individually as they are of LED design and soldered to a printed circuit board. It is not possible to replace a single LED. If an LED is not functioning, the complete instrument cluster must be replaced.

Switch illumination

13 The switches are illuminated by LEDs, and cannot be replaced separately.

Heater/air conditioning control panel illumination

14 The control panel is illuminated by non-replaceable LEDs. If defective, the control panel must be replaced.

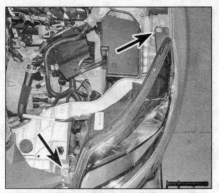

8.1 Headlight retaining bolts

8.3 Use a small screwdriver to disconnect the headlight electrical connector

8.7 Remove the mounting bolts

8.11 The taillight housing thumbwheels on hatchback models. Sedan models are similar

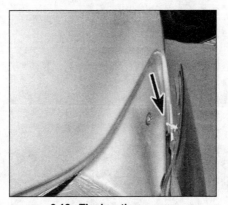

8.12a The locating peg on hatchback models...

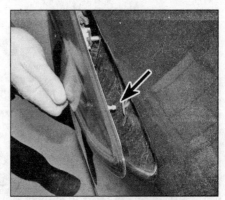

8.12b ...and on sedan models

8   Exterior light housings – removal, installation and beam adjustment

Warning: *Some models use High Intensity Discharge (HID) bulbs instead of conventional halogen bulbs. The high voltages produced by this system can be fatal in the event of shock. Also, the voltage can remain in circuit even after the headlight switch has been turned to OFF and the ignition key has been removed. Therefore, for your safety, we don't recommend that you try to replace one of these bulbs yourself. Instead, have this service performed by a dealer service department or other qualified repair shop.*

Headlight housing

1   Open the hood and locate the 2 headlight retaining bolts **(see illustration)**.
2   Remove the bolts, and pull the headlight forward, while slightly lifting the rear to remove it.
3   Disconnect the electrical connectors from the rear of the headlight as it's withdrawn **(see illustration)**.
4   Installation is the reverse of the removal procedure. On completion check for proper operation, and have the headlight beam

adjustment checked as soon as possible (see steps 24 through 26)).

Front foglight

5   Apply the parking brake, raise the front of the vehicle and support it securely on jackstands.
6   Remove the engine undershield and then remove the air deflector from beneath the bumper cover.
7   Undo the 2 mounting bolts, withdraw the foglight from the front bumper, and disconnect the electrical connector **(see illustration)**.
8   Installation is the reverse of removal, but have the foglight beam setting checked at the earliest opportunity. An approximate adjustment can be made by positioning the car 32 feet in front of a wall marked with the center point of the foglight lens. Turn the adjustment screw as required. Note that only height adjustment is possible – there is no lateral adjustment.

Side turn signal

9   The procedure is as described for bulb replacement in Section 6.

Taillight housing

10   Open the liftgate or trunk and remove the cover from the side panel

8.12c Disconnect the electrical connector

11   Remove the upper and lower light retaining thumbwheels **(see illustration)**. These are difficult to access and often very tight. Provisions are made for a slotted screwdriver to be used to loosen the thumbwheels. A short stubby screwdriver will be required.
12   Pull the light unit outward (to release the unit from the locating peg) then rearwards. Disconnect the electrical connector **(see illustrations)**.
13   Installation is the reverse of removal.

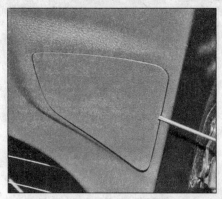

8.14 Use a screwdriver to carefully remove the cover

8.15a Disconnect the electrical connector...

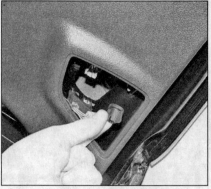

8.15b ...and remove the thumbwheel

8.22 Squeeze the clips to release it from the trunk lid

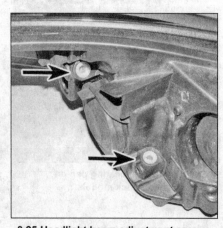

8.25 Headlight beam adjustment screws

Trunk light – Sedan models

14   Open the trunk and remove the cover from the trunk trim panel (see illustration).
15   Disconnect the electrical connector. Release the thumbwheel (see illustrations) and remove the light.
16   Installation is the reversal of removal.

License plate light

17   To replace the light remove the liftgate handle as described in Chapter 11.

High-level brake light

Liftgate models

18   Remove the screws, remove the light, disconnect the electrical connector and the screen washer jet (see illustration 6.46).
19   Installation is the reverse of removal.

Sedan models

20   Carefully pry out the trunk lid trim panel pin-type fasteners, then remove the trunk lid trim panel.
21   Disconnect the electrical connector for the light.
22   Squeeze the clips and push the brake light housing out of the trunk lid (see illustration).

23   Installation is the reverse of removal.

Beam adjustment - halogen headlights

24   Accurate adjustment of the headlight beam is only possible using optical beam setting equipment, and this work should therefore be carried out by a dealer or suitably-equipped workshop.
25   For reference, the headlights can be adjusted using the adjuster screws, accessible via the top of each light unit (see illustration).
26   All models are equipped with an electrically-operated headlight beam adjustment system which is controlled through the switch in the instrument panel. Ensure that the switch is set to the basic O position before adjusting the headlight aim.

9   Xenon (HID) headlights - general information

Some models use High Intensity Discharge (HID) bulbs instead of conventional halogen bulbs. The high voltages produced by this system can be fatal in the event of shock. Also, the voltage can remain in circuit even after the headlight switch has been turned to OFF and the ignition key has been removed. Therefore, for your safety, we don't recommend that you try to replace one of these bulbs yourself Instead, have this service performed by a dealer service department or other qualified repair shop.

10   Instrument cluster – removal and installation

Note: *The instrument panel and its function is included in the vehicle's self-diagnosis program. If the instrument panel has a fault, it would be prudent to have the vehicle's fault code memory checked by a dealer or specialist, prior to removing the panel.*

Note: *If the instrument panel is being replaced with a new or exchange unit, the assistance of a dealer or specialist is required to download necessary software, and initialize/adapt the various instrument panel functions.*

1   Disconnect the negative battery cable from the remote ground terminal (see Chapter 5).
2   Fully extend the steering column, and move it to its lowest position.
3   Rotate the steering wheel and the release column upper shroud (see Section 23).
4   Remove the upper shroud complete with the trim panel from below the instrument panel (see illustration 23.4).
5   Undo the 2 retaining bolts on the lower edge of the instrument cluster, then using either a suitable trim tool or the round end of a stainless steel ruler, release the upper mounting clip and carefully pull the top edge of the panel rearwards. Remove the instrument cluster (see illustrations).
6   Disconnect the electrical connector(s) as the cluster is removed.
7   Installation is the reverse of removal, but see the Notes at the beginning of this section.

10.5a Undo the mounting bolts...

10.5b ...and release the clip

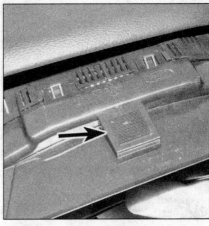

10.5c Note that the retaining clip is part of the instrument panel. The clip locates on the serrated section of the instrument cluster

11.2a Pull off the rubber cap, remove the nut...

11.2b ...and remove the wiper arm

11.2c A small two jaw puller can be used to remove the arm if necessary

11   Windshield wiper components – removal and installation

Wiper arms

1   If the wipers are not in their parked position, switch on the ignition, and allow the motor to automatically park.

2   Before removing an arm, mark its parked position on the glass with a strip of adhesive tape. Pry off the cover and unscrew the spindle nut **(see illustrations)**. Ease the arm from the spindle by rocking it slowly from side-to-side.

3   Installation is the reverse of removal, but before tightening the spindle nuts, position the wiper blades as marked before removal. Note that the driver's arm must be installed above the passenger side arm.

Wiper motors

Note: *If the wiper motors are replaced, they must be initialized using a suitable diagnostic tool. This task should be done by a dealer or suitably equipped specialist.*

Note: *While the motors are physically identical, they are programmed differently. This means it is not possible to swap the motors over from side to side.*

4   Remove the wiper arms as described above.

5   Disconnect the negative battery cable from the remote ground terminal (see Chapter 5).

6   Remove the clips at the front edge of the cowl panel, then pull it upwards to release it from the base of the windshield **(see illustrations)**. The panel is a tight fit at the base of the windshield and is best released by working it free at one end first.

7   At the appropriate side, remove the single bolt from the lower panel **(see illustration)**.

8   On models equipped with a electric

11.6a Remove the screws...

11.6b ...and the push-pin fasteners...

11.6c ...then remove the cowl cover

11.7 Remove the lower panel

11.9 Remove the windshield wiper motor

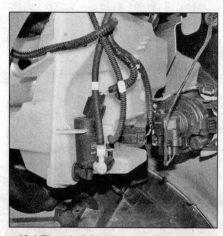

12.1 The windshield washer fluid pump

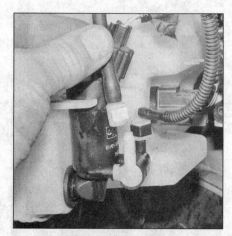

12.4 Pull off the hoses

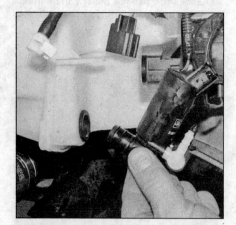

12.5 Pull the pump from the grommet in
the reservoir

windshield defroster, disconnect the electrical connector for the heated windshield from the wiper motor support bracket.

9   Unbolt the wiper motor support bracket (2 bolts). Pull the motor and bracket free from the partially hidden rubber mounting **(see illustration)**. Disconnect the electrical con-

nector as the motor is removed.
10   Remove the mounting grommet if necessary.
11   Remove the 3 bolts securing the motor to the bracket and remove the motor from the bracket.
12   Installation is the reverse of removal. If a replacement motor (or motors) has been installed, the wipers must be initialized using suitable diagnostic equipment.

12 Washer system – general information

1   The fluid reservoir for the windshield/ headlight washer is located behind the right-hand end of the bumper cover. The windshield washer fluid pump is attached to the side of the reservoir body **(see illustration)**. On hatchback models, the liftgate washer is fed by the same reservoir, with a dual output pump. Models with a headlight washer system have an additional pump installed on the reservoir. Access to the reservoir and pump(s) is made from below.
2   The reservoir fluid level must be regu-

larly topped-up with windshield washer fluid containing an antifreeze agent, but not cooling system antifreeze.
3   Loosen the right front wheel lug nuts, raise and support it safely on jackstands. Remove the right-hand wheel and the wheel arch liner (see Chapter 11).
4   The supply hoses are attached by quick release connectors. Have a suitable container ready beneath the washer reservoir to catch spilled fluid. Release the locking clip and pull off the appropriate connector **(see illustration)**.
5   Work the pump free from the retaining grommet **(see illustration)**.
6   Remove the grommet and check that the filter is clear **(see illustrations)**.
7   To remove the reservoir, remove the front bumper cover, then remove the reservoir filler neck (see Chapter 11). Disconnect the electrical connectors from the pump(s) and the fluid level sensor. Remove the washer hoses and the 2 mounting bolts. Unhook the reservoir from the upper mounting and remove it from the vehicle.
8   The windshield washer jets can be adjusted by inserting a pin into the jet and

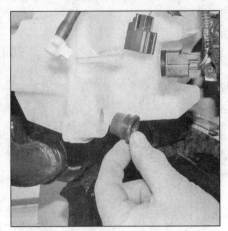

12.6a Pull the grommet from the reservoir

12.6b The grommet incorporates a coarse filter

12.9 Press the jet forwards and lift the rear edge

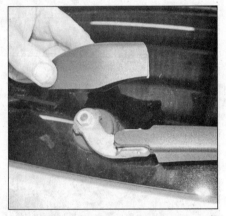

13.2a Remove the cover...

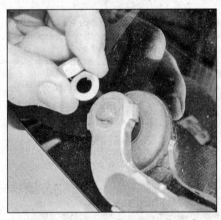

13.2b... and remove the nut and washer

13.3a Rock the wiper arm free...

13.3b... or use a suitable puller

13.6a Remove the bolts...

altering the aim as required. To remove a washer jet, open the hood, and disconnect the hose from the jet. Note that on some models, the hood insulation panel must be unclipped and removed.

9   Disconnect the electrical connector, then push the jet forwards, and lift the rear edge.

Remove the jet from the hood **(see illustration)**.

10   The headlight washer jets are removed by pulling the cover forward and removing it. Depress the locking tabs and remove the jet assembly, releasing the washer hose as the jet is removed.

11   The rear window washer jet is bonded to the high mounted brake light. If a problem develops with the washer jet the high mounted brake light will have to be replaced (see Section 6).

13   Liftgate wiper motor – removal and installation

1   Make sure the liftgate wiper is switched off and in its rest position. Mark the position of the wiper blade on the liftgate window glass using masking tape.

2   Remove the wiper arm cover, nut and washer **(see illustrations)**.

3   Gently rock the wiper arm free from the spindle. If necessary use a puller to free the arm from the spindle **(see illustrations)**.

4   Open the liftgate and remove the trim panel as described in Chapter 11.

5   Disconnect the electrical connector from the wiper motor.

6   Remove the 3 wiper motor mounting bolts and remove the wiper motor from the liftgate **(see illustrations)**. Check the condition of the spindle rubber grommet in the liftgate, and if necessary, replace it.

13.6b ...and remove the wiper motor

14.2 The horns

17.5a The parking aid module on hatchback models...

7   Installation is the reverse of removal. Install the wiper arm and blade so that the arm is in the position noted during removal.

---

14   Horns – replacement

---

1   The horns are located behind the front bumper cover on the right-hand side. Raise the front of the vehicle and support it securely on jackstands.

2   Access may be possible if the right-hand side wheel arch liner is removed **(see illustration)**. It may be necessary to remove the front bumper cover as described in Chapter 11.

3   Disconnect the horn electrical connector, remove the mounting bolt and remove the horn from the vehicle.

4   Installation is the reverse of removal. Check for satisfactory operation on completion.

---

15   Sunroof motor – removal and installation

Removal of the sunroof motor requires the headliner to be removed. This is an involved task, requiring patience and dexterity. Consequently, we recommend you entrust this task to a dealer or upholstery specialist.

---

16   Central locking system – general information

---

1   All models are equipped with a central door locking system, which automatically locks all doors and the rear liftgate/trunk lid in unison with the manual locking of the driver's front door. The system is operated electronically with motors/switches incorporated into the door lock assemblies. The system is controlled by the BCM (Body Control Module – formerly referred to by the manufacturer as the Generic Electronic Module - GEM) and the Keyless Vehicle Module (KVM) – where

equipped. The BCM and the KVM communicate with the vehicle's other control modules via an information network known as a Databus. Control modules integral with electric window motors receive signals from the BCM via the databus, and directly control the operation of the door locks. The liftgate/trunk lid has its own control module, integral with the lock assembly. If any module is replaced, new software for the unit must be downloaded from the manufacturer. This task should be preformed by the dealer or suitably-equipped specialist.

2   The control unit is equipped with a self-diagnosis capability. Should the system develop a problem, have the control unit checked by a dealer or suitably-equipped specialist. Once the problem has been established, refer to the relevant Section of Chapter 11 to replace a door module or liftgate/trunk lid lock as applicable.

---

17   Parking aid components – general information and replacement

---

General information

1   The parking aid system is equipped as standard on higher specification models. It is also an optional extra on most models within the range. Top of the range models also are equipped with a parking assist system. The manufacturer calls this system Active park assist. The system uses ultra sound sensors, a control module and the ability of the electric power steering system to turn the vehicles wheels with no driver assistance. Under the right conditions the system will identify a suitable parking space and reverse the car into the space with no driver control of the steering wheel.

2   Four ultrasound sensors located in the bumpers measure the distance to the closest object behind or in front the car, and inform the driver using acoustic signals from the audio system speakers. The information dis-

17.5b ...and on sedan models

play will also show a moving graphic or text message. The nearer the object, the more frequent the acoustic signals.

3   The system includes a control module and self-diagnosis program, and therefore, in the event of a problem, the vehicle should be taken to a dealer or suitably-equipped specialist who will be able to interrogate the system.

Replacement

Parking Aid Module (PAM)

4   The control unit is located behind the right-hand luggage compartment side trim panel. Remove the luggage compartment side panel trim as described in Chapter 11, and remove the foam padding behind the panel.

5   Remove the 2 retaining bolts, and remove the PAM **(see illustrations)**. As the unit is removed, disconnect the electrical connectors.

6   Installation is the reverse of removal.

Range/distance sensor

7   Remove the relevant bumper as described in Chapter 11.

8   Disconnect the sensor electrical connector, push the retaining clips apart, and pull out

17.8 A typical parking sensor

18.3a Remove the screws...

18.3b ...and release the control panel

18.4 Disconnect the electrical connector(s)

18.7 Remove the mounting screws

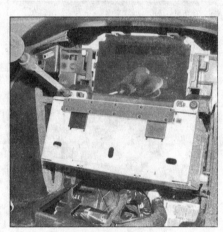

18.10a Remove the screws

the sensor **(see illustration)**.

9   Installation is the reverse of removal. Press the sensor firmly into position until the retaining clips engage.

18   Audio system – removal and installation

Note: *This Section applies only to factory-installed audio equipment.*

Note: *If a new audio unit is to be installed, it must be configured using Manufacturer diagnostic equipment (IDS). Have this done by a dealer or suitably equipped specialist.*

1   All audio units installed in the vehicle feature a front control panel, an information display unit and the main audio unit. All models have a minimum of 6 speakers. Higher specification models also have additional rear tweeters and on some models, a spare wheel well mounted subwoofer speaker.

Removal

2   Disconnect the negative battery cable from the remote ground terminal (see Chapter 5).

Front control panel

3   Remove the 2 screws and gently work the control panel free from the instrument panel **(see illustrations)**.

4   Pull the panel forward and disconnect the electrical connector(s) **(see illustration)**.

5   Place the panel on a soft surface and remove the 4 mounting screws to release the control panel from the trim panel.

Information display unit

6   Remove the control panel as described above.

7   Remove the mounting screws **(see illustration)**, pull the unit forward, note the location and routing of the electrical connectors, and disconnect the electrical connectors.

8   If required, the display can now be removed from the mounting bracket.

Audio unit

9   Remove the control panel as described above.

10   Remove the mounting screws. Pull the unit forward, noting the location and routing of the electrical connectors, and disconnect the electrical connectors **(see illustrations)**.

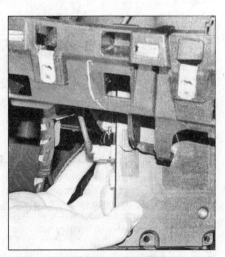

18.10b Disconnect the electrical connectors

Media synchronization module

11   Remove the heater control panel as described in Chapter 3.

12   Remove the mounting screws and lower

18.12a Remove the screws..

18.12b ...and lower the module

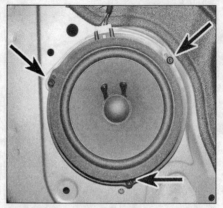

20.2 Remove the screws and remove the speaker. Some models use rivets that must be drilled out

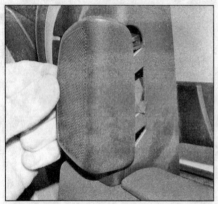

20.5 Remove the trim panel

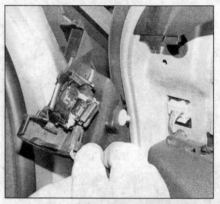

20.6 Disconnect the electrical connector

the module **(see illustrations)**, disconnecting the electrical connector as the module is removed.

Installation

13   Installation is the reverse of removal, but if a new unit has been installed, suitable software must be downloaded from the manufacturer. Have this done by a dealer or suitably-equipped specialist.

19   Antenna – removal and installation

Removal and installation of the antennal requires the headliner to be removed. This is an involved task, requiring patience and dexterity. Consequently, we recommend you have this done by a dealer or upholstery specialist.

20   Speakers – removal and installation

Door speakers

1   Remove door panel as described in Chapter 11.

2   Remove the screws (or on some models drill out the rivets) securing the speaker to the door **(see illustration)**.
3   Disconnect the electrical connecter as the speaker is withdrawn.
4   Installation is the reverse of removal.

Front tweeter speakers

5   Pull the trim panel covering the door mirror speaker **(see illustration)**.
6   Disconnect the electrical connector **(see illustration)**.
7   Release the retaining clips and remove the speaker.
8   Installation is the revese of removal.

Rear tweeter speakers

9   Remove the door trim panel as described in Chapter 11.
10   Disconnect the electrical connector and unclip the tweeter from the door panel.
11   Installation is the reverse of removal.

Instrument panel speaker

12   Using a suitable plastic trim tool pry off the speaker grille (complete with the speaker).
13   Disconnect the electrical connector and unbolt the speaker from the grille.
14   Installation is the reverse of removal.

Subwoofer

15   Remove the trunk area cover.
16   Disconnect the electrical connector, remove the single bolt and remove the speaker.
17   Installation is the reverse of removal.

21   Airbags - general information

1   These models are equipped with a Supplemental Restraint System (SRS), more commonly known as airbags. This system is designed to protect the driver and the front seat passenger from serious injury in the event of a head-on or frontal collision. It consists of an airbag module in the center of the steering wheel and another airbag module on the right side of the instrument panel plus, on some and later models, side airbags and curtain shield airbags designed to protect the occupants in a side impact and a sensing/diagnostic module which is mounted in the center of the vehicle below the instrument panel. These models are also equipped with a pair of impact sensors that are located at the front of the vehicle.
2   Some later models are equipped with seatbelt pre-tensioners, also part of the airbag system. The pre-tensioners are pyrotechnic (explosive) devices designed to retract the seat belts in the event of a collision.
3   On models equipped with pre-tensioners, do not remove the front seat belt retractor assemblies. Problems with the pre-tensioners will turn on the SRS (airbag) warning light on the dash. If any pre-tensioner problems are suspected, take the vehicle to a dealer service department.

Airbag module

Steering wheel-mounted

4   The airbag inflator module contains a housing incorporating the cushion (airbag) and inflator unit, mounted in the center of the steering wheel. The inflator assembly is mounted on the back of the housing over a hole through which gas is expelled, inflating

22.4a Insert a flat-bladed screwdriver and push the handle down to release the airbag clip

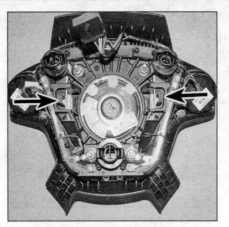

22.4b The airbag clips must be pushed outwards

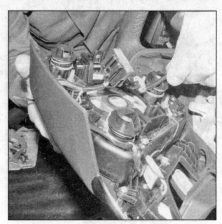

22.5 Disconnect the electrical connector

the bag almost instantaneously when an electrical signal is sent from the system. A spiral cable assembly on the steering column under the module carries this signal to the module. This spiral cable assembly can transmit an electrical signal regardless of steering wheel position.

Instrument panel-mounted

5   The passenger side airbag is mounted above the glove compartment and designated by the letters SRS (Supplemental Restraint System). It consists of an inflator containing an igniter, a bag assembly, a reaction housing and a trim cover.

6   The passenger airbag is considerably larger than the steering wheel-mounted unit and is supported by the steel reaction housing. The trim cover has a molded seam which splits when the bag inflates.

Side and curtain airbags

7   The side airbag and inflator modules are mounted on the sides of the front seats and contain an inflator containing an igniter and bag assembly. The curtain shield airbag assemblies run along the interior of the roof from the front A-pillar to the rear of the passenger compartment. In the event of a side impact, both airbag assemblies are activated by the sensors mounted at the base of the center pillar behind the seats.

Sensing and diagnostic module

8   The sensing and diagnostic module supplies the current to the airbag system in the event of the collision, even if battery power is cut off. It checks this system every time the vehicle is started, causing the "AIR BAG" light to go on then off, if the system is operating properly. If there is a fault in the system, the light will go on and stay on, flash, or the dash will make a beeping sound. If this happens, the vehicle should be taken to your dealer immediately for service.

Seat belt pre-tensioners

9   Some models are equipped with pyrotechnic (explosive) units in the front seat belt retracting mechanisms. During an impact that would trigger the airbag system, the airbag control unit also triggers the seat belt retractors. When the pyrotechnic charges go off, they accelerate the retractors to instantly take up any slack in the seat belt system to more fully prepare the driver and front seat passenger for impact.

10   The airbag system should be disabled any time work is done to or around the seats. **Warning:** *Never strike the pillars or floorpan with a hammer or use an impact-driver tool in these areas unless the system is disabled.*

Precautions

Disabling the SRS system

Warning: *Failure to follow these precautions could result in accidental deployment of the airbag and personal injury.*

Warning: *Never install a memory-saver device, used to preserve PCM memory and radio station presets, when working on or around any of the airbag system components.*

11   Whenever working in the vicinity of the steering wheel, instrument panel or any of the other SRS system components, the system must be disarmed. To disarm the system:

a) *Point the wheels straight ahead and turn the ignition key to the LOCK position.*

b) *Disconnect the negative battery cable from the remote ground terminal (see Chapter 5).*

c) *Wait at least five minutes for the back-up power supply capacitor to be depleted.*

12   Whenever handling an airbag module, always keep the airbag opening (trim side) pointed away from your body. Never place the airbag module on a bench or other surface with the airbag opening facing the surface. Always place the airbag module in a safe location with the airbag opening (trim side) facing up.

13   Never measure the resistance of any SRS component. An ohmmeter has a built-in

battery supply that could accidentally deploy the airbag.

14   Never use electrical welding equipment on a vehicle equipped with an airbag without first disconnecting the negative battery cable (see Chapter 5).

15   Never dispose of a live airbag module. Return it to your dealer for safe deployment, using special equipment, and disposal.

---

22   Airbag system components – removal and installation

Warning: *Refer to the warnings in Section 21 before carrying out the following operations.*

1   Disconnect the negative battery cable from the remote ground terminal (see Chapter 5). Wait at least 5 minutes for any residual electrical energy to dissipate before commencing work.

Note: *If removing the driver's airbag, turn the steering wheel 90° from straight-ahead before disconnecting the battery, otherwise the steering lock will engage.*

Driver's airbag

2   Set the steering wheel and front wheels in the straight-ahead position.

3   Rotate the steering wheel 90° in each direction to access the steering column upper shroud retaining clips. Release the clips and remove the shroud **(see illustration 23.3)**.

4   Locate the access hole in the reverse side of the steering wheel, and insert a flat-bladed screwdriver into the hole, then push the handle downwards to release the retaining clip **(see illustrations)**. Turn the steering wheel 180° and release the clip on the other side.

5   Temporarily touch the striker plate of the front door to discharge any electrostatic electricity. Return the steering wheel to the straight-ahead position, then carefully lift the airbag assembly away from the steering wheel and disconnect the electrical connectors from the rear of the unit **(see illustration)**. Note that the airbag must not be knocked or dropped, and should be stored the correct way up with its padded surface facing up.

22.9 Disconnect the electrical connector

22.14 Ensure the yellow mark is visible in the window

22.17 Remove the clockspring

22.21 Remove the control module

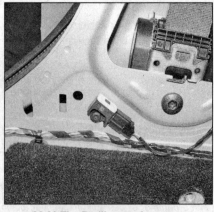

22.30 The B-pillar crash sensor

6   On installation, reconnect the electrical connectors and locate the airbag unit in the steering wheel, making sure the wire does not become trapped, and push the airbag into place to engage the retaining clips. Reconnect the cable to the negative battery terminal (see Chapter 5). Ensure no one is in the vehicle when the battery is reconnected.

Passenger airbag

7   Pry off the instrument panel end panel on the passenger side.
8   Remove the passenger's glovebox as described in Chapter 11.
9   Disconnect the airbag electrical connector **(see illustration)**.
10   Remove the 6 bolts that hold the airbag up and then remove the 2 bolts from the support bracket.
11   Installation is reverse of removal. Ensure that no one is inside the vehicle and then reconnect the cable to the negative battery terminal (see Chapter 5).

Airbag clockspring

12   Remove the airbag and then the steering wheel as described in Chapter 10.
13   Remove the upper and lower steering column shrouds (see Chapter 11).
14   Ensure that the yellow mark is visible

through the window in the clockspring **(see illustration)**.
15   Disconnect the electrical connector from the clockspring and the steering angle sensor.
16   If the clockspring is to be re-installed, apply tape to lock the unit in position. Do not attempt to rotate the unit.
17   Undo the screws and remove the clockspring **(see illustration)**.
18   Installation is the reverse of removal, but if there is any doubt as to the correct position of the clockspring it must be centered as follows:
a) *Rotate the clockspring clockwise until a resistance is felt.*
b) *Rotate it counterclockwise 2 and a half turns – the colored marking will be visible in the window at the 7 o'clock position.*
c) *Tape the clockspring in position.*

Restraint Control Module (RCM)

19   Refer to Chapter 11 and remove the center console.
20   Release the locking devices and disconnect the electrical connector for the control unit.
21   Undo the retaining bolts and remove the

clockspring **(see illustration)**.
22   Installation is the reverse of removal, ensuring the module is installed with the arrow mark on the top pointing forwards. Note that if a new module has been installed, software for it will need to be downloaded from the manufacturer. Have the job done by a dealer or suitably-equipped specialist. Note also that if any of the airbags have deployed it is possible to reset the control module (up to a maximum of 5 times) using suitable diagnostic equipment.

Side airbags

23   The side airbags are incorporated into the side of the front and rear seats. Removal of the units requires the seat upholstery to be removed. We recommend this task be done by dealer or specialist.

Head/overhead curtain airbags

24   Renewal of the head airbags/inflatable curtain requires removal of the headlining. This is a specialist task, and should be entrusted to a dealer or specialist.

Crash/lateral acceleration sensors

Front sensor

25   Open the hood, remove the 2 bolts and remove the hood catch.
26   Remove the retaining bolt and remove the sensor.
27   Installation is the reverse of removal.

Side sensors

28   The side sensors are located in the vehicle's B-pillars on each side.
29   Remove the B-pillar trim panel (see Chapter 11) and unbolt the seatbelt lower mounting.
30   Disconnect the sensor electrical connector, then remove the bolt and remove the sensor **(see illustration)**. Take great care not to damage the sensor wiring harness. Note that the sensor must be handled carefully. Do not install a sensor that has been dropped or knocked.
31   Installation is the reverse of removal.

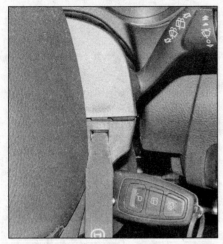

23.3 Rotate the steering wheel and release the upper shroud retaining clip each side

23.4 Lower steering column shroud bolts

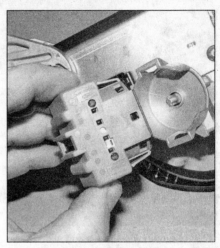

23.5 Release the clips and pull the switch from the lock

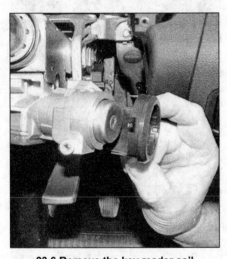

23.6 Remove the key reader coil

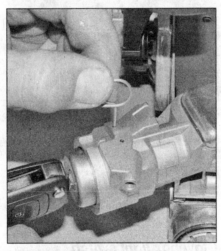

23.8a Release the lock cylinder...

23.8b ...and remove it

23   Ignition switch – replacement

Key-type ignition

1   Disconnect the negative battery cable from the remote ground terminal (see Chapter 5), then turn the ignition switch to position I.

2   Fully extend and lower the steering column.

3   Rotate the steering wheel as necessary to access the column upper shroud retaining clips. Release the clips and remove the shroud (**see illustration**).

4   Remove the bolts and remove the steering column lower shroud (**see illustration**). Release the steering column adjustment lever to remove the shroud.

5   Disconnect the electrical connector, then depress the clips and remove the ignition switch (**see illustration**). Do not turn the lock cylinder (key) from position I while the ignition switch is removed.

6   Disconnect the electrical connector from the key reader coil and then pry the coil assembly from the lock cylinder housing (**see illustration**).

7   Remove the snap-ring, cover plate and small interlock plate from the rear of the lock cylinder.

8   With the key still in position I, insert a thin rod into the hole in the lower part of the cylinder housing and depress the spring-loaded locking lug, and pull the cylinder from the housing (**see illustrations**).

9   Installation is the reverse of removal. Note that the lock cylinder (key) must be in position I prior to installing the ignition switch.

Push Button Start System

10   Remove the steering column trim panel and the steering column covers (see Chapter 11).

11   Reach behind the instrument panel and release the tabs securing the switch, then push the switch out of the instrument panel.

12   Disconnect the electrical connector from the switch.

13   Installation is the reverse of removal.

24   Switches – removal and installation

Steering column switches

1   Release the locking lever and fully extend and lower the steering column.

2   Rotate the steering wheel as necessary to access the column upper shroud retaining clips. Release the clips and remove the shroud (**see illustration 23.3**).

3   Remove the 2 bolts and remove the steering column lower shroud (**see illustration 23.4**). Release the steering column adjustment lever to remove the shroud.

24.4 Remove the screws and slide the relevant switch from place

24.6 Removing the switches and clock spring as a complete assembly

24.8 Remove the screw

24.10 Remove the switch

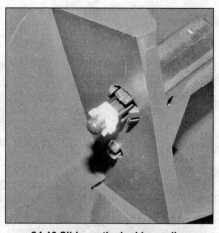

24.13 Slide up the locking collar

24.17 Release the trim

4   Remove the screws and slide the relevant switch from the assembly **(see illustration)**.

5   If the multifunction switch/rotary contact carrier is to be removed as a complete assembly, begin by removing the steering wheel as described in Chapter 10.

6   Disconnect the electrical connectors, undo the 4 bolts and slide the complete assembly from the steering column **(see illustrations)**.

7   Installation is the reverse of removal.

Multifunction light switch

8   Remove the instrument panel end panel (see Chapter 11) and then remove the single screw from the air distribution vent **(see illustration)**.

9   Use a plastic trim removal tool to carefully pry out the vent, complete with the switch from the instrument panel. Disconnect the electrical connector as the vent is removed.

10   With the vent and switch assembly on the bench, squeeze together the upper and lower switch retaining clips and remove the switch from the vent **(see illustration)**.

11   Installation is the reverse of removal.

Glovebox light switch

12   Remove the glovebox as described in Chapter 11.

13   Using a small screwdriver, pull up the white locking clip from the switch assembly **(see illustration)**.

14   Release the clips and remove the switch.

15   Installation is the reverse of removal.

Door mirror adjuster

16   The door mirror adjusters are integral with the window switch assemblies on the the door panels.

17   To remove the switch assemblies, carefully pry away the grab handle outer trim **(see illustration)**.

18   Pry off the switch panel and disconnect the electrical connector. With the assembly on the bench, remove the screws and release the switch panel from the door pull handle trim **(see illustration)**.

19   Installation is the reverse of removal.

Instrument panel center panel switches

20   The switch panel is part of the heater

24.18 Remove the switch assembly from the panel

control panel. It is not possible to remove the switches without first removing the control panel.

21   Remove the audio unit as described in Section 18. Remove the left-hand center console upper trim panel as described in Chapter 11.

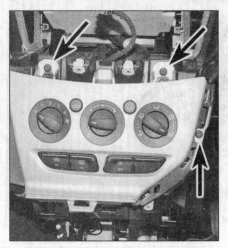

24.22a Remove the screws and...

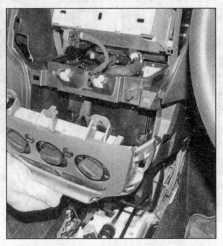

24.22b ...remove the control panel

24.23a Depress the locking tabs with a trim tool...

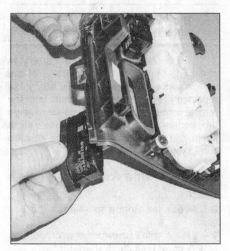

24.23b ...and remove the switch

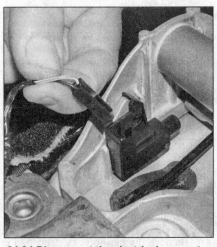

24.34 Disconnect the electrical connector

24.35 Remove the switch

22   Remove the 2 upper retaining screws and the single screw from the side of the panel. Pull the switch panel from the instrument panel (see illustrations). Disconnect the electrical connectors as the panel is removed.
23   Release the clips and pull the relevant switch from the panel (see illustrations).
24   Installation is the reverse of removal.

Sunroof control switch
25   Open the storage compartment in the overhead console and remove the 2 screws.
26   Lower the switch panel and disconnect the electrical connector.
27   With the panel on the bench separate the switch from panel.
28   Installation is the reverse of removal.

Central locking switch
29   The switch is part of the audio unit control panel.

30   Removal is the same as the removal of the audio unit control panel (see Section 18).

Window switches
31   Removal is the same procedure as the removal of the door mirror adjuster and is described earlier in this Section.

Courtesy light switches
32   The courtesy lights are controlled by microswitches incorporated into the door locks. The switches are not available separately. If defective, the door lock assembly must be replaced (see Chapter 11).

Handbrake warning switch
33   Remove the center console as described in Chapter 11.
34   Disconnect the electrical connector from the switch (see illustration).
35   Release the locking tab and detach the switch (see illustration).

36   Installation is the reverse of removal.

Brake light switch
37   Refer to Chapter 9.

Headlight control/foglamp/ instrument illumination
38   These switches are integral with the multifunction light switch. Removal is described earlier in this Section.

Hazard warning switch
39   The hazard warning switch is an integral part of the audio control panel. If it is faulty, the audio control panel must be replaced (see Section 18).

Steering wheel switches
40   Remove the driver's airbag as described in Section 22.

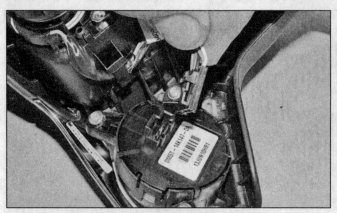

24.41 Disconnect the electrical connector

24.42 Remove the screws

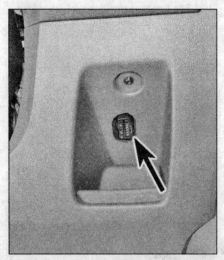

26.00 The diagnostic plug is located under the driver's side of the instrument panel

41   Disconnect the electrical connector **(see illustration)**.
42   Remove the screws and remove the relevant switch pad **(see illustration)**.
43   Installation is the reverse of removal.

Seat heating switches
44   Remove the upper rear section of the center console as described in Chapter 11.
45   Remove the 4 screws and remove the switch panel.
46   Installation is the reverse of removal.

25   Anti-theft alarm system – general information

An anti-theft alarm and immobilizer system is installed as standard equipment. Should the system become faulty, the vehicle should be taken to a dealer or specialist for examination. They will have access to a special diagnostic tester which will quickly trace any fault present in the system.

26   Electronic control modules – removal and installation

Note: *All of these modules are included in the vehicle's sophisticated self-diagnosis system. Should a fault occur, have the system checked using a fault code reader/manufacturer test equipment, via the diagnostic plug located under the driver's side of the instrument panel, above the pedals (see illustration).*

Removal
1   Disconnect the negative battery cable from the remote ground terminal (see Chapter 5).

Body control module (BCM)
2   Remove the end panel from the facia on the passenger side.
3   Remove the trim panel above the passenger's side footwell.
4   Remove the glovebox as described in Chapter 11.
5   Note their installed positions, and disconnect the electrical connectors.
6   Release the locking pegs and remove the BCM
7   If a new BCM is to be installed, the unit must be configured and initialized using the manufacturer diagnostic equipment (IDS). Entrust this task to a dealer or suitably-equipped specialist.

Keyless vehicle module (KVM)
8   Remove the left-hand side load area trim panel as described in Chapter 11.
9   Note the locations of the electrical connectors and disconnect them.
10   Remove the 2 mounting bolts and remove the KVM from the vehicle.

Climate control module (CCM)
11   Removal of the CCM is described in Chapter 3, Section 10.

Installation
12   Installation is the reverse of removal. If a new module has been installed, software will need to be downloaded from the dealer.

Entrust this task to a dealer or suitably-equipped specialist.

27   Remote keyless entry fob - battery replacement

1   We recommend that the battery is changed every 2 years, regardless of the vehicle's mileage. However, if the door locks repeatedly fail to respond to signals from the remote control at the normal distance, change the battery in the remote control before attempting to troubleshoot any of the vehicle's other systems.

Models with a folding key blade
2   Press the button to release the key blade.
3   Use a small screwdriver and open the battery cover **(see illustrations)**.
4   Fully remove the battery cover and remove the battery.
5   Install a new battery; the positive (+) side of the battery must face up **(see illustration)**.
6   Install the battery compartment cover and check the operation of the remote.

Models without a key blade
7   The emergency key blade is located beneath a cover. Press and hold the small buttons on the side of the remote to remove the key cover **(see illustration)**.
8   Remove the key blade and then use a small screwdriver, first at the end of the narrow end of the key blade compartment and then on the side of the remote **(see illustration)**.
9   Fully separate the two halves of the remote and use the screwdriver to remove the battery **(see illustrations)**.
10   Install a new battery; the positive (+) side of the battery must face down **(see illustration)**.
11   Reassemble the two halves of the remote and install the emergency key blade. Install the blade compartment cover and check the operation of the remote.

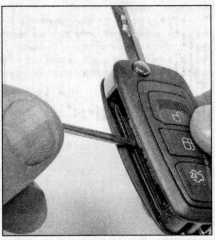

27.3a Insert a screwdriver into the slot. . .

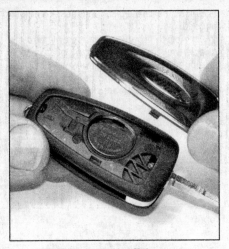

27.3b. . . and pry off the cover

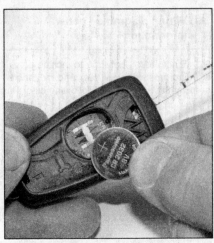

27.5 The battery installs positive side up

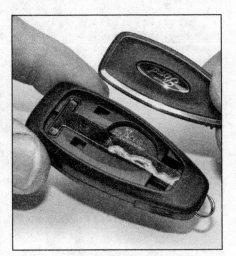

27.7 Remove the key cover

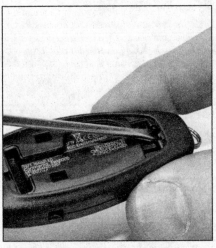

27.8 Release the upper half at the end first

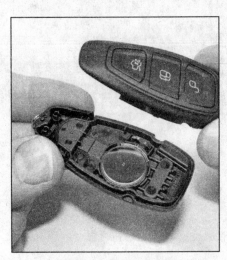

27.9a Separate the 2 halves…

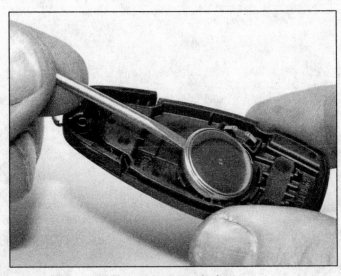

27.9b …and remove the battery

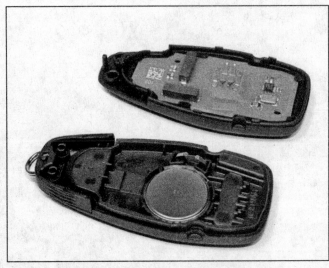

27.10 The battery installs positive side down

31 Wiring diagrams - general information

1   Since it isn't possible to include all wiring diagrams for every year and model covered by this manual, the following diagrams are those that are typical and most commonly needed.

2   Prior to troubleshooting any circuits, check the fuses and circuit breakers (if equipped) to make sure they are in good condition. Make sure the battery is properly charged and has clean, tight cable connections (see Chapter 1).

3   When checking the wiring system, make sure that all electrical connectors are clean, with no broken or loose pins. When unplugging an electrical connector, do not pull on the wires, only on the connector housings themselves.

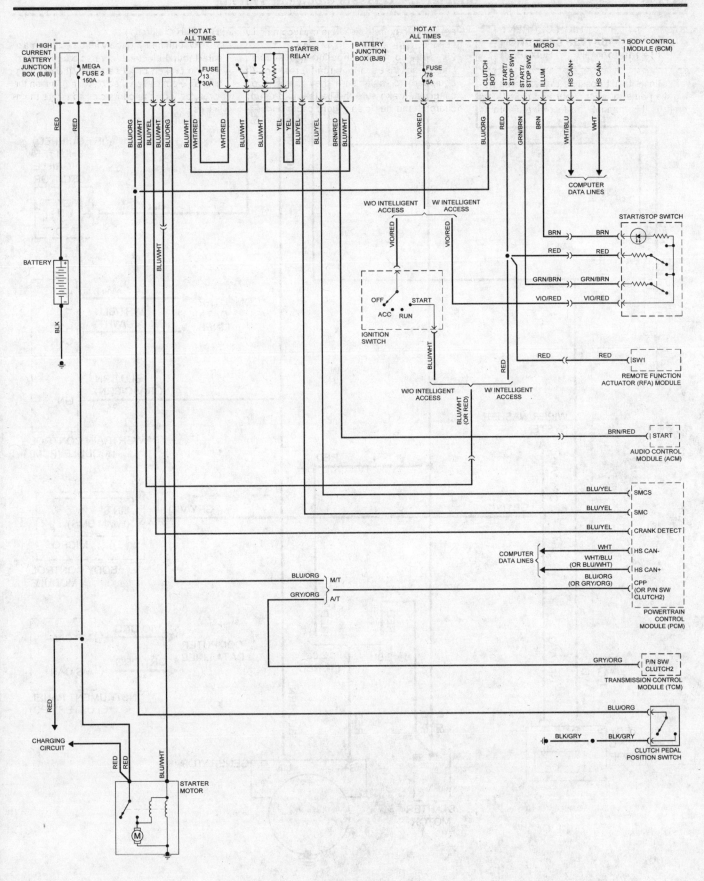

Starting system

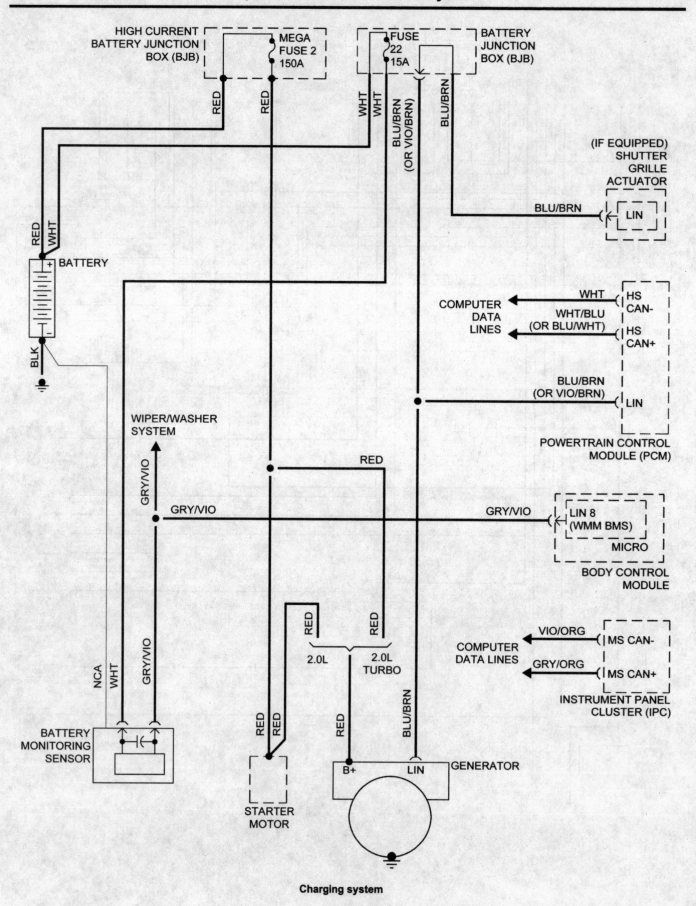

Charging system

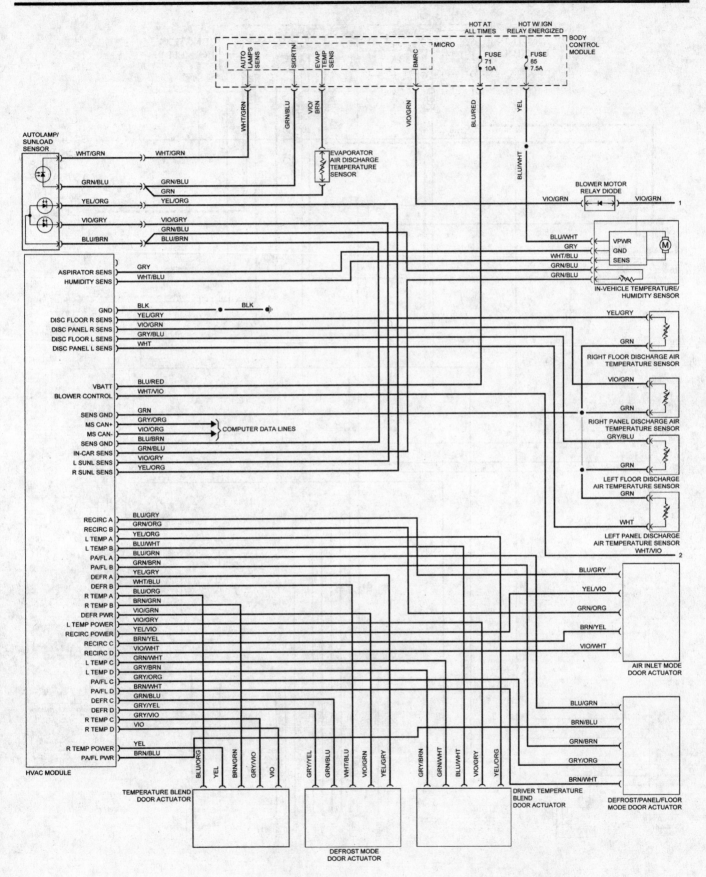

Air conditioning system - automatic (1 of 2)

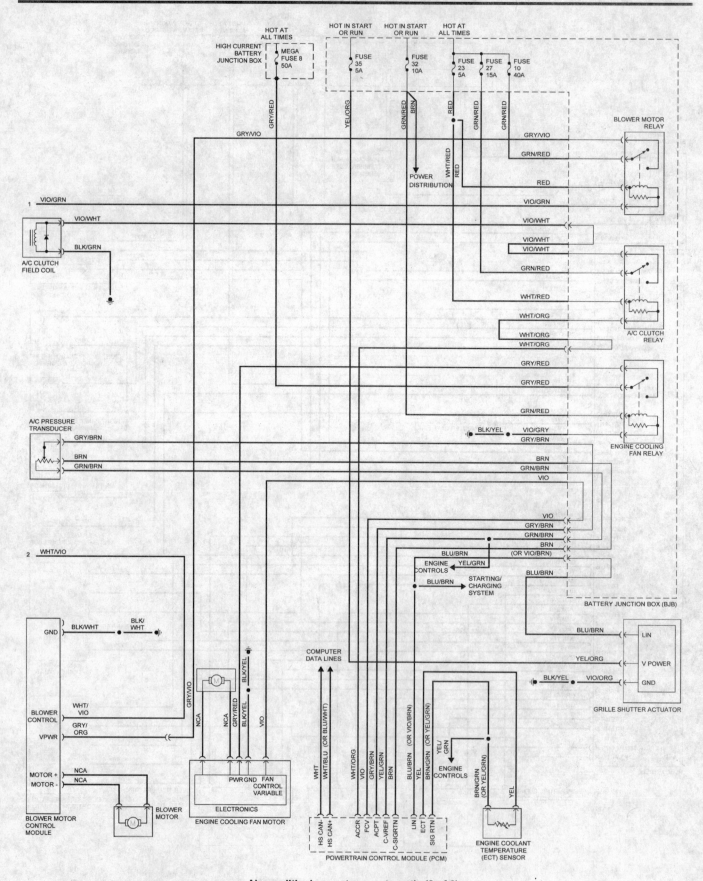

Air conditioning system - automatic (2 of 2)

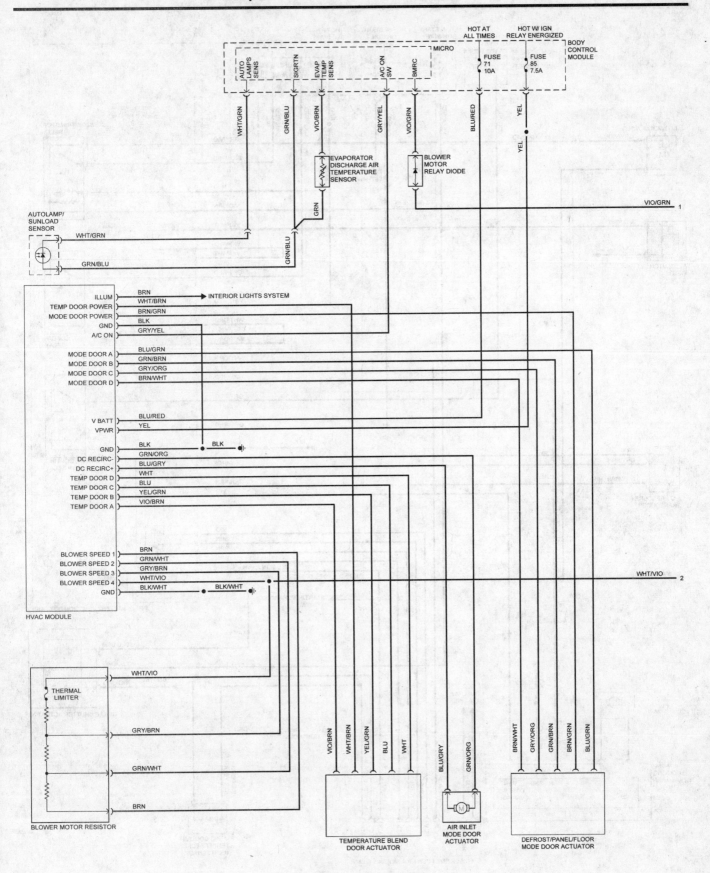

Air conditioning system - manual (1 of 2)

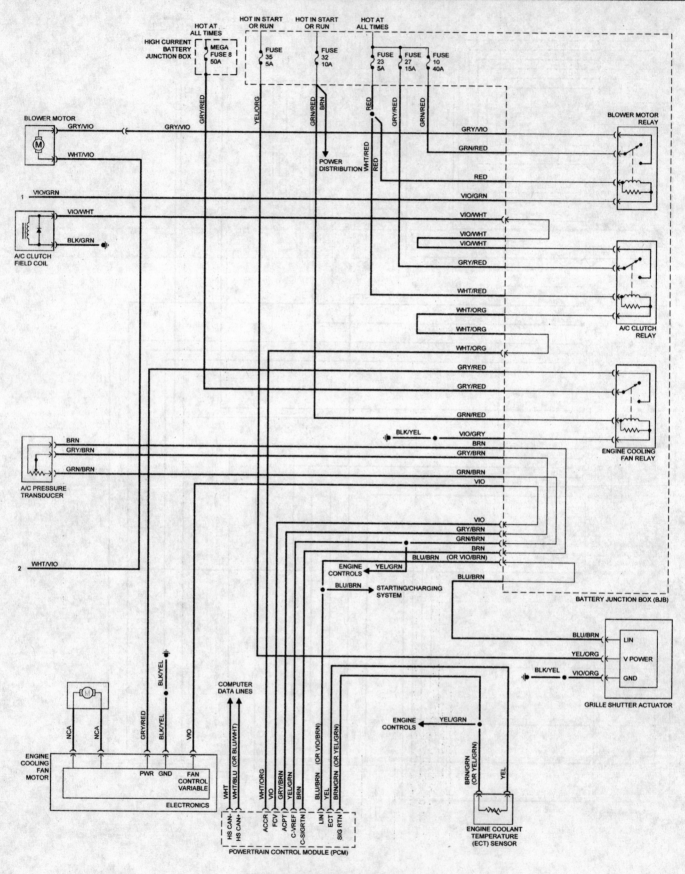

Air conditioning system - manual (2 of 2)

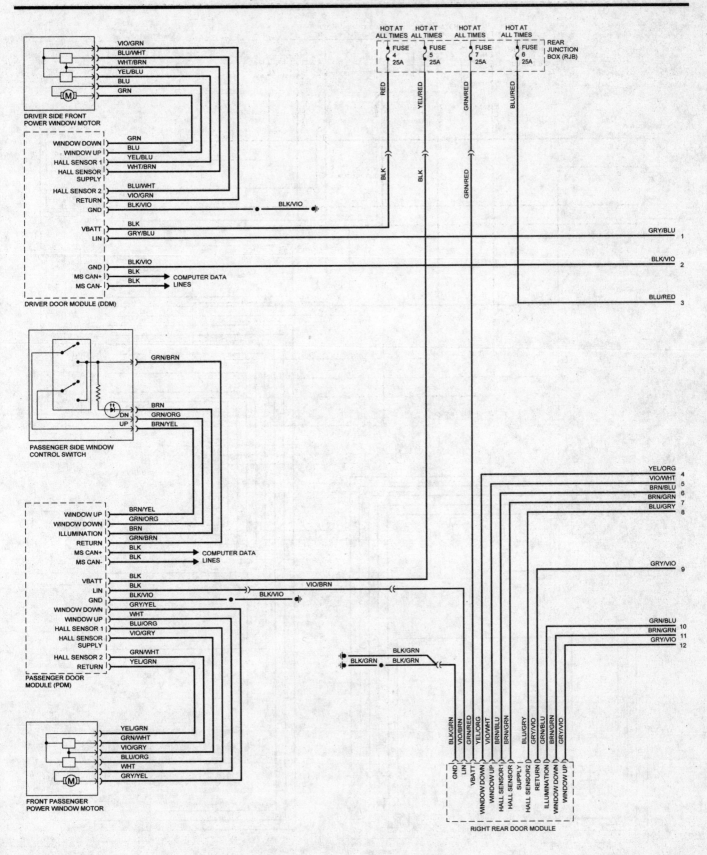

Power windows with door module (1 of 2)

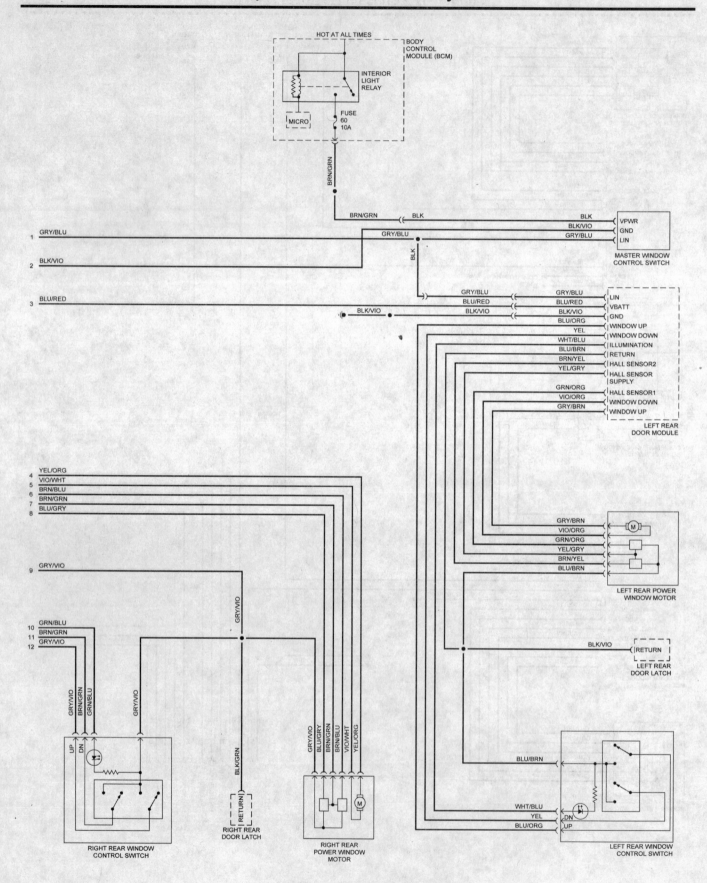

Power windows with door module (2 of 2)

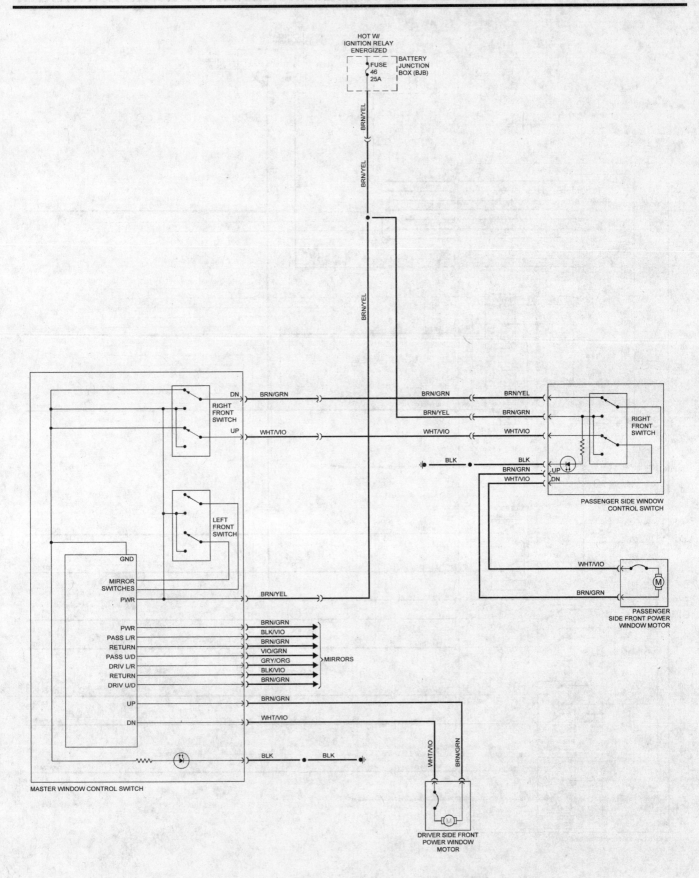

Power windows without door module or rear power windows

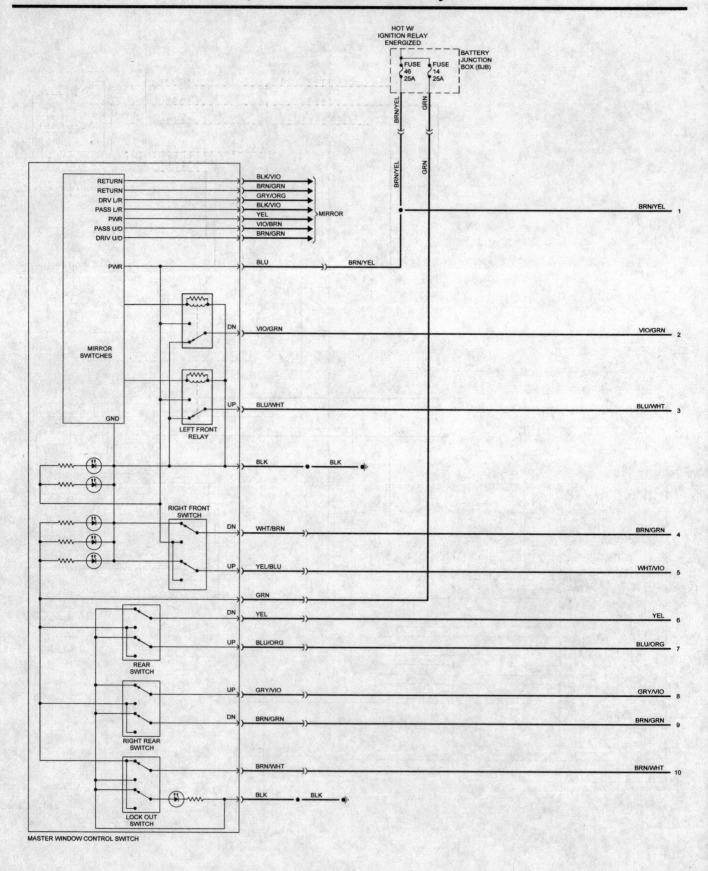

Power windows without door module with rear power windows (1 of 2)

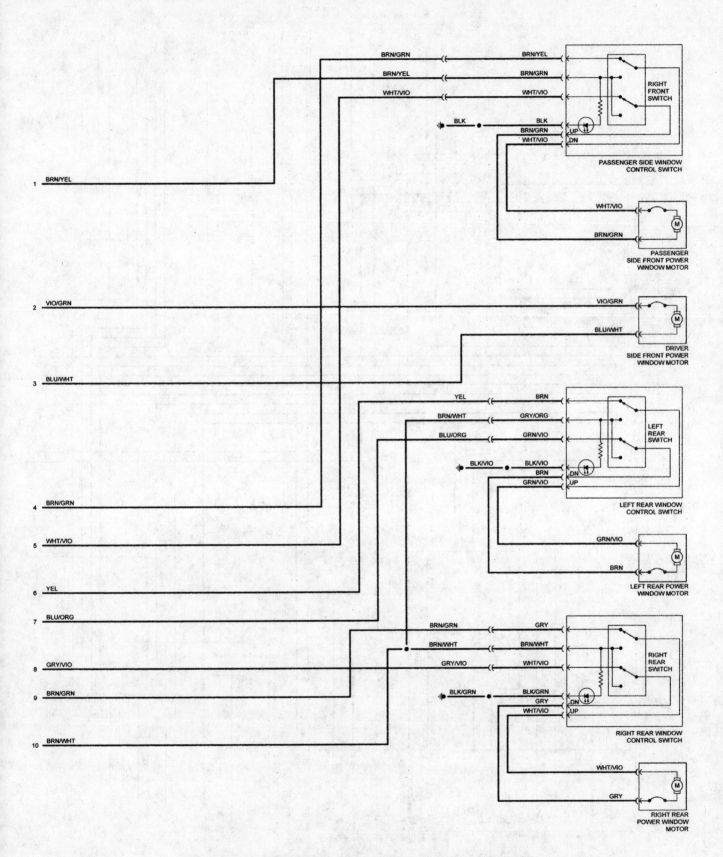

Power windows without door module with rear power windows (2 of 2)

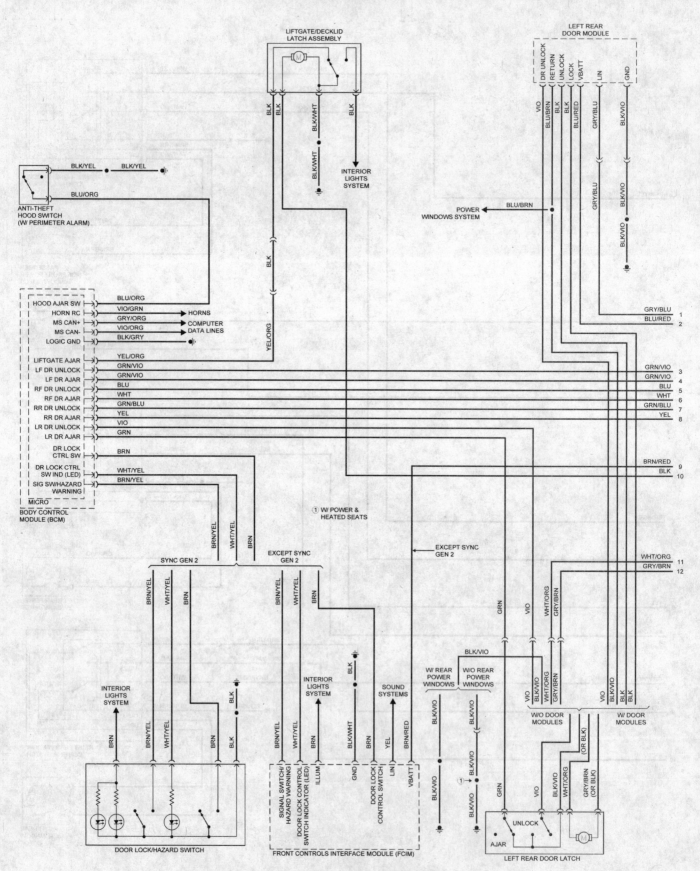

Power door locks without intelligent access (1 of 3)

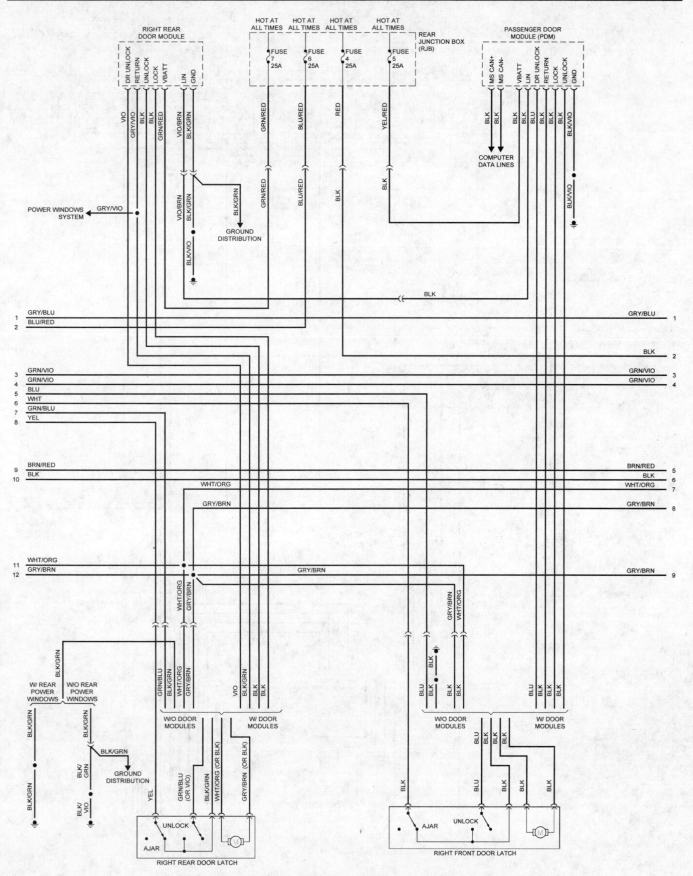

Power door locks without intelligent access (2 of 3)

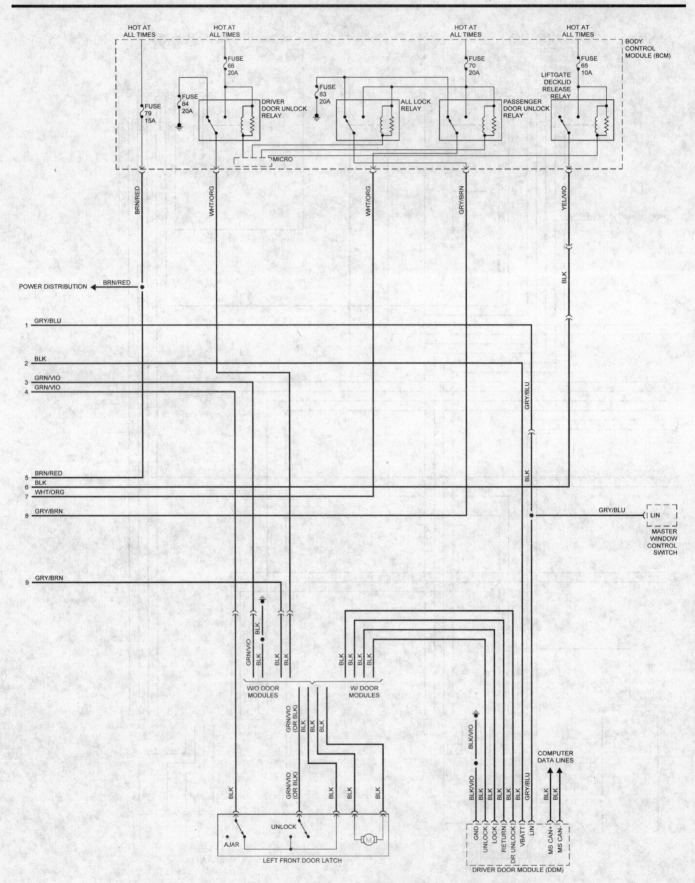

Power door locks without intelligent access (3 of 3)

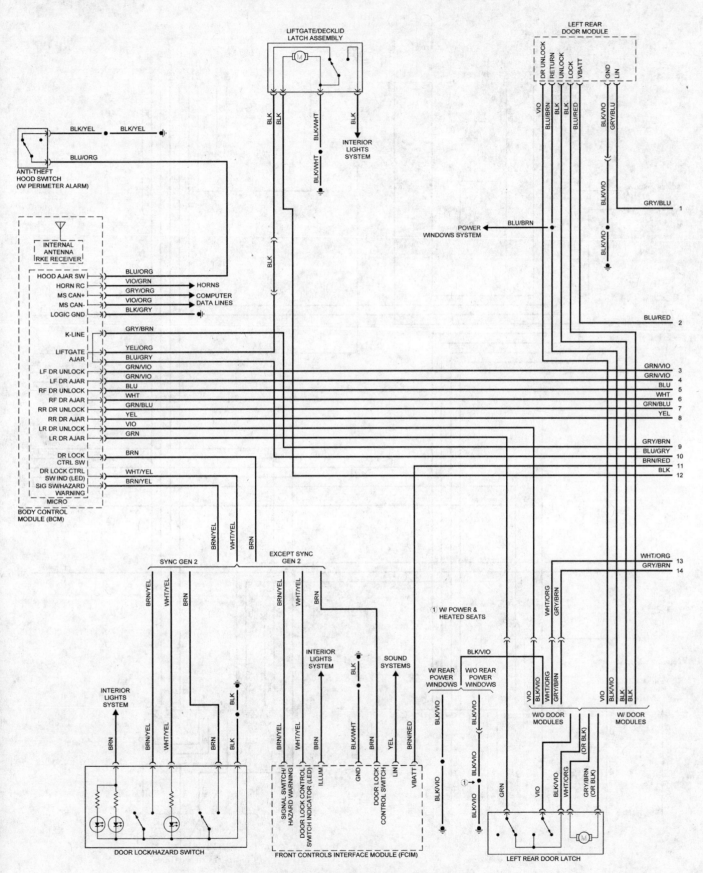

Power door locks with intelligent access (1 of 5)

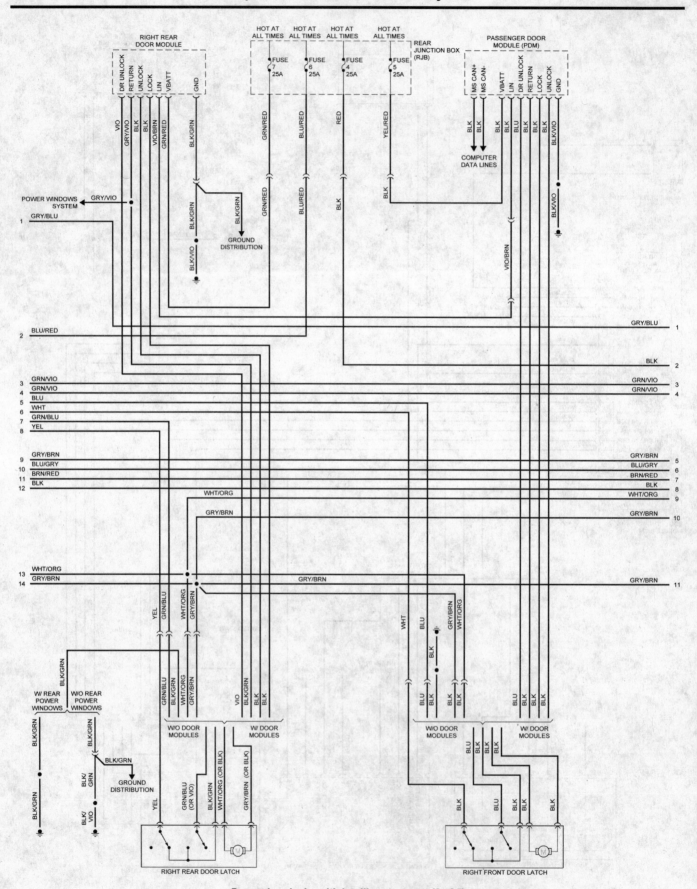

Power door locks with intelligent access (2 of 5)

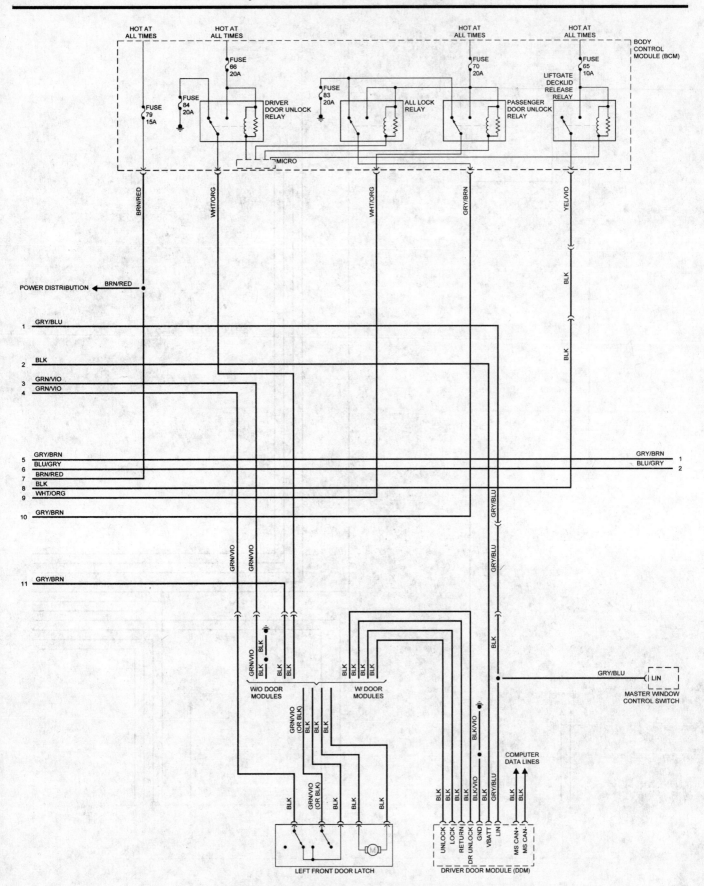

Power door locks with intelligent access (3 of 5)

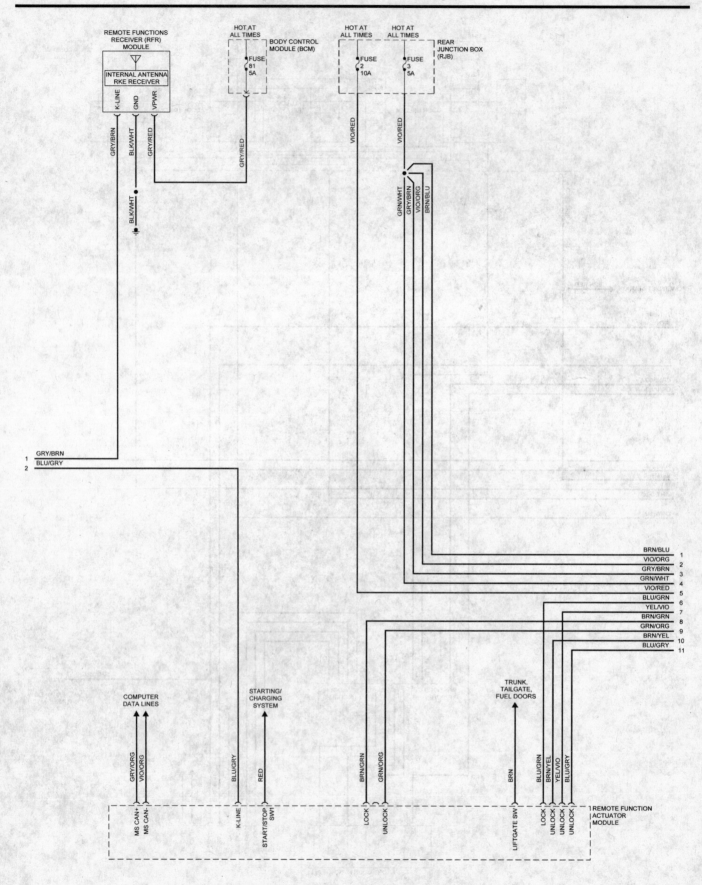

Power door locks with intelligent access (4 of 5)

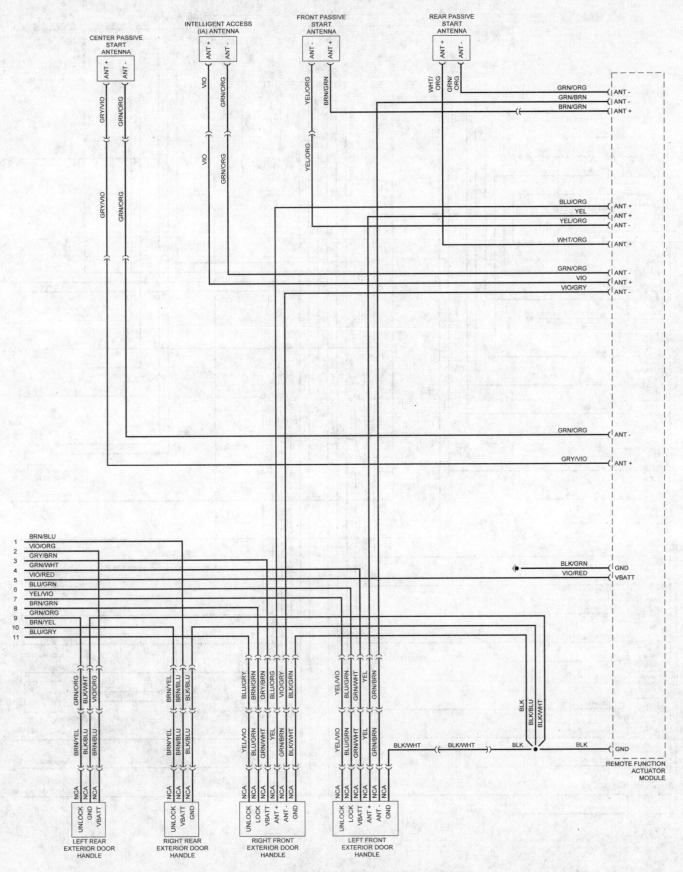

Power door locks with intelligent access (5 of 5)

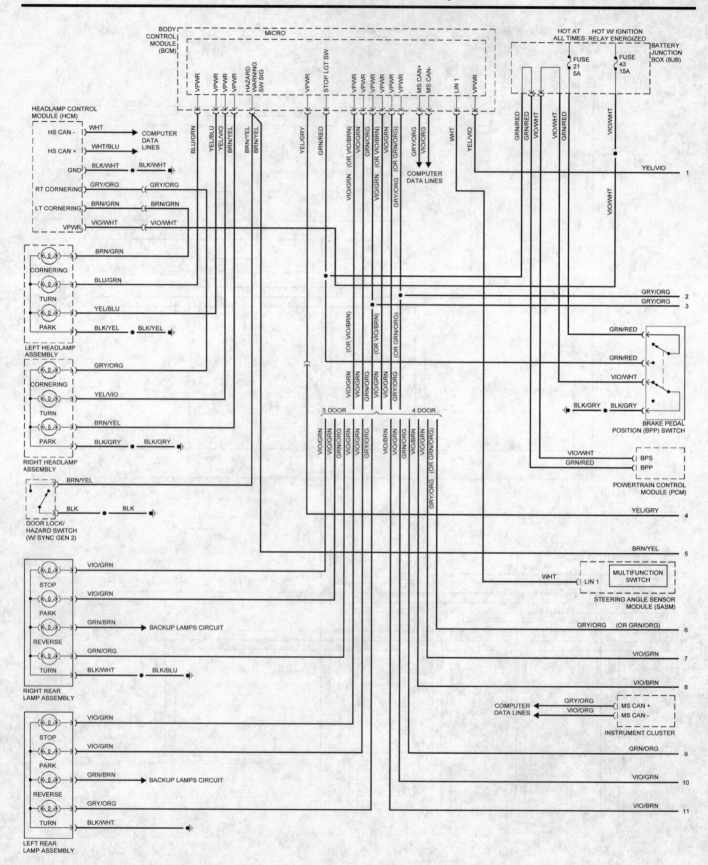

Exterior lights (1 of 2)

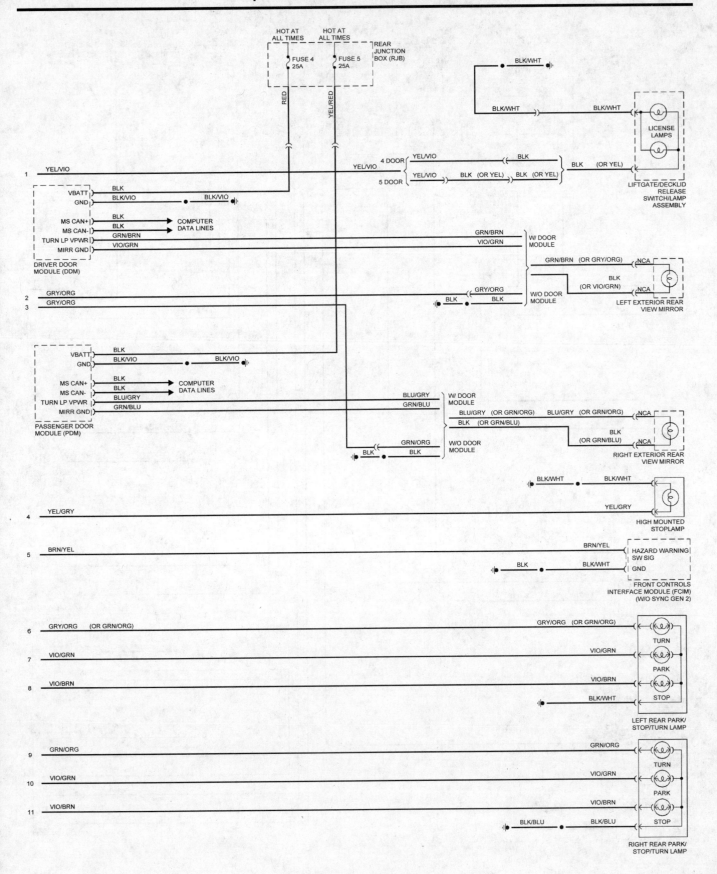

Exterior lights (2 of 2)

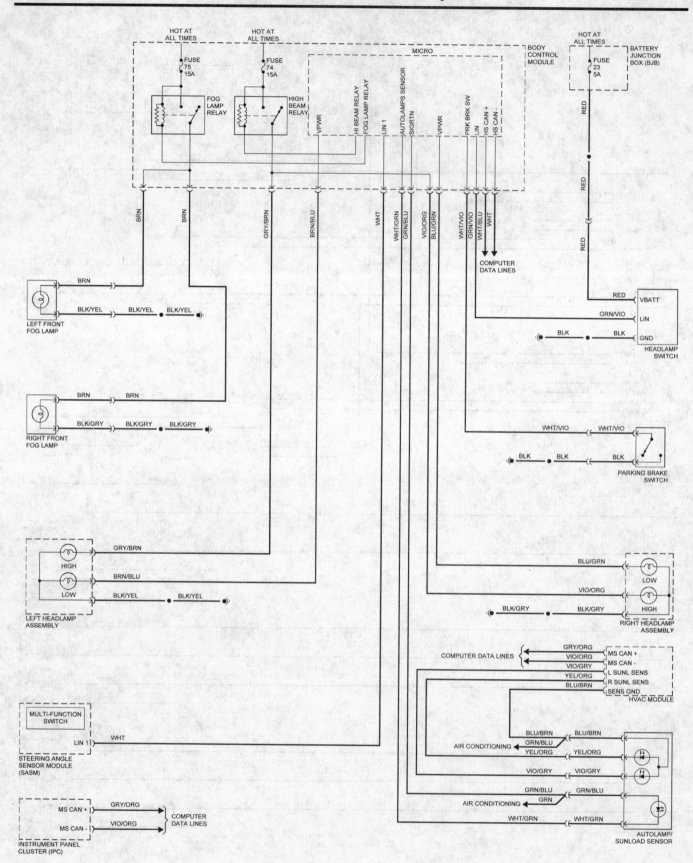

Headlights - without HID

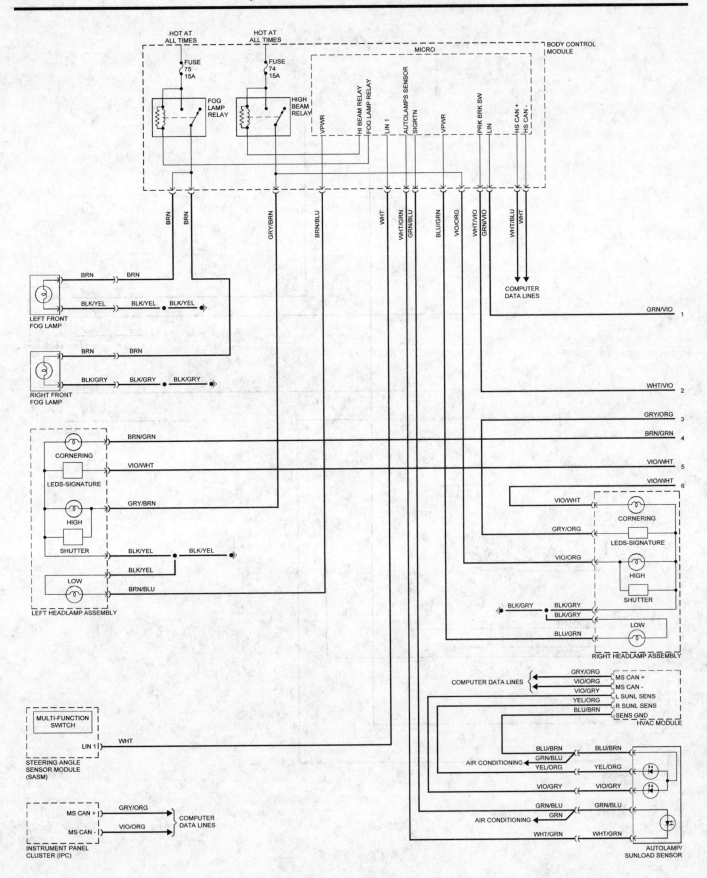

Headlights - with HID (1 of 2)

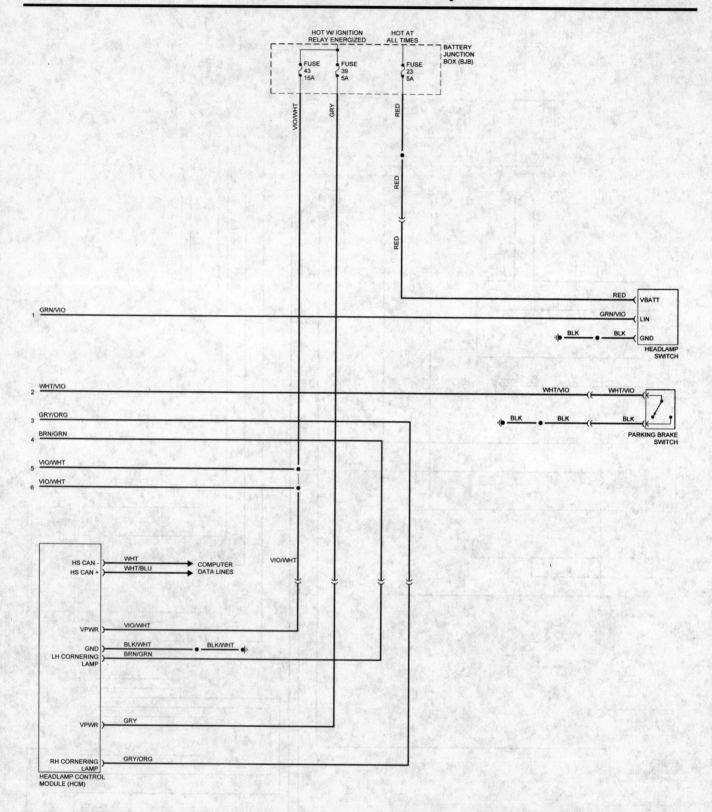

Headlights - with HID (2 of 2)

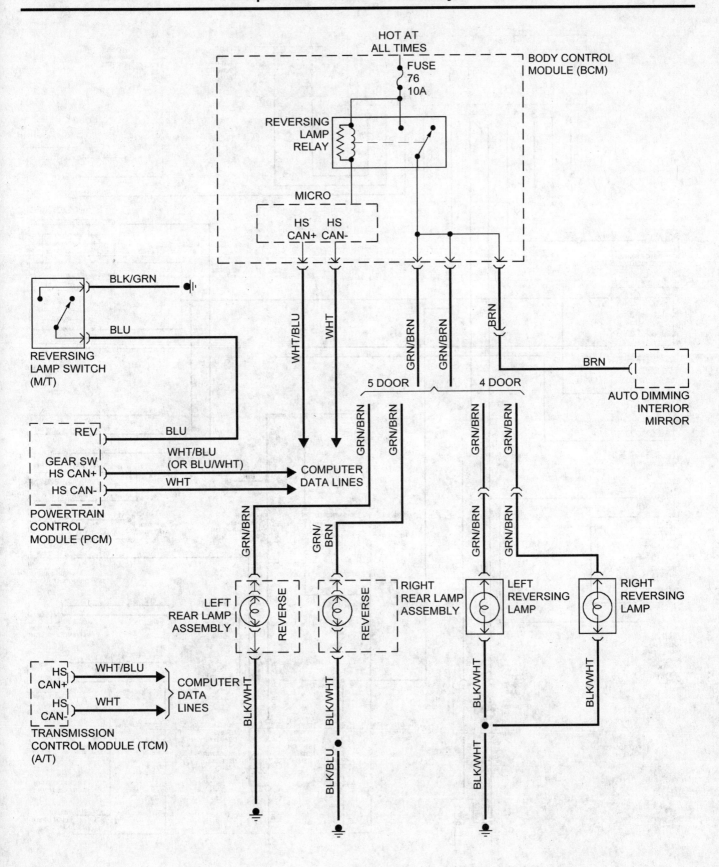

Backup lights

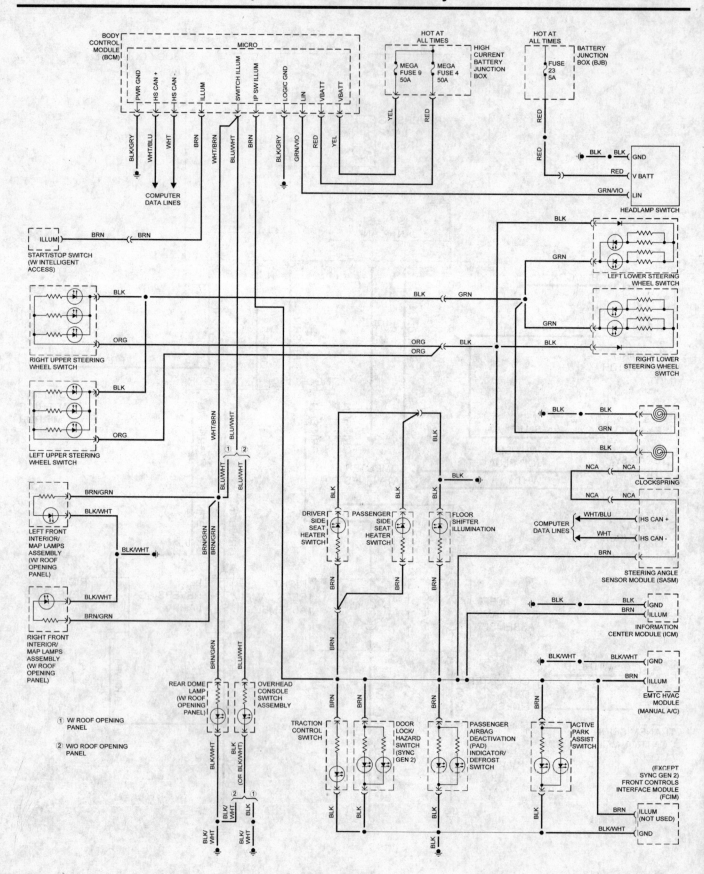

Instrument illumination circuit

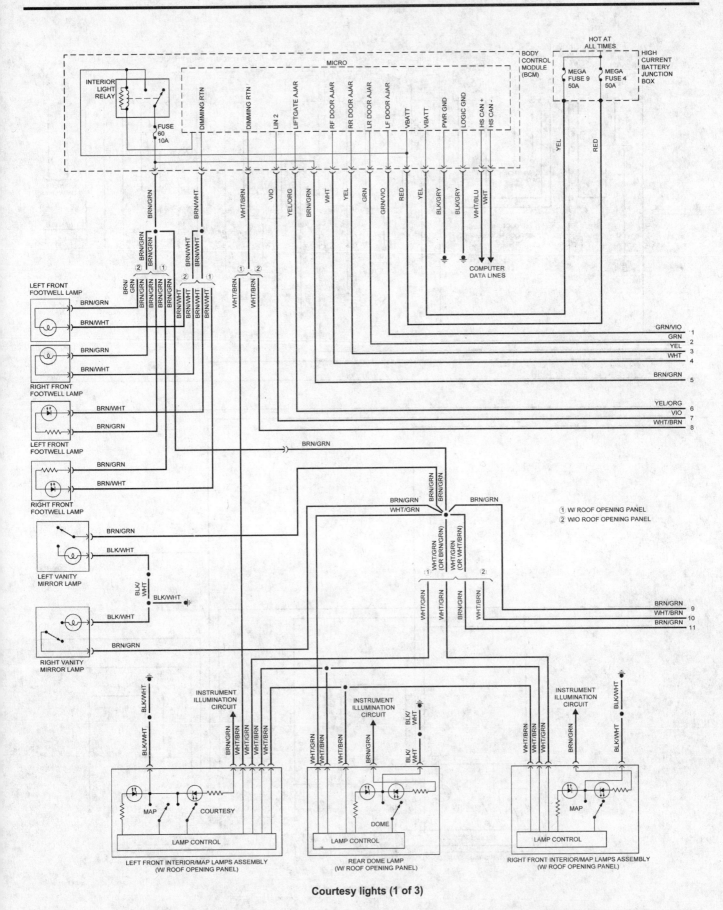

Courtesy lights (1 of 3)

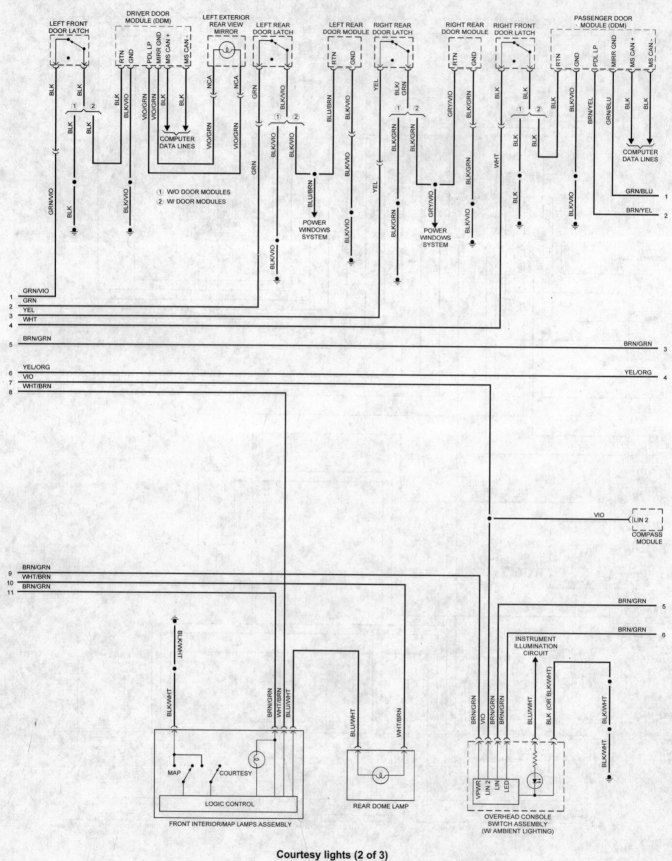

Courtesy lights (2 of 3)

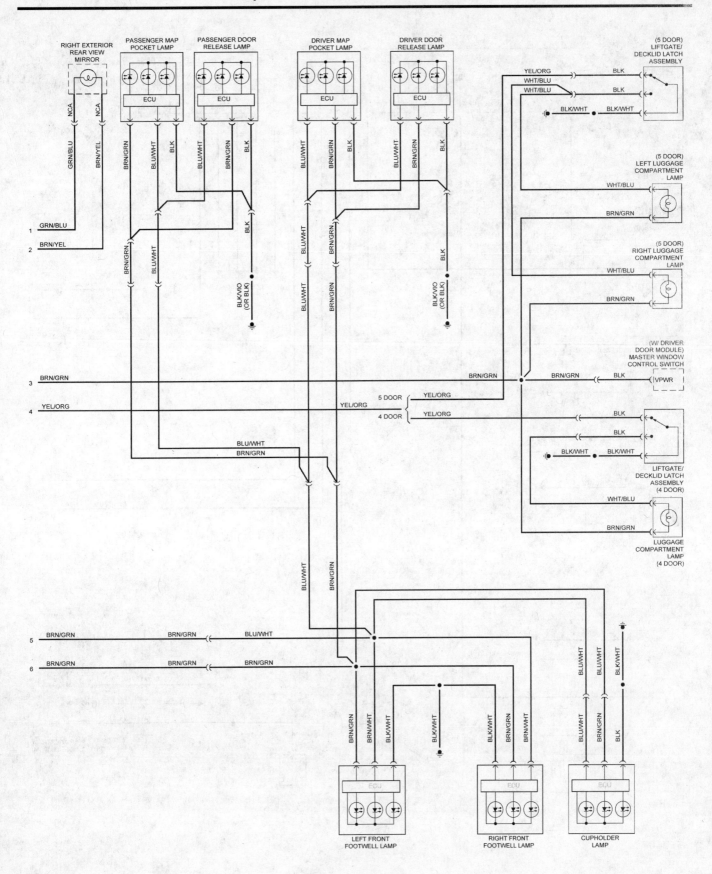

Courtesy lights (3 of 3)

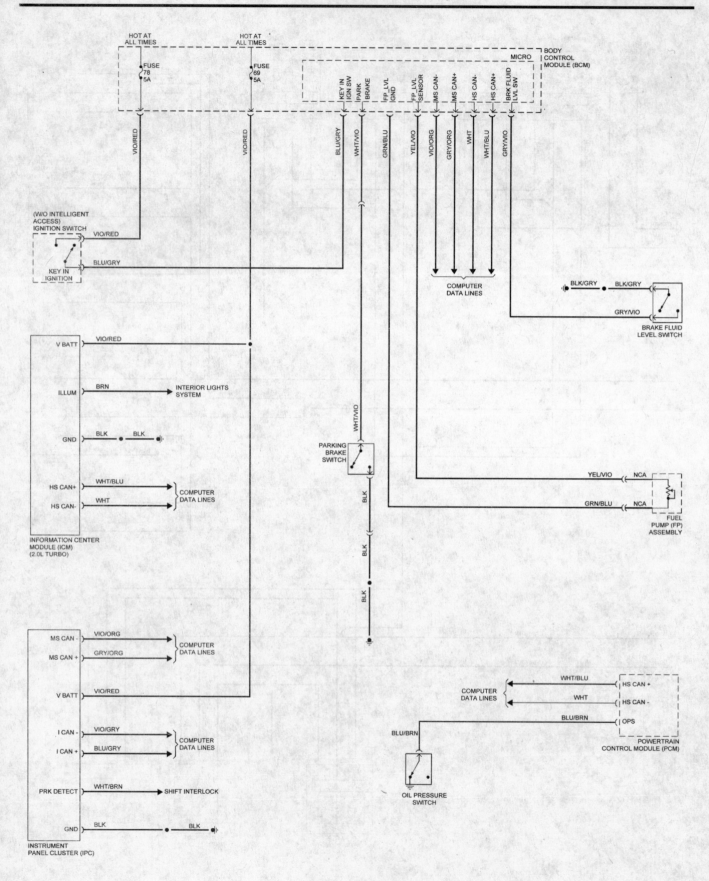

Warning system

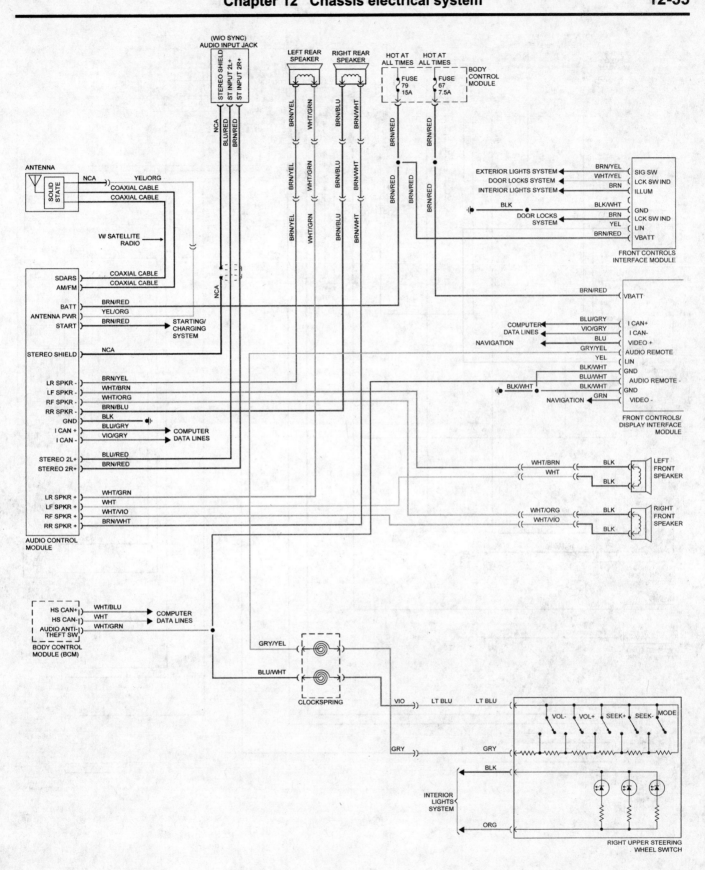

Audio system

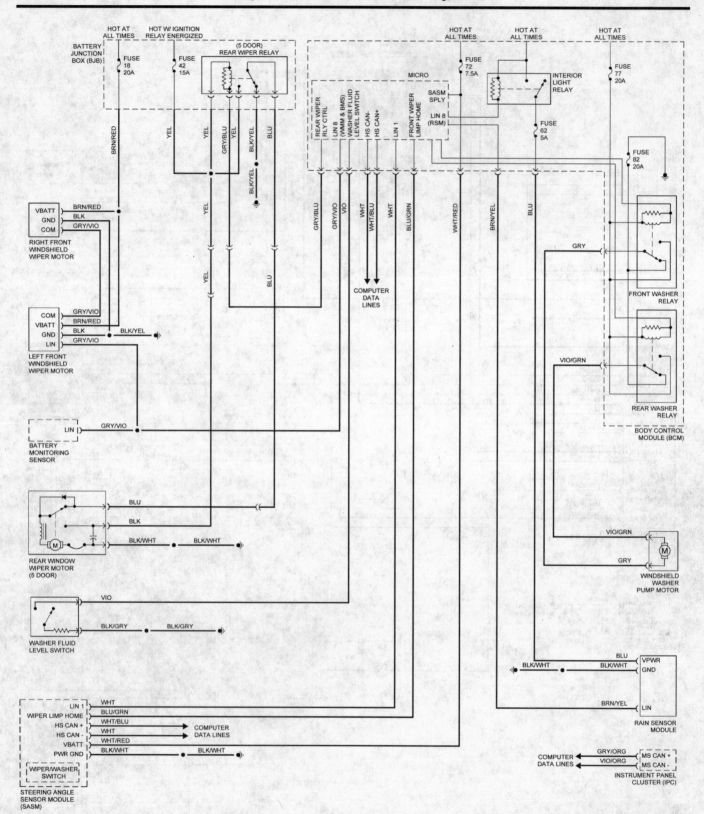

Wipers

Notes

Notes

Index

Notes

Haynes Automotive Manuals

NOTE: If you do not see a listing for your vehicle, consult your local Haynes dealer for the latest product information.

ACURA
- **12020 Integra** '86 thru '89 **& Legend** '86 thru '90
- **12021 Integra** '90 thru '93 **& Legend** '91 thru '95
  - **Integra** '94 thru '00 - *see HONDA Civic (42025)*
  - **MDX** '01 thru '07 - *see HONDA Pilot (42037)*
- **12050 Acura TL** all models '99 thru '08

AMC
- **Jeep CJ** - *see JEEP (50020)*
- **14020 Mid-size models** '70 thru '83
- **14025 (Renault) Alliance & Encore** '83 thru '87

AUDI
- **15020 4000** all models '80 thru '87
- **15025 5000** all models '77 thru '83
- **15026 5000** all models '84 thru '88
  - **Audi A4** '96 thru '01 - *see VW Passat (96023)*
- **15030 Audi A4** '02 thru '08

AUSTIN-HEALEY
- **Sprite** - *see MG Midget (66015)*

BMW
- **18020 3/5 Series** '82 thru '92
- **18021 3-Series** incl. Z3 models '92 thru '98
- **18022 3-Series** incl. Z4 models '99 thru '05
- **18023 3-Series** '06 thru '10
- **18025 320i** all 4 cyl models '75 thru '83
- **18050 1500 thru 2002** except Turbo '59 thru '77

BUICK
- **19010 Buick Century** '97 thru '05
  - **Century** (front-wheel drive) - *see GM (38005)*
- **19020 Buick, Oldsmobile & Pontiac Full-size (Front-wheel drive)** '85 thru '05
  - **Buick** Electra, LeSabre and Park Avenue; **Oldsmobile** Delta 88 Royale, Ninety Eight and Regency; **Pontiac** Bonneville
- **19025 Buick, Oldsmobile & Pontiac Full-size (Rear wheel drive)** '70 thru '90
  - **Buick** Estate, Electra, LeSabre, Limited, **Oldsmobile** Custom Cruiser, Delta 88, Ninety-eight, **Pontiac** Bonneville, Catalina, Grandville, Parisienne
- **19030 Mid-size Regal & Century** all rear-drive models with V6, V8 and Turbo '74 thru '87
  - **Regal** - *see GENERAL MOTORS (38010)*
  - **Riviera** - *see GENERAL MOTORS (38030)*
  - **Roadmaster** - *see CHEVROLET (24046)*
  - **Skyhawk** - *see GENERAL MOTORS (38015)*
  - **Skylark** - *see GM (38020, 38025)*
  - **Somerset** - *see GENERAL MOTORS (38025)*

CADILLAC
- **21015 CTS & CTS-V** '03 thru '12
- **21030 Cadillac Rear Wheel Drive** '70 thru '93
  - **Cimarron** - *see GENERAL MOTORS (38015)*
  - **DeVille** - *see GM (38031 & 38032)*
  - **Eldorado** - *see GM (38030 & 38031)*
  - **Fleetwood** - *see GM (38031)*
  - **Seville** - *see GM (38030, 38031 & 38032)*

CHEVROLET
- **10305 Chevrolet Engine Overhaul Manual**
- **24010 Astro & GMC Safari Mini-vans** '85 thru '05
- **24015 Camaro V8** all models '70 thru '81
- **24016 Camaro** all models '82 thru '92
- **24017 Camaro & Firebird** '93 thru '02
  - **Cavalier** - *see GENERAL MOTORS (38016)*
  - **Celebrity** - *see GENERAL MOTORS (38005)*
- **24020 Chevelle, Malibu & El Camino** '69 thru '87
- **24024 Chevette & Pontiac T1000** '76 thru '87
  - **Citation** - *see GENERAL MOTORS (38020)*
- **24027 Colorado & GMC Canyon** '04 thru '10
- **24032 Corsica/Beretta** all models '87 thru '96
- **24040 Corvette** all V8 models '68 thru '82
- **24041 Corvette** all models '84 thru '96
- **24045 Full-size Sedans** Caprice, Impala, Biscayne, Bel Air & Wagons '69 thru '90
- **24046 Impala SS & Caprice and Buick Roadmaster** '91 thru '96
  - **Impala** '00 thru '05 - *see LUMINA (24048)*
- **24047 Impala & Monte Carlo** all models '06 thru '11
  - **Lumina** '90 thru '94 - *see GM (38010)*
- **24048 Lumina & Monte Carlo** '95 thru '05
  - **Lumina APV** - *see GM (38035)*
- **24050 Luv Pick-up** all 2WD & 4WD '72 thru '82
  - **Malibu** '97 thru '00 - *see GM (38026)*
- **24055 Monte Carlo** '70 thru '88
  - **Monte Carlo** '95 thru '01 - *see LUMINA (24048)*
- **24059 Nova** all V8 models '69 thru '79
- **24060 Nova and Geo Prizm** '85 thru '92
- **24064 Pick-ups** '67 thru '87 - Chevrolet & GMC
- **24065 Pick-ups** '88 thru '98 - Chevrolet & GMC
- **24066 Pick-ups** '99 thru '06 - Chevrolet & GMC
- **24067 Chevrolet Silverado & GMC Sierra** '07 thru '12
- **24070 S-10 & S-15 Pick-ups** '82 thru '93, **Blazer & Jimmy** '83 thru '94,
- **24071 S-10 & Sonoma Pick-ups** '94 thru '04, including **Blazer, Jimmy & Hombre**
- **24072 Chevrolet TrailBlazer, GMC Envoy & Oldsmobile Bravada** '02 thru '09
- **24075 Sprint** '85 thru '88 **& Geo Metro** '89 thru '01
- **24080 Vans - Chevrolet & GMC** '68 thru '96
- **24081 Chevrolet Express & GMC Savana** Full-size Vans '96 thru '10

CHRYSLER
- **10310 Chrysler Engine Overhaul Manual**
- **25015 Chrysler Cirrus, Dodge Stratus, Plymouth Breeze** '95 thru '00
- **25020 Full-size Front-Wheel Drive** '88 thru '93
  - **K-Cars** - *see DODGE Aries (30008)*
  - **Laser** - *see DODGE Daytona (30030)*
- **25025 Chrysler LHS, Concorde, New Yorker, Dodge Intrepid, Eagle Vision,** '93 thru '97
- **25026 Chrysler LHS, Concorde, 300M, Dodge Intrepid,** '98 thru '04
- **25027 Chrysler 300, Dodge Charger & Magnum** '05 thru '09
- **25030 Chrysler & Plymouth Mid-size** front wheel drive '82 thru '95
  - **Rear-wheel Drive** - *see Dodge (30050)*
- **25035 PT Cruiser** all models '01 thru '10
- **25040 Chrysler Sebring** '95 thru '06, **Dodge Stratus** '01 thru '06, **Dodge Avenger** '95 thru '00

DATSUN
- **28005 200SX** all models '80 thru '83
- **28007 B-210** all models '73 thru '78
- **28009 210** all models '79 thru '82
- **28012 240Z, 260Z & 280Z Coupe** '70 thru '78
- **28014 280ZX Coupe & 2+2** '79 thru '83
  - **300ZX** - *see NISSAN (72010)*
- **28018 510 & PL521 Pick-up** '68 thru '73
- **28020 510** all models '78 thru '81
- **28022 620 Series Pick-up** all models '73 thru '79
  - **720 Series Pick-up** - *see NISSAN (72030)*
- **28025 810/Maxima** all gasoline models '77 thru '84

DODGE
- **400 & 600** - *see CHRYSLER (25030)*
- **30008 Aries & Plymouth Reliant** '81 thru '89
- **30010 Caravan & Plymouth Voyager** '84 thru '95
- **30011 Caravan & Plymouth Voyager** '96 thru '02
- **30012 Challenger/Plymouth Saporro** '78 thru '83
- **30013 Caravan, Chrysler Voyager, Town & Country** '03 thru '07
- **30016 Colt & Plymouth Champ** '78 thru '87
- **30020 Dakota Pick-ups** all models '87 thru '96
- **30021 Durango** '98 & '99, **Dakota** '97 thru '99
- **30022 Durango** '00 thru '03 **Dakota** '00 thru '04
- **30023 Durango** '04 thru '09, **Dakota** '05 thru '11
- **30025 Dart, Demon, Plymouth Barracuda, Duster & Valiant** 6 cyl models '67 thru '76
- **30030 Daytona & Chrysler Laser** '84 thru '89
  - **Intrepid** - *see CHRYSLER (25025, 25026)*
- **30034 Neon** all models '95 thru '99
- **30035 Omni & Plymouth Horizon** '78 thru '90
- **30036 Dodge and Plymouth Neon** '00 thru '05
- **30040 Pick-ups** all full-size models '74 thru '93
- **30041 Pick-ups** all full-size models '94 thru '01
- **30042 Pick-ups** full-size models '02 thru '08
- **30045 Ram 50/D50 Pick-ups & Raider and Plymouth Arrow Pick-ups** '79 thru '93
- **30050 Dodge/Plymouth/Chrysler RWD** '71 thru '89
- **30055 Shadow & Plymouth Sundance** '87 thru '94
- **30060 Spirit & Plymouth Acclaim** '89 thru '95
- **30065 Vans - Dodge & Plymouth** '71 thru '03

EAGLE
- **Talon** - *see MITSUBISHI (68030, 68031)*
- **Vision** - *see CHRYSLER (25025)*

FIAT
- **34010 124 Sport Coupe & Spider** '68 thru '78
- **34025 X1/9** all models '74 thru '80

FORD
- **10320 Ford Engine Overhaul Manual**
- **10355 Ford Automatic Transmission Overhaul**
- **11500 Mustang** '64-1/2 thru '70 Restoration Guide
- **36004 Aerostar Mini-vans** all models '86 thru '97
- **36006 Contour & Mercury Mystique** '95 thru '00
- **36008 Courier Pick-up** all models '72 thru '82
- **36012 Crown Victoria & Mercury Grand Marquis** '88 thru '10
- **36016 Escort/Mercury Lynx** all models '81 thru '90
- **36020 Escort/Mercury Tracer** '91 thru '02
- **36022 Escape & Mazda Tribute** '01 thru '11
- **36024 Explorer & Mazda Navajo** '91 thru '01
- **36025 Explorer/Mercury Mountaineer** '02 thru '10
- **36028 Fairmont & Mercury Zephyr** '78 thru '83
- **36030 Festiva & Aspire** '88 thru '97
- **36032 Fiesta** all models '77 thru '80
- **36034 Focus** all models '00 thru '11
- **36036 Ford & Mercury Full-size** '75 thru '87
- **36044 Ford & Mercury Mid-size** '75 thru '86
- **36045 Fusion & Mercury Milan** '06 thru '10
- **36048 Mustang V8** all models '64-1/2 thru '73
- **36049 Mustang II** 4 cyl, V6 & V8 models '74 thru '78
- **36050 Mustang & Mercury Capri** '79 thru '93
- **36051 Mustang** all models '94 thru '04
- **36052 Mustang** '05 thru '10
- **36054 Pick-ups & Bronco** '73 thru '79
- **36058 Pick-ups & Bronco** '80 thru '96
- **36059 F-150 & Expedition** '97 thru '09, **F-250** '97 thru '99 **& Lincoln Navigator** '98 thru '09
- **36060 Super Duty Pick-ups, Excursion** '99 thru '10
- **36061 F-150 full-size** '04 thru '10
- **36062 Pinto & Mercury Bobcat** '75 thru '80
- **36066 Probe** all models '89 thru '92
  - **Probe** '93 thru '97 - *see MAZDA 626 (61042)*
- **36070 Ranger/Bronco II** gasoline models '83 thru '92
- **36071 Ranger** '93 thru '10 **& Mazda Pick-ups** '94 thru '09
- **36074 Taurus & Mercury Sable** '86 thru '95
- **36075 Taurus & Mercury Sable** '96 thru '05
- **36078 Tempo & Mercury Topaz** '84 thru '94
- **36082 Thunderbird/Mercury Cougar** '83 thru '88
- **36086 Thunderbird/Mercury Cougar** '89 thru '97
- **36090 Vans** all V8 Econoline models '69 thru '91
- **36094 Vans** full size '92 thru '10
- **36097 Windstar Mini-van** '95 thru '07

GENERAL MOTORS
- **10360 GM Automatic Transmission Overhaul**
- **38005 Buick Century, Chevrolet Celebrity, Oldsmobile Cutlass Ciera & Pontiac 6000** all models '82 thru '96
- **38010 Buick Regal, Chevrolet Lumina, Oldsmobile Cutlass Supreme & Pontiac Grand Prix (FWD)** '88 thru '07
- **38015 Buick Skyhawk, Cadillac Cimarron, Chevrolet Cavalier, Oldsmobile Firenza & Pontiac J-2000 & Sunbird** '82 thru '94
- **38016 Chevrolet Cavalier & Pontiac Sunfire** '95 thru '05
- **38017 Chevrolet Cobalt & Pontiac G5** '05 thru '11
- **38020 Buick Skylark, Chevrolet Citation, Olds Omega, Pontiac Phoenix** '80 thru '85
- **38025 Buick Skylark & Somerset, Oldsmobile Achieva & Calais and Pontiac Grand Am** all models '85 thru '98
- **38026 Chevrolet Malibu, Olds Alero & Cutlass, Pontiac Grand Am** '97 thru '03
- **38027 Chevrolet Malibu** '04 thru '10
- **38030 Cadillac Eldorado, Seville, Oldsmobile Toronado, Buick Riviera** '71 thru '85
- **38031 Cadillac Eldorado & Seville, DeVille, Fleetwood & Olds Toronado, Buick Riviera** '86 thru '93
- **38032 Cadillac DeVille** '94 thru '05 & **Seville** '92 thru '04 **Cadillac DTS** '06 thru '10
- **38035 Chevrolet Lumina APV, Olds Silhouette & Pontiac Trans Sport** all models '90 thru '96
- **38036 Chevrolet Venture, Olds Silhouette, Pontiac Trans Sport & Montana** '97 thru '05
  - **General Motors Full-size Rear-wheel Drive** - *see BUICK (19025)*
- **38040 Chevrolet Equinox** '05 thru '09 **Pontiac Torrent** '06 thru '09
- **38070 Chevrolet HHR** '06 thru '11

GEO
- **Metro** - *see CHEVROLET Sprint (24075)*
- **Prizm** - '85 thru '92 *see CHEVY (24060)*, '93 thru '02 *see TOYOTA Corolla (92036)*
- **40030 Storm** all models '90 thru '93
- **Tracker** - *see SUZUKI Samurai (90010)*

GMC
- **Vans & Pick-ups** - *see CHEVROLET*

HONDA
- **42010 Accord CVCC** all models '76 thru '83
- **42011 Accord** all models '84 thru '89
- **42012 Accord** all models '90 thru '93
- **42013 Accord** all models '94 thru '97
- **42014 Accord** all models '98 thru '02
- **42015 Accord** all models '03 thru '07
- **42020 Civic 1200** all models '73 thru '79
- **42021 Civic 1300 & 1500 CVCC** '80 thru '83
- **42022 Civic 1500 CVCC** all models '75 thru '79

(Continued on other side)

Haynes North America, Inc., 861 Lawrence Drive, Newbury Park, CA 91320-1514 • (805) 498-6703 • http://www.haynes.com

Haynes Automotive Manuals (continued)

NOTE: If you do not see a listing for your vehicle, consult your local Haynes dealer for the latest product information.

42023 **Civic** all models '84 thru '91
42024 **Civic & del Sol** '92 thru '95
42025 **Civic** '96 thru '00, **CR-V** '97 thru '01,
    Acura Integra '94 thru '00
42026 **Civic** '01 thru '10, **CR-V** '02 thru '09
42035 **Odyssey** all models '99 thru '10
    Passport - *see ISUZU Rodeo (47017)*
42037 **Honda Pilot** '03 thru '07, **Acura MDX** '01 thru '07
42040 **Prelude CVCC** all models '79 thru '89

HYUNDAI
43010 **Elantra** all models '96 thru '10
43015 **Excel & Accent** all models '86 thru '09
43050 **Santa Fe** all models '01 thru '06
43055 **Sonata** all models '99 thru '08

INFINITI
    G35 '03 thru '08 - *see NISSAN 350Z (72011)*

ISUZU
    Hombre - *see CHEVROLET S-10 (24071)*
47017 **Rodeo, Amigo & Honda Passport** '89 thru '02
47020 **Trooper & Pick-up** '81 thru '93

JAGUAR
49010 **XJ6** all 6 cyl models '68 thru '86
49011 **XJ6** all models '88 thru '94
49015 **XJ12 & XJS** all 12 cyl models '72 thru '85

JEEP
50010 **Cherokee, Comanche & Wagoneer Limited**
    all models '84 thru '01
50020 **CJ** all models '49 thru '86
50025 **Grand Cherokee** all models '93 thru '04
50026 **Grand Cherokee** '05 thru '09
50029 **Grand Wagoneer & Pick-up** '72 thru '91
    Grand Wagoneer '84 thru '91, **Cherokee &**
    Wagoneer '72 thru '83, **Pick-up** '72 thru '88
50030 **Wrangler** all models '87 thru '11
50035 **Liberty** '02 thru '07

KIA
54050 **Optima** '01 thru '10
54070 **Sephia** '94 thru '01, **Spectra** '00 thru '09,
    Sportage '05 thru '10

LEXUS
    ES 300/330 - *see TOYOTA Camry (92007) (92008)*
    RX 330 - *see TOYOTA Highlander (92095)*

LINCOLN
    Navigator - *see FORD Pick-up (36059)*
59010 **Rear-Wheel Drive** all models '70 thru '10

MAZDA
61010 **GLC Hatchback** (rear-wheel drive) '77 thru '83
61011 **GLC** (front-wheel drive) '81 thru '85
61012 **Mazda3** '04 thru '11
61015 **323 & Protogé** '90 thru '03
61016 **MX-5 Miata** '90 thru '09
61020 **MPV** all models '89 thru '98
    Navajo - *see Ford Explorer (36024)*
61030 **Pick-ups** '72 thru '93
    Pick-ups '94 thru '00 - *see Ford Ranger (36071)*
61035 **RX-7** all models '79 thru '85
61036 **RX-7** all models '86 thru '91
61040 **626** (rear-wheel drive) all models '79 thru '82
61041 **626/MX-6** (front-wheel drive) '83 thru '92
61042 **626, MX-6/Ford Probe** '93 thru '02
61043 **Mazda6** '03 thru '11

MERCEDES-BENZ
63012 **123 Series Diesel** '76 thru '85
63015 **190 Series four-cyl gas models, '84 thru '88**
63020 **230/250/280 6 cyl sohc models** '68 thru '72
63025 **280 123 Series gasoline models** '77 thru '81
63030 **350 & 450** all models '71 thru '80
63040 **C-Class:** C230/C240/C280/C320/C350 '01 thru '07

MERCURY
64200 **Villager & Nissan Quest** '93 thru '01
    All other titles, see FORD Listing.

MG
66010 **MGB** Roadster & GT Coupe '62 thru '80
66015 **MG Midget, Austin Healey Sprite** '58 thru '80

MINI
67020 **Mini** '02 thru '11

MITSUBISHI
68020 **Cordia, Tredia, Galant, Precis &**
    Mirage '83 thru '93
68030 **Eclipse, Eagle Talon & Ply. Laser** '90 thru '94
68031 **Eclipse** '95 thru '05, **Eagle Talon** '95 thru '98
68035 **Galant** '94 thru '10
68040 **Pick-up** '83 thru '96 & **Montero** '83 thru '93

NISSAN
72010 **300ZX** all models including Turbo '84 thru '89
72011 **350Z & Infiniti G35** all models '03 thru '08
72015 **Altima** all models '93 thru '06
72016 **Altima** '07 thru '10
72020 **Maxima** all models '85 thru '92
72021 **Maxima** all models '93 thru '04
72025 **Murano** '03 thru '10
72030 **Pick-ups** '80 thru '97 **Pathfinder** '87 thru '95
72031 **Frontier Pick-up, Xterra, Pathfinder** '96 thru '04
72032 **Frontier & Xterra** '05 thru '11
72040 **Pulsar** all models '83 thru '86
    Quest - *see MERCURY Villager (64200)*
72050 **Sentra** all models '82 thru '94
72051 **Sentra & 200SX** all models '95 thru '06
72060 **Stanza** all models '82 thru '90
72070 **Titan pick-ups** '04 thru '10 **Armada** '05 thru '10

OLDSMOBILE
73015 **Cutlass** V6 & V8 gas models '74 thru '88
    For other OLDSMOBILE titles, see BUICK,
    CHEVROLET or GENERAL MOTORS listing.

PLYMOUTH
    For PLYMOUTH titles, see DODGE listing.

PONTIAC
79008 **Fiero** all models '84 thru '88
79018 **Firebird** V8 models except Turbo '70 thru '81
79019 **Firebird** all models '82 thru '92
79025 **G6** all models '05 thru '09
79040 **Mid-size Rear-wheel Drive** '70 thru '87
    Vibe '03 thru '11 - *see TOYOTA Matrix (92060)*
    For other PONTIAC titles, see BUICK,
    CHEVROLET or GENERAL MOTORS listing.

PORSCHE
80020 **911** except Turbo & Carrera 4 '65 thru '89
80025 **914** all 4 cyl models '69 thru '76
80030 **924** all models including Turbo '76 thru '82
80035 **944** all models including Turbo '83 thru '89

RENAULT
    Alliance & Encore - *see AMC (14020)*

SAAB
84010 **900** all models including Turbo '79 thru '88

SATURN
87010 **Saturn** all S-series models '91 thru '02
87011 **Saturn Ion** '03 thru '07
87020 **Saturn** all L-series models '00 thru '04
87040 **Saturn VUE** '02 thru '07

SUBARU
89002 **1100, 1300, 1400 & 1600** '71 thru '79
89003 **1600 & 1800** 2WD & 4WD '80 thru '94
89100 **Legacy** all models '90 thru '99
89101 **Legacy & Forester** '00 thru '06

SUZUKI
90010 **Samurai/Sidekick & Geo Tracker** '86 thru '01

TOYOTA
92005 **Camry** all models '83 thru '91
92006 **Camry** all models '92 thru '96
92007 **Camry, Avalon, Solara, Lexus ES 300** '97 thru '01
92008 **Toyota Camry, Avalon and Solara and**
    Lexus ES 300/330 all models '02 thru '06
92009 **Camry** '07 thru '11
92015 **Celica Rear Wheel Drive** '71 thru '85
92020 **Celica Front Wheel Drive** '86 thru '99
92025 **Celica Supra** all models '79 thru '92
92030 **Corolla** all models '75 thru '79
92032 **Corolla** all rear wheel drive models '80 thru '87
92035 **Corolla** all front wheel drive models '84 thru '92
92036 **Corolla & Geo Prizm** '93 thru '02
92037 **Corolla** models '03 thru '11
92040 **Corolla Tercel** all models '80 thru '82
92045 **Corona** all models '74 thru '82
92050 **Cressida** all models '78 thru '82
92055 **Land Cruiser FJ40, 43, 45, 55** '68 thru '82
92056 **Land Cruiser FJ60, 62, 80, FZJ80** '80 thru '96
92060 **Matrix & Pontiac Vibe** '03 thru '11
92065 **MR2** all models '85 thru '87
92070 **Pick-up** all models '69 thru '78
92075 **Pick-up** all models '79 thru '95
92076 **Tacoma, 4Runner, & T100** '93 thru '04
92077 **Tacoma** all models '05 thru '09
92078 **Tundra** '00 thru '06 & **Sequoia** '01 thru '07
92079 **4Runner** all models '03 thru '09
92080 **Previa** all models '91 thru '95
92081 **Prius** all models '01 thru '08
92082 **RAV4** all models '96 thru '10
92085 **Tercel** all models '87 thru '94
92090 **Sienna** all models '98 thru '09
92095 **Highlander & Lexus RX-330** '99 thru '07

TRIUMPH
94007 **Spitfire** all models '62 thru '81
94010 **TR7** all models '75 thru '81

VW
96008 **Beetle & Karmann Ghia** '54 thru '79
96009 **New Beetle** '98 thru '11
96016 **Rabbit, Jetta, Scirocco & Pick-up** gas
    models '75 thru '92 & Convertible '80 thru '92
96017 **Golf, GTI & Jetta** '93 thru '98, **Cabrio** '95 thru '02
96018 **Golf, GTI, Jetta** '99 thru '05
96019 **Jetta, Rabbit, GTI & Golf** '05 thru '11
96020 **Rabbit, Jetta & Pick-up** diesel '77 thru '84
96023 **Passat** '98 thru '05, **Audi A4** '96 thru '01
96030 **Transporter 1600** all models '68 thru '79
96035 **Transporter 1700, 1800 & 2000** '72 thru '79
96040 **Type 3 1500 & 1600** all models '63 thru '73
96045 **Vanagon** all air-cooled models '80 thru '83

VOLVO
97010 **120, 130 Series & 1800 Sports** '61 thru '73
97015 **140 Series** all models '66 thru '74
97020 **240 Series** all models '76 thru '93
97040 **740 & 760 Series** all models '82 thru '88
97050 **850 Series** all models '93 thru '97

TECHBOOK MANUALS
10205 **Automotive Computer Codes**
10206 **OBD-II & Electronic Engine Management**
10210 **Automotive Emissions Control Manual**
10215 **Fuel Injection Manual** '78 thru '85
10220 **Fuel Injection Manual** '86 thru '99
10225 **Holley Carburetor Manual**
10230 **Rochester Carburetor Manual**
10240 **Weber/Zenith/Stromberg/SU Carburetors**
10305 **Chevrolet Engine Overhaul Manual**
10310 **Chrysler Engine Overhaul Manual**
10320 **Ford Engine Overhaul Manual**
10330 **GM and Ford Diesel Engine Repair Manual**
10333 **Engine Performance Manual**
10340 **Small Engine Repair Manual, 5 HP & Less**
10341 **Small Engine Repair Manual, 5.5 - 20 HP**
10345 **Suspension, Steering & Driveline Manual**
10355 **Ford Automatic Transmission Overhaul**
10360 **GM Automatic Transmission Overhaul**
10405 **Automotive Body Repair & Painting**
10410 **Automotive Brake Manual**
10411 **Automotive Anti-lock Brake (ABS) Systems**
10415 **Automotive Detailing Manual**
10420 **Automotive Electrical Manual**
10425 **Automotive Heating & Air Conditioning**
10430 **Automotive Reference Manual & Dictionary**
10435 **Automotive Tools Manual**
10440 **Used Car Buying Guide**
10445 **Welding Manual**
10450 **ATV Basics**
10452 **Scooters 50cc to 250cc**

SPANISH MANUALS
98903 **Reparación de Carrocería & Pintura**
98904 **Manual de Carburador Modelos**
    Holley & Rochester
98905 **Códigos Automotrices de la Computadora**
98906 **OBD-II & Sistemas de Control Electrónico**
    del Motor
98910 **Frenos Automotriz**
98913 **Electricidad Automotriz**
98915 **Inyección de Combustible** '86 al '99
99040 **Chevrolet & GMC Camionetas** '67 al '87
99041 **Chevrolet & GMC Camionetas** '88 al '98
99042 **Chevrolet & GMC Camionetas**
    Cerradas '68 al '95
99043 **Chevrolet/GMC Camionetas** '94 al '04
99048 **Chevrolet/GMC Camionetas** '99 al '06
99055 **Dodge Caravan & Plymouth Voyager** '84 al '95
99075 **Ford Camionetas y Bronco** '80 al '94
99076 **Ford F-150** '97 al '09
99077 **Ford Camionetas Cerradas** '69 al '91
99088 **Ford Modelos de Tamaño Mediano** '75 al '86
99089 **Ford Camionetas Ranger** '93 al '10
99091 **Ford Taurus & Mercury Sable** '86 al '95
99095 **GM Modelos de Tamaño Grande** '70 al '90
99100 **GM Modelos de Tamaño Mediano** '70 al '88
99106 **Jeep Cherokee, Wagoneer & Comanche**
    '84 al '00
99110 **Nissan Camioneta** '80 al '96, **Pathfinder** '87 al '95
99118 **Nissan Sentra** '82 al '94
99125 **Toyota Camionetas y 4Runner** '79 al '95

Over 100 Haynes
motorcycle manuals
also available

7-12